PRAISE FOR *PRISONS O*

"This is an important book, extremely well researched, documented, illustrated, and argued. It provides a deep and thorough understanding of poverty governance and the mechanisms by which inequality is institutionally organized and reproduced. The ethnography and interviews are expertly woven through the text to provide rich, and at times dramatic, testimonies of the institutional processes central to the book."

TIMOTHY BLACK, coauthor of *It's a Setup: Fathering from the Social and Economic Margins*

"An incredibly important book, both with respect to its rigor and multilayered analysis and the importance of its findings. *Prisons of Debt* successfully shows how child support orders are core to understanding the long reach or aftermath of mass incarceration experiences."

SARA WAKEFIELD, coauthor of *Children of the Prison Boom: Mass Incarceration and the Future of American Inequality*

"In Haney's beautifully written *Prisons of Debt*, we learn what the merger of the criminal legal and child support systems has wrought for formerly incarcerated parents, especially low-income fathers of color, who bear the brunt of the dual systems' mutually reinforcing modes of surveillance and control. Punitive state policies both deny indebted parents' financial citizenship and deprive them of their liberty. The result: it is near impossible to resolve their ever-accumulating debt; it is also extremely difficult to contribute to their children's lives in satisfying and meaningful ways. It is a system that produces few, if any, winners: fathers struggle mightily to show up for their children; mothers continue to raise their children with meager support; and their children fail to get the resources and protections they need and deserve to survive and thrive. *Prisons of Debt* is a compelling and devastating account and a must-read for students of punishment and beyond."

SANDRA SUSAN SMITH, Daniel and Florence Guggenheim Professor of Criminal Justice and Faculty Chair for the Program in Criminal Justice Policy and Management, Harvard Kennedy School

"*Prisons of Debt* is an absolutely compelling and tragic account of how the child support and criminal legal systems jointly produce mass indebtedness among the most disadvantaged fathers, thereby exacerbating the problems they are supposed to solve. Lynne Haney's astute ethnographic observations and gripping in-depth interviews with fathers caught up in these intersecting systems dismantle the 'deadbeat dad' trope, echoed in media and in court, to reveal the exceptionally high cost of our current child support policies for children, families, and society."

MONA LYNCH, author of *Hard Bargains: The Coercive Power of Drug Laws in Federal Court*

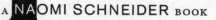

A NAOMI SCHNEIDER BOOK

Highlighting the lives and experiences of marginalized communities, the select titles of this imprint draw from sociology, anthropology, law, and history, as well as from the traditions of journalism and advocacy, to reassess mainstream history and promote unconventional thinking about contemporary social and political issues. Their authors share the passion, commitment, and creativity of Executive Editor Naomi Schneider.

Prisons of Debt

Prisons of Debt

THE AFTERLIVES
OF INCARCERATED FATHERS

Lynne Haney

UNIVERSITY OF CALIFORNIA PRESS

University of California Press
Oakland, California

Library of Congress Cataloging-in-Publication Data
Names: Haney, Lynne A. (Lynne Allison), 1967– author.
Title: Prisons of debt : the afterlives of incarcerated fathers / Lynne Haney.
Identifiers: LCCN 2021042438 (print) | LCCN 2021042439 (ebook) | ISBN 9780520297258 (cloth) | ISBN 9780520297265 (paperback) | ISBN 9780520969681 (epub)
Subjects: LCSH: Child support—United States. | Prisoners—Family relationships—United States. | Child welfare—United States. | Prisoners' families—United States.
Classification: LCC HV8886.U5 H44 2022 (print) | LCC HV8886.U5 (ebook) | DDC 362.82/9086927—dc23
LC record available at https://lccn.loc.gov/2021042438
LC ebook record available at https://lccn.loc.gov/2021042439

Manufactured in the United States of America

31 30 29 28 27 26 25 24 23 22
10 9 8 7 6 5 4 3 2 1

For Tristan

Contents

Acknowledgments

As I look back on the many debts I've accumulated while working on this book about debt, I'm filled with more gratitude than I can relay in a few pages. Thankfully, my debts did not produce the loops of disadvantage of the kind the fathers I write about here got stuck in. Just the opposite: they've created loops of advantage that have nurtured and sustained me over many years.

Unlike the institutions I discuss in this book, those I've had access to were extraordinarily supportive during this long-running (and expensive) research. The project's bookends were supported by two outstanding research foundations: the idea for the project began to percolate while I was a Straus Fellow at the NYU Institute for the Advanced Study of Law, and the writing took shape years later during my stay at the Russell Sage Foundation. In between these foundation stays, the research was supported by generous funding from the National Science Foundation and the National Institute of Justice (grant no. SES-1424309). Of course, institutions are only as good as the people in them—and these were filled with some of the best minds in academia. At Straus, I thank Maximo Sozzo, John Pratt, David Green, Sonja Snacken, and David Garland for helping me formulate the idea for the research—and then, in Budapest and Bologna, for offering valuable feedback on it. At RSF, my fellow fellows Richard Wilson, Issa Kohler-Hausmann, Yari Bonilla, and Dara Strolovitch read parts of the book and pushed me on many of its arguments. I also thank Kathy Edin, Maria Cancian, Suzanne Nichols, Sandra Danziger, and Sheldon Danzinger for being so supportive during my time at RSF. And at NSF, I'm grateful to Marjorie Zatz for being such a strong advocate of this work from the start.

NYU has for more than two decades been my intellectual home, where many friends, colleagues, and students have kept me engaged. John Halushka helped conduct some of the New York interviews, and I am beyond grateful for his assistance. Other current and former NYU graduate students contributed to this project, both formally and informally, including Sabrina Dycus, Marie Mercier, Allison McKim, Chris Seeds, Jon Gordon, and Poulami Roychowdury. My excellent undergraduate RAs Krysta Camp, Vaclav Masryk, and Elie Bartlett kept the policy data updated and produced a steady stream of research briefs. I'm fortunate to have Ruth Horowitz, Kathleen Gerson, and Ann Morning as wonderful colleagues and friends—and I owe them an enormous thanks for keeping me sane and grounded over the years. Other colleagues from NYU Sociology have been supportive of me and this research, including Iddo Tavory, Jeff Manza, Gianpaolo Baiocchi, Tom Ertman, Paula England, Harvey Molotch, Steven Lukes, Sarah Cowan, and Larry Wu. Across NYU I've benefited from the support of so many, especially Kirk James, Jane Anderson, Gene Jarrett, Linda Gordon, Richard Kalb, and the late great Jim Jacobs and Sally Merry—who are both dearly missed.

Beyond NYU, I have received valuable feedback from many colleagues and scholars. I am especially grateful to the brilliant members of the Gender, Theory, and Power Workshop—particularly to Ann Orloff, Talia Shiff, Julia Adams, Jenny Carlson, Rhacel Parrenas, Leslie Salzinger, Raka Ray, and Kimberly Hoang—for their support and feedback on several chapters. Over the years, I've given many talks on this research and received insightful comments on it. There is no way I could possibly thank everyone who contributed, but to name a few: Sara Wakefield, Tim Black, Marie Gottschalk, Nancy Hirschmann, Patricia Fernandez-Kelly, Elizabeth Clemens, Armando Lara-Millan, Mona Lynch, Kelly Hannah Moffat, Nathan Link, Megan Comfort, Jill McCorkel, Rickie Solinger, Nina Eliasoph, Christina

Ewig, Robert Vargas, Eva Fodor, and Kimberly Spencer-Suarez. As always, I am indebted to everyone at UC Press and especially to Naomi Schneider for her unwavering support and brilliant input—and for continuing to publish books that make sociology such a rich and interesting field.

This research was very much a collective endeavor. Even if I was the one to do the observations and interviews, it took several villages to make it all happen. For help accessing courts, locating fathers, and teaching me so much about this policy terrain, thanks to Pam Posehn, Margie McGranahan, Esteban Nuñez, Collette Carroll, Lonnie Tuck, Ebony Branner, Lourdes Castaneda, Anne Manning, Randall Briggins, Katherine Burns, Freda Randolph Glenn, Alisha Griffin, and Jim Garrison. For creating a formidable force for policy reform, thanks to Hellan Dowden, Brantley Choate, Amber Williams, Jessica Bartholow, Greg Wilson, Anne Stuhldreher, Christa Brown, Anne Price, and Tara Eastman. Of course, my biggest debt here is to the fathers who took the time to speak with me and trusted me with their stories. I'm especially grateful to a few of them: Lamar, Ali, Tyrice, Ronnie, Reggie, Manny, and Sonny. Although I can't use your real names, you surely recognize yourselves in this book—and I am beyond grateful for your time, insight, and generosity.

This book about fathers owes a tremendous amount to the extraordinary father figures I've had in my life. My dad, Craig Haney, began his parenting journey not unlike many of the men in this book—as a young, unexpected father—so I am enormously grateful that our father/daughter bond has remained so strong and loving. This book bears his imprint in so many ways, especially in his commitment to social justice and insight into the criminal justice system. My grandpa Haney was the first man to teach me the joy of small, simple acts of love—as well as how to endure the heartbreak of being a Phillies fan. My stepfather, Rudy Peritz, was a calming, comforting, and consistent figure in my life, and I miss him tremendously. And I remain grateful to Michael Burawoy, whom I will always consider my sociological father.

As this book makes clear, good fathering emerges from a larger social and familial context. So it is in my life: surrounding my great fathers are incredible mothers and family members. My gratitude to my mother, Janice Peritz, for her many sacrifices and for becoming my confidant and co-parent is deep. My siblings have grown into rock stars in their own fields, and after decades of being the big sister, I am thrilled to learn from them: from Jessica's stunning academic accomplishments, to Erin's awe-inspiring work on criminal justice reform, to Matt's phenomenal political work. I'm also lucky to have a big extended family on both coasts. Thanks to the Haney–Hurtado clan, especially to Aida Hurtado, for all the support, Sunday Zooms, and Mexico vacays. And my Yurko family continues to be a source of great food and good times, despite the loss of our beloved matriarch, Grandma Kay, whom we all miss dearly.

In addition to my family, I am fortunate to have strong support systems that have kept me happy and grounded over the years. I thank my five-year LAFamilia—Olivier, Daniel, Alex M, Angie, and Sam—for providing a warm, supportive home environment; Gita and Nina for keeping me sane in SoCal; Thea for our yearly meetups in Prague; Budapest Kati for fighting the good fight for more years than I can count; Alex K for the times he came through for me; Hilary and Meg for our monthly meals; Norm for our long talks and fantastic dinners; and Anne and Joan for always listening. Special thanks to Ali, Coco, Saatchi, and Penny for becoming our second family—and for getting us through one of the scariest periods of our lives, with our covid bubble safe and well-fed.

A decade ago, just as I was beginning to contemplate this project, my partner, Andras Tapolcai, died unexpectedly. In the more than twenty years that we were together, Andras passed on many amazing things to me, and I am especially thankful for his example of caring, consistent fathering. It is an example I often came back to as I wrote this book about fathers—and as I've parented for both of us over the years. Which leads to Tristan, our incredible son, who grew up along with this book. During the research, I dragged him across the country and stuck him in all sorts of crazy camps—from alligator camps to baseball camps to surf camps. Yet he always rolled with it, happy to join my seemingly never-ending research trips. As Tristan grew older, we talked about the book's findings, and he eventually became my graph and map maker extraordinaire. He continues to enrich my life every day and reminds me of the joys of parenting. And so, Tristan, I dedicate this book to you: in honor of the outstanding young man you have grown into and the future caregiver you will become—in whatever form you decide it will take.

Introduction

FROM DEADBEAT TO DEAD BROKE

"You lookin' for Ronnie Jones?" the man at the cash register asks me, in a tone that rings of suspicion. "And who would you be?" Sensing his distrust, I shower him with explanation: how I am a researcher interested in talking to fathers in the area, how I spoke to Ronnie earlier, and how I was referred to him by a trusted confidant. Still doubtful, he instructs me to wait while he disappears into the back of the otherwise empty bodega. I follow his instructions, lingering for what seems like eternity in the sweltering Jacksonville summer heat, occasionally noticing as someone peeks out at me from behind the aisle of canned food, only to scurry away. Finally, the man from the cash register emerges alongside a tall African American man with a broom in his hand. "We weren't sure who you really are," the cashier explains. Then the man with the broom adds, "My boss was just being careful. 'Cause you never know what they'll do to find me."

At his boss's encouragement, Ronnie puts down the broom and joins me outside at a small table in front of the store. After we talk for a bit, it becomes clear what they were so worried about: the Jacksonville Sheriff's Office. Given their fear, one might assume Ronnie is wanted for some serious offense, but his crime is financial: he owes back child support. Due to that debt, Ronnie has been dodging law enforcement for almost a decade. A few years earlier, they captured him during one of their "Father's Day roundups." Ronnie was in the front of the family house, barbecuing with his kids and extended kin, when the sheriff's car pulled up. "It was like the cops came right to our street, looking for us with warrants," Ronnie remembers. The police found him, handcuffed him, and took him to jail. His kids watched it all. "I should have been smarter," Ronnie recalls. "I shouldn't have been exposed.... My kids shouldn't have seen something like that." He promises never to make that mistake again.

Indeed, throughout our discussion, Ronnie admits to making many mistakes in his life. He also concedes that those mistakes underlie his large child support debt. A series of robberies he committed in his twenties got him incarcerated for much of his thirties. That time in local jail and state prison took a toll on his work and family life. They took an even greater toll on Jackie, the mother of his children, who was left to raise their three kids alone. As Ronnie went in and out of prison, she went on and off public assistance, food stamps, and Medicaid as needed. This was years ago, when Florida still had some semblance of a welfare system and, as required by federal law, the state charged the costs of those public benefits to Ronnie in the form of child support. While in prison, Ronnie was totally unaware that he had a support order, much less child support debt. Later, as he cycled through jail and prison, his address changed so often that mail never reached him. He kept moving, and his child support debt kept mounting, unbeknownst to him.

Ronnie's account of his child support woes is largely structured around the times they landed him back in jail. He initially learned about his order and the accompanying debt the first time he got arrested for it—and the judge informed him that he owed over $25,000. The second time, he was picked up on an outstanding warrant and learned that the debt had climbed to over $40,000, in large part because Florida charged 10 percent interest on outstanding child support debt owed to the state. Several more child support arrests followed, more than he could count. But the last one, the Father's Day roundup a few years earlier, had been perhaps the most consequential. This time it took him two weeks in jail to come up with the $1,000 the judge required him to pay in order to purge himself of contempt and be released. In fact, the cost was much higher than that: he lost his job and his apartment during that stint in jail, which put him further behind on his support payments as he struggled to get back on his feet. All of this infuriated Jackie, who received next to nothing from Ronnie's payments. "This money I keep paying . . . all goes to Tallahassee. None of it [goes] to my kids," Ronnie laments, with his head down. "So I try to help out in other ways."

One of those "other ways" led him here, to this bodega on the outskirts of Jacksonville. Jackie and his children live nearby, so he came to the area after losing his job downtown. Unable to afford an apartment in the area, Ronnie resides in a nearby homeless shelter. But he considers himself fortunate, and his life on the upswing, since the situation allows him to walk his kids to and from school every day, so that Jackie can get to work early and return late. Sometimes he even escorts other kids in the neighborhood to school, painting the image of himself as a "big duck with all these little ducklings" following him down the street. His job in the bodega enables all of this: his boss pays Ronnie under the table and lets him off for a few hours every afternoon to accompany his kids from school. And he is protective of Ronnie, always watching out and running interference for him. "He's the best worker I got," his boss yells to us from inside the bodega. Taking this comment as a hint that he should return to work, Ronnie grabs his broom and wraps up our interview. But not before making one thing very clear: "My kids are everything to me. I may be a felon, but I'm no deadbeat!"

Fathers like Ronnie Jones rarely come to mind when we think of men with large child support debt—his age, his poverty, and his commitment to his children are not usually captured in images of such fathers. Far more common is the image of a man of means who chooses not to pay child support, like millionaire internet entrepreneur Joseph Stroup, who, after being on the run for over twenty years, was caught in Canada and extradited to Michigan for running up $540,000 in child support debt.[1] Yet for every Joseph Stroup there are hundreds of thousands of Ronnie Joneses. Or men like Walter Scott, the South Carolina man who was shot and killed by police after running from a routine traffic stop—all because he feared that his child support debt, which he had been unable to repay, would be discovered and land him back in jail.[2] Men like Ronnie Jones and Walter Scott are in fact the norm: it is estimated that 70 percent of the $115 billion in child support debt owed by Americans is in fact owed by parents with incomes under $10,000, half of whom reported no income at all, largely due to imprisonment.[3]

This book tells the collective story of the millions of parents who fall into this latter category: indebted fathers who live at the intersection of the child support and criminal justice systems. These are two of the largest state systems in the United States today. More than 7 million citizens live under some form of correctional supervision, and close to 6 million live with child support debt. Yet we don't know how many parents actually fall into both groups, as indebted parents with incarceration histories. In part, this is because neither system collects reliable data on the other. But it is also because parents themselves try to keep a low profile. When dealing with child support, they are leery of mentioning their criminal justice histories; when interacting with criminal justice officials, they rarely admit to owing child support. They struggle to avoid being detected by either system. While their resulting behavior might seem odd and even a bit paranoid—with fathers like Ronnie Jones peering out from behind the canned food aisle of a bodega, or Walter Scott running off during a routine traffic stop—it is actually quite sensible given the realities of the systems they live under and the punishing consequences of any misstep.

For four years, between 2014 and 2018, I studied those systems and the fathers enmeshed in both of them. To do this, I moved across state terrains, examining the policies and laws established by the federal and state governments as well as the practices of local child support courts. I also sought out men like Ronnie Jones, with histories of incarceration and child support debt, and persuaded them to sit down with me for interviews. And I did this in different parts of the country, to account for variations in state criminal justice and child support systems. By the end, I had conducted three years of ethnographic research in child support courts in New York, California, and Florida and observed roughly four hundred cases in each state—more than twelve hundred in all.[4] I also carried out 145 qualitative interviews with formerly incarcerated fathers with child support debt.[5] These fathers came from the three states where I had conducted my research, around the same number from each. The interviews probed men's experiences with the penal and child support systems as well as their lives as parents. Always emotional and often angry, regretful, and desperate, these men offered me a window onto the lived realities of parenting while imprisoned in both of these massive state systems.

• • •

"These men are like runaway slaves," exclaimed Lamar, a former indebted father turned social advocate. "So in that book you're writing, you need to show them as human." I take Lamar's directive seriously and have tried to heed his call—to reveal how those reviled as "deadbeat dads" are in fact real people who lead real lives with real stories behind them. Of course, this does not mean idealizing or romanticizing these fathers and their struggles. And it certainly does not mean excusing their mistakes, misdeeds, or missteps, which should never be the goal of social scientific analysis. Instead, one of my goals is to expose how these men have complex and layered lives that too often get flattened out in portrayals of them, be it in court assessments, bureaucratic formulas, or media accounts. The portrayals I relay here show these fathers in all of their complexity: sometimes doing bad things and making bad decisions; sometimes breaking the law, over and over again; sometimes neglecting their children; and sometimes hurting people. Yet they are also men who have been hurt by others: by court officials who refuse to see them as fully human; by judges who insist on humiliating them as they enforce compliance; by policies that fail to acknowledge the realities of their lives; and by state bureaucracies that seem to conspire against them. These fathers are left grappling with seemingly contradictory feelings of anger and guilt, frustration and remorse, rage and hopelessness.

These fathers' stories reveal a great deal about how systems of social exclusion and punishment operate. Their accounts expose the webs of inequality entrapping their lives. To start with the basics: the fathers in this study had an average of $36,500 in child support debt—three times more than the support debt owed by other low-income fathers. The additional debt was a byproduct of their contact with the criminal justice system. Some of them had done long stints in prison, during which time their debt skyrocketed. Others cycled in and out of jail, during which time their debt accumulated incrementally. No matter which route they took, the path through criminal justice ended in massive debt.

The first set of findings in this book relate to how exactly this happens: how the material costs of imprisonment build up to create a perfect storm of debt. The overwhelmingly majority of fathers in prison receive no modification of child support orders, which means those orders go unpaid during their incarceration. Most states then charge interest on the accumulated debt, at rates between 4 and 12 percent, leading to an exponential increase in what fathers owe. Incarcerated fathers often do not realize their debt is growing until their release, at which point they encounter all sorts of bureaucratic and legal hurdles that further disadvantage them in getting a handle on their debt. Together, their experiences reveal how the physical confinement of prison leads to the financial confinement of child support debt, creating what I call the *debt of imprisonment.*

Complicating the situation even more are the punitive costs associated with child support debt that can deepen fathers' criminal justice involvement. My second set of findings revolve around those costs: how the punishments of child support become their own prison. Child support debt is accompanied by an enforcement apparatus that rivals criminal justice in its scope and reach. As Ronnie Jones was all too aware, these apparatuses intersect and merge. They draw on each other to regulate and surveil fathers—support officials issue arrest warrants for the non-compliant, then sheriff officers reel in indebted parents. From the revocation of driver's licenses and passports, to the seizure of property, to liens on bank accounts, to interceptions of state benefits, enforcement measures can make parents feel like they are being processed and punished without end. For fathers with criminal records, the combined effects of debt accumulation and debt enforcement can seem inescapable, creating what I call the *imprisonment of debt.*

Indeed, for many fathers, debt accumulation and debt enforcement are so tightly linked that they amount to a single system. These fathers are quite literally doubly indebted: having paid their "debt to society" through incarceration, they emerge from prison and find themselves facing enormous child support debt, much of which is owed to the state itself and not to their families.[6] Their indebtedness thus overlaps and crisscrosses. In a sense, this is not entirely surprising: social scientists and criminologists have long argued that incarceration has debilitating "collateral consequences" or "spillover effects" higher than the prison walls themselves. Like a leaky faucet, the mark of a criminal record can continue to drip and spill into work life, family life, civic life, and political life, until it collects into a pool that then expands to become an ocean that drowns the formerly incarcerated.

However, the intersections analyzed here work a bit differently. Instead of dripping in one direction, from one institution to the next, they flow back and forth. Some of these flows begin with men's involvement in the criminal justice system, others with child support, and still others through a combination of the two. Men's entanglements also emerge from federal and state policies as reflected in public assistance payback policies, state modification laws, and local enforcement measures. These policies are then implemented through local judicial practices in ways that are both uneven and consistently disadvantageous to this group of fathers. The sanctioning power of these practices blends civil, administrative, and criminal law—combining fines, fees, revocations, and reincarceration—to create a legal hybridity that adds to the institutional complexity. Rather than simply "piling onto" men's lives, these practices work in circular ways to form feedback loops of disadvantage.

In fact, the looping nature of these entanglements is what makes them so consequential for so many fathers. These loops are difficult to detect or disentangle and are even harder to escape. And the effects of getting caught in them can be devastating. This would be true for even the most stable and committed of parents. But for those who are already disadvantaged, and who are trying to reintegrate after imprisonment, these loops can lead to major derailments. They can exclude parents from the most basic forms of financial citizenship, denying them the ability to transport themselves to work, keep property, or maintain bank accounts. They can undermine relations of social support and put pressure on familial networks, frequently to the breaking point. They can push fathers underground, disconnecting them from community support and deepening their estrangement. These entanglements can thus become their own form of imprisonment, making poor men feel dehumanized and invisible—indeed, like runaway slaves.

A central claim of this book is that the promise of child support as familial support vanishes when it merges with criminal justice. When fathers are enmeshed in both state systems simultaneously, they can end up doubly imprisoned—confined by incarceration and by unmanageable debt. Once enmeshed, they confront seemingly inescapable obstacles that make their lives as fathers even more challenging. This can have ripple effects, ultimately harming those who need the most support. When fathers' lives are broken, mothers rarely get the financial support they need and deserve. Children no longer receive what they need to feel safe, secure, and nurtured. Everyone suffers when the law and state policy undermine those bonds proven most essential for social well-being: relationships of care, reciprocity, and interdependence.

PUNISHMENT AS CONFINEMENT, PUNISHMENT AS DEBT

The merging of criminal justice and child support is not entirely unexpected. Over the past forty years, as the criminal justice system has grown in size and scope, it has shown itself to be uncontainable. It has seeped into all areas of social life, particularly in poor communities of color. Unable to restrain its practices of confinement, the criminal justice system has gobbled up more and more lives: at last count, more than 2 million American citizens were in prison or jail and another 5 million were under correctional supervision through parole, probation, and community programs.[7] In the process, the logic of confinement has moved into new institutional spaces. From schools to hospitals to social services, a punitive approach has changed the form and focus of institutional practice.[8] Sociologists Lara-Millan and Gonzalez van Clev call this "penal-welfare hybridization"—a process of governance that adds new levers of punishment to state sectors that, once upon a time, were oriented toward social support and rehabilitation.[9]

Another way the tentacles of criminal justice have extended out is through the collateral consequences of confinement—the cascading effects of removing millions of people from social life have been as punishing as the experience of confinement itself. Social scientists have spent decades researching these effects and the ways they spill into work, civic, and public life to weigh down people as they struggle to reintegrate.[10] More recently, scholars have turned their attention to the effects of carceral confinement on families, showing how punishment is not limited to prisoners themselves. For instance, feminist scholars have shown how the carework of mass incarceration has been feminized, placing pressure on women who are already overburdened financially and straining kin relationships.[11] Others have revealed how the formerly incarcerated can become the conduits along which the negative effects of incarceration spread in families—effects ranging from disease to poverty to emotional turmoil to social stigma.[12] For years, data from the Fragile Families Survey have documented how incarceration exacerbates childhood disadvantage, familial instability, domestic violence, and parental depression.[13] Indeed, when it comes to children, scholars have revealed how parental incarceration adds new levels of disadvantage to already disadvantaged kids at every developmental stage, from infancy through adolescence.[14]

Clearly, the effects of penal confinement are vast and varied. Yet confinement is not the only form of punishment pulsating through the contemporary penal state. As Issa Kohler-Hausmann so astutely notes, the fixation on mass incarceration has both understated the reach of criminal justice and misrepresented the modal experience of it.[15] It has also made other forms of control seem minor and trivial despite their far-reaching consequences. For instance, as Kohler-Hausmann reveals, the world of mass misdemeanor arrest is governed by its own logic of control, which sorts, tests, and monitors its subjects. With this logic comes a unique set of techniques that rely on marking, procedural hassle, and performance to exact punishment. While not based on confinement *per se*, these penal practices curtail behavior through ongoing surveillance, compliance, and evaluation—all of which carry their own consequences.

Indeed, a similar argument can be applied to a host of other punishments ranging from community corrections to parole to mandatory programming to public shaming. I would put punishment by debt in this category. While not based on the same removal or incapacitation as prison, its practices are extremely punishing nonetheless. Particularly when tied to the criminal justice system, debt as a consequence of confinement can be enormously damaging and debilitating. Criminal justice financial obligations (CJFOs), whose use has been surging since the 1990s, can take a variety of forms, from court fees to restitution to fines related to the costs of incarceration. Most of what we know about CJFOs, and the debt arising from them, relates to their prevalence and implications. And the trends here have been eye-opening: 66 percent of federal prisoners and 30 percent of state prisoners leave prison with such debt.[16] While reliable national data on the amount of these debts is limited, state-level CJLOs average somewhere between $5,000 and $10,000, making these fees as onerous as they are pervasive.

Yet at the conceptual level, social scientists know far less about how criminal justice debt acts as its own form of social control—that is, the dynamics of what Karin Martin terms "pecuniary justice."[17] Most often, debt is conceptualized as one of the collateral consequences of confinement, as a monetary mark of a criminal record that follows people from prison.[18] Yet debt involves much more than this. Although it is linked to these other punishments, it has its own logic: it both monetarizes accountability and holds the sanctioned responsible for the costs of their own sanctioning. It couples the loss of liberty with the denial of financial citizenship, since debt can relegate people to life without credit, property, or bank accounts. Debt defines how one should be answerable to the state, in terms of both what is owed (money) and what repayment connotes (retribution).[19] It also sets in motion its own techniques of control, in that it tethers people to the justice system based on their inability to pay for their transgressions, while using the monetary as a means to monitor social relationships and alter behavior.

To some extent, child support debt is yet another example of pecuniary justice. Indeed, scholars often list it among the many types of CJLOs. At one level, this seems justified: like criminal justice fees, child support debt links economic disadvantage to the incapacitation of prison. Since a large portion of arrears are owed to the government (and not to custodial parents), it binds parents to the state through financial liability. It monetarizes accountability. It becomes a means to deny parents their rights and to dictate their behavior. It conflates the inability to pay with all sorts of other failures and transgressions. And if anything, child support debt does all of this on an even larger scale than CJLOs. For instance, the overall amount of child support debt in the United States exceeds $115 billion, which is much more than other criminal justice debt.[20] For individuals, child support debt exerts stronger financial pressure, given that it averages three times more than even the highest CJLO estimates. Unlike CJLOs, which tend to be one-time assessments, child support accrues in an ongoing and seemingly endless way. So given its enormous size and broad reach, child support debt could be seen as a case of pecuniary justice writ large.

Yet lumping these types of debt together obscures what is most unique about child support debt as a form of punishment, as well as what makes it so fraught for so many. Besides exacting an economic toll, child support debt creates feedback loops of disadvantage that cross institutions and can seem impossible to escape. Perhaps more importantly, child support debt has moral and political connotations that other forms of criminal justice debt do not. This makes it uniquely constraining on indebted fathers' lives and identities.

To begin with the feedback loops: for incarcerated parents, child support debt is largely the product of the collision of two massive state systems. As I analyze throughout this book, the physical confinement of prison breeds the financial confinement of child support, and vice versa. As these systems collide, their modes of regulation mesh and begin to complement each other. This leads to fathers' double indebtedness and a series of institutional entanglements that work in unison: criminal justice sanctions loop through those of child support, while the enforcements of child support loop back through criminal justice. Once caught in these webs, indebted parents find it exceptionally hard to disentangle themselves. In the chapters that follow, I describe many cases in which a parent resolves one set of entanglements only to discover others festering, or in which a parent grapples with one part of their debt only to learn that other parts have mushroomed. In this way, these loops of disadvantage expose the institutional processes underlying debt as punishment.

These same loops also unmask the particular kind of power this debt can wield. Indebtedness is always disempowering, for it is based on the inability to uphold one's end of a relationship. When this relationship is based on money, additional connotations surface. As many social scientists have theorized, money carries unique moral significance and moral expectations. Vivianna Zelizer, a prominent social theorist of money, argues that money categorizes significant social relations in that it assigns a value to specific relations.[21] She claims that this is done by states in a "top down" way characterized by constraint, whereas the "bottom up" valuing of everyday social relations can be more creative.[22] With child support debt, the state uses money to do this relational work, monitoring the indebted through computations and calculations of what they owe in familial relationships. The state also models what those relationships should look like, defining parental obligations in strictly financial terms that value monetary contributions above all else. When those models are not followed, it then monetarizes the punishment. And it does so in the most discretionary and far-reaching of ways—by linking nonpayment of child support to a host of other moral failures, from laziness to neglect to desertion to abandonment.

Although this moralization could apply to other forms of criminal justice debt, those debts do not invade social or personal relationships the way child support debt does. As sociologists have also shown, the moral connotations of debt vary according to the perceived nature of that debt.[23] These moral connotations relate to who is owed and for what reason. The more personal a debt, the more likely it is to be viewed as a moral obligation; the more a debt is owed for something of value, the more morally suspect its nonpayment becomes.[24] All of this makes child support debt unique in its connotations. This debt is assumed to involve the most personal relations of care: those between parents and children. It is imagined to be a debt owed to mothers for the care of children and thus collected by the state on behalf of those most in need. Never mind that much of this debt is in fact owed to the state as repayment for public assistance benefits. Even when owed to the state, and when children will see little of its payment, it is still called *child* support. The inclusion of "child" invests the debt with moral urgency. Special names then apply to those who fail to pay it: the deadbeat dad, the absentee father, the daddy-b-gone. Television shows track them down and bring them to "justice." Most-wanted signs warn the public about them, while "man up and pay" police raids capture them. State registries are constructed to expose them—California proposed a new registry as recently as 2019.[25]

These public acts are unimaginable with other types of criminal justice debt. Yet they are standard with child support debt, largely because those who owe it are thought to be moral threats. They are perceived as having violated the most personal of relationships by failing to support their children. So they are moral threats cast as parental threats, and vice versa. Racialized undercurrents only add to this moralization. These threats are often expressed through racialized tropes: the deadbeat dad, the absentee father, and the daddy-b-gone all become racially marked categories, and such marking makes the moralization of debt all the more potent. It also provides state officials with a way to draw impenetrable boundaries around debtors: the imposition of enforcement measures on fathers is justified as a way to protect children; the impugning of men's parental identities is framed as a way to help mothers; and the stigmatizing of fathers is disguised as a way to force men to comply with familial obligations. Again, this all transpires even when the debt being collected is owed to the government and not to children or families. Thus, the moral connotations of debt obscure both its penalization and its racialization.

These moral connections are so strong and run so deep that indebted fathers often defend themselves from stigmatization by reasserting them. Most of the indebted fathers I interviewed insisted that child support was a moral obligation—indeed, that it was *their* moral obligation.[26] Fathers told me as much whether they could afford their support orders or not and whether they paid those orders or not. Almost all men accepted this moral imperative and often resorted to it to condemn other fathers for nonpayment, drawing on the same racialized tropes to denounce other men. Yet even while doing so, they acknowledged their own struggles with these tropes and the damage they had done to their own sense of self as parents. So while men insisted that *their* poverty not be conflated with bad parenting—and that *their* failure to pay not be misconstrued as deadbeat behavior—they rarely extended other fathers the same understanding. The moral overlay was so thick that it concealed the similarities in fathers' experiences and bred division among fathers.

Indeed, this moral overlay also masked what so many fathers found most troubling about their debt: how their roles as parents had been completely monetarized. Finances became both the cause and the consequence of their problems. State officials viewed money as the source of men's inability to meet their responsibilities as parents and stable breadwinners. These officials deemed them failures as parents and as people because of their failure to pay. Most-wanted signs and public registries shamed them for the same failures. But finances also became the consequence of these failures: fathers were fined and charged as punishment for the failure to pay. In the process, money eclipsed everything they did as parents, from caregiving to showing commitment to expressing love. At times, this shaming pushed men to try harder and to defend their parenting models even more vociferously. Other times, it fostered a sense of failure and unrelenting guilt and remorse, which then bred a cyclical parenting that only seemed to confirm the worst suspicions of them as unreliable and inconsistent. And this led to a sense of hopelessness that state policies would ever reflect the realities of their lives as fathers.

THE STATE POLITICS OF DISADVANTAGED FATHERHOOD

Public stereotypes about the supposed irresponsibility of poor parents are mainstays of American culture.[27] Social scientists have worked for decades to debunk the myth of the "unwed mother" embedded in these portrayals, documenting how such misrepresentations are used to stigmatize poor mothers in both welfare and criminal justice policy. But less has been said of fathers. Fatherhood surfaced on occasion in classic accounts of disadvantaged men, from those on Tally's corner to those on Jelly's corner to those on Hakim's corner, but it was rarely the focus of analysis.[28] The same is true of depictions of the incarcerated: most accounts highlighted men's struggle for control, dignity, and respect while saying little about their lives as caregivers.[29] These silences have left gaps in our understanding of men as fathers and allowed stereotypical images to remain uninterrogated for decades.

Over the past several years, however, more attention has focused on disadvantaged men as fathers. With the rise in concern over the "crisis of fatherhood" in the 1990s and the subsequent focus on "responsible fatherhood" in the 2000s, researchers began to study the factors shaping disadvantaged fatherhood.[30] Unlike work on poor mothers, which tends to focus on the state and social policies affecting them, research on fathers has centered on the economic and cultural context of men's parenting.[31] From policy documents to social scientific studies, research is exposing the many economic, community, and cultural constraints faced by poor fathers.[32] Perhaps most prominent is research on the economic obstacles affecting them: from structural economic shifts to limited paid employment to wage depression to educational barriers, these men face serious material challenges to meeting their parenting ideals.[33] Also important are the social and community pressures men face, especially those that make them vulnerable as well as insecure about becoming fathers.[34] Then there are the cultural expectations they encounter—from the bravado of hegemonic masculinity to the demands of the breadwinning ideal to the condemnation of the deadbeat, the paternal expectations placed on these men are as contradictory as they are unachievable.[35]

In addition, social scientists have begun to chart how fathers manage these contradictions. Taking the economic and cultural context as a backdrop, they have analyzed disadvantaged fathers' experiences of parenting. Here the emphasis is more on the relational and social psychological aspects of men's parenting, with researchers pointing to important tensions in men's lives as fathers.[36] They describe how the lure of fatherhood can draw men in even while unrealistic expectations push them away. They explore how men's search for redemption or for a way out of their tumultuous lives can lead them to engage as parents; yet their inability to follow through can then push them to move on and create new families. They show how their need for self-esteem and self-respect can push men to contribute as parents, even while their lack of psychological resources can leave them unable to do so consistently or reliably. Yet as Edin and Nelson argue, men continue to find pleasure in fatherhood despite the challenges, with some redefining a new "package deal" that highlights their caregiving role.[37]

All of this research on disadvantaged fatherhood has revealed a great deal about the constraints and possibilities of poor men's caregiving. By highlighting the economic and cultural context, and men's personal responses to it, researchers have shown how struggles with intimacy, self-respect, and masculinity influence their lives as fathers. Yet men's struggles are not merely personal—they are also bound up with public policies and laws, which are in the background of most accounts of disadvantaged fathers. We are thus left without a clear sense of how poor men are governed as fathers, or what feminist scholars Barbara Hobson and David Morgan call the "social politics of fatherhood."[38] We know more about men's bad choices and failed attempts to meet their familial obligations and less about the concrete policies and practices that can derail them. Like all familial relationships, parenting is embedded in social systems, state institutions, and state policies. This is particularly true for disadvantaged fathers.

There are several dangers to ignoring this social embeddedness. First, it overestimates fathers' autonomy. It can lead to the sense that men's responses to economic and cultural constraints are primarily a question of their motivation to overcome adversity. It is as if what stands between them and the management of massive social inequality are personal strength and perseverance—and, by extension, as if what underlies their mistakes are simply personal demons and psychological limitations. This emphasis is perhaps clearest in "responsible fatherhood" programs, which emerged in full force during the Obama era to teach men how to construct new paternal identities, to increase their motivation, to become breadwinners, and to enhance their "marital masculinity."[39] While social scientists are not this explicitly prescriptive, they can end up overemphasizing men's agency by stressing the personal obstacles fathers encounter as they struggle to overcome economic and cultural disadvantage.

This leads to another danger: the underestimation of how fatherhood can be constrained by state policy. Poor men's lives as fathers are shaped not only by broad, abstract economic and cultural forces, but also by very concrete state provisions. These policies can stand in the way of men persevering through hardship and can derail the most motivated of fathers. While social research might mention the public provisions targeting fathers, it rarely disentangles the many webs of policies and laws that structure fathers' lives. These webs are precisely what I highlight in this book: how fatherhood is doubly mediated for so many poor men, experienced from behind prison walls and under the heavy weight of support orders. I also analyze the specific entanglements that form across state institutions and the concrete ways they make it even harder for poor fathers to weather the perfect storm of economic and cultural adversity.

For instance, regarding the economic arena, research has shown repeatedly that the mark of a criminal record adds new challenges to reentry, making it exceedingly difficult to find and maintain employment and housing. Sociologists have done exceptional research on the bias and discrimination underlying this struggle, particularly as meted out by employers and landlords.[40] Yet alongside individuals who discriminate are state processes of discrimination. The data here are too staggering for researchers not to notice: Of the more than 5 million men who live under correctional supervision, 56 percent are parents of minor children. Of these fathers, close to half have open child support cases. And of those open cases, nearly half of the arrears are owed to the state as repayment for public benefits. These fathers are thus shouldered with repaying what was once *state* assistance. Yet they cannot afford such repayment: it is estimated that 40 percent of them have little or no reported income.[41] Their economic lives are mediated by these realities; their parenting lives are structured by these state practices. State systems of criminal justice and of child support are so pervasive in the lives of poor men that few remain untouched by their dictates. So while poor fathers try to navigate the perfect storm of economic constraints, state policies can cause those waves to surge.

The same is true of cultural constraints: state practices shape how they are experienced and managed. In fact, the cultural trope of the deadbeat is frequently deployed when state actors target and punish these fathers. As when the sheriff's department rounds them up in "man-up-and-pay" or "deadbeat" raids. Or when fathers are brought before judges who berate them as broken-down breadwinners who choose to keep their families impoverished, calling them everything from failures to losers to liars to scumbags. Or when they meet with state attorneys who assume they are conniving and accuse them of deceit, immaturity, and selfishness. If such things were said or done to any other population, there would be public outrage. But not with this group: indebted fathers are thought to deserve such treatment. Their inability to meet the one standard they are held to, the breadwinning ideal, feeds cultural stereotypes of their parenting as somehow unregulated by common norms or obligations.[42] This can set into motion a vicious cycle: state practices provoke culturally overdetermined responses in fathers, from distrust to cynicism to frustration to escape, which then harden the stereotypes. As this goes round and round, the state policies underlying the conflicts appear to vanish; the state processes that exacerbate the cultural contradictions seem to disappear.

When we highlight these state processes, the flip side also becomes clear: state policies can *help* fathers manage economic and cultural constraints. State interventions can be both constraining and enabling, which is difficult to see when we focus narrowly on men's autonomy and agency. We know a lot about this from feminist work on state policies that target poor women: however damaging state policies can be for women as parents, the absence of policies can be far more damaging.[43] The contemporary retrenchment in public assistance, public housing, and social services reveals how mothers' lives can get worse when states withdraw and retreat. Something similar applies to poor fathers. As I reveal in part 3, men's access to public resources is a key intervening variable shaping their experience as fathers. Men construct and perform fatherhood through interactions with state institutions, by emulating or rejecting state definitions of good parenting. Indeed, through these interactions, some fathers are able to gain valuable tools to become the fathers they want to be.

As I show throughout this book, even the most disadvantaged men who find themselves confronting seemingly insurmountable obstacles often become exceptional caregivers when given the right kind of support. They can protect the most vulnerable of children; they can provide care in the most difficult of circumstances. Hence, the story of these men's experiences as fathers is not only one of constraint and control—it is also one of ingenuity. It is one in which many men find creativity within constraint. In which they harness the social resources they need to feel confident as parents and to care for their children as they see fit. And in which they use state conceptions of fatherhood to model their own parental practices and behavior. From local-level programs to state-level provisions, public policy can help indebted fathers secure their families' well-being. So while it can seem as if massive economic and cultural shifts must occur for their lives to improve, once we shift our sights to concrete state policy, meaningful reform becomes visible.

Highlighting the state politics of disadvantaged fatherhood might also go a long way to address the complicated racial and gender politics that child support often evokes. The racial politics here seem all too clear: men of color are overrepresented in the criminal justice and state child support systems; they are also overrepresented among indebted fathers. Their parenting is shaped by all the familiar cultural stereotypes, from the deadbeat to the absentee dad, and this often makes them defensive and vulnerable as parents. In this way, racialization propels the state politics of indebted fatherhood. Yet this racialization is also what shapes the myths about these fathers: the conflation of race and paternal irresponsibility marks them no matter what they actually do as parents. Racial injustice can thus be both the cause and the effect of indebted fatherhood. This state arena is also the terrain of poor parents more generally—terrain onto which dead-broke fathers are drawn irrespective of their race. So the stigma can travel to reach all indebted fathers. On occasion, this can breed even harsher punishment for those thought to defy racialized expectations, be they extremely committed fathers of color or extremely negligent white fathers. As in so many areas of social life, race and class work in layered ways to create intersections that complicate the politics of parental debt.

Further complicating this politics are the gendered dynamics at play, which are themselves fraught and layered. It goes without saying that women shoulder the familial burdens brought on by mass incarceration and impoverishment. Some fathers have exacerbated those burdens by refusing to provide the kind of care mothers need. This is particularly true for never-married mothers, who receive only a tiny fraction of the support owed to them by their children's fathers. Overburdened and unsupported, these women have been failed by so many, which only deepens the gender distrust separating disadvantaged mothers and fathers. Add to this women's own experiences of racial and class injustice, and their gender distrust can intensify. Then there are all the ways that this distrust is appropriated by others to further entangle race, class, and gender, thus pitting one set of vulnerabilities against another. As when policy-makers use mothers' poverty to justify public assistance payback laws. Or when judges rationalize their harsh enforcement measures as protecting mothers and children. Or when parents then echo these state actors, using the cultural tropes of the deadbeat or the welfare cheat to regulate and resist each other. In the process, the layers of gender, race, and class injustice fuse together so tightly that they become seemingly impossible to separate.

Indeed, discussions of child support too often get tangled up in these layers. The battle lines then get drawn, which only exacerbates the conflict between parents and divides those advocating for them. For instance, over the course of this research, I was repeatedly asked which "side" I was on, as if there were only two sides and the lines separating them were clear. Such dichotomies emerged decades ago, in the 1990s, when one sector of feminist politics took on the child support issue as a way to address the feminization of poverty. But, as I discuss in chapter 1, even that history is complicated and misunderstood. Certainly, feminists did push for gender equity in caregiving and familial support. Many of them did advocate for stronger child support enforcement policies as part of this push. And some feminist advocates may even have contributed to the nasty deadbeat politics of the period. But the child support system was certainly not of their making. In fact, their advocacy was often appropriated by others for their own political ends. At times, it was even used by social scientists as cover for their welfare reform agendas, making the feminist role as misread and unclear now as it was back then.

Yet one thing is quite clear: since the 1990s, child support has been transformed in ways that few anticipated. As the child support system merged with criminal justice, it became exceedingly punitive; as it expanded in size and scope, its reach extended far beyond what anyone ever expected. In doing so, it captured a majority of poor fathers and made them indebted to the state, which has arguably deepened women's poverty. So while the political dividing lines were never clear, they are even less so now. It is possible to acknowledge that these state systems can hurt fathers *and* fail to help mothers.[44] It is possible to see them as interconnected: as fathers get trapped in loops of disadvantage, their capacity to form familial bonds of care and reciprocity is depleted. It is also possible to recognize that this makes indebted fatherhood itself a feminist issue: it is a neglected aspect of the "crisis of care" and an example of the public's refusal to ascribe social value to caregiving.[45] The twist here is that men are now experiencing a refusal that women have encountered for decades: their contributions as caregivers are being negated, and their families' need for nurturance has been turned into monetary calculations of debt.

Again, no one knows this better than the mothers involved in child support cases. Although I did not interview them, I observed thousands of mothers in court vacillate from anger to hurt to sympathy and back. Judges rarely encouraged them to speak, but they expressed their ambivalence with their facial expressions and body language. For good reason, they seemed ambivalent toward and distrustful of fathers, yet they also acknowledged men's importance to their kids' lives. Some mothers seemed conflicted as the personal betrayal they felt collided with these men's public humiliation. They seemed pained as they watched their personal anger toward these men being harnessed to public tropes of them as careless, oversexed deadbeats. They seemed distraught as they listened to judges characterize their personal lives as destroyed by male abandonment and neglect. Since many of them were women of color who had themselves been stigmatized by controlling stereotypes of their parenting, these mothers likely related to the damage being done. They thus seemed genuinely uncertain how to proceed in these state spaces—some backed off their demands or dropped their cases entirely, neither of which was a desirable outcome.

Recognizing the state politics at play here may provide a way to proceed through this muddled terrain—or at least ways around some of its political roadblocks. At their core, the processes analyzed in this book are part of a more general war on the impoverished and communities of color. This war encompasses more than the racialized tropes of popular culture and the economic discrimination of financial institutions. It also includes the concrete policies enacted by state criminal justice and child support systems. Its battleground includes specific laws that criminalize marginalized men and treat them as failed fathers or broken work machines. State actors wage this war in part by holding poor men up to outdated parenting ideals and by punishing them through the very fatherhood standards they are least able to meet. In the end, this is a war that harms all sides—fathers, mothers, and children. In this way, Lamar was right on point: the first step is "to show these men as human." This must be accompanied by another step: breaking down the state processes that underpin this view of indebted fathers as untouchables, with few allies or defenders willing to be associated with them. And this might then lead to yet another step: opening up sufficient political space to make state policy more reflective of the lives of those it is designed to improve and protect.

NAVIGATING THROUGH INDEBTED FATHERHOOD

Given the size and scope of the system of indebted fatherhood, unpacking the institutional processes underlying it and the parental effects emerging from it is quite an undertaking. So I will cover this ground in three stages, moving my analysis from the accumulation of debt to the enforcement of debt to the parental consequences of indebtedness.

Part 1 begins by tracing how the United States created a child support system through which poor fathers accumulate so much debt and disadvantage. It focuses on the debt of imprisonment, revealing how a perfect storm of debt floods the lives of disadvantaged parents in general and how that storm becomes a tsunami for incarcerated fathers. Chapter 1 examines the successive waves of child support reform over the past forty years and the increased federal involvement in the child support system. It also examines how the paternal politics of poverty in the 1980s and 1990s ushered in a shift in child support so that it no longer served as a replacement for public assistance but instead became a conduit for repaying state benefits. It also exposes the racial undercurrents that often fueled this shift in welfare payback policies and ultimately the criminalization of debt. This is followed by an analysis of key divergences in child support policy within and across states—differences that help explain why the experience of child support, and its accumulated debt, is so dependent on parents' state of residence. In the end, this chapter argues that federal and state child support policies work together to create a system in which poverty, and not necessarily neglect or desertion, leads to massive debt.

Chapter 2 then zooms in on the subgroup of indebted parents at the center of this book: incarcerated fathers. It dissects how and why debt accumulates so much more quickly for fathers with the mark of a criminal record. To do this, I pull apart the specific laws and policies underlying the debt of imprisonment, showing how incarcerated fathers become ensnarled at every stage of the child support process, from the setting of their orders to their post-release modification. This chapter also ventures into the messy world of child support courts to explore how state practices exact a much greater toll on incarcerated fathers. From their inability to appear in court, to their lack of legal know-how, to their inability to code switch from prison to court, incarcerated fathers are at an enormous disadvantage in negotiating these interlocking systems. And the enormity of their post-prison debt is testament to this disadvantage.

Child support debt comes with an enforcement apparatus that is itself quite punitive. Part 2 focuses on this arena of enforcement, what I term the imprisonment of debt. Chapter 3 disentangles *how* and *what* this system punishes. It begins by unpacking the continuum of enforcement measures and describing the financial, remedial, and custodial modes of punishment that operate at different state levels; then it reveals how they are applied in quite unpredictable and inconsistent ways. This chapter also analyzes variations in the targets of state punishment. For this, I go inside the child support systems of New York City and Florida to explore what support courts end up sanctioning. Here I show how New York courts frequently use child support to punish parents for being poor and for failing to work hard enough to rise out of this poverty. Florida courts, by contrast, are more fixated on male breadwinning and on fathers' failures as providers. In this way, I argue that child support enforcement penalizes much more than the nonpayment of support: it also impugns indebted fathers' work lives and parental identities.

Chapter 4 extends the analysis of the criminalization of fathers to include the financial, familial, and legal loops created by the imprisonment of debt. It reveals how these loops crisscross among institutions to form cycles of disadvantage for indebted fathers. From the financial obstacles that can draw fathers underground, to the familial pressures that can dislodge them from vital networks, to the legal hurdles that can land them back in prison, I show how fathers' attempts to manage debt frequently undermine their social reintegration. Throughout this analysis, I also point to an enduring irony of the enforcement system: as fathers respond to it by retreating underground, violating rules, and committing crime, the system ends up producing the kind of subjects it most fears. Thus, the chapters in part 2 expose how the enforcement system creates criminals where there were once only indebted parents.

In part 3, I turn to men's lives as fathers. Indebted fathers face a common set of economic, familial, and legal challenges to their social reintegration, yet they deal with those struggles in diverse ways. Chapter 5 examines fathers who parent at opposite ends of a continuum. At one end are those who confront the constraints on their lives in heroic, almost superhuman ways. These men parent under the most trying of circumstances but find ways to care for their kids reliably and lovingly. At the other end are fathers who respond with the opposite: already unresponsive or ambivalent parents, they deal with the challenges brought on by child support debt and enforcement by acting in the most stereotypically neglectful ways. Instead of viewing these parental trajectories solely as outgrowths of men's individual ability to be dependable and resilient, I connect them to fathers' access to social, familial, and public resources and to how those resources shape men's confidence and competence as fathers.

In between these two groups of men we find the vast majority of fathers: those who parent in between the extremes of "good" and "bad" fathering, often vacillating between them. Chapter 6 turns to these men, who have the best parental intentions but often get ensnarled in the entanglements of debt and punishment. It traces how these men cycle through their kids' lives, fluctuating between feeling committed as parents and overwhelmed as indebted fathers. While these fathers' lives are some of the messiest, they are also quite patterned. When they have resources to bolster their confidence and value as caregivers, they cycle up; when that support dwindles, they cycle down and can derail as parents. As this chapter also shows, no matter what the source of men's cyclical parenting, it exacerbates the distrust in their intimate relationships. This is particularly true of relationships with mothers, as gender distrust can propel and worsen men's episodic fathering. Together, the chapters in part 3 highlight the role of the state in shaping how men conceptualize, judge, and conduct themselves as fathers, as well as the consequences of this conduct for familial well-being more broadly.

This book comes at a time when criminal justice reform is at the forefront of many political agendas. Gaining more support and attention than ever, advocates of reform cross the ideological spectrum, from the Black Lives Matter movement to the Koch brothers. The concluding chapter harnesses the political will of the moment to argue for the inclusion of child support in larger projects to reform the criminal justice system. This chapter makes a case for why child support must be central to reform conversations; it also suggests concrete reforms to disrupt the spiraling of parental debt and the never-ending cycle of punishment. After suggesting a road map for reform at both the federal and state levels, the book ends by recalling the importance of linking policy reform to the reimagining of fatherhood, in the hope of bringing about a real change in how men with criminal records are viewed and valued as fathers.

PART I Accumulation

"Sir, can you hear me?" Judge Chen yells into the speakerphone. "Why couldn't you come to court today? Why are you appearing by phone?" The man on the other end of the line explains that his driver's license had been suspended due to back child support so he could not drive to court. "What about public transportation, Mr. Garcia? We have that in Los Angeles, you know?" Judge Chen responds, unpersuaded. "Yes, but I just had heart surgery," the man explains. "So I can't move very well. It takes me three buses to get down there." The state attorney sitting across from Judge Chen confirms that her records indicate Mr. Garcia has been on disability assistance for several years. "Well, then, I guess I understand. I suppose this is why you haven't worked in years?" Judge Chen responds, her question sounding more like an accusation than a query. Mr. Garcia corroborates that he has indeed been disabled for the past few years.

The state attorney then reads the details of Mr. Garcia's case for the entire courtroom to hear: Mr. Garcia owes over $500,000 in arrears on orders for his children, who are now twenty-eight, thirty-three, and forty-one years old. Gasps ripple across the courtroom, including from Judge Chen, who rarely shows any reaction to the cases before her. She does a quick calculation and announces that, given the 10 percent interest that

California charges on child support debt, Mr. Garcia's interest-only payment on his debt would approximate $2,300 per month. "Damn, that's like having a mortgage on an expensive house," the man sitting next to me whispers. "But I bet he don't live in no expensive house." Silence then falls over the courtroom as everyone contemplates what it means for a man living on a disability pension to be charged that amount by the state. The silence is broken by Mr. Garcia who, almost on cue, reveals his place of residence: "I rent a small studio in the back of the auto body shop I used to work at.... It's loud and dirty but it's a place to live."

Finally, the state attorney gets to the actual point of the hearing: Mr. Garcia would like his license back, but because of his spotty payment history, the state is not inclined to reinstate it and might actually consider holding him in contempt of court for nonpayment. A lively discussion ensues, with Judge Chen and the state attorney going back and forth about what Mr. Garcia has paid on the debt and how much he receives in disability every month. During it all, Mr. Garcia remains silent. Finally, they conclude by offering him a "deal": if he pays $500 every month on his debt, which is half his disability benefit, they will lift the hold on his driver's license and not hold him in contempt. Mr. Garcia tries to get them down to $300, explaining that he cannot work to increase his income, but they won't budge. "Well, I can try," he concludes, "if it means I get my license back after all these years."

As the phone call ends, Judge Chen looks dismayed. She then asks the attorney if anything can be done about Mr. Garcia's arrears. "A $2,300 interest payment seems, well, a bit excessive," she notes. The attorney shakes her head, explaining that she'll look into the case but the arrears are a mixture of welfare debt and parental debt. "They're from the 1980s and 1990s so our hands are tied."

Indeed, it appears little can be done to reduce Mr. Garcia's debt: once accumulated, his support debt seems set in stone. Child support is one of very few types of debt that cannot be discharged, so it follows those who cannot pay it to their grave. Even filing for bankruptcy does not absolve a parent of this debt. This is perhaps why Mr. Garcia seems resigned to a life in debt. At no point in the proceedings did he try to get his debt reduced, modified, or altered; all of the negotiations were over how large his monthly payment on it would be. While it was unclear from the hearing whether his debt continues to accrue interest after all these years, it has profound consequences nonetheless. Living $500,000 in the red to the state meant living without a driver's license, without a professional license, without the ability to get a federal loan or private credit, and often without a bank account. It meant living without the possibility of owning his place of residence; Mr. Garcia's mortgage was to the State of California. In essence, it meant living without financial citizenship and all the rights and responsibilities that come with it.

Although few indebted fathers have amassed as much debt as Mr. Garcia, nothing else was particularly unique about his case. Like millions of other men, his life included many bouts of unemployment, a few stints in jail, ongoing health problems, and lots of years of poverty. The one exceptional thing about Mr. Garcia's case was its longevity: it began in the late 1970s, when his first son was a toddler, and lasted into his sixties, when his grandson could have himself been a father. In fact, over the years, his support debt had become something of a family affair, with Mr. Garcia's oldest son sometimes making payments on a decades-old debt once intended to support him as a child. He did so simply to keep his elderly father out of legal trouble.

The longevity of the Garcia case is precisely what makes it such a good preview of what is to come in part 1. It offers a window onto the successive waves of child support reform that have emerged over the past forty years: from the rise of child support as a federal issue, to its use as a replacement for public assistance, to its recasting as a repayment of state benefits. Add to this the many machinations of state-level policies. Mr. Garcia has ridden these waves from the beginning and lived through a storm of policy change—and has half a million dollars of debt to show for it. The next two chapters tell the story of how this storm formed: chapter 1 reveals how the storm has flooded the lives of poor families in general, while chapter 2 details how the storm has become a tsunami for formerly incarcerated parents.

1 Making Men Pay

> One of the main reasons single mothers go on welfare is that fathers have failed to meet their responsibilities to the children. . . . If every parent paid the child support they should, we could move 800,000 women and children off welfare immediately.
>
> Bill Clinton, at the 1996 Announcement of the Personal Responsibility and Work Opportunity Act

There are very few policy areas, particularly when it comes to families and children, that are characterized by complete bipartisan agreement. Throughout the 1980s and 1990s, child support policy was one such area: politicians and legislators broadly agreed that the "problems" of sole parenthood, poverty, and welfare could be addressed by "making men pay."[1] While their emphases differed in terms of whom men should pay and what they should pay for, policy-makers agreed that the support system needed revamping. After decades of leaving child support to state legislatures and agencies, the federal government entered this arena, setting out to build a policy apparatus alongside the state systems. That policy apparatus remains largely intact today as few lawmakers have had the political will to criticize or reform it.

In particular, federal involvement in child support was intricately linked to welfare politics from the start. But, as I show in this chapter, the nature of the link shifted over time. Initially, child support was framed as a *replacement* for public assistance—as a form of support that would help poor families avoid public assistance. Federal policies used mandates and oversight to ensure compliance with support orders between parents. Over time, the federal focus shifted and child support became a form of *repayment* for public assistance—a way to pay back the state for benefits it provided to poor families. Often with the encouragement of academic researchers invested in ending welfare as they knew it, child support politics were interwoven with welfare reform politics. This resulted in a system in which more parents became indebted to the state itself. Filing a child support order became a requirement for applicants for public aid, who then had to give up their right to support payments. This shift to child support as "state payback" is largely what has underpinned the massive increase in child support debt since the 1970s.

The federal government's role in child support became considerable, but individual states retained significant control over implementation and enforcement. Some key policies of the national child support system amounted to mandates—that is, they dictated what states had to include in their support programs. But many other directives were merely advisory. States used this maneuvering room to leave their mark on the form and focus of child support systems. Clear patterns of divergence then arose, with some states taking a law and order approach designed to "make men pay" in the punitive sense. Other states set out to moderate the effects of national policies by designing state systems that would "make men pay" in strictly the financial sense. These state patterns also varied and evolved over time, with states engaging in punitive child support politics at different moments.

The policy divergences within and across states are described in the second part of this chapter, where my analysis shifts to those state policies that have had the strongest impact on debt accumulation. These include divergent policies on how child support orders are set—in particular, on how they define a parent's "ability to pay" and how orders are calculated for low-income parents whose families are on public assistance. Equally pronounced are variations in state procedures for modifying a support order once it's on the books. Given the differences in how states define a "significant change of circumstance" that warrants the modification of an order, parents confront inconsistent legal standards as they manage support payments and the debt that can arise from them. There are also huge variations in the interest rate applied to support debt, which ranges from 0 to 12 percent, depending on where the order was filed. All of these differences make the experience of child support, and its accumulated debt, dependent on the parents' state of residence.

Amidst all these differences, one outcome is consistent: federal and state child support policies have worked together to create a system in which poverty, and not necessarily neglect or desertion, leads to massive child support debt. Whether this was the intention or not, these policies have been woven together into a net that captures dead-broke parents, who are subsequently cast as deadbeats. Child support debt is unique in that a small number of parents owe the majority of it: close to 60 percent of support debt is owed by only 10 percent of obligors. And they are not the privileged few; indeed, the overwhelming majority of these obligors are poor—one study found that 70 percent of them reported little or no income in the previous year.[2] These are also the parents with the most debt: 76 percent of parents who owe more than $100,000 in back support made less than $10,000 per year.[3] The child support system thus generates a perfect storm of debt, with arrears accumulating rapidly and from multiple directions until they submerge low-income parents. So, how did that storm emerge? How did the child support system become the terrain of the poor?

A PERFECT STORM OF DEBT

The story of how the federal child support system was built is a complex one, largely because the policies that comprise it are themselves very complicated. Since the mid-1970s, there have been dozens of pieces of federal legislation dealing with child support specifically, as well as countless others that affect the system indirectly. There has also been a vast amount of research on the form and focus of these policies.[4] Amidst all this legislation and policy analysis, two developments at the federal level stand out as especially consequential: policies enacted to regulate the payment of private support and to mandate the repayment of public assistance.

In the late 1970s and 1980s, the political mantra of "make men pay" spurred the federal government to enter the child support arena. Initially, its main target was child support paid between parents, what I refer to as "private" support.[5] The first wave of federal policies set out to standardize child support procedures and address the power imbalances among judges, mothers, and fathers. Here "getting men to pay" implied ensuring that fathers paid mothers the support they needed to raise children. The state stepped in to help parents obtain that support, and the funds thereby gathered were to be channeled to and used by custodial parents. For disadvantaged families, the plan was to get fathers to pay so that mothers would not have to go on public assistance—or could go off assistance if they were already receiving it. That imperative was embedded in a broader call to hold men accountable for their children's financial well-being.

This broad approach began to narrow as another series of policy waves developed in the 1980s, reaching their peak in the 1990s. These waves were launched by welfare reform politics that ushered in child support policies linked to state-owed support; parents would now be charged for the public assistance received by their families. While there had always been "welfare payback" provisions for families enrolled in Aid to Families with Dependent Children (AFDC) and food stamp programs, they were uneven and often unenforced at the state level. In the 1980s, these payback provisions were extended and mandated—the federal government required them and funded their collection. Child support thus became a form of cost recovery for both federal and state governments. This marked a profound shift in the meaning of "making men pay." Fathers were no longer only paying mothers to support their children or to get them off public assistance. The state now demanded to be paid back and reimbursed for the public aid it gave to families. Those who failed to pay back the money were then constructed not only as failing to support their children but also as stealing from the public—and thus as needing "to pay" in both the financial and punitive sense.

With this shift, the child support system bifurcated: it became a two-tiered program, split between support owed to parents and support owed to the state. The child support program then experienced the largest expansion in its history, with public payback at times overtaking other support in size and scope and causing overall debt to surge to $117 billion by 2020. In the process, child support became thoroughly racialized and, ultimately, criminalized. And the iconic deadbeat, notorious for neglecting his family and robbing taxpayers, had been created.

Child Support as a Replacement for Public Assistance

Most people, when they think of child support, imagine it as an exchange between two parents—the noncustodial parent, usually the father, provides a set amount of financial support to the custodial parent, usually the mother.[6] Indeed, forty years ago this *was* the main type of child support. In 1974, when the federal government formalized its involvement in child support policy, this was the support it targeted. Given the state's long history of involvement in familial welfare—from mothers' pensions to Aid to Dependent Children (ADC) to AFDC to food stamps—child support entered the state arena relatively late. But with divorce rates rising, out-of-wedlock birth rates increasing, and welfare rolls swelling, policy-makers started to look for links among these trends. Never mind that these shifts were largely affecting different socioeconomic groups, with divorce rates and sole parenthood rising primarily among the middle class. The assumption was that public spending was exploding in large part because fathers weren't doing their part to support women and children and that something needed to be done to force them to do so.

At the time, child support programs were small and run at the state level, with enormous variation.[7] There was a patchwork of local-level support practices, with different ways of establishing and enforcing support orders. In fact, many social welfare policies of the period discouraged and even penalized paternal involvement, through "man in the house rules" and stringent means tests that punished poor families with resident fathers. With the Social Services Amendments of 1974—in particular, Title IV-D of the Social Security Act—Congress sought to create consistency in parental support obligations and to regulate the financial contributions of nonresident fathers. There was clearly a need for this, given that at the time, fewer than 20 percent of never-married mothers received any child support.[8] The rationale for the federal enforcement of fathers' support was to get more payments to these mothers to reduce familial poverty and reliance on public assistance.[9]

More specifically, Title IV-D established several mandates for states to follow in their child support programs. It created the federal Office of Child Support Enforcement (OCSE) and required states to have their own OCSE offices.[10] It channeled federal funds to states to assist them in locating nonresident fathers, establishing paternity, and enforcing support orders. It even created a Parent Locator Service that made federal records available to states to assist them in collection efforts. To justify these new expenses, policy-makers and politicians argued that child support could decrease the use of public assistance. As the Act declared: "The problem of welfare... is, to a considerable extent, a problem of the non-support of children by their absent parents."[11] Casper Weinberger, Secretary of Health, Education, and Welfare, put it this way in his memo on the Act:

> Studies indicate that existing state and local child support programs can produce child support collections far in excess of corresponding administrative expenses. Therefore, the new child support program could reduce AFDC costs by substantially increasing child support collections.... Over 75 percent of the AFDC caseload involves an absent parent. Less than 15 percent of the cases are receiving any child support payment.... Certain parents have shifted their support obligation to the public.[12]

Hence, the first federal response to the child support issue was to mandate payment collection and ensure that fathers supported their families. Given how uncontroversial this mandate would become, it is somewhat surprising that it was initially contentious—it passed Congress quite narrowly in 1974. A political balance had to be struck for it to pass. On the one hand were those invested in using child support to get poor families off public assistance. To appease them, support collections for families on AFDC were to be turned over the state; this would reduce costs and discourage "double dipping" by AFDC recipients. But to gain broader political support, this system could not be seen as entirely the terrain of the poor; child support could not be framed only as a means to reduce costs. So lawmakers insisted that child support was also a women's issue, claiming that making men pay was a move toward gender equity. They thus expanded the target of Title IV-D and included provisions to assist non-AFDC families with child support collections.[13]

But this wider casting of the state's net troubled conservative lawmakers, who objected to its potential to impinge on family life. Never mind that the government had a long history of intrusion into the lives of poor families—from man-in-the-house regulations to mandatory paternity establishment.[14] It was the prospect of middle-class intrusions that prompted concerns about privacy. For instance, when contemplating the bill, then President Gerald Ford expressed concern over the Act's parental locator service, writing that it might "interject the Federal Government too deeply into domestic relations."[15] He thus insisted that Congress find a way to protect people's personal lives from government intrusion. Again, this insistence had everything to do with the Act's relatively broad paternal target. Indeed, in the first years of Title IV, fewer than half of all support collections came from poor parents; 60 percent came from parents not receiving AFDC or other public assistance.[16]

Even with these federal mandates, state child support systems remained all over the map.[17] In large part, this was because child support orders—both their setting and their enforcement—were largely at the discretion of local judges.[18] Moreover, there were vast differences in participation rates among low-income parents, especially those who relied on state welfare programs—their participation rates remained low despite attempts to pull them into the system. So ten years after Congress passed Title IV-D, it enacted the Child Support Amendments of 1984. When it came to families receiving AFDC, these amendments tried to incentivize support compliance by mandating that states transfer the first $50 in collected support to families. A decade of experience had taught policymakers that turning over all support payments to the state discouraged both parents from complying with the child support system: why would mothers cooperate when their children received none of the support withheld? And why would fathers pay support if it went to the state and not to their families? It was thought that the $50 "pass-through" would act as an incentive. Some states went further, allowing an even larger portion of support payments to go to families receiving AFDC.[19]

The 1984 Amendments also established procedures to even out state variations in the setting of support orders. They included a federal mandate for income withholding and state procedures to calculate support orders. They required states to set guidelines based on a combination of parents' income, or potential income, and the child's needs—but also gave states the discretion to determine the content of their guidelines and the extent to which judges could deviate from them. Two general models emerged to calculate orders between parents.[20] First, there was the "percentage of income" model, which included only the noncustodial parent's income when calculating the order amount. Some states used a flat percentage formula that applied to parents of all income levels; others used a varying percentage that applied different rates to parents with different incomes. Second, there was the "income shares" model, which used both parents' incomes to set support. Here officials used fixed tables to estimate childrearing expenses and parents' obligations. As with most else, states varied in the implementation of both models, with differences in everything from how income was computed, to how childrearing expenses were set, to whether there were minimum order amounts. Again, these models have shifted over time and across states since first being established.

The Title IV and the Child Support Amendments were federal attempts to increase compliance and uniformity across child support systems. Another law to do this was the Bradley Amendment, passed by Congress in 1986. In fact, Bradley remains one of the most consequential pieces of child support legislation, particularly for disadvantaged fathers. Yet Bradley was not even its own legislation; it was one of thirteen amendments to the Omnibus Budget Reconciliation Act. It introduced three federal mandates for state support systems. First, it required all child support orders to be considered judgments by operation of law—thus, they could be pursued with the full force of the state, including through civil and criminal contempt actions. Second, it required states to enforce unpaid support orders as legal judgments, which meant they could be pursued by state officials the moment a payment was missed. And third, it barred retroactive modification of support orders and arrears, which meant that support debt could remain unchanged irrespective of an obligor's social circumstances. Interestingly, Bradley was uncontroversial at the time: introduced by Senator Bill Bradley, it sailed through Congress uncontested. As the *New York Times* put it, "a vote against the Bradley amendment was politically impossible: it zipped through the Senate without recorded dissent."[21]

Bradley was only the first of several seemingly small, uncontentious reforms that had ramifying effects and that would alter the child support system for decades. It created some of the most significant state mandates to date. By defining child support as judgments of law, it opened up a Pandora's box of enforcement tools that could be used in child support cases, including asset seizures, credit reporting, issuance of property liens, suspension of state-issued licenses, and contempt of court filings.[22] It also allowed these tools to come into play when an order went unpaid, thus giving enormous authority to child support officials.[23] And it curtailed judicial discretion, even that of bankruptcy judges, thereby enhancing the power of enforcement workers. The prohibition against retroactive modification meant that once debt had accrued, obligors were constrained from negotiating it down retrospectively. If a parent was unable to petition for modification before the debt accrued, federal law seemed to foreclose the possibility of debt reduction.

Like previous pieces of federal legislation, the Bradley Amendment was a sign of the times. In its push to create more consistency in state child support programs, the amendment targeted local judges, who were thought to be using their discretion too freely to dismiss fathers' child support arrears. In Congress, the discussion of Bradley was laced with accusations that states had poor records of collecting child support debt in part because judges were routinely dismissing support orders and debt. It was also alleged that absentee fathers had begun to count on these dismissals—amassing huge debt in hopes that sympathetic judges would retroactively forgive it. Yet there is little evidence that judicial favor was in fact the reason for states' poor collection efforts.[24] The politics of child support reflected the larger criminal justice politics of the time, as well as the broader preoccupation with renegade, "activist" judges who used their discretion to undermine the legal system. From the introduction of sentencing guidelines to the establishment of mandatory minimums, criminal justice reforms in the 1980s sought to tie the hands of judicial officials in order to protect "the public."[25] In the child support arena, Bradley was symptomatic of this political preoccupation.

Yet the Bradley Amendment did not promise to protect some mythical public. Indeed, the object it was protecting was quite specific: women and children. This is another way in which Bradley was a sign of the times. By assuming that child support orders were only between parents, it targeted the power imbalance that enabled men to deny support to women. Indeed,

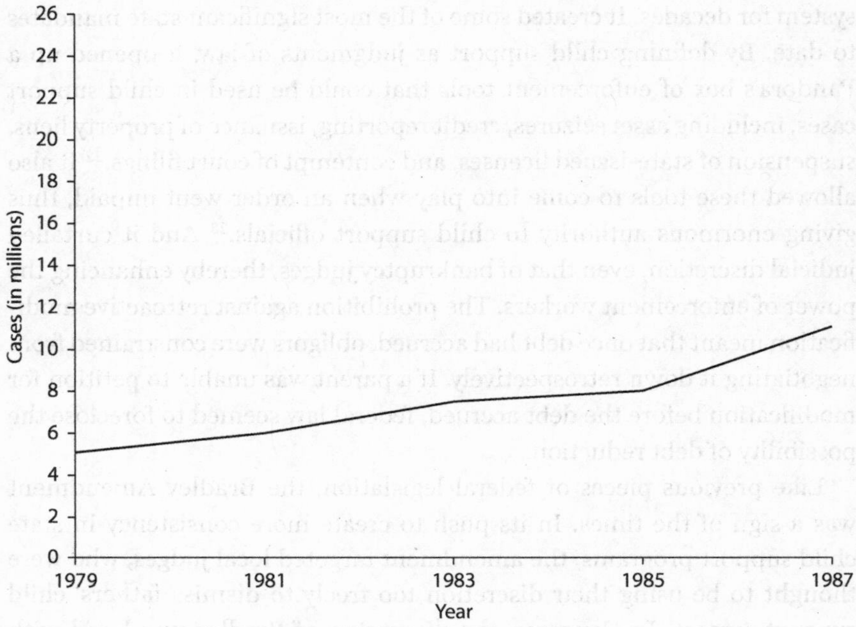

Figure 1. National Child Support Caseload, 1979–1988. SOURCE: OCSE 2004

Senator Bradley justified his amendment in precisely this way, claiming it would break the "shocking spiral of poverty for women and children who were not receiving support to which they were legally entitled."[26] The state as "protector" would step in to halt this spiral and make sure women got what men owed them. Even then-president Ronald Reagan echoed these claims, noting how "shocking" and "unacceptable" it was that so many women received "less than what they're due."[27]

Given the amendment's focus on women and children, it is not surprising that some feminists and child advocates ended up backing Bradley.[28] They did so for good reason: in the late 1980s, only a minority of mothers with support orders were receiving the full amount, and over 20 percent were receiving no payments at all.[29] Feminists traced this to the way in which support orders were set, pointing out that orders were being established inconsistently yet always inadequately to meet children's needs. They offered up effective examples to buttress these claims—for example,

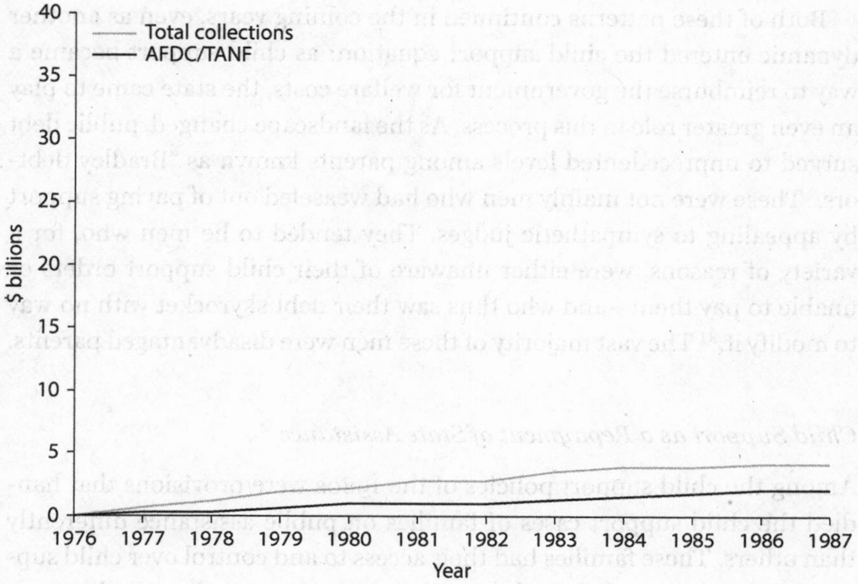

Figure 2. National Child Support Collections, 1976–1987. SOURCE: OCSE 2004

in some states fathers' support payments amounted to less than their car payments. Still, feminists' role has also been overstated by opponents of Bradley—opponents like Phyllis Schlafly, who blamed "feminists and their docile liberal male allies" for inflicting such an "injustice on men" with the amendment.[30] Yet not all women's groups supported Bradley at the time. Those that did tended to support it for orders between parents as a way of curtailing court practices that disadvantaged mothers. Instead of seeking to inflict injustice on men, feminist advocates sought to equalize an imbalance of power by tying judges' hands.

These federal policies—from Title IV-D to the Child Support Amendments to the Bradley Amendment—had a clear impact on child support caseloads and collections. As figure 1 reveals, the overall caseload size doubled in the first decade of federal involvement.

Moreover, as figure 2 indicates, the overall amount of support collections also rose steadily during this period for AFDC and non-AFDC cases.

Both of these patterns continued in the coming years, even as another dynamic entered the child support equation: as child support became a way to reimburse the government for welfare costs, the state came to play an even greater role in this process. As the landscape changed, public debt surged to unprecedented levels among parents known as "Bradley debtors." These were not mainly men who had weaseled out of paying support by appealing to sympathetic judges. They tended to be men who, for a variety of reasons, were either unaware of their child support orders or unable to pay them—and who thus saw their debt skyrocket with no way to modify it.[31] The vast majority of these men were disadvantaged parents.

Child Support as a Repayment of State Assistance

Among the child support policies of the 1980s were provisions that handled the child support cases of families on public assistance differently than others. These families had their access to and control over child support payments curtailed. Such curtailments were applied unevenly across states and locales. For instance, while all states passed through the first $50 in collected child support to families, some states ended up passing through more to support poor families. This began to change in the late 1980s and 1990s as the purpose of child support broadened. In addition to enforcing the payment of support orders between parents as a mode of *cost avoidance*, the child support regime become a form of *cost recovery.* This shift was profound. Mandated child support was no longer justified simply as a way to lift women out of poverty—it also became a way to reimburse taxpayers, or the state itself, for the assistance provided to poor families.

The first sign of this federal shift in focus came in 1988, when Congress passed the Family Support Act (FSA). Best known as a precursor to "welfare reform," the FSA had complete bipartisan support; it sailed through the Senate with a near-unanimous vote. Then-Senator Daniel Patrick Moynihan directly linked together poverty, welfare, and single parenthood:

> We knew that poverty in the United States was now concentrated in single-parent families. . . . Welfare dependency is endemic in the United States today. It is a common experience of children. . . . We talk about the drug

crisis, the education crisis, and the problems of teen pregnancy and juvenile crime. But all these ills trace back predominantly to one source: broken families.[32]

The centerpiece of the FSA was the Job Opportunities and Basic Skills (JOBS) program, which required states to establish work and training programs and introduce work requirements for two-parent families on public assistance. Often overlooked were the FSA's child support provisions, which also produced far-reaching changes. The FSA required states to garnish the wages of parents in all public assistance cases; it mandated paternity establishment in a proportion of assistance cases; and it penalized states that failed to do so. Some states already adhered to these practices; now, the FSA penalized those that did not.[33] The FSA had little impact on AFDC use but a big impact on child support debt, which rose the year after it passed from $14.2 billion in 1988 to $18.9 billion in 1989.[34]

The FSA marked a shift in the nature of child support but did not provide states with the resources to fully actualize the change. As states implemented FSA mandates, public debt continued to rise, inching up steadily in the early 1990s. The big change did not come until 1996, with the Personal Responsibility and Work Opportunity Reconciliation Act (PRWORA). Like other reforms, PRWORA has been analyzed mainly for its effects on welfare policies. Indeed, its impact on those policies was profound: PRWORA overhauled the welfare system by replacing AFDC with Temporary Assistance for Needy Families (TANF) and instituting new time limits and work requirements on assistance. But PRWORA also initiated critical changes in the child support system. It firmly established the principle of public assistance as a "loan" the state provided to poor families, one that was to be repaid by the absent head-of-household in the form of child support.

Overall, PRWORA was a complex piece of legislation, and quite a lot has been written about it and the politics surrounding it.[35] In the child support arena, it ushered in a series of changes expressed as federal mandates and not simply recommendations. It required states to comply with child support enforcement. It mandated that states monitor child support payments and enact universal wage withholding from obligors' paychecks.[36] And it required states to participate in paternity establishment through new procedures such as paternity acknowledgment forms in hospitals, birth register centers, and welfare offices. Failure to do so would lead to new federal sanctions. For instance, states had to establish paternity in a large percentage of nonmarital births, presumably to increase the number of those obligated to pay child support or to repay the cost of public assistance. States that missed the threshold faced additional penalties.

Connected to this, PRWORA required that TANF recipients assign child support payments to the state—so the cost of everything from TANF to Medicaid was calculated as child support and owed to the state.[37] It could also be owed retroactively for public assistance received before the child support order had been established.[38] This debt was federally mandated; states could not allow parents to opt out of it. PRWORA eliminated the requirement that states pass through $50 of child support payments to families; this allowed them to keep all of recipients' child support payments. The large majority of states followed suit and ended pass-throughs.[39] In fact, they were encouraged to do so by a new funding structure: the "proceeds" from payback were now to be split between state and federal governments, so states had to cover the federal portion if they wanted to pass through more child support to families. In this way, PRWORA marked a shift from incentivizing state participation to punishing noncompliance.

The same shift applied to parents who did not comply: instead of incentivizing their cooperation, PRWORA used penalties to enforce it. The legislation introduced an arsenal of enforcement tools. It expanded the Parent Locator Service. It created a national directory of new hires to ensure that all eligible orders were issued and collected through universal withholding. It expedited the issuance of property liens and seizures as well as the appropriation of tax refunds. It required the revocation of state-issued licenses, including driver's licenses. And it allowed states to deny food stamps to those behind in their child support payments. Together, these provisions ensured that the role of welfare payback would become more significant and that those parents "indebted" to the public would be tracked down and punished.

PRWORA also dramatically increased the size of this indebted group. As figure 3 shows, close to 8 million cases had been added to the child support caseload by the time PRWORA passed.

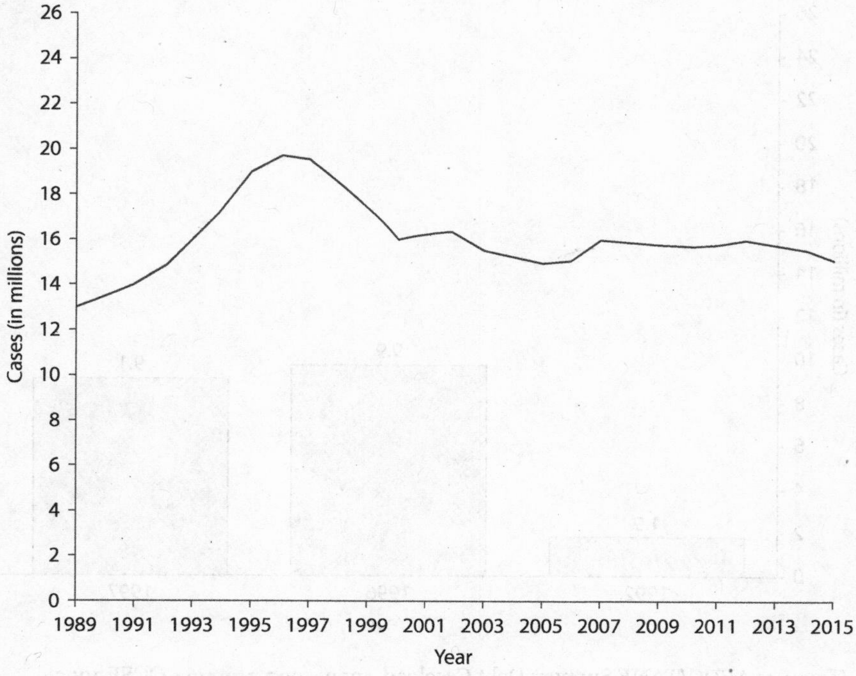

Figure 3. National Child Support Caseload, 1989–2015. SOURCE: OCSE 2004, 2015

Importantly, the overwhelming majority of these new cases involved families who received public assistance. As figure 4 indicates, within only five years, the size of the caseload involving AFDC/TANF arrears had surged by 364 percent. The child support politics surrounding the PRWORA reforms were similar to those of the Bradley Amendment a decade earlier, but on a larger scale. Here, too, there was broad bipartisan support for the legislation, with almost all Republicans and half of Democrats in Congress voting for the Act.[40] Child support reforms garnered even more consensus; there was little disagreement expressed about the core principles guiding them. Prominent academics and policy experts backed these provisions, offering up research that linked poverty to out-of-wedlock births and absentee fathers, thus buttressing the arguments of "family values" advocates concerned about rising divorce rates and nostalgic for a mythical era of male breadwinners. For instance, Harvard pro-

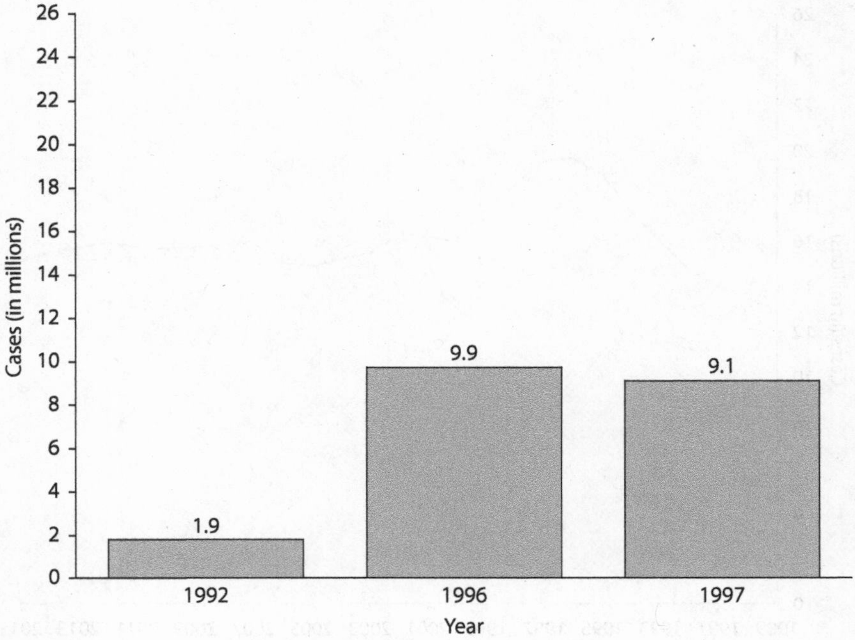

Figure 4. AFDC/TANF Support Debt Caseload, 1992–1997. SOURCE: OCSE 1997

fessor and policy adviser David Ellwood argued that strengthening support enforcement was not simply about economic efficiency; it was also "a matter of right and wrong," since "parents have obligations."[41] Never mind that even at the time there was an abundance of research showing that most of those who were failing to pay support did not question their obligations—they were simply poor fathers whose child support orders far exceeded their ability to pay them.[42] Yet this research rarely made it into the political debate over PRWORA.

Also missing from the discussion was a feminist analysis of PRWORA's child support provisions. Some women's groups did support those parts of the legislation that claimed to be advancing gender equity and fairness. A few groups, like the National Women's Law Center and the Children's Defense Fund, and a few prominent female politicians, like Hillary Rodham Clinton, came out in support of the child support reforms. Again, they saw those reforms as advancing gender equity in caregiving.[43] Yet, as was true with Bradley, the feminists' role here tends to be overstated.[44] Most feminist policy-makers failed to interrogate the changes in child support or to lift the cloak of gender equity that obscured them. Some simply overlooked the significance of the child support reforms and the impact public welfare debt could have on poor families. Others were more focused on challenging other parts of PRWORA, centered on how its work requirements undercut motherhood and wage labor as well as how they undermined the basic principles of public assistance.[45]

Had feminist lawmakers looked a bit more closely at the child support reforms, they would have seen how the same ideas that so troubled them about PRWORA's welfare reforms also characterized its child support reforms. Both reforms were guided by a distrust of poor women, who were not to be trusted to decide when to name the fathers of their children—so the state had to force them to do so. Nor were they to be trusted to decide how to spend the $50 child support pass-through they might have received—so the state had to claim it from them. They were not entitled to basic privacy rights—so the state could enlist them in tracking down their indebted partners and then refuse to pay them anything from what was retrieved of their debt.

Perhaps most importantly, PRWORA's welfare and child support reforms marked a shift in understandings of what public assistance connoted. They signified an end to what little entitlement poor families had to state assistance. For female recipients, this meant new requirements to work off their benefits and time limits regarding how long they could receive them. For their male partners, it meant that whatever the state paid in benefits they would have to repay as child support. For both parents, state assistance was now cast as a loan from the state and other taxpayers. Jennifer Dunn, a Member of Congress from Washington, perfectly summarized the newly merged logic of welfare and child support:

> What these deadbeat parents do is . . . force you, the American taxpayer, to pick up the tab for their irresponsibility. . . . They force the Government to become the parent. . . . The child support provision of our bill, which I am pleased to say has great bipartisan support, will begin the process of ending welfare as we now know it and putting our children first by requiring both parents to support their own children.[46]

It is no coincidence that this shift in the logic of assistance was accompanied by a more punitive approach to its collection. With shocking speed, the notion that parents were *borrowing* from the state morphed into the notion that they were *robbing* the state. Not by chance, the construct of the deadbeat now emerged as the symbol of men with child support arrears. This is one way the child support politics of the 1990s were unique. Unlike discussions of Title IV reforms, concerns were no longer being raised about protecting parents' privacy or expanding the child support system to encompass middle-class parents. Those concerns had disappeared, which was both a cause and a consequence of who deadbeats were thought to be. The iconic deadbeat of the period was marked by his race and class: he was the absentee male partner of the iconic "welfare queen." He had many kids from many women, none of whom he supported. He was always conniving and villainous, and he was usually a man of color. And he was all over the media, with episodes of *Cops* and *America's Most Wanted* devoted to apprehending him and bringing him to justice.

Once deadbeats were framed as stealing from the public, it was only a matter of time before they were criminalized. Politicians and government officials began talking about "tracking them down" and giving them "no place to run."[47] Nonpayment of child support was now being equated with serious crimes, like robbery. Such men were to be combated using tactics of war—capture them, detain them, and force them to pay. There is no better articulation of this than these comments by then-president Bill Clinton the week before he signed PRWORA:

> Non-payment of child support is a serious crime, like robbing a bank or even a 7-Eleven store.... If you owe child support, you better pay it. If you deliberately refuse to pay it, you can find your face posted in the Post Office. We'll track you down with computers. We'll track you down with law enforcement. We'll find you through the Internet.[48]

Needless to say, there was no serious attempt to figure out who these parents actually were. There was no attempt to break down representations of them or to make differentiations among them. There was no discussion of why some fathers were unable to pay their child support orders. It was rarely considered that some fathers might be unable to pay because they were incapacitated, institutionalized, or incarcerated. There was no

WANTED
In Hamilton County, Ohio
FOR NON-PAYMENT OF CHILD SUPPORT
If you have information on the whereabouts of any of these offenders, please contact the Hamilton County Sheriff's Fugitive Warrants Unit
513-946-5350
FIRST TIME EVER, 2ND POSTER ISSUED IN A YEAR!
Thanks to community response, all offenders from Aug 2006 poster have been apprehended!
For a full listing of local parents with outstanding child support, visit the Hamilton County Sheriff's Office website at www.hcso.org and choose "Deadbeats" from the Public Services menu.
This poster is a public service of the Hamilton County Child Support Services.
JOB & FAMILY SERVICES

Figure 5. Ohio Wanted Sign, 2006

discussion of whether they were otherwise good parents or caregivers. There was no mention that much of their debt was owed to the state, not to mothers and children. So, as promised, "Wanted" posters like this one, from Ohio, did indeed go up in child support departments, post offices, and police precincts across the country (figure 5).

This image of the deadbeat soon became enshrined in federal law. In 1998, two years after PRWORA, Congress passed the Deadbeat Parents Punishment Act. Besides using the term "deadbeat" for the first time in federal legislation, the Act made nonpayment of child support a felony. As the Act put it, the goal was to "establish felony violations for the failure to pay legal child support obligations."[49] The Act targeted nonpayment across state lines, since willful non-payment had been a felony in most states since the early 1990s. The Act also created gradations of punishments, making it a more serious felony to move across state lines to avoid

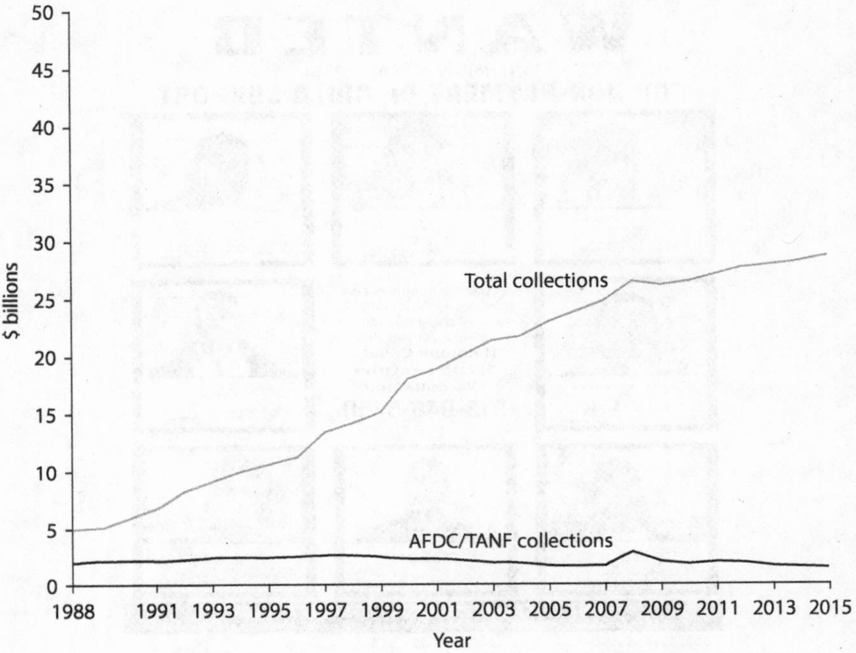

Figure 6. National Child Support Collections, 1988–2015. SOURCES: OCSE 2004, 2015

paying a support order. Like so many child support policies of this period, it received bipartisan support. One Democratic senator from Wisconsin offered this defense of the Act: "This measure sends a clear message to deadbeat dads: ignore the law, ignore your responsibilities, and you will pay a high price. In other words, pay up or go to jail."[50]

With the Deadbeat Parents Punishment Act, the foundations of the federal child support system were laid. Into the 2000s, that system would continue to focus on public assistance payback and on corresponding punishments for failure to pay.[51] As a consequence, the amount of collections and the amount of debt both rose steadily. As figure 6 reveals, there was a steady increase in the overall amount of child support collected over this period, while the amount collected in TANF debt remained relatively flat.

While overall collections increased steadily, the amount of support debt surged. As figure 7 shows, between the late 1980s and 2015 there was a

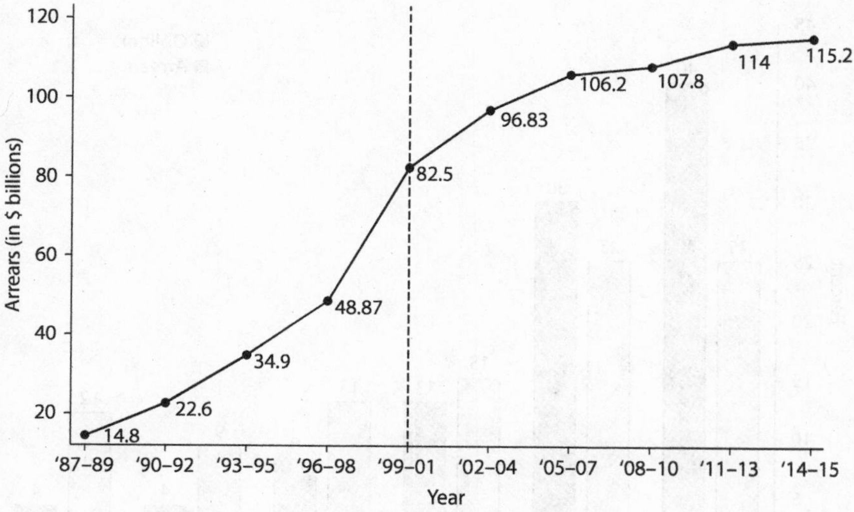

Figure 7. National Child Support Debt, 1987–2015. SOURCES: OCSE 2004, 2015

significant increase in support debt: the $14.8 billion owed in 1987–1989 had risen to $115.2 billion by 2015.[52] By that year, support debt exceeded federal expenditures on TANF and food stamps combined. And much of this increase was due to the sharp increase in public assistance debt owed to the government.

These policy shifts turned *public* assistance into *private* debt in ways that disproportionally affected disadvantaged parents. As figure 8 indicates, this state arena became the terrain of the poor, with most debt owed by parents making poverty-level wages or reporting no income at all.

The targeting of poor parents through welfare debt continued throughout the 2000s. No major federal reforms were made to reduce the accumulation of welfare debt. Instead, that reduction ended up happening because of something else—the end of welfare itself. Bill Clinton had kept at least part of his promise—many of the 800,000 women and children he so infamously promised to move off welfare through PRWORA did in fact leave assistance. But it was not because they exited poverty; in fact, poverty rates actually rose during this period. Nor was it because mothers became flush from all the child support payments they were now receiving; in fact,

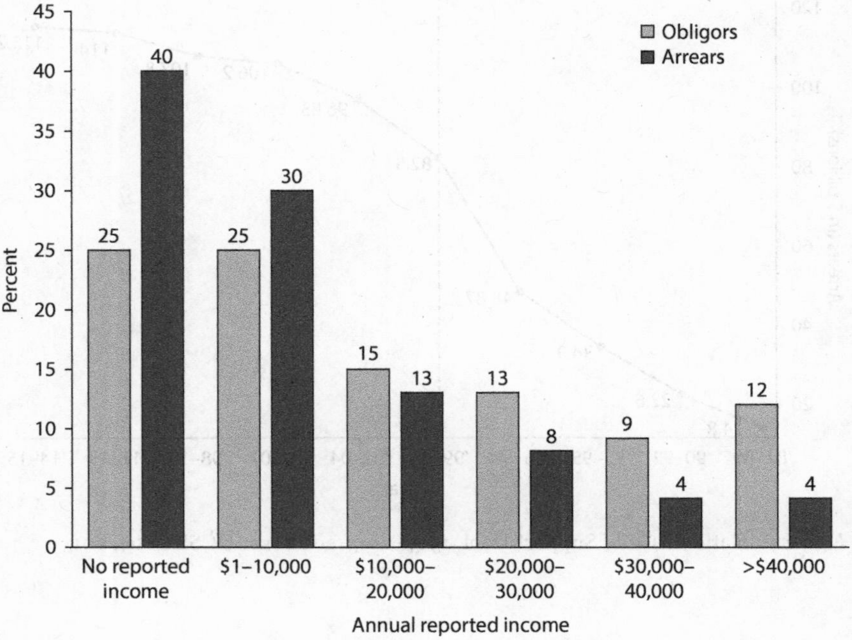

Figure 8. Child Support Obligors and Arrears (Nine State Sample) by Income 2003–2004. SOURCE: Sorenson, Sousa, and Schaner 2007

the back support owed to them *rose* during this the period. Instead, many women were pushed off assistance by new eligibility requirements and time limits. Others left with their feet, refusing to participate voluntarily in child support enforcement. As a result, the portion of family income coming from TANF funds shrunk, as figure 9 reveals.

As the use of public assistance declined, the ratio of private to public debt shifted, with more poor families turning to private support. While these families had always cobbled together funds from both public and private sources, by the late 2000s the latter had overtaken the former. The decline in TANF use had led to increased reliance on child support and a shift in the site of re/distribution from the state to the family. Vulnerable families now had to rely on a more precarious and inconsistent source of income. Between 2000 and 2016 there was a 62 percent decrease in child support cases involving TANF-assisted families.[53] Again, while overall child support debt continued to rise, TANF debt declined in the 2010s.

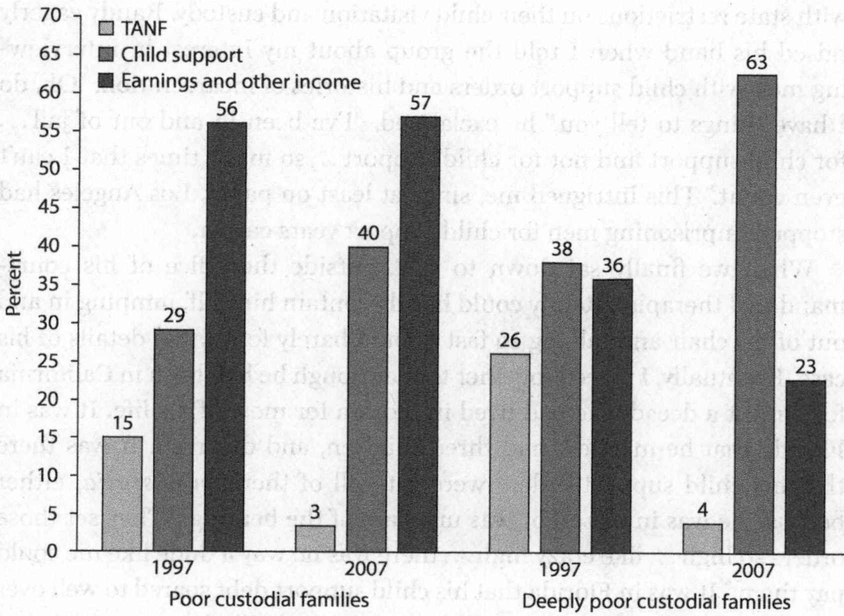

Figure 9. Family Income from TANF and Child Support, 1997 and 2007.
SOURCE: Sorenson 2010

That decline had less to do with shifts in child support policy and more to do with reforms to welfare provisions adjacent to it.

Moreover, after decades of trying to forge consistency among state systems, in the 2000s the federal government began to encourage state variation. As with welfare programs, the federal government allowed states to be "inventive" when it came to setting and collecting public child support debt. With much of the action occurring at the state level, the child support story became even more complicated as it weaved its way through state legislatures, political cultures, and court systems.

WHAT A DIFFERENCE A STATE MAKES

I had been looking forward to talking with Randy for weeks. We met at a Los Angeles meeting of the Fatherhood Initiative, held for men faced with state restrictions on their child visitation and custody. Randy eagerly raised his hand when I told the group about my interest in interviewing men with child support orders and histories of incarceration. "Oh, do I have things to tell you," he exclaimed. "I've been in and out of jail... for child support and not for child support... so many times that I can't even count." This intrigued me, since at least on paper, Los Angeles had stopped imprisoning men for child support years earlier.

When we finally sat down to talk, outside the office of his court-mandated therapist, Randy could hardly contain himself, jumping in and out of his chair and talking so fast I could barely follow the details of his case. Eventually, I pieced together that although he had been in California for almost a decade, he had lived in Florida for most of his life. It was in Florida that he married, had three children, and divorced. It was there that his child support orders were set—all of them *in absentia,* either because he was in prison or was unaware of the hearing. "They set those orders so high... like crazy high... there was no way a dude like me could pay them." It was in Florida that his child support debt soared to well over $50,000. "Whenever I lost a job or went in [to jail], the amount I owed just grew and grew." It was in Florida that he was held in contempt of court for nonpayment of support more times than he could remember. "They jailed me like ten times, I swear, for child support." It was also in Florida that he racked up a felony conviction for crossing state lines, which the state insisted was to avoid paying child support. "Moving to Georgia had nothing to do with child support, I swear. It was for a job... okay, and also for a girl. But they said it was [for child support] and brought me back in cuffs... threw me away for a long time." A casualty of the 1998 Deadbeat Parent Act.

By the time Randy came to Los Angeles in the 2000s, the California system, which had been one of the most punitive programs in the United States, was undergoing reform. As Randy recalls, he got things done there that were unimaginable in Florida. He worked out a low-income "payment plan" to pay down his debt over time, with a $100 monthly payment. He reduced his welfare debt by proving he was homeless with no reportable income. Each time he went to jail in California, which happened a few times for minor, non–child-support-related offenses, he had his order set at $0 during incarceration simply by filling out paperwork.

So even though he was homeless when we spoke, he ended the interview by exclaiming, "They don't call California the Golden State for nothin'"—without even a tinge of irony.

While California is far from the Golden State of child support, and has certainly not always been as accommodating as Randy encountered, his experience points to the difference a state can make in the arena of child support. The United States is very much a collection of fifty child support systems, all of them loosely guided by varying degrees of federal oversight. While federal guidance over child support reached its peak in the 1990s with the passage of PRWORA, that oversight still allowed for states to craft the form and focus of their support systems. By the 2000s vastly different state child support systems had emerged. While these differences are multitudinous, three areas of divergence have the greatest consequences for debt accumulation: state policies on setting child support orders, on modifying orders, and on charging interest on debt.

Setting Orders

One of the first things the federal government did when it got involved in child support in the 1980s was to mandate that states set clear guidelines for how orders are established. But it stopped short of dictating the content of those guidelines. This has led to the use of different income calculations, with states computing orders according to "percentage of income" or "income shares." And among these models are all sorts of permutations. Policy analysts Pirog and Ziol-Guest write that fifty-four state models are in use, when Guam, US Virgin Islands, Puerto Rico, and the District of Columbia are included.[54] They also provide a concrete example of the consequences of the lack of standardization, showing how a low-income father in New York could end up paying as little as $30 in support while his counterpart in Indiana could pay upwards of $325.

Part of the reason for these massive differences in order amounts is the absence of federal mandates regarding how states should proceed when confronted with insufficient information to set an order. What should be done when the parents are not in court or cannot provide complete income documentation? Or when they are deemed unemployed or underemployed? States have ended up dealing with these issues very differently, leading to sharp variation in the amount of support orders. Lest we think such issues are exceptional, a California study found the majority of support orders for low-income parents were set by default, meaning they were issued at a time when at least one parent (usually the father) was not present and/or did not provide complete income information.[55]

One of the most comprehensive studies of state-level variation in default orders was conducted by the Office of the Inspector General. It found that most states (48 of them) set these orders through income imputation—that is, they used a combination of factors to determine how much the noncustodial parent *should* be earning.[56] Of these, the majority imputed income based on the assumption that parents should work a minimum wage job for forty hours per week. States also looked at the parents' skills and experience, as well as their most recent employment, to set an order above the minimum wage rate. Here, too, there was large variation in how courts interpreted the information: Did they use it as contextual material to assess a parent's real ability to earn income or to justify an increase in a parent's order? Did states define underemployment in light of labor market realities? Or did it reflect what parental employment should look like in an ideal world? Some states also introduced minimum orders, under which no support order could go. These orders could be issued irrespective of parental income and used when sufficient wage information was unavailable.

In 2016, in an effort to even out the variation across states in the setting of child support orders, the Obama administration included guidelines for it in the Final Rule. While most were advisory, some guidelines offered stronger advice than others. Although it deemed the use of income imputation acceptable, the Final Rule restated the need to set child support orders with an accurate sense of the obligor's ability to pay. It recommended that states increase their efforts to determine this ability and that they take steps to verify information about parents rather than simply assume its accuracy.[57] It also singled out low-income parents, suggesting that states make a special effort to determine their circumstances prior to setting orders. Since these directives were only recommendations, it remains unclear whether they will shape actual state practices on order setting.

Randy's case is a perfect example of why these differences in order-setting matter and why evening them out is so crucial. When his first two orders were set, the Florida court imputed income to him. He recalls the process as enormously complicated—it required him to submit years of tax returns and pay stubs, many of which he did not have and thus could not give the court. So those orders were set at around $300/month on the presumption that he *could* work a forty-hour-per-week job at minimum wage, which he did not. For his third order, he was in jail and claimed to have no idea that a support hearing was being held. This order was for public assistance—what Florida called a "welfare order"—since his ex-wife had gone on temporary aid while Randy was doing time. This order was even higher, closer to $400, and also set by default. Altogether, Randy's combined child support order was more than $1,000, which Florida continued to bill him despite his inability to work to pay it off.

This leads to another area of state variation in the setting of orders, related to whether they offer income adjustments for low-income parents. The majority of states have instituted some sort of low-income support policy for parents who have become impoverished. But those policies vary significantly in terms of how often they are used and what their low-income thresholds are. For instance, some states leave minimum orders to the court's discretion, which has led to all kinds of inequities. In addition, the range of income thresholds varies from state to state, with some setting them so low that few parents were eligible, and others setting them at the poverty level.[58] In addition, there is considerable variation in the amount of minimum orders—some states set them at around $200, although the average is in the $25 to $100 range. And there are differences in how long orders can remain in effect—some states grant them for a fixed period, while others require parents to engage in court-mandated programs or job searches as a condition of keeping them.[59]

Here, too, Randy's experience reveals why low-income adjustments matter. When his child support orders were set, he lived in Florida, which did not have a minimum order policy. So although Randy lived well below the poverty line, and did several stints in jail, his orders were set as if he was working full-time. Had he lived in one of those states that offered minimum orders, his situation could have been different. For instance, had he lived in California, where the income threshold at the time was $1,000 per month, he would have been eligible for a $100 low-income order—making his cumulative order $300 as opposed to $1,000. This could have changed the entire trajectory of his child support case, and much of his subsequent life.

The fate of low-income parents like Randy is shaped by yet another order-setting policy: retroactive child support provisions. When a new support order is established, it rarely starts at $0. Most states set orders retroactively and charge parents back support for a period prior to the actual filing of the order. Policy-makers call these "front end costs," and the states vary in terms of what support they charge parents for and how far back they charge that support.[60] When it comes to nonpublic support orders, there is considerable variation in timing—some states project support orders back to the child's birth, others to a specified number of years, and still others to the date the order was first filed. This means a parent's child support order can start with thousands of dollars owed. And retroactive debt can be calculated according to the parent's imputed income, so even if parents had no income in the preceding years—due to unemployment or incarceration—they are charged retroactive support as if they did.

With public debt owed to the state, there is more uniformity, largely because more federal mandates apply to it. Until 2009, families had to assign all pre-assistance support to the state as a condition of public aid. So states were permitted to charge back support on public assistance costs incurred *prior to* a support order being filed. Most states did this, which meant that the cost of all prior TANF and Medicaid payments was added to a child support order before it even began. Parents then had to pay off this retroactive "welfare debt" in addition to their monthly support obligation. This was exactly what happened to Randy, who was charged back child support for public assistance that caused his order amount to balloon to a point he considered "crazy high." It was not until 2009 that the federal government halted this practice, allowing states to bill parents only for the current public assistance received by their families.[61]

This leads to a final important area of state variation in the setting of child support: how they process public assistance payback orders. While states must issue public orders, they have retained considerable control over how to manage those orders. Just as state welfare programs differ—in terms of their eligibility requirements, work requirements, and time limits for recipients—so do their procedures for setting public child support

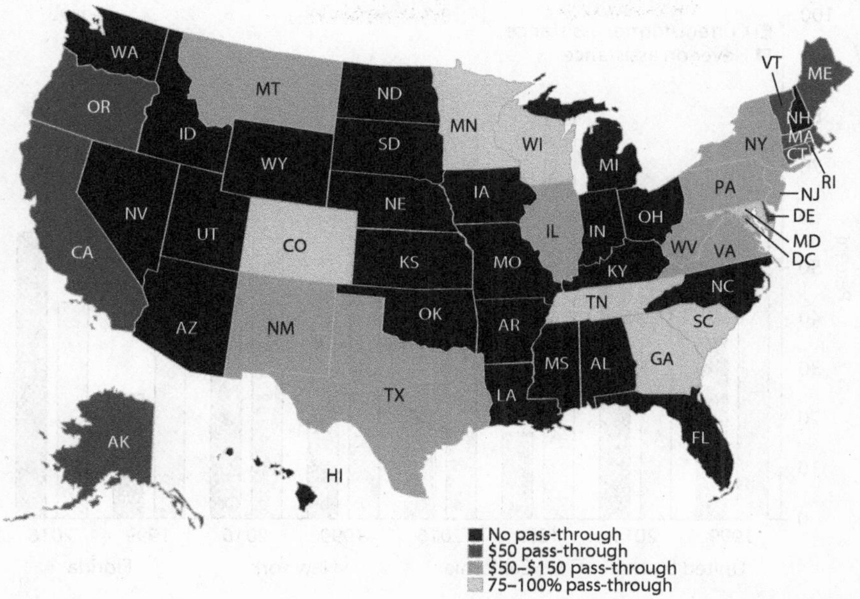

Map 1. Public Assistance Payback Given to Families (pass-throughs).
SOURCE: NCSL 2020b

orders. One of the many ways states differ here is with regard to the extent to which they keep all or part of the child support funds they collect. As discussed earlier, prior to PRWORA, states passed through at least the first $50; after PRWORA, the majority of states kept all child support payments. More recently, states have begun to experiment with passing through more to families, with a 2006 law supporting state pass-throughs of $100 to poor families. Several states have also experimented with passing through the entire amount of child support.[62] Map 1 reveals just how much variation there continues to be in this area of state policy.

Another way states vary in the processing of public support orders relates to the structure of their TANF programs. Throughout the 2000s, some states used federal welfare reforms to phase out their programs almost completely—pushing families off assistance or derailing them from applying for it. The rate of public payback orders then reflected this decline. For instance, in Florida the number of families eligible for TANF plummeted in the late 1990s and 2000s, so payback assistance orders also

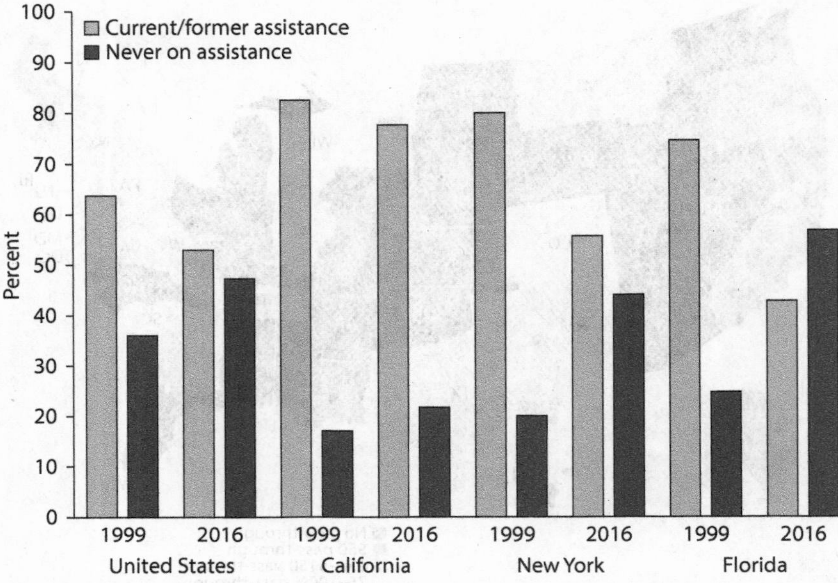

Figure 10. Percentage of Child Support Caseload with Assistance, 1999 and 2016.
SOURCE: OCSE 2017c

declined, dropping by more than half between 2000 and 2016.[63] Other states used a two-pronged approach to achieve similar ends, tightening TANF requirements and enacting procedures to lure parents off public assistance. New York City is an excellent example of this: the city's child support system referred public assistance cases to its Manhattan courthouse, where parents were "encouraged" to leave public assistance with promises of what child support orders could yield. Judges sold them on the benefits of child support by claiming it would give them more and be easier to receive. Never mind that they portrayed the *ideal* of the child support payments as opposed to the *reality* of what families actually received.[64] Still, many states took this approach, thereby significantly decreasing the use of public support orders.[65]

In a few states, though, the use of TANF remains high and thus the issuing of public payback orders is steady. California is the iconic case of this: its TANF program (CalWORKS) is relatively robust, constituting close to 60 percent of all national TANF expenditures. As a result, its number of public child support orders also remains high, with the overwhelming majority of child support cases involving some public assistance. Still, in the 2000s, fewer than 15 percent of noncustodial parents made enough to pay their public orders.[66] So California's public child support debt soared. The irony is obvious: the more generous a state's welfare system, the more disadvantaged parents owe in public assistance payback. By 2016, close to 70 percent of California's caseload included some state-owed debt.[67]

Modifying Orders

After a child support order is set, there are two ways for it to be changed: prospectively and retroactively. Orders between parents can be reviewed when formally requested by either parent. Support reviews can also be ordered by a judge for specific reasons, for example, in cases of low-income adjustments. In public assistance cases, these reviews are supposed to occur automatically every three years. In fact, prior to PRWORA, federal law required three-year reviews to ensure that orders were modified in line with parents' economic lives. But once the mandate was lifted, states could decide when these reviews occurred and required them only when requested by a parent.

Once initiated, modification reviews should be relatively standard and adjustments made according to preset methods. Yet complications can and do surface over how to adjudicate claims about a parent's ability to pay. Most complicated are modification reviews initiated due to a significant "change of circumstance." Here there is enormous variation across states in what counts as a change that alters the parent's ability to pay.[68] Does the change warrant a new order amount? Is the request for a change being made in "good faith" or to avoid paying support? Was the change foreseeable or voluntary? This last standard is perhaps the most contentious and inconsistently applied, since periods of unemployment can be deemed "voluntary" or willful. A finding of voluntary unemployment can then be grounds for rejecting a parent's request for a downward modification or a low-income adjustment. In these cases, child support will continue to accrue at the original order's amount, despite any change in circumstances.

Indeed, the in/voluntary unemployment standard has become the basis for one of the most controversial modification issues: what to do with

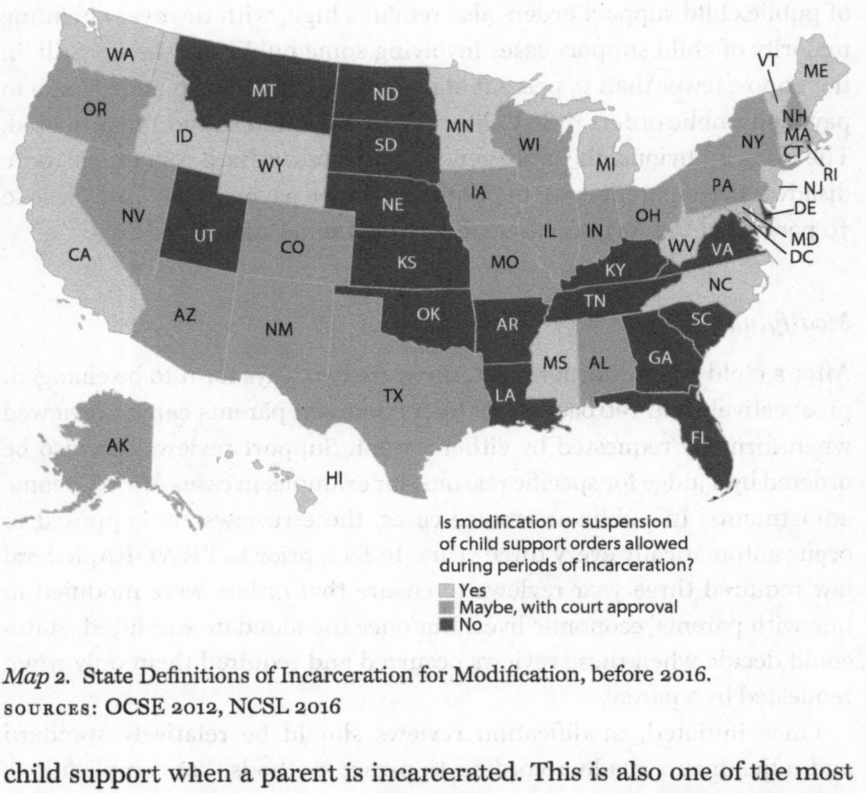

Map 2. State Definitions of Incarceration for Modification, before 2016.
SOURCES: OCSE 2012, NCSL 2016

child support when a parent is incarcerated. This is also one of the most consequential state policies for many parents, since it determines whether imprisonment in itself warrants a modification. State policies vary here. Prior to 2016, policies fell into three categories, which varied according to whether incarceration was grounds for order modification.[69] As map 2 indicates, roughly one third of all states forbade consideration of order modification by deeming incarceration a form of "voluntary unemployment" due to the presumed voluntary nature of criminal behavior and the "foreseeable loss of income resulting from criminality." This shut off even the possibility of modification during imprisonment, so child support continued to accrue at the previous order amount for the length of the parent's sentence.

A second category of states classified incarceration as a *possible* justification for modification. These states defined incarceration as "involuntary unemployment," so it was theoretically possible to modify a child support order prospectively. But it was subject to judicial discretion, since courts decided whether parents deserved a modification. Since the burden of proof of deservedness was on prisoners, who had to apply and make the case for modification from prison, such changes were granted inconsistently and infrequently.

In the final category of states, imprisonment was a fixed justification for modification and thus considered a change in circumstances. But even here there were critical variations: in most of these states, prisoners had to initiate a judicial process to seek a modification. The burden was placed on them to notify child support authorities of their imprisonment and file for the legal modification. While some states offered legal assistance to incarcerated parents, they did so in uneven and inconsistent ways that often ended up reaching very few prisoners. In only a handful of states was the modification process administrative—that is, support orders could be suspended or set at $0 for incarcerated parents with little judicial involvement.

After the 2016 Final Rule, the policy terrain became more difficult to categorize. Here the rule went a bit further than in its recommendations for order-setting: it forbade states from a blanket definition of incarceration as "voluntary" unemployment. The rule thus required states to hold open the possibility of reviewing orders for modification. Yet it stopped short of requiring such reviews or mandating how states define incarceration in relation to order modifications. As a result, the modification issue shifted from one of formal *eligibility* to one of *accessibility*. And the latter is far more difficult to track and document. As map 3 shows, most states have put in place some modification policy, but it is unclear whether these new policies have increased access to support modifications.[70] So while thirty-six states now define incarceration as involuntary unemployment, they still have vastly different rules for when and how modifications can be requested by incarcerated parents.

In addition to prospective modification, states differ in their approach to retroactive modification. Since many states refused to modify the orders of low-income or incarcerated parents prospectively for decades, they essentially guaranteed the accumulation of debt. The question then became what could be done on the back end, once debt was on the books. The Bradley Amendment placed serious restrictions here by seeming to

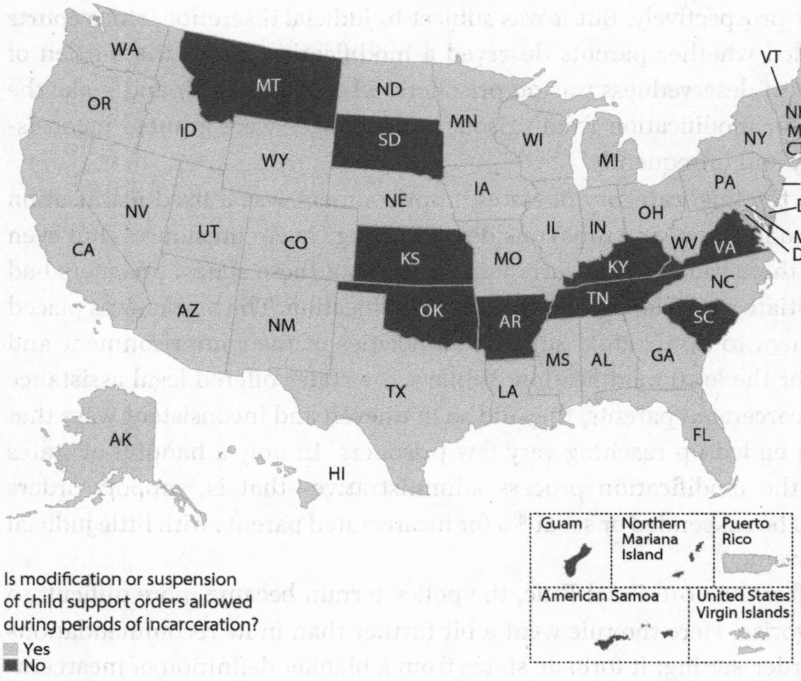

Map 3. State Definitions of Incarceration for Modification, after 2016.
SOURCE: NCSL 2019

forbid debt forgiveness. Many states have indeed interpreted it in this way, claiming that all retroactive modification of arrears is tantamount to a violation of federal law. This is especially true with debt owed to parents, which states have not been inclined to reduce or modify.[71]

Yet the realities of debt accumulation for low-income parents have pushed states to develop formal mechanisms of retroactive debt relief for public assistance debt. In 2007, twenty states operated some sort of child support debt compromise program; by 2011, the number had more than doubled; and by the late 2010s, most states had a program on the books.[72] Yet the actual programs run the gamut. Some target low-income parents in general, like California's Compromise of Arrears Program (COAP), which provides pay-off plans to parents who can demonstrate an ability to pay back some of their arrears. Other state programs target parents

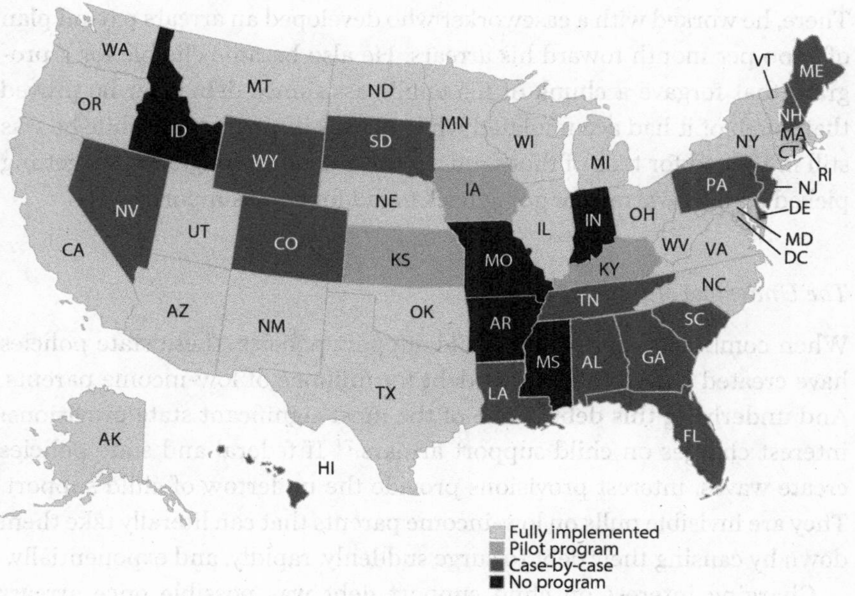

Map 4. State Debt-Relief Programs. SOURCE: OCSE 2018

with particular hardships—such as institutionalization and incarceration. Here, too, the 2016 Final Rule offered some recommendations for states, "urging" them to have policies on the books that allow arrears to be compromised, particularly those of low-income parents and arrears owed to the state itself. Map 4 shows the states with debt-relief programs in 2017.

These state differences in modification policies are enormously consequential for parents since they structure how much they owe and how that debt can be paid off. Here, again, Randy's case is illustrative. At the time that most of his debt accrued, Randy was living in Florida, which essentially considered incarceration a form of "voluntary unemployment."[73] Each time he went to prison, his child support accrued at the order's rate of $1,000 per month. Since Florida took a narrow interpretation of the Bradley Amendment, it had no state-wide program to modify arrears retroactively. "Every judge I saw turned me down," Randy recalled. "Seemed like whenever I'd make a request [in Florida], they'd throw me in jail . . . so I just stopped askin'." It was not until Randy moved to California that he saw any change.

There, he worked with a caseworker who developed an arrears pay-off plan of $100 per month toward his arrears. He also became eligible for a program that forgave a chunk of his public assistance debt after he proved that much of it had accumulated while he was incarcerated. While he was still in the red for tens of thousands of dollars, he no longer feared getting picked up on a warrant or going back to jail for child support.

The Undertow of Interest

When combined with federal child support policies, these state policies have created a perfect storm of debt for millions of low-income parents. And underlying this debt is one of the most significant state provisions: interest charges on child support arrears.[74] If federal and state policies create waves, interest provisions provide the undertow of child support. They are invisible pulls on low-income parents that can literally take them down by causing their debt to surge suddenly, rapidly, and exponentially.

Charging interest on child support debt was possible once arrears became judgments by operation of law. This placed support debt in a special category, allowing states to treat it as non-negotiable and to charge interest on it. And thirty-five states did just that by authorizing interest charges be added to both private and public debt. Crucial state variation occurs here as well: What interest rates do states charge? Do they charge it on the debt principle or on the accumulated debt? What about retroactive support? How often do they assess interest? And do they do so on both current and past debt?

As map 5 indicates, states use a range of interest rates for child support debt. These rates can be set by state statute, state constitution, or the state Child Support Director. Most rates are fixed, although a few charge a variable rate. Since interest is usually charged on compounded debt, it is easy to see how debt can grow exponentially. This helps to explain why, in states like California, which has an interest rate of 10 percent, researchers have estimated that up to half of support debt is accumulated interest.[75]

In addition, states assess interest charges differently. And most of the surge in child support debt is attributable to states that routinely assess interest—their debt has increased sixfold over the past two decades. In fact, interest assessment explains much of the state-level variation in

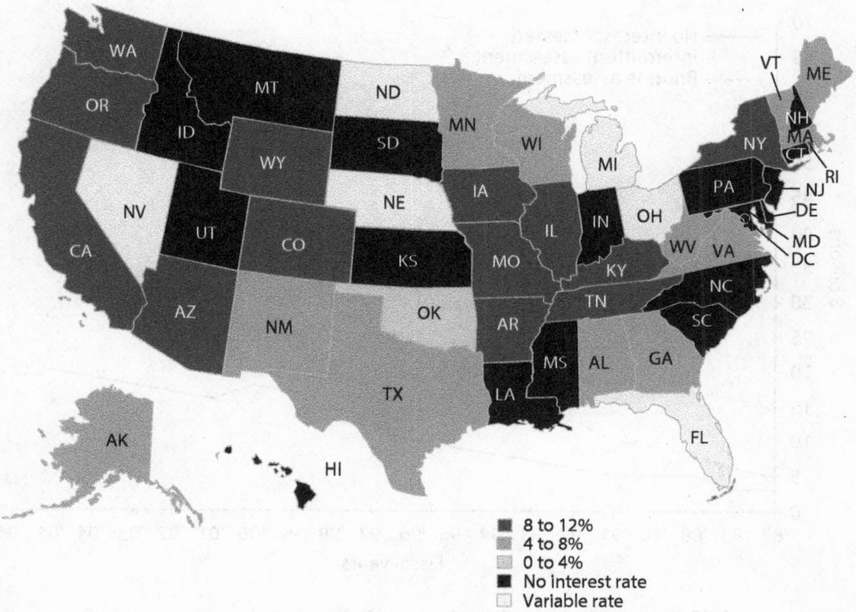

Map 5. State Interest Rates on Child Support Debt. SOURCE: NCSL 2019a

arrears in figure 11: all states with high arrears regularly compute interest on child support debt.

Policy-makers and child support officials justify the application of interest on child support debt in several ways. With parental debt, state officials often point out that failure to pay support to custodial parents can push them to go into debt and subject them to high interest charges on those debts. They thus insist it is only fair that parents with child support debt face similar penalties. Of course, this logic does not neatly apply to public debt. A few judges did tell me they felt indebted parents owed "the public" these additional charges since it had fronted them money, as public assistance, which they had failed to repay.[76] But with public debt, a far more common justification was that indebted parents would have no reason to repay this debt unless there were interest charges. "They would always pay other debts that accrue interest first, like credit cards or payday loans," a high-ranking California policy-maker explained to me. "We would be the last to be paid . . . which is unfair for the citizens of our

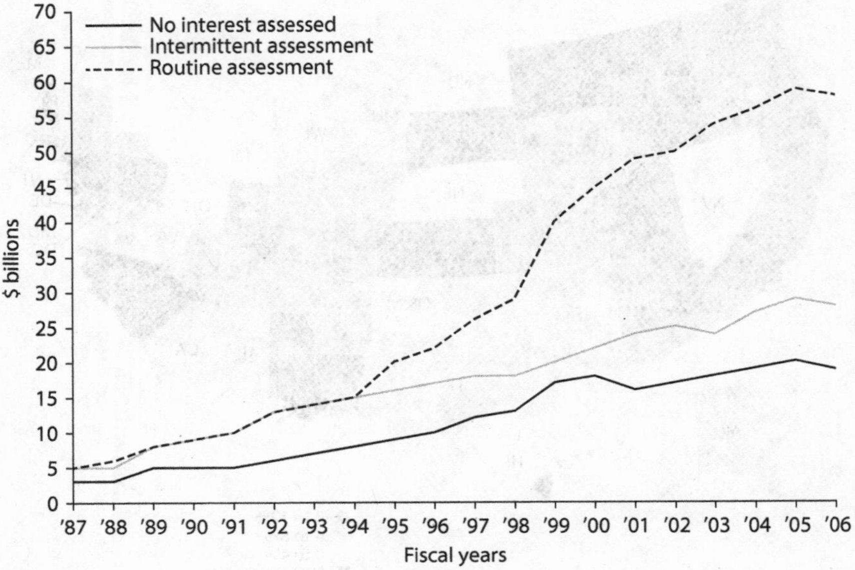

Figure 11. Child Support Debt by State Interest Policy, 1987–2006. SOURCE: Sorenson, Sousa, and Schaner 2007

state." What this logic fails to acknowledge is that those other loans do not come with child support's enforcement apparatus—those lenders do not have the power to seize debtors' driver's licenses, tax returns, property, or paychecks the way child support can and does with great frequency, all of which I outline in later chapters.

Indeed, of the hundreds of indebted parents I encountered, I met very few who understood how interest charges affected their debt. And not one who felt pressured by interest charges to repay it. Far more common were parents like Raymond, an African American father of two who was facing over $28,000 in arrears, which were continuing to increase even though he was making the court-ordered minimum monthly payments. He did not grasp why, so he came to court in Oakland to point out the error to the judge. Luckily for Raymond, he got an unusually sympathetic judge, who spent nearly half an hour explaining compound interest to him:

JUDGE ROBINSON: It works like this: interest gets added to your "principal," or the amount you originally owe. If that isn't paid, interest is

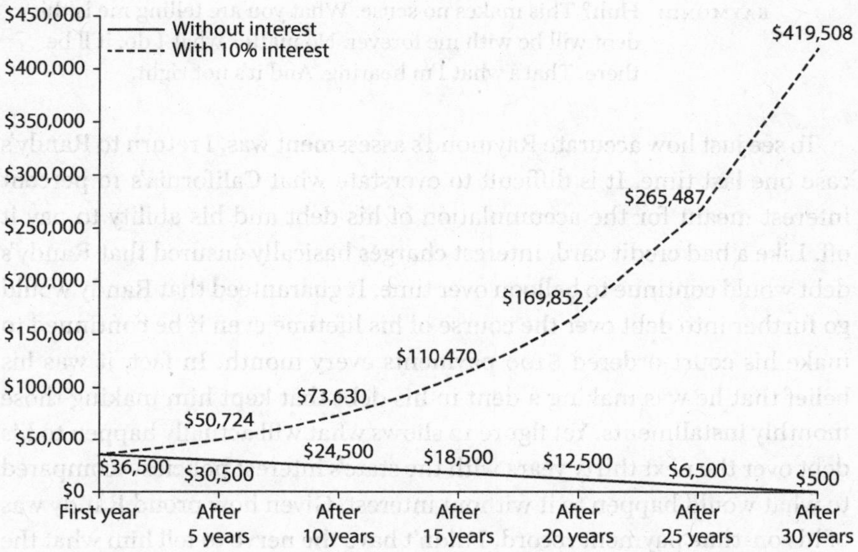

Figure 12. Paying Off Randy's Child Support Debt (or Not), with a $100 Monthly Payment

added to the new balance. So it's compounded.... If you don't pay at least the interest amount every month, it's like interest charged on interest.

RAYMOND: I still don't get why it's going up. Your honor, I am paying. Every month... the amount the court tells me to. That should reduce it. Why doesn't it reduce it?

JUDGE ROBINSON: It only reduces it if you pay more than the interest each month. If your interest is $125, you need to pay $150 so $25 goes towards your debt.

RAYMOND: But $150 should go to my debt. Where's the extra money going? Who is taking it?

JUDGE ROBINSON: No one is taking it. That money is interest.

RAYMOND: So what you are saying is that because of this interest thing, it just keeps going up no matter what? What's the point of paying then? There are times I don't have food in the house... so I'm not gonna pay this if it ain't make a difference.

JUDGE ROBINSON: No, it does make a difference because it means your debt won't grow as fast as it could grow if you paid nothing.

RAYMOND: Huh? This makes no sense. What you are telling me is this debt will be with me forever. No matter what I do, it'll be there. That's what I'm hearing. And it's not right.

To see just how accurate Raymond's assessment was, I return to Randy's case one last time. It is difficult to overstate what California's 10 percent interest meant for the accumulation of his debt and his ability to pay it off. Like a bad credit card, interest charges basically ensured that Randy's debt would continue to balloon over time. It guaranteed that Randy would go further into debt over the course of his lifetime even if he continued to make his court-ordered $100 payments every month. In fact, it was his belief that he was making a dent in his debt that kept him making those monthly installments. Yet figure 12 shows what will actually happen to his debt over the next thirty years with the state's interest policies—compared to what would happen to it without interest. Given how proud Randy was of his on-time payment record, I didn't have the nerve to tell him what the undertow of interest was doing to his debt. Somehow, it seemed preferable to let him continue to think he was living in the Golden State of child support.

THE POLITICS OF DEBT ACCUMULATION

Analyzing child support policy is very much like taking aim at a moving target. This chapter has revealed many of the twists and turns in state provisions designed to "make men pay." As child support provisions weaved their way through different federal agencies, state legislatures, and court systems, their form and focus changed. Some of the most consequential changes came at the federal level—from its standardization of support orders to its mandate of public assistance payback. Others came at the state level—from their policies to set and modify support orders to the charging of interest. But however complicated the child support story became, its end was clear enough: a perfect storm of debt for low-income parents, with their arrears accumulating rapidly and from multiple directions. The well-being of women and children was used to justify these policy shifts, but they did not weather the storm very well either. Their poverty rates rose, while their income became more inconsistent and their lives more precarious.[77]

It is impossible to analyze the evolution of child support policy as distinct from welfare politics. Indeed, this chapter has shown them to be interwoven. Yet they were woven together in different ways over time, with different consequences. Initially, child support policy was framed as a way for families to avoid public assistance and for mothers to get their fair share of childrearing expenses. Here the imperative to "make men pay" was embedded in a broader call to hold men accountable for children's well-being. Over time, that was accompanied by a mandate for men to repay the state for the "loan" of public assistance. These were different projects with different targets and different logics. It was largely the welfare payback project that led to the massive accumulation of debt for poor parents. This project also pushed women out of the equation, with fathers paying the state and the state turning over next to nothing to families in need. This then led to the criminalization and racialization of child support.

It would take a very different type of analysis to explain these shifts. In documenting them, this chapter has pointed to a few possible explanations, from the role of "family values" politicians to those of conservative policy-makers and feminist lawmakers and social scientists. Even here, it is not entirely clear whether their impacts were intentional. In fact, a mixture of motives seemed to characterize child support reforms. Some policy-makers were genuinely concerned about the feminization of poverty, while others appeared more invested in punishing the poor. Child support policy bears the mark of this collusion of intentions. And this collusion changed over time. At least in the beginning, the imperative to collect child support was guided by an ethos of fairness and a sense that those raising children after divorce or separation were entitled to support. Over time, this ethos became entangled with other political imperatives. In this mean season of punitive criminal justice and welfare reform, child support absorbed and incorporated other agendas. Ultimately, it also reflected the stigmatization and criminalization of poor families.

But unlike welfare and criminal justice reform, which provoked considerable debate, child support remained under the political radar. As did the massive accumulation of debt it generated. There was little fanfare associated with it, even when it came to the most consequential policies.

Perhaps child support provisions seemed more minor and administrative than changes in criminal law or welfare policy. Indeed, child support reforms frequently surfaced as additions to other bills, such as the 1986 Omnibus Budget Reconciliation Act, the Family Support Act, and PRWORA. The child support changes these bills introduced were often eclipsed by other parts of those bills.

Moreover, child support reforms happened at multiple state levels simultaneously: the federal government was doing one thing, state legislatures another, state prosecutor's offices another, and court systems yet another. Few of these changes were understood or acknowledged, much less coordinated. But while no one seemed to be looking across state spaces, these seemingly small changes had massive confounding effects as the accumulation of debt surpassed expenditures on many of the biggest state programs. In the case of child support, it was the small changes that often had the most significant consequences. So a perfect storm led to poor parents' debt accumulation, yet it was a relatively quiet storm.

That said, the assumptions underlying this policy storm of reform were quite consistent across state levels. These reforms were united by at least two assumptions about poverty and parenthood. And these uninterrogated ideas probably had more to do with the rapid accumulation of parental debt than any nefarious intentions among lawmakers. The first was embedded in the Clinton quotation I began this chapter with: the assumption that familial poverty was due to the absentee male or, more precisely, to the absent male wage. If this wage returned to the family, the "problems" of welfare and poverty would be solved. If this wage was pursued with vigor—and mandated from men whose families used public assistance—those families would eventually benefit from its repayment. Yet in their vigor to collect that wage, no one bothered to ask what had happened to the family wage of yesteryear: was it in fact absent, or had wages declined in real value for all sorts of people? No one bothered to ask whether the men being targeted by these new child support policies had ever been capable of earning those wages and whether their families had any chance of seeing them in the foreseeable future. In effect, no one bothered to acknowledge how the socioeconomic changes occurring across the United States might complicate the plan to use child support as a replacement for state re/distribution in the alleviation of poverty.

This leads to a second uninterrogated assumption guiding child support politics: the insistence that if the male wage was absent, it was intentionally so. If child support was not being paid, it was because fathers did not want to pay up. This assumption was so fundamental to federal and state policy that it undergirded the penalties of nonpayment and the high interest rates charged on debt. It undergirded the punitive approach to debt collection. Yet no one bothered to ask if nonpayment was in fact a choice. Or if all the penalties gave fathers the push they needed to pay. If lawmakers had asked these questions, they would have learned that this group of parents was far from homogenous. They would have learned that the vast majority of parents did not question their obligation to pay support; the problem, rather, was support orders that far exceeded their ability to pay. The assumption of intentional neglect blinded lawmakers to all of this.

Indeed, the assumption of intentionality was so strong it even applied to a group of parents for whom choice was literally out of their hands: incarcerated parents. Instead of recognizing the limitations on these parents' ability to pay support, federal and state policies doubled down. As a result, the perfect storm of reform that submerged so many poor parents developed into a tsunami for the incarcerated.

2 The Debt of Imprisonment

"Damn, I hate it when they don't give us warning. Who's there? Is that Attica calling?" Officer Gordon asks as she points to a large video screen facing the courtroom. Staring back on the screen is a bewildered African American man, wearing a prison jumpsuit and with his hands shackled together. The slamming of steel doors and the screams of prisoners and guards echo through the video feed, filling the courtroom. Suddenly, a voice booms out from behind the shackled man on the screen: "Yes, this is Attica calling for our 10:15." Judge Maddox then takes over, delivering a speech she repeats countless times a day:

> This is New York City family court. We are here to inform you that we are issuing a child support order against you. New York State, and not the mother of your child, is seeking this order because of public benefits received by your minor son. You are entitled to hire an attorney for these proceedings if you see fit, but you will have to cover the cost yourself. Since you are incarcerated, your order will be $0. Do you accept the order?

Perplexed, the man responds, "Huh, a child support order?" Judge Maddox confirms. "For my son, Malik?" he continues. "For $0? Then, yeah, I guess it's ok." As soon as he approves, the Attica video cuts out and a man from another prison shows up on the screen. This goes on for three hours, with different prisons calling at eight-minute intervals to stream in images of unsuspecting prisoners who are instructed that child support orders have been issued against them as a result of public assistance cases. And this goes on every Friday morning in Judge Maddox's Manhattan courtroom. "We've been on a prison tour across New York State," she jokes with me one day. "Courtesy of the New York Office of Child Support Enforcement."

When federal and state policy-makers built their child support systems in the 1980s and 1990s to "make men pay," they made few distinctions among men: they lumped indebted fathers into one category—the deadbeat—irrespective of their circumstances. In the process, support policies made many assumptions about these parents. If they weren't paying support, it was because they had chosen not to; if they were not in their families' lives, it was because they were neglectful. While this might have been true of some, the one thing that definitely united these parents was poverty. By the late 2000s, studies were finding that 70 percent of child support debt was owed by parents who made less than $10,000 year—and 40 percent of those families reported no income at all.[1] This was largely because around the time state child support systems were emerging, the United States was undergoing dramatic social changes.

In the 1970s, family structures began changing and economic sectors began shifting. Divorce rates rose, especially among the middle class, and female-headed households became more common across socioeconomic groups. As manufacturing declined and the service sector expanded, the family wage approached extinction, ushering in the era of the two-wage-earner family. The decades that followed saw a series of economic recessions, often referred to as "man-cessions" since they hit traditionally male sectors of the economy particularly hard. So at the precise moment the government set out to make men pay, fewer men were *able* to pay. This was particularly true of disadvantaged, low-income fathers.[2]

Another important development was happening in the United States around this time, one that is seen clearly every Friday in Judge Maddox's Manhattan courtroom: the social and political project of mass incarceration. The statistics regarding its impact are quite familiar by now: starting in the 1980s, the imprisonment rate in the United States surged to unprecedented levels. By the late 2000s, more than 2.2 million citizens were in prison or jail and another 5 million were under correctional supervision.[3] More than 68 million US citizens now live with the mark of a criminal record. And that mark affects not only the formerly incarcerated but also those connected to them. Mass imprisonment coats families with a broad brush: there are nearly as many children with parents in prison as there are prisoners.[4] Put another way, around 10 percent of all children have a parent under correctional supervision, and 3 percent have a parent in prison.[5]

As a result of these changes, the child support system began to reach deep into US prison and jails—as Malik's father, and millions of men like him, would learn. Yet the extent of its reach is difficult to document. Child support systems do not keep reliable information on the percentage of their caseloads that are incarcerated, and departments of corrections do not document how many prisoners have child support orders. Parents try not to "come out" in either system. When dealing with child support, they are leery of mentioning their criminal justice histories; when interacting with criminal justice officials, they rarely admit to owing child support. Absent a comprehensive, centralized database connecting these systems, we are left to estimate these numbers, though we can say without hesitation that they are quite high.

Estimates of the number of parents with criminal records and child support obligations can be computed in two ways (see figure 13). From the criminal justice side, we know that 55 percent of men in state and federal prisons have minor children and that 40 to 50 percent of those prisoners face child support orders.[6] This puts the number of indebted parents currently in prison at somewhere between 450,000 and 550,000.[7] When the same figure for the jail population is added, the number rises by several hundred thousand, bringing it closer to 800,000.[8] When we add to this estimate those indebted fathers who were previously incarcerated, that figure more than doubles. According to national estimates, up to 50 percent of fathers with support orders have some criminal justice background and around 20 percent of nonpaying, indebted fathers were recently incarcerated.[9] Given that there are roughly 5.5 million parents with child support debt, this middle category of indebted parents with criminal justice histories grows to more than 1 million parents when approached from the child support side.[10]

Although the precise numbers may be unclear, one thing is certain:

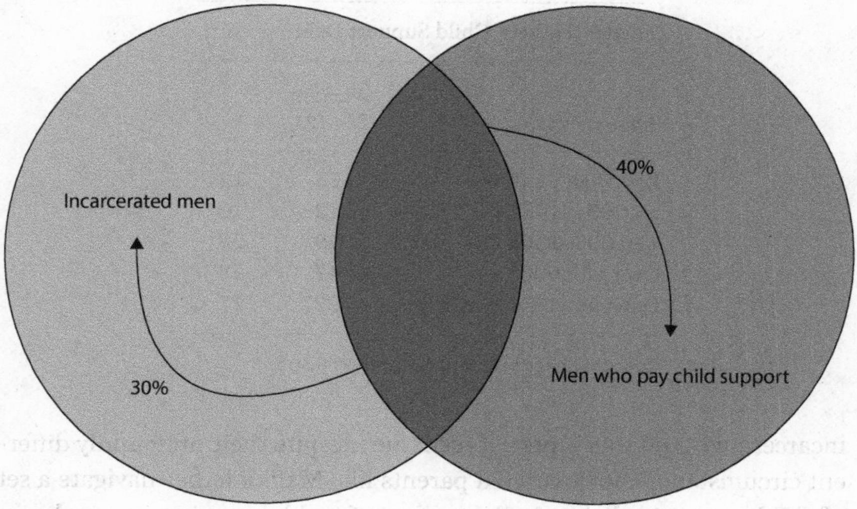

Figure 13. How Many Parents with Criminal Records and Child Support?

living in the middle area where these systems overlap is both perilous and costly. The policy landscape of child support is fraught for low-income fathers and even more so for incarcerated fathers. Traversing that landscape leads most parents into extreme debt. Here, too, it is hard to know the extent of this debt, since few studies separate the formerly incarcerated from other low-income parents.[11] National-level data are limited; however, state-level studies indicate that incarcerated fathers' support debt more than doubles during imprisonment, averaging $20,000.[12] Yet as table 1 indicates, the fathers in my sample had a much higher average debt of $36,500.[13] To put this in context, their debt was roughly three times more than the average child support debt of low-income fathers, which is between $10,000 and $12,000.[14] The additional debt for those in my sample was a byproduct of their contact with the criminal justice system. I call this the debt of imprisonment.

Why does incarceration lead to so much debt? This is a somewhat vexing question since there are few child support policies aimed specifically at the incarcerated. Except for the in/voluntary unemployment clauses and the $0 incarceration support orders discussed earlier, child support provisions do not treat the incarcerated much differently than the non-

Table 1 Fathers' Child Support Debt

Amount owed	*Number N = 125*	%
Less than $5,000	15	12
$5,000–$10,000	12	10
$10,000–$30,000	29	23
Over $50,000	47	38
Don't know/Can't estimate	22	17

NOTE: Average of known arrears = $36,500.

incarcerated. And this is part of the issue: despite their profoundly different circumstances, incarcerated parents like Malik's father navigate a set of child support policies similar to those faced by non-incarcerated parents. So to understand how the debt of imprisonment emerges, we need to pull apart these policies and trace their effects on this group of parents. For this, we need to delve into policy implementation and the ways in which actual state practices place incarcerated fathers at a disadvantage as they negotiate the dynamics of parenthood, punishment, and debt.

Social scientists have not spent much time analyzing these dynamics or showing how the physical confinement of imprisonment leads to the financial confinement of child support debt. Instead, most research remains focused on child support and criminal justice as separate entities in terms of their processes and outcomes. We know a lot about the trajectory and consequences of child support policy, from how it emerged as a federal issue in the 1970s, to how enforcement measures expanded in the 1980s, to how the accumulation of debt surged in the 1990s, particularly for the poor. And we know even more about developments in criminal justice, from the economic and political forces propelling mass incarceration, to the specific policies underlying it, to its far-reaching effects on family and community life. Yet we know less about the connections and overlaps between these systems. To the extent that social scientists do examine institutional overlaps, they do so by tracking the "spillover effects" of incarceration—that is, how imprisonment affects work, family, and civic life and weighs down people as they struggle to reintegrate.

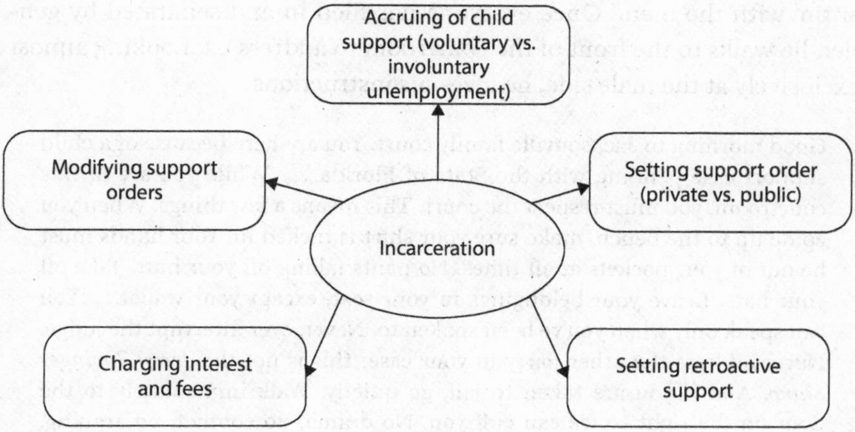

Figure 14. The Debt of Imprisonment

As I will show in this chapter, these state systems operate somewhat differently and the ways they are linked have generated complex entanglements for fathers. Instead of spilling over in a linear way from one institution to the other, these entanglements are multidirectional. Instead of piling up in fathers' lives, they work in circular ways to form feedback loops of disadvantage. Incarcerated fathers get ensnarled at every stage of the child support process, from the setting of their orders to their post-release modification. Figure 14 provides a visual representation of the processes that comprise the debt of imprisonment. To understand how this debt accumulates, we need to start at the beginning of the process—in the messy, conflictual world of child support courts.

ABSENCE MAKES THE DEBT GROW LARGER

"Women on the left, men on the right!" bailiff Frank barks as several dozen of us shuffle into the Jacksonville courtroom. Couples that came to court together are told to separate and sit on opposite sides of the courtroom. When I mistakenly take a seat on the men's side, I am immediately reprimanded: "Respondents on the left, ma'am." I explain that I am an observer, not a respondent, but bailiff Frank still insists I move. "You shouldn't be sittin' with the men." Once everyone has filed in and separated by gender, he walks to the front of the courtroom to address us. Looking almost exclusively at the male side, he gives his instructions:

> Good morning to Jacksonville family court. You are here because of a child support case pending with the State of Florida.... While you are in this courtroom, you must respect the court. This means a few things. When you come up to the bench, make sure your shirt is tucked in. Your hands must be out of your pockets at all times. No pants falling off your butt. Take off your hats. Leave your belongings in your seat, except your wallet.... You can speak only when you've been spoken to. Never, ever interrupt the judge. Never address the other party in your case: this is not the *Jerry Springer Show*. And if you are taken to jail, go quietly. Walk immediately to the door on the right so we can cuff you. No drama, no conflict, no arguing. Understood?

Courtrooms are sites of power. They are places where key decisions about people's lives and livelihoods are made and punishment is meted out. They are also spaces where people get marked; and as social psychologist Shadd Maruna contends, that marking can involve rituals of condemnation.[15] As they adjudicate, courts often engage in ceremonies to publicly mark some as "deviant" and "criminal." Because these judicial markings can be interpreted as societal judgments, they are frequently experienced as especially meaningful.[16] Because much of what transpires in court is about forming these judgments, representation is a key type of courtroom power. After all, courts are essentially storytelling arenas where different narratives compete and collide. This is most obvious in criminal courts, but it is also key in civil and family courts, where representations breed particular judicial decisions about who is a law-abiding citizen or who is a fit parent or how children should be raised. Such representation is closely tied to legal knowledge and the ability to narrate. Participants must know how to engage, what to share, what to hide, and how to construct a story. They must know what's at stake in this storytelling. They must appreciate how effective narratives can make a case and how ineffective ones can break it.

As part of the family court system, child support courts are at once highly bureaucratic and highly performative. In terms of the law, they address all aspects of the child support process: the setting, modifying, and/or enforcing of support orders. They are thus a unique blend of other courts: they impinge on terrain covered by civil, family, and criminal courts and hold sanctioning power that merges civil, family, administrative, and criminal law. Much of what takes place in them involves shaping representations in order to decide who owes how much to whom, who should be punished for failure to pay, and what that punishment will consist of. Led by a judge or a magistrate, support proceedings are public and thus played out in front of audiences of varying sizes.[17] As bailiff Frank made clear in his daily speech, rules and expectations govern these proceedings to dictate how parents should engage with the court and represent themselves.

Yet those rules are not the same in all support courts. One distinctive feature of child support courts is their enormous variation—judicial, prosecutorial, and administrative. This leads to wild divergences in processes and outcomes. What is standard procedure in some states is unimaginable in others; what is an acceptable legal interpretation in one court is unthinkable in others. The cast of characters is usually similar in all support courts—alongside the judge or magistrate is a state child support lawyer, a representative of child support services, as well as one or both parents. But their roles can vary quite dramatically. The same is true of court dynamics.[18] Some courts have an assembly-line quality to them, with judges and state attorneys rushing through as many cases as possible. Other courts include long judicial lectures about the meaning of family and parental responsibility. Many hearings end with discussions about parental problems and failures, particularly those of fathers. And in most courts, no one has a name (not even children) and everyone is presented as a financial computation.

Despite these differences, the representation of self is key to the legal process in all child support courts. Parents are expected to behave in certain ways, even without bailiff Frank to outline expectations for them. Parents must know how to deliver an effective performance—and to do so as flawlessly as possible. In all of the courts I observed, incarcerated fathers' disconnection from this legal process, and their corresponding lack of knowledge about the expectations of legal representation, brought them to the first step in the debt of imprisonment.

Where's Daddy?

The most basic precondition for delivering an effective court performance is making an appearance. Yet this is precisely what incarcerated parents can't deliver: in an event where they are usually the central figure, they are almost always absent. This brings about one of three scenarios. In the first, which is the most common, the court doesn't know why the parent is absent but proceeds with the case anyway. In the second, the court knows the parent is incarcerated but proceeds anyway. In the third, the court discovers a parent is incarcerated and then facilitates his testimony from prison. In all of these scenarios, incarcerated parents must negotiate their absence, which presents obstacles that often prove insurmountable.

When I began observing child support courts, it seemed inconceivable that judges and lawyers would not know whether someone was incarcerated. They knew so much about parents, from their past employers to their family structure, that it seemed impossible they would not know that a parent was in prison or jail. As it turns out, this was not only possible but very common. State institutions are notoriously distrustful of one another, so they often fail to share critical information. For instance, few states have integrated databases to link the Department of Corrections to Child Support Services. As a result, state attorneys and child support workers often don't know which parents are incarcerated, and prison officials don't know which prisoners have pending child support cases. Nor are there any easy ways for them to find out. So when these cases get to court, officers can have no idea of parents' whereabouts. This is so common that they often don't even ask: if the father is a no-show, they simply assume he is an absentee parent and forge ahead with the case. No-shows are usually adjudicated at the end of the daily court calendar, when they can be whizzed through in minutes, with decisions made without delay or contestation. "Whew, that was a whirlwind," a Bronx judge exclaimed after running through more than a dozen no-shows in the hour before her lunch break. "All that work made me hungry."

In theory, this should never happen, since due process guarantees require that proof of service be secured prior to legal proceedings. But that is in theory. In reality, cases need to be resolved—so rules are bent, ignored, or waived to allow cases to go forward. Forging ahead like this is especially common in states like Florida, which has extremely lax service notification protocols. Yet it is not uncommon in other states for hearings to proceed after service is either overlooked or waived because a parent seems "unlocatable."[19] There are hundreds of thousands of unlocatable fathers on the books in state child support offices. In fact, in 2016 California had to commission an outside firm to track down 100,000 of its "unlocatables"—and found that 45 percent had histories of incarceration and that close to 20 percent were currently incarcerated.[20]

Most of the cases I observed went ahead and established support orders without the parent. This is so common that another study found that 70 percent of all support orders for low-income fathers in California were set by default or based on imputed income due to the parent's absence or insufficient information.[21] While the percentage was closer to half of that in my court observations, most of these cases were of a missing parent whose whereabouts was unclear. Yet the cascading effects of their absence were clear: because they were unable to provide accurate income information, their support orders were set higher than those of parents who were present. In part, this was because judges came down harder on them. "If he doesn't have enough respect to show up," a Miami judge once explained to me, "then I will show him the same lack of respect." The case he referred to was of an unlocatable father ordered to pay a temporary support order of $425 for two kids, based on full-time, minimum wage work, whether he actually worked that much or not.

In this way, the large support orders given to no-shows reflected common assumptions about parents. Others represented these parents' lives for them. Others represented their earning capacity. Others represented them as "underemployed" if they did not work forty hours per week or as "unsuitably employed" if they worked in jobs not on par with their education or work experience. These representations were based on an ideal world, not local labor market realities. That is, even in cities with high unemployment rates, courts set default orders based on the assumption that the missing parent was working full-time. This could become surreal in cities like Miami and Los Angeles, which have relatively large populations of undocumented workers. Here, too, courts imputed income based on a minimum wage job at forty hours per week, even if they were fully aware that a parent was undocumented and thus unable to work legally.

"Sometimes I realize how crazy it seems that I am issuing an order that demands an illegal [parent] to work," a Miami judge admitted to me. "I am ordering him to break the law. But that's the only decision I can make." Again, such decisions remained uncontested when the parent was a no-show.

In addition to setting support orders by default, courts often applied the maximum retroactive support to parents not in court. Again, if a parent was a no-show, judges assumed he was neglectful and threw the book at him with retroactive support. This is a key area of judicial discretion, since the law allows courts to add retroactive support to new child support orders but does not require it. Yet judges usually did so with absent parents. This was particularly true in public support cases: when back support was owed to the state, attorneys for the state almost always asked for the maximum amount of allowed back support to be applied. Until 2009, they could add all past public assistance received by the family; after this, states were only supposed to add current assistance. But well into the 2010s, many courts were still recovering the full cost. Once again, with no one there to contest the fairness, the amount of the order was increased.

It is unclear how many fathers were no-shows because of incarceration. That is the point: no one bothered to investigate. And while not all no-shows were incarcerated fathers, close to all incarcerated fathers were no-shows. During my interviews, a large majority of incarcerated fathers told me their child support orders were set by default, *in absentia*. Many claimed to have no idea they had child support cases pending while in prison. Even more complained about how those orders were being set based on wildly inaccurate income calculations: "I never made that kinda money in my whole life . . . but especially not after serving time," Jonah exclaimed when describing the wages imputed for him. They recounted gross exaggerations of their skills and earning potential: "Since when does a GED mean I'll make that kinda money?" Sean asked incredulously. Fathers with multiple orders compared those set when they were present to those set *in absentia*. Mike, for example, insisted that the order set while he was incarcerated was much more than his previous one. "Nothing changed about me, except I earned nothing in prison. . . . I was helpless to do anything about [the second order]." Devon, a Florida father incarcerated during his support hearing, put these words to his feelings of helplessness: "There I was, sitting in my cell, and there was some man sitting at his desk down in Tallahassee adding up everything I owed. They went to court without me. Then they sent me a bill. It was waiting for me when I got out. And there ain't nothing I can do about it."

This sense of shock and helplessness was most common among men who had public assistance payback orders.[22] They insisted that prior to imprisonment, they had contributed to their kids' upbringing informally, without a support order—what Edin and Nelson refer to as the "as needed" model of support.[23] Once incarcerated, that informal support stopped and their kids' mothers turned to public assistance. Many men claimed to be unaware of this use of public assistance; others had no idea they would be charged for it. In both cases, fathers were shocked to learn they had support orders. Like Martin, who had not spoken to his son's mother in years when he got notification while in prison. "I got a letter from social services, saying I owed this money. I was like 'Not me, must be a mistake.' So I ignored it. Until I couldn't [ignore it] anymore." Or like Omar, who was unaware his kids had moved to another state until he got a letter in prison. "I'm like, Kansas? Why is Kansas writing me in prison? Why are they asking me for money?" Men like Martin and Omar told me they had repeatedly sent letters to state child support offices but had got no response.[24] As incarcerated father Earl Harris asked a journalist reporting on incarcerated fathers: "Didn't they know I was in prison? Weren't they the ones that put me there?"[25]

In fact, "they" probably didn't know Earl was in prison. And even if they had known, cases like these might not have transpired much differently, especially in states that viewed incarceration as "voluntary unemployment." In Florida, incarcerated fathers who were unable to provide accurate information were held to exaggerated calculations of their income potential. Their income estimates were usually based on either their last recorded employment or wages listed in social security records, as opposed to what they could earn in prison. They were unable to contest any of this because, while it is quite possible that the court knew they were in prison, the reverse was rarely true: incarcerated fathers often had no idea their cases were being heard in court. So their support orders were set just as high as for the no-shows.

Some of the most aggressively prosecuted cases I observed involved incarcerated fathers. In court, the announcement that a parent was incarcerated could change the judicial tone. This was especially true in Florida, where these cases proceeded with an almost vindictive tone. Judges set orders at the maximum amount, effectively putting fathers on the hook for reimbursing the state for all assistance received by their families, even that predating incarceration. They also used these cases as occasions to launch into a defense of these payback policies. "This may seem like a lot [of debt] to put on a sorry soul in prison," Florida Judge Matthews explained after setting an order for an incarcerated parent. "But what about the money the citizens of Florida spent paying for his family? Where's the fairness there?" Or as Brooklyn Judge Patros proclaimed one morning, in a celebratory tone: "I just read that the child support system brought over $16.3 million last year alone. For every $5 we collected, only $1 was spent collecting it.... That should make us proud of what we do here and how we do it. We spend our time going after these deadbeats to help the kids... and all New Yorkers."

At times, aggressive prosecution morphed into misconduct. Indeed, some of the most egregious examples of judicial misconduct I observed involved incarcerated fathers. Custodial parents could be pushed to do things they seemed otherwise uninterested in doing. While mothers had little influence when it came to setting or modifying a public support order (these decisions were left to the state itself), they had considerable influence over support orders for their children.[26] In cases where the father was incarcerated, many mothers seemed genuinely concerned about adding too much to fathers' debt. Some asked that orders be set at lower amounts; others asked that retroactive support not be added to the case. "I mean, he's in jail," a Miami mother pointed out to the judge after he calculated her support order. "Is it really right to charge him all that? Could we lower it, just for now?" When judges encountered this sort of wariness, they often tried to convince mothers to change their minds. They lectured mothers about protecting the welfare of their children and the importance of fathers paying their fair share. "You know what it costs to raise children," the Miami judge responded to the mother. "Why would you deny your kids their due... to protect some low-life in prison?"

In Florida, judges went so far as to force mothers to undergo waiting periods before changing their orders—or even to overrule their decisions on the amount of new orders by claiming to protect what was best for mothers. "Don't be shy ma'am," Judge Myers exclaimed to a woman seeking to waive her right to back support because the father was in prison. "I am going to guess you have not received any money from this deadbeat. So I will do what I can to get all you deserve, no matter how nice you think you should be." Judge Matthews was notorious for replacing women's requests with his own plans. This was especially common with white women, with whom he often became quite condescending, overriding their decisions by claiming to know what was best for them. "I will get you your money," he said after nixing a mother's decision not to seek back arrears. "What kind of man leaves his family with nothing to get by? Don't worry, I am here for you." In an especially inappropriate comment, Matthews once explained to a white single mother of three: "You're gonna get money soon, ma'am. So you can go down to Dillards and buy some nice shoes for yourself."

Such indiscretions were far less common in California and New York courts. In these courts custodial parents, especially those on public assistance, could be subjected to other kinds of pressure. This occurred most often with women of color: court officials frequently tried to convince them of the benefit of child support over public assistance. For instance, judges in New York City made strong cases that these mothers could receive more money if they went off public benefits.[27] "How much do you get from Family Assistance?" a Bronx judge once asked a woman whose partner was serving a one-year sentence at Rikers. "That would double under the [child support] guidelines I'm looking at." Never mind that this woman had little hope of seeing that money for a while, if ever. The goal was to lower TANF usage rates and shift the financial burden to fathers. As this judge explained to me after referring the mother to the Manhattan public assistance support court: "In so many cases, when the mother hears how much she can get if she leaves welfare, she goes off. . . . She really can get more. When she comes back to court, I guarantee that she'll be off. That is success . . . to get them off assistance as often as we can."

Judges used yet another tactic to convince women to go off public assistance: they reminded women that the amount of their orders would be less if any of the fathers' other "baby mamas" filed first. Here, too, judges tended to use this tactic with women of color. It was also a way courts pitted mothers against one another: since new child support orders take into account existing support obligations, the later a mother files her order, the more she risks a lower amount in cases of multiple kids. Judges often explained the chain of support to women, urging them to "get at the front of the line" by filing a guideline order. "You need to get ahead of other [baby] mamas," a Manhattan judge warned one mother. "'Cause if you don't, they'll get more than you.... And they'll get it first 'cause he'll just pay down the list. If you're at the bottom, you'll never see the money."

Indeed, this approach to getting women off public assistance has been largely successful across the nation. As I noted in chapter 1, the percentage of poor families' budgets that come from public assistance has steadily declined over the past two decades while the percentage from child support has increased.[28] Although there are no quantitative data on whether these percentages vary for incarcerated parents, from the perspective of the courtrooms I observed, the push to leave public assistance was used more often when the father was absent from court—an absence often due to imprisonment.

Phoning from Prison

In a handful of cases I observed, incarcerated fathers coordinated among institutions to appear for their hearing. This happened rarely: fewer than two dozen of the cases I observed involved incarcerated fathers making an audio or video appearance. It was not for the setting of a child support order—they called in to question an existing order they had been notified of while in prison. Their goal was to "set the record straight," as one incarcerated Florida father put it. They wanted to correct misrepresentations: of their earning capacity, previous employment, or commitment to their children. Most of all, they wanted to reclaim some control over a process from which they had been excluded. Ricardo, a New York father who had served a decade in prison, described the importance of phoning in:

> I have this saying when it comes to the justice system... it's not that we want to get away with anything, but they just look at us in a whole other light. We're not productive people. That's why I have a lot to prove, because when I show up for that court date, I want to go there and say... see me in a different light. If you don't see me as anything else, see me as taking care of my business as a father.

hearings. Since the video feeds often streamed minutes before the father came on the screen, the court got a jarring glimpse of prison life: the sounds of clanking chains, slamming metal doors, and screaming guards and prisoners. When men appeared, they were pushed into a chair, handcuffed, and chained up. Guards yelled at them to lift their heads, look at the camera, and talk into the microphone. After being told about the child support order, fathers seemed stunned and shocked. Some bowed their heads in silence, but many responded with anger. Their initial response was to fight back. Some denied paternity or any relationship to the custodial parent. Others resisted by recounting everything they did for their children, even while behind bars. Still others questioned the court's legitimacy. Defiance may have been in line with the prison code, but it clashed with the representation of self required by courts.

The most extreme case I saw of such resistance involved an African American father who used the "sovereign citizen" defense in defiance of the court during a video hearing.[29] When asked, he refused to give Judge Maddox his name or prison identification number. He refused to admit to having any children. He refused to hire a lawyer. And he refused to agree to the support order of $0. "This court is illegitimate," he answered to all questions. "These proceedings are illegitimate. I am a sovereign citizen." This went on for nearly thirty minutes, with Judge Maddox peppering him with questions, only to get his prepackaged response. By the end, everyone in the courtroom was laughing at him and shaking their heads in disbelief. "Stupid advice inmates give each other," the state lawyer explained after the video feed ended. "They tell each other this crap will stop the case from going forward. [It is] delusional." In the end, a note went in the man's file that he was a belligerent parent, and his support order was issued.

The Letter

Most incarcerated fathers recall the first time they got The Letter. Whether their support orders had been set with or without their knowledge, this official communication from the state child support office was a definitive statement of how much they owed in child support debt. The letters could also be the first time some fathers heard of these orders—as well as their first notice of how much their orders had ballooned while in prison. So they recounted the time they opened these letters with precision. "At first, I thought it was a mistake," explained Jesse, a Los Angeles father of three. "Or a bad joke. I don't have child support. I don't owe anything, I've been in prison. This must be a mistake, the wrong name. Too many zeros in what I owe." Or as Leroy, a Miami father of two who had served ten years in prison, remembered: "When I opened that letter, and found out how much they wanted me to pay, my eyes jumped out of my head."

For some, the letters arrived while they were still in prison. These men described how everyone in prison dreaded mail from the Department of Child Support.[30] "You get so happy to receive mail," Martin recalled, referring to the day he got his letter. "Until you saw who it was from." Confused, incarcerated fathers often asked other prisoners how they should deal with the letters. This was rarely a good idea: Misinformation fed off misinformation, leading parents to do inadvisable things. In Florida prisons, rumor had it that child support stopped automatically during incarceration. No matter how far-fetched it seemed, some fathers thought that if they did nothing, their debt would just go away. "I heard they don't charge [child support] when you're in jail," a Miami father of three explained to me. Or, as one man explained to a judge berating him for not paying child support for five years. "But, your honor, I was incarcerated. . . . Child support stops while I'm in prison. That's what I was told." Laughing, the judge responded, "Well, I don't know who told you that. But listening to him just cost you a lot of money."

Others took the opposite tactic: enraged by the letter, they wrote back letters of protest to child support authorities to advocate for themselves. Usually to no avail—they rarely heard back from these authorities. "I wrote letter after letter to the child support authorities," incarcerated Earl Harris once told a journalist. "Never got one single letter back."[31] I heard something similar from many incarcerated fathers—even letters of inquiry rarely got a response. When they did, it was usually just another copy of the judgment. As Ricardo described it:

> They sent me a notice in prison. I wanted to stop the payments, so I sent a letter [back]. I said, look I'm looking to stop these payments because when I get home my license is going to be suspended and I'm going to need it for work. They wouldn't stop it. They just sent me back another letter, "No, we aren't going to stop it. When you come home, go to court, but New York State law says you can't take any arrears off." So that killed it.

Fathers like Ricardo then put the issue aside. Given their sense of powerlessness, they didn't follow up. "What was I gonna do?" Ricardo asked. "Nothing more I could do from the inside."

Fathers who found the letter waiting for them when they returned home had similar reactions. They vividly remembered the first time they opened it, and their shock and awe at the amount they owed. These fathers often interpreted the letter as another sign of the obstacles they would face and how "the system" conspired against them. "I couldn't deal," explained Raymond, an Oakland father, when describing the time he discovered the letter. "I gave it to my mom . . . and told her to put it away. I don't want to see it." Fathers like this felt paralyzed in the face of their documents of debt. In fact, the letter was so symbolic of men's sense of defeat that some pulled them out during our interviews, all crumpled up, torn, or ripped in fits of anger. As Luis, a Los Angeles father of two, explained as he pulled out his letter:

> I'm sorry it's all ripped up. . . . I got so upset when I read it. I lost my temper. Here I am just out of prison and doing everything right. I got a good job with the city. . . . I am living with my mom so I can see my kids. Then I get this letter from child support. How am I ever going to pay this? It gives me so much stress to think of it . . . how much I owe.

WHAT YOU DON'T KNOW CAN HURT YOU

Letters in hand, most incarcerated fathers embarked on post-prison life with some sense of how deep in debt they had become. Or, perhaps more accurately, as they moved in and out of the criminal justice system, these letters reminded them of the accumulation of their debt. The large majority of people end up recidivating, with more than half returning to prison within the first year alone. Indebted fathers also did repeated stints behind bars. With each stint, they were more likely to experience the debt of imprisonment, with new support orders issued, orders set by default, and retroactive support applied to those orders. Unable to advocate for themselves when back in prison, men's cycles of recidivism mirrored their cycles of debt, with the former exacerbating the latter in immeasurable and often undetected ways.

What, then, could fathers do to contain the financial damage? In some states, there was almost nothing they could do. While imprisonment should be the kind of "change in circumstance" that justifies the modification of a child support order, prior to 2016 one-third of all states defined incarceration as "voluntary unemployment" and thus forbade it to be used as grounds for support modification.[32] With the 2016 Final Rule, the federal government compelled states to put policies on the books to at least consider modifying support orders for the incarcerated, although their actual accessibility remained subject to enormous judicial discretion.

Modification decisions are unpredictable, which creates real obstacles for parents who seek changes to their child support orders. These obstacles were particularly consequential for incarcerated parents, blocking many from receiving the support modifications they might have been entitled to. In fact, a 2015 national study found that 27 percent of parents had been granted modifications while incarcerated and another 11 percent after release, despite the fact that many more were entitled to modifications.[33] The percentage was even lower in my sample: only 26 percent of the fathers I interviewed reported any kind of modification.[34] This meant that nearly three-quarters of fathers left prison with child support debt they had been unable to modify. To understand how this happens, we must once again go inside the messy, conflictual world of child support courts.

Becoming a Bradley Debtor

For child support workers and judges, the modification process seems clear and straightforward: eligible incarcerated parents apply to have their orders held in abeyance until release (in Florida) or to have them set at $0 while incarcerated (in California and New York). Over and over again, officials told me the process was obvious and transparent. From their desks, with their neat stacks of modification forms and paperwork, the process did seem simple. "What on earth stops these men from filling out a few damn forms?" a California judge once exclaimed. "You cannot tell me that prison so handicapped them . . . or they cannot figure this out!"

The clarity of the process for state officials stood in stark contrast to the experience of fathers. These men exhibited a shocking lack of knowledge about their child support orders. The majority of incarcerated parents left prison without even realizing they had an open child support order.[35]

Unaware of these orders, parents also had little understanding of the modification process or their right to request that their orders be held in abeyance.[36] The few who knew about modifications lacked the requisite knowledge to file the necessary paperwork to initiate the process.[37] This explains why a 2015 national survey found that assistance with child support is one of the most pressing needs for incarcerated parents: 86 percent of them reported being in need of such assistance and 30 percent reported it as their most pressing need, yet only 11.5 percent claimed to have actually received help with debt modification.[38] Without assistance, fathers confronted contradictory pulls on them that undermined their ability to contain their debt of imprisonment. Many then became "Bradley debtors"—that is, fathers with debt they could not retroactively modify due to the 1986 amendment's classification of support debt as judgments of law.

The first and strongest of the pulls on fathers was their inclination to do nothing about their child support woes. Those who got the letter while in prison faced the temptation to ignore it. With so many things confronting them in prison, dealing with child support seemed one of the least urgent. In fact, pretty much everything else in prison seemed more pressing than child support: from adjusting to prison life, to negotiating the power dynamics behind bars, to dealing with the details of their criminal case, to maintaining a connection to loved ones on the outside. Child support didn't factor into the long list of things bearing down on them. These men also described being totally unaware of the legal process involved in child support modification. They had no idea how to initiate the process; they were confused by the filing procedures and requirements. They felt unable to affect a process that had gone on for so long in their absence, without their input. Or they were simply unable to read the complicated modification instructions. "Ma'am, there is no way I'm gonna get through all that," a prisoner at Florida's Baker Correctional Institution whispered as a legal aid worker handed him stack of papers to file. "I'm gonna have to wait until I get help with them forms."

Yet waiting was quite literally the worst thing this father could do. During the delay, his debt would continue to pile up and accrue interest. While Florida did not have a standard modification policy for the incarcerated, other states did. And most required that judicial reviews be initiated while the parent was still incarcerated or *before* the debt accumulated. The obstacles here are obvious: incarcerated parents had a hard time organizing their cases, collecting documentation, obtaining financial affidavits, and negotiating court dynamics from prison.

For instance, I conducted child support workshops at the Manhattan Detention Center to teach prisoners about the state's modification process. As I explained the legal process to the fathers, their eyes always glazed over. Within minutes, most of them checked out amidst the bureaucratic complexities. Over and over, these fathers told me they had decided to "lay low" and deal with their support debt upon release. No matter how carefully I explained that laying low would leave them with lifelong debt, they insisted it was too much to handle from jail. As David, a father of two who hovered around our workshop for weeks without joining in, explained to me:

> I got child support too.... But I just can't think about that shit while I'm in here. I want to listen to what you're telling [other inmates] needs to be done, but I'm not doin' it now. Nah, that needs to wait. Until I can go out, talk to my baby mama, and work it out with the court.... From in here, I can't even deal. Not with that anyways.

The tension between doing something and doing nothing also plagued fathers upon release from prison. Here, too, the inclination was to avoid the documents of debt waiting for them. They let those documents accumulate, unopened. They told themselves they would wait to deal with those documents until their post-prison life was back together. The list of things they needed to prioritize over child support was long: getting a job, finding a place to live, repairing familial ties. Fathers told me about their elaborate post-prison plans to get their economic lives in order before addressing other obligations. This is how Darden, a San Francisco father of five who had left San Quentin after twenty years with enormous debt to repay foster care costs, explained the dilemma:

> I gotta pay back my auntie for everything she gave me all these years.... And I'm livin' with her now so that's the first thing to do. Then I gotta get a car 'cause I can't find work without a car.... I got debts to settle before this one [the public assistance payback].... But the judge tells me it's been years that the "citizens of California" have waited to be paid back [for foster care].... I gotta plan but she won't listen.

For others, the decision to do nothing was less commendable: they went underground after their release because they just could not deal with everything facing them. These fathers felt overwhelmed by the magnitude of the problems they confronted. They felt angry at how hard their reentry and reintegration seemed to be. "It's like you got so much shit comin' at you," Julio explained after doing seven years in Florida State Prison. "It's hard to take it all in." So they developed avoidance tactics. They threw away letters from child support without opening them. They tore up child support notifications before reading them carefully. They ignored court summons. They convinced themselves that if the notices stopped coming, they would be magically out of the red. And they refused to tell anyone about their accumulated debt. If asked about child support by criminal justice, they avoided the question or denied having any outstanding arrears.

Here, too, avoidance tactics just worsened their problems. Incarcerated parents fortunate enough to secure a $0 order while in prison lost it upon release, since support orders quickly spring back to their original amount, often within 30 days. So to stay out of the red they had to develop ways to keep current on their support. For fathers who had not obtained $0 orders—and they were the large majority—debt continued to accrue rapidly. What is more, enforcement measures halted during incarceration—from license suspension to wage garnishment to asset liens to passport revocations to arrest warrants—are rebooted as soon as child support offices learn of parents' release. So while fathers prioritized other obligations that seemed more pressing, their child support debt festered in the shadows. By the time they learned of their missteps, it was too late: they had become Bradley debtors, with no ability to retroactively modify their debt.

Although I encountered this Bradley trajectory in every legal system I studied, it was especially pronounced in Florida. Here the modification process was unusually complicated: at the time, it required that parents appeal to a judge immediately upon entering prison to request that their support payments be held in abeyance for later review. Incarcerated parents then had to petition for a legal review of their arrears upon release from prison. The outcome of this review was left to judicial discretion. Thus, the modification process was dependent on incarcerated parents knowing what was required of them and having the legal wherewithal to pursue modification appeals. In my interviews with Florida fathers, I did not encounter a single one who knew they were supposed to apply for an abeyance upon entering prison.[39] And no one knew they could appeal to have their debt reviewed upon release.

This complete lack of understanding was demonstrated to me on a grand scale during a reentry forum I participated in at Baker Correctional Facility, a large Florida prison for those approaching release. Consisting of several hundred men jammed into a sweltering prison auditorium, the forum was designed to provide a sense of the legal landscape awaiting them upon release. As an introduction, I took a survey of the room, asking how many of them had been on child support while in prison. Over half the men raised their hands. Then I asked how many had applied for debt modification. Silence. So I elaborated: "Did anyone apply to put their child support on hold by the court? Did anyone know you could do this?" I was met with hundreds of blank stares. As soon as the panel ended, the silence broke and I was bombarded with questions from the men: What did I mean by modification? Could they do it now? "How come no one told me about this when I could do something about it?" an incarcerated father exclaimed. "I got five kids.... I can't even count how much I owe. Now I can't do nothing?" Indeed, he was right: since he had not applied for an abeyance upon entering prison, it was too late to do anything.

In effect, Florida's modification policy was designed to be inaccessible. Yet fathers in the two "modification friendly" states I researched did not understand the process much better. Both California and New York allowed parents to request $0 modifications for public orders while in prison as well as modification reviews after prison. Yet only a small minority of them actually got their orders modified. Of the fifty New York fathers I interviewed, only six reported having their orders modified by the court after prison. They had all been assisted by a committed child support worker who crossed the state to advise incarcerated fathers on managing their child support debt. Most incarcerated fathers in New York lacked basic knowledge of their rights when it came to child support. In our interviews, some insisted that their support had stopped automatically while in prison, while others claimed they just had to go to court to get their debt wiped out. Indeed, the Friday video prison tours described earlier were to *set* new support orders, not to *modify* existing orders. For the latter, there were few procedures to make the process accessible for incarcerated parents.

Moreover, as with support order hearings, modification reviews often worked against incarcerated parents. Very few fathers got far enough even to apply for one: in the more than 250 support adjudication cases I observed in New York courts, only three involved modification requests justified explicitly on the basis of incarceration. In all three cases, fathers had little sense of what they could request and what they were entitled to. Their cases thus became spectacles. One father called in from Rikers to the jokes and jeers of everyone in the courtroom. Another father insisted that all his child support arrears should be wiped out, retroactively, because he was in prison when they accrued—only to be admonished by the judge for demanding the impossible. In another memorable case, a father who did submit the necessary financial statements from prison provoked condescension when the judge asked about the $15,000 he listed under "charitable contributions" on his statement—a category he had interpreted as the amount he would offer to resolve his case. "Are you kidding me?" the state lawyer scoffed. "Paying child support is not a charity." Not surprisingly, all of these men's appeals were denied: for waiting too long to apply, for filling out the paperwork improperly, or for asking for the wrong thing.

Fathers' lack of knowledge not only deterred them from reaching court but also undermined the few who did find their way there. These men encountered a series of stumbling blocks as they tried to make their case for modification. Men tripped over them largely because they were unaware of the process. Keeping track of what is permitted, and where, when, and for whom, is difficult for legal experts—and nearly impossible for incarcerated parents. Cases also require an enormous amount of paperwork to adjudicate: from W2s to expense statements to tax returns from multiple years. Parents rarely kept such records, so the bureaucratic barriers seemed insurmountable. Very few parents came to court with counsel; they appeared in court on their own without knowing what to ask for and how to advocate for themselves.

Take, for instance, the Bradley Amendment. On the surface, this legislation seems to forbid retroactive modification. Yet I encountered enormous variation across states in terms of how Bradley is interpreted and implemented. In Florida, Bradley was often used to justify a ban on modifying retroactive debt. In New York, this seemed true of private debt, which was rarely modifiable, but public debt could be modified at the discretion of judges and administrators. Then there was California, which facilitated the modification of public debt and even some private debt. Here state officials often encouraged custodial parents to negotiate the debt owed to them. Officials in all three states cited the Bradley Amendment as the rationale for their approach. One federal mandate had led to three divergent state practices, and parents did not have a clear sense of what they had a right to because those rights varied by state.[40]

Even within states there was significant variation in how courts adjudicated Bradley. Here, too, it was deployed strategically: sometimes courts used Bradley to reject a modification request, claiming that federal legislation forbade it. Other times, Bradley was referenced to justify a modification. For instance, despite New York officials' insistence that Bradley restricted them from modifying private debt, I watched numerous courts encourage mothers and fathers to agree to a reduction in arrears (although rarely in cases involving incarceration). Like the Brooklyn judge who convinced a mother to write off $5,000 of the $23,000 owed to her provided that her ex-husband agreed to pay her $1,000 immediately. "You haven't seen any money for your child in four years," the judge prodded. "Wouldn't you rather have money in your pocket now than waiting for more?" This interpretation of Bradley was codified in New York City's Arrears Cap Initiative, which allowed state officials to write off public debt if they could show that a parent was living below the poverty line when it accrued.[41] But few incarcerated fathers knew about it, so modifications were left to judicial discretion, dependent on whether judges decided to use their wiggle room to modify an order.

Incarcerated fathers encountered yet another snag when trying to secure modifications: how much to reveal about their histories of incarceration. As with the infamous "box" on employment applications, many fathers feared that admitting to having been incarcerated would stigmatize them further. So they took a don't-ask-don't-tell approach, making no mention of their imprisonment unless forced to. In court, I observed hundreds of cases where there were long gaps in fathers' payments that seemed related to incarceration. Yet fathers made no mention of it.[42] "Why would I cop to being a convicted felon, in front of a JUDGE?" Julio exclaimed to me when I asked how he explained his spotty payment history in his post-prison support hearing. "If he didn't have [the information], why would I turn it over to him? It'll just make him hate me even more." In many respects, Julio's logic made sense: some judges were more suspicious and punitive when fathers had criminal records. These fathers were subjected to more scrutiny and longer lectures about personal responsibility and familial neglect.

But not sharing incarceration information could also make the plight of fathers like Julio *more* difficult. Because of their long absences from their kids' lives, these men came across as neglectful, irresponsible parents. The huge gaps in their payment histories made them look like iconic deadbeats. What is more, these fathers didn't realize that serving time might actually entitle them to a modification hearing—that far from being something to hide, incarceration could serve them as a path to debt modification. Even in Florida, which refused to consider incarceration as the basis for a modification review, courts often used prison to contextualize a large arrears balance or a long child support rap sheet. But few fathers knew enough about the legal process to realize they should share the information.

This was made clear one afternoon in Judge May's Florida courtroom. Notoriously punitive, even to the point of indiscretion, May prided himself on "givin' the deadbeats hell." On this July day, I watched him do just that to James, an African American father of three who owed more than $32,000 in back child support. "You are a sorry excuse for a man," May began. "Leaving your babies with nothing. For how many years?" May then calculated that it had been years since the state disbursement unit had received a child support payment from James, which prompted May to launch into a fifteen-minute tirade during which he called James everything from "scum" to a "disease" who engaged in "irresponsible sexual behavior." Amidst the relentless judicial attacks, James said nothing. He kept his head down, occasionally muttering "I am sorry, sir" and "I don't know why I did this, sir." The case ended with May issuing a $2,000 purge, which James had to deliver to him in court within two weeks or else face jailtime.

The next day, I sat down with James at a nearby Burger King for a two-hour interview. He described spending much of the prior fifteen years in and out of prison, first for drug arrests from his decade-long crack addiction and then for drug trafficking. Interspersed throughout his long rap sheet were numerous stints in jail for child support. "I could never get ahead of the debt," he explained while looking down at his half-eaten hamburger. "It just seemed to get bigger and bigger no matter what I did." He described a route to debt common of so many fathers, where his debt grew exponentially with each stint in jail. He lost track of who he owed and why. Mail stopped reaching him given his residential instability, stays in rehab, and stints in jail. He stopped reading his mail when it did find its way to him. "I'd come back to court ... and that's when they'd tell me these crazy ass numbers [of his debt]. They just got bigger." Then I asked him about his most recent hearing with May, and why he hadn't explained his history of incarceration to the court. "It wouldn't have mattered," he claimed. "That just would have made it worse." James insisted that he needed to keep his incarceration history to himself. "If I told them, I'd be a felon and a deadbeat ... The worst man on earth."

The Curious Case of the California $0 Order

The inability of fathers like James to secure modifications on their orders and debt was not only due to their lack of information about the legal process. There were also institutional barriers that blocked incarcerated parents from managing their child support. Nowhere are these institutional barriers clearer than in California, which has a quite progressive modification policy on the books. In 2010, California was one of the first states to introduce $0 child support orders for eligible incarcerated parents.[43] Initially, modification requests had to be initiated by the parent while incarcerated. Their requests then underwent judicial review that required incarcerated parents to provide evidence of their imprisonment as well as other financial documentation. Parents could participate in this review via telephone, although it was not required since the $0 order was granted for those who qualified for it without much discretion.

A few years after its introduction, a legislative review of the California policy by the Department of Child Support Services (DCSS) raised concerns that few incarcerated parents were utilizing the modification option.

Initially, there had been an uptick in modification requests coming from jails and prisons, due at least in part to a coordinated effort between DCSS and the California Department of Correction and Rehabilitation (CDCR) to inform prisoners of their right to a $0 modification.[44] But those quickly leveled off, prompting state officials to propose the removal of the judicial review altogether. The state assembly then passed a temporary law to experiment with allowing modifications to be granted administratively by caseworkers. The idea was to bypass the legal hurdles that made it so difficult for incarcerated parents to modify their orders. With this reform, California's policy became one of the most progressive in the country.

In 2019, when the pilot policy was due to expire, another congressional review of the policy was done by DCSS, yet again finding that only a small percentage of those eligible for $0 orders actually received them.[45] So despite having the most accommodating modification policy on the books, California's modification rates were not very different from those of other states. While this perplexed many of the state officials, the lack of change is more explicable when viewed from an institutional perspective. Under both policies, parents were responsible for initiating the modification process: they needed to file a legal petition or notify child support workers of their incarceration.[46] Some of them then needed to provide financial documentation such as tax returns, which they frequently did not have. These parents not only lacked information about their support orders but also were entangled in institutional nets and caught between two systems with competing demands.

State institutions are notoriously suspicious of one another. This is especially true of punitive ones like child support and criminal justice institutions. In my work with officials in both institutions, I was struck by how often they blamed each other for the barriers to support modification. On the one hand, child support workers insisted that prisons refused to assist them. They accused prison officers of not giving parents information about support orders and modifications; they claimed that prisons were refusing to allow child support workers into their facilities to counsel fathers; and they suggested that guards were jealous of the assistance given to prisoners and thus subverted it. "At every stage, there was resistance [from CDCR]," an agency director explained to me. "They would cancel our child support workshops or fail to inform inmates about them. It was so frustrating. . . . I eventually gave up." As another child support official put it:

> They [corrections officers] don't want the inmates to get help with this. They thought helping them understand child support was like being too soft on them. Like we were favoring them or something. . . . Sometimes I felt like maybe the officers and guards were jealous that inmates were getting help. Like they were angry 'cause they needed help too, since many of them had child support as well. As if they thought it was unfair that [inmates] were getting all this "special" help.

Exacerbating these challenges were structural shifts in California's criminal justice system. Around the time of the introduction of the $0 incarceration orders, criminal justice realignment dispersed inmates across the state and from prisons to jails. Prisoners were also moved across state lines. After 2011, it became difficult to trace the state's carceral landscape or to track where a prisoner would land in it. Such dispersion made it harder for fathers to figure out whom to contact about support orders and modifications. It created difficulties locating incarcerated parents eligible for modifications. Even after caseworkers could modify orders on their own, they struggled to find parents. They also needed cooperation from the local jails, which could be even more challenging than CDCR. One San Francisco child support official recalled going on "jail fieldtrips" to search for incarcerated parents: she'd go from cell to cell, asking if anyone had child support issues. Needless to say, she got few takers.

Similar sentiments were echoed on the prison side of the institutional divide. "Child support is ruining our rehab programs," a New York corrections commissioner once exclaimed to me. "We give [inmates] money if they attend rehabilitation workshops prior to release. But then child support comes in and garnishes their prison accounts. How can we work like this?" Correctional officers across states viewed child support agencies as fixated on debt recovery and enforcement. In California, they also accused the child support system of being so excessively punitive that it inhibited prisoners' reentry. "When they [inmates] get out, how are they supposed to stay out [of prison] when they can't drive?" a high-ranking CDCR official asked me. "Or when they can't keep most of their income 'cause of child support?" As another correctional supervisor told me while we worked on a new child support intake program at his prison:

> [It] seems like every year something is changing with child support. I don't understand why they need to make it all so complicated. . . . We can print up information now but I bet it'll change by the time we give it out. We're gonna need to revise what we tell them [inmates] all the time 'cause child support just can't decide what they're doing.

The distance separating these state systems was not merely symbolic: they literally had no way to connect to one another. Unlike other state bodies, like the DMV, CalWORKS, and Social Security, these institutions operated largely in isolation from each other. Most importantly, there was no computer interface linking the CDCR and DCSS.[47] So there was no straightforward way to locate incarcerated parents with open child support orders. While caseworkers could modify orders administratively and allow parents to avoid court, they could only do so if they found these parents. Without access to data on who was incarcerated, their hands were tied. The same goes for CDCR. Without a direct way to access who had open support orders, correctional staff could not assist with modification appeals or debt relief even if they wanted to.

In this way, as is often the case with policy reform, California's attempt to address one part of debt accumulation ended up exposing the other issues. Simply giving incarcerated parents the option to modify their support orders while in prison did little to change the amassing of their debt. Instead, it revealed the many complications parents faced in managing child support—some were informational, others contextual, and others structural. It also exposed how addressing the debt of imprisonment requires confronting the institutional obstacles that cause parents to fall through the cracks without receiving the modifications they are entitled to. Unless those barriers are addressed, the accumulation of these parents' debt will remain as certain as it is crushing.

THE POLITICS OF DEBT FORGIVENESS

The reform attempts in California expose something of more general significance: the complex entanglements of the debt of imprisonment. While child support and criminal justice institutions might insist on their separateness, parents experience their interconnections. Indeed, part of the power of these state systems lies in their denial of those intersections. Each system has its own separate demands and expectations, yet parents living between the two of them encounter these demands as crisscrossing. From setting support orders *in absentia* to the legal processes of child support court, these systems feed off each other. This makes incarcerated parents' relationship to child support different from that of other low-income parents. Incarcerated parents are situated across institutions in ways that consistently trip them up: from the perils of code-switching, to the trajectory of the Bradley debtors, to the traveling stigma of prison, these parents stumble as they try to manage it all. With each stumble, the debt of imprisonment accumulates to levels unknown by other disadvantaged parents.

The institutional loops connecting child support and criminal justice are not just conceptually important—they also have policy implications for how to address the debt of imprisonment. Given the immense size of this debt, some state officials have begun to think seriously about policy reforms for this group of parents. Perhaps the most common way states have done this is with $0 incarceration orders of the kind California experimented with.[48] Yet as the California experience shows, incarceration orders are hardly a panacea; they often expose larger institutional entanglements. Addressing these entanglements means recognizing the unique context of incarcerated parents and the multiple obstacles they confront. This might mean rethinking the Bradley Amendment, especially for institutionalized parents who are unable to advocate for themselves. It might involve ending public assistance payback for institutionalized parents, thus acknowledging the unique constraints incarceration places on earning income. Or it might mean waiving interest on incarcerated parents' support debt, also as a recognition that charging interest on a debt that parents have no capacity to repay is excessively punitive.[49]

While these policy reforms might chip away at the amassing of future debt, new policies are also needed for the millions of incarcerated parents who have already accumulated debt. For this, debt forgiveness programs are promising options, particularly for those deep in the red due to incarceration and poverty. Even if done only for public arrears, debt relief can make a dent in the debt of imprisonment—since much of the debt owed by incarcerated parents is in fact to the government. Indeed, some states and locales have experimented with such relief, albeit on a small scale, but no program operates across states or at the national level.[50]

This is largely because the politics involved such programs are enormously fraught. On one end are proponents of debt forgiveness, who tend to be sensitive to the precariousness of reentry and to how saddling fathers with so much debt complicates their reintegration. They also argue that easing parents' debt burden will ultimately benefit poor families and children.[51] Evaluation research backs up both sets of claims: studies show that debt forgiveness leads to better reentry outcomes by reducing debt, enabling employment, reducing stress, and improving familial relationships.[52] In addition, debt relief can be beneficial to the state itself. Fiscal conservatives are often troubled by the large amount of debt owed to state governments and its drain on state budgets. With only 6 percent of all arrears repaid yearly, most of this debt sits unpaid as interest accrues.[53] When it comes to public debt, repayment rates are even lower.[54] For instance, of the $12 billion owed in public debt in California, over 95 percent has been deemed uncollectable.[55] Getting this debt off the books through retroactive forgiveness can thus be in the state's interest.

Yet resistance to debt relief is fierce. Some of it comes from the usual suspects: from "law and order" policy-makers, who insist that any sort of debt relief would reward indebted parents for their irresponsible behavior and incarcerated parents for their illegal behavior. These arguments harken back to claims from the 1980s about the need to "make men pay" for their negligence. In fact, some lawmakers rejected the 2016 Final Rule by insisting it "gave prisoners a break" from their obligations and incentivized bad behavior.[56] Then there are those who viewed debt relief as an attack on the core principles of welfare reform. Here the echoes are from the 1990s, and claims about the need for public assistance payback. As senator Orrin Hatch proclaimed in his opposition to the 2016 Final Rule, child support reform undermined the idea that "single mothers can avoid welfare if fathers comply with child-support orders."[57]

In this way, despite decades of unmanageable debt accumulation, the political debate continues to be stymied by claims about how reform might reward bad behavior and negligent parents. While I revisit this debate in the concluding chapter, for now it is critical to note that underlying these reform debates are competing ideas about the role of child support. Is child support a form of behavior modification? A way to make men pay for their past mistakes, from nonpayment to criminal behavior? Or is child support a tool to assist families and ensure children get the care they need? Without agreement on these questions, it is difficult to agree on what debt forgiveness implies: what kind of debt is being forgiven? Is it a debt to the custodial parent, the child, or the state? Or is it forgiving a behavior, such as parental irresponsibility or criminality? For decades, child support provisions veered toward behavior modification, which resulted in the massive accumulation of public and private debt. Moreover, the state's attempts at behavior modification then gave rise to an enforcement apparatus that rivals criminal justice in scope and punitiveness. I turn to this enforcement system in part 2.

PART II Enforcement

It is a hot summer day in the Jacksonville area, and everyone in court is a bit on edge. Especially Judge Matthews, who has already sent three fathers to jail for nonpayment of child support—and it is not yet noon. "I'm fixin' to break for lunch, so let's do one more," Matthews proclaims. Bailiff Frank obliges and calls the next case. As the parents walk up to the bench to take their places in front of Matthews, he starts to read their file. He shakes his head and lets out a loud sigh before summarizing it: "So, Mr. Casey, you owe $481 a month on an order for one minor child, with arrears of $24,000 because you failed to pay anything for six years, correct?" As Mr. Casey starts to explain that he's made two payments since getting out of jail, Matthews interrupts him. "How much money did you bring with you to court today? No, come to think of it, take out your wallet." He then instructs bailiff Frank to open the wallet and show him what's inside: "I want to see the money . . . " As Frank pulls out $200, Matthews tells him to hand it to the mother. "Here ma'am, this belongs to you," he declares.

Matthews turns to Mr. Casey and bombards him with questions: Where does he work? How does he support himself? Why didn't he pay support for so many years? Did he know how much it costs to raise a child? How does it feel to leave a child without the means to be supported and cared for? With each of Mr. Casey's answers, Matthews's disapproval builds. "Excuses, excuses," he exclaims. "Your child can't eat excuses." Finally, he erupts with an order: "Frank, cuff him right now. I'm finished listening to your excuses.... Stand over there and face the wall. You're going to jail now.... But first who brought you to court today?... Your girlfriend? Is she in the waiting area right now? Okay, Frank, bring her into court."

After escorting Mr. Casey to the wall, Frank exits the courtroom and returns minutes later with a frightened woman. Matthews points to Mr. Casey as he issues his instructions to the woman:

> Did you come to court today with this man? 'Cause he's your boyfriend, right?... Well, how much money do you have on you, ma'am? 'Cause that man of yours owes a lotta money to the mama of his baby.... [You have] $300? Well, give that over. 'Cause I bet this loser told you to hold this money for him. 'Cause he knew I was fixin' to take all his money away.... You see that man of yours over there? Facing the wall? Well, he's about to go to jail. You are the only one who can save him.... How much money can you come up with over the lunch break?... Let me make this easy for you: if you come back to court with $2,000, I won't send him away. Otherwise, he's going to jail.

As court adjourns for lunch, I walk out with Mr. Casey's girlfriend. She is crying. I ask if she expected any of this. "My god, no," she exclaims. "I had no idea... I'd be brought into court too. And, now, this? How am I gonna get all that money to save him?" She starts to cry harder as she runs through all the people she could call for loans. His aunt in Tallahassee? His father in Miami? His cousin in Virginia? "But how am I gonna get them to send the money so fast?" she asks while frantically scrolling through her phone. "I can't ask my family 'cause they just hate him.... My mama warned me about him, told me he'd be nothin' but trouble." She then runs off to her car to start the fundraising. When court resumes an hour later, there is no sign of her. At the end of the day, I ask bailiff Frank what happened to Mr. Casey. "Oh, he's in jail," he responds, shaking his head. "How's a woman like that gonna come up with all that money?"

Indeed, this was a question I often found myself asking as I observed child support courts across the country: how could fathers like Mr. Casey, and those connected to them, possibly raise the amount of money being demanded of them? This question frequently led to another: given the impossibility of getting out of debt, can parents just resign themselves to living deep in the red? After all, many Americans live in debt—in 2020, the United States became the world's eleventh most indebted nation, with an average household debt of $155,000. So could child support debt perhaps become like a car loan or credit card debt, something that one just learns to live with? Like Mr. Garcia, the Los Angeles man I highlighted in part 1, who lived while owing the state of California half a million dollars? Or all of the other fathers I interviewed, who owed anywhere from a few thousand to several hundred thousand dollars in back support?

The problem with this logic is that child support debt is unlike any other sort of debt. In contrast to credit card or mortgage debt, obligors cannot walk away from child support debt if they go underwater; bankruptcy law does not apply to support debt. More importantly, child support debt is accompanied by an enforcement apparatus that rivals the criminal justice system in its punitive reach. When a child support order goes unpaid, even if only for a month, it sets off a slew of enforcement measures that can ensnare parents and those connected to them with extraordinary speed and effectiveness—as Mr. Casey and his girlfriend came to learn.

In previous chapters, I described the accumulation of child support debt as a kind of tsunami for incarcerated fathers, surging fast and high to submerge them. The metaphor is even more apt when enforcement is considered. Tsunamis overwhelm not only because their initial tidal wave takes people under, but also because the subsequent waves can be equally disruptive and destructive. The same is true of the tsunami of child support debt: the initial accumulation of debt is followed by additional waves as parents are brought into court, lose basic rights, and are held in contempt. These secondary waves can seem relentless as they keep coming at parents for years, even decades, throwing their lives into disarray without a moment's notice.

These subsequent waves emerge from the enforcement system that accompanies child support debt. Just when parents think they've weathered the waves, they get hit by another; when they think it's smooth sailing, another wave comes at them. The next two chapters explain how and why these waves keep rising: chapter 3 details the different parts of the enforcement apparatus and the variability in it targets, while chapter 4 analyzes how some fathers are able to ride out these waves, while others end up riding them right back to illegal activity and prison.

3 Punishing Parents, Creating Criminals

> If you don't pay the child support you owe, we will garnish your wages, take away your driver's license, track you across state lines and, if necessary, make you work off what you owe.
>
> Bill Clinton, at the 1996 Announcement of the Personal Responsibility and Work Opportunity Act

In the 1980s and 1990s, when the government set out to direct the child support system to "make men pay," it had a dual focus. First and foremost, it sought to make men pay in the monetary sense. Through a series of policies and practices, it tried to make men financially responsible for their children. But there was also a punitive connotation to making men pay—through measures to enforce child support orders, it punished those who failed to pay. In theory these two arms were to work in unison: the enforcement apparatus was to kick in once parents failed to pay, thus buttressing and supporting the financial arm. But as often occurs with punitive state measures, enforcement took on a life of its own. It began to operate according to its own logic and with its own consequences. Unlike the monetary arm, which at least followed some fixed steps and formulas, the enforcement arm operated with almost total discretion. The adjudication process frequently skipped steps and changed course, seemingly at the whim of child support administrators and court officials.

As a result, parents rarely knew what they would encounter when the nonpayment of support brought them into the enforcement realm. As I made my way into child support courts across the country, I rarely knew what I would encounter. From New York to Florida to California, the divergence in state practices was stunning: what was standard practice in one state could be unthinkable in another. For instance, what Mr. Casey and his girlfriend experienced in Florida was unimaginable in most of New York and California. Similarly, the degree of variation within states surprised and baffled me: the enforcement measures used in northern and southern Florida could bear little resemblance to each other, just as those in northern and southern California could differ dramatically. And the differences between rural and urban courts were so stark they could seem unrecognizable. Even within the same locale and court system, variations between courts were striking. This was not true just of judicial style, tone, and demeanor—that was to be expected. Courts also adhered to different adjudication processes and took different routes to the enforcement of child support orders, and officials had particular intolerances that shaped those processes. For instance, one Florida judge had a deep prejudice against interracial couples—they so enraged him that he threw all protocol out the window when he faced one. A Brooklyn magistrate was so fixated on bureaucracy that even a minor mistake on legal paperwork could lead him to jump several steps in the process and punish the wrongdoer harshly. Then there was the Los Angeles judge who was so troubled by gang affiliations that the smallest sign of one prompted him to come down hard on a parent without warning.

Power and punishment are at their most damaging when wielded unpredictably. Social scientists have demonstrated this in an array of social relations: whether it involves parent and child or doctor and patient or dictator and citizen or guard and inmate, the unpredictable application of power in a relationship can seem especially cruel and abusive to those it targets. It can make them profoundly vulnerable; unclear about what to expect, they can feel discombobulated and sideswiped. Inconsistent control can be experienced as arbitrary and lead to the sense that the system is rigged. Indeed, this was often the case with child support enforcement: as parents came to court expecting a predictable process only to encounter unpredictability, they complained vociferously that the system was erratic, unjust, and deceitful. While this unpredictability might seem like simple legal capriciousness, it was also enormously consequential.

Overall, the unpredictability of child support enforcement took two main forms. First, there was grave inconsistency in *how* punishment occurred. The enforcement measures available in the child support system varied in both degree and kind. To some extent, they fell along a continuum, with mounting levels of punitiveness. But the steps leading from one end of the continuum to the other were not always followed. Moreover, the sanctioning power underlying these measures blended civil, administrative, and criminal law. Because of this legal hybridity, it was never clear which form of power would prevail or what combination of fines, revocations, or confinement would be applied. The first part of this chapter analyzes these punitive measures, describing the financial, remedial, and custodial sanctions of child support enforcement.

As significant as fluctuations in *how* enforcement transpired were inconsistencies in *what* was punished. In theory, enforcement should be limited to the collection of support. In reality, it became much more. In many cases, it was used to punish poverty, which here meant punishing parents for not meeting their financial obligations. Cases often began with nonpayment and devolved into indictments of parents' economic choices. This was especially true of incarcerated fathers, for whom a criminal record frequently led to the criminalization of poverty. The second part of the chapter documents this slippage in the nation's largest child support program: New York City's system, where a poverty discourse prevailed to blame parents for not working hard enough for their children.

Yet child support enforcement was not simply about punishing poverty—it was also about enforcing a particular form of fatherhood. Parents considered to be in violation of the breadwinning ideal became the targets of their own scolding and rebuke. Here, too, there was frequent slippage, with officials moving from the enforcement of a support order to the condemnation of a father's parental commitment. The final part of this chapter describes how this conflation occurred in another state child support program: the Florida system, where courts often used support enforcement to dictate a specific model of fatherhood.

THE ENFORCEMENT ASSEMBLAGE

When a parent falls behind on child support, even for only a month or two, a system of enforcement measures kicks in. This enforcement appa-

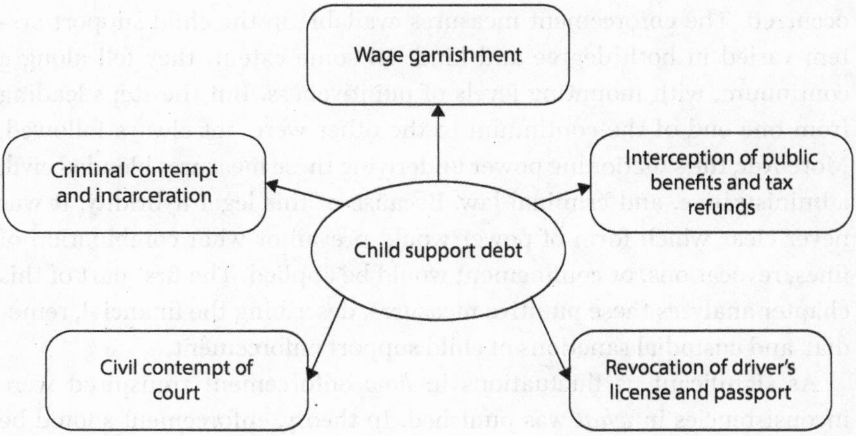

Figure 15. The Imprisonment of Debt

ratus is a complex assemblage of local, state, and federal actions that vary according to the type and severity of the sanction. Not all courts use all these measures to the same degree, although they have access to them. While these measures are supposed to be deployed incrementally, with punishment escalating from financial to remedial to custodial sanctions, some steps get jumped over or bypassed without reason. Yet no matter which tools get used, this assemblage produces an inescapable net of punishments, what Ronald Mincy has called a "heat-seeking missile" due to its ability to track and destroy targets.[1] Figure 15 illustrates the different dimensions of enforcement.

Financial Sanctions

The first line of offense against parents failing to pay their child support are a series of financial actions to intercept funds. The most common of these is wage garnishment, which is mandated at the federal and state levels. These withholdings are administrative sanctions and can be done automatically, in a computerized and centralized fashion. Whatever amount of money the parent owes in an already established order is withdrawn as a salary garnishment. This is true of public and private orders, as funds to pay both custodial parents and public assistance payback can be taken from paychecks. States work with different guidelines for what percentage of a parent's income can be withheld, with most allowing garnishments up to 65 percent of the obligor's wages if multiple children or arrears are involved. They also work with varying policies as to where the garnished funds end up going in public assistance cases—some states "pass through" a small amount to the family, while others use all recovered funds to repay the state.

Because wage garnishment is mandated and centrally administered, it is one area where support magistrates and judges have limited discretion. And they complain vociferously about this. Some are angered by being constrained by state guidelines set for them. So they blame faceless bureaucrats—"the people over in Tallahassee" or "politicians in Albany"—for tying their hands. Judge Matthews, the most punitive judge I encountered, had a special name for them: "Those folks down in Tallahassee are like the Gestapo.... They tell me what to do and there ain't no reasoning with them." Other judges complained because they viewed the fixed guidelines as unfair and unreasonable. As they ordered the withholding of huge chunks of fathers' wages, some judges apologized and advised parents how to modify their orders. As an Oakland judge explained to a father whose income was cut in half after he lost overtime hours:

> I am going to order a downward departure in your case, sir. Do you know what this means?... I will depart from what the guidelines tell me to order because I am very worried about you becoming homeless if you have to pay the $580 guideline order. If you become homeless, that helps no one.... So for now, I will set it at half that. But I can only do this for a short period. You must consider modifying your order, based on your new income. The court officials can give you the paperwork for that.... While I can see that you still see this as very unfair, you must understand that this is all I can do. My hands are tied otherwise.

Obviously, income withholding only applies to parents with formal employment. For parents who are unemployed, or who lose their jobs and fall behind on child support, additional financial measures can kick in. There is far more discretion in the administration of these measures. When confronted with a parent without formal employment, court officials have several options. First, they can do nothing, thus leaving the support order unchanged. In this way, nonaction can be punitive: most unemployed parents can no longer pay their existing orders, so their debt mounts. Second, officials can issue low-income orders to reduce the support order while the parent remains unemployed. Many child support hearings begin as enforcement cases and end with judges recommending low-income orders for parents without work. Third, court officials can delay the start of an enforcement measure by giving unemployed parents time to start paying their orders. Here judges may order parents to attend a job-readiness program or conduct job searches for a set amount of time, during which time enforcement measures are suspended.[2] This option is especially critical for formerly incarcerated parents, who often need time to get on their feet after being released from prison.

Because judges have the ability to decide which approach to take in these cases, they usually require parents to demonstrate their worthiness before ruling. These hearings are thus devoted to sussing out if parents are deserving of a "break." And this involves all sorts of questions: Why isn't the parent working? Has he really tried to find work? Is he willing to do any kind of work, or is he being too picky? Most of all, is he working informally and hiding his income? These questions usually involve parents submitting all sorts of written records, from job search diaries to employer statements to financial affidavits. Parents often have a hard time collecting all this documentation. Perhaps the most difficult of these requests were for tax returns, which some parents failed to file or keep records of. This added another layer of discretion to the process. Is the judge willing to excuse incomplete documentation or missing tax returns? Does the judge view these lapses as evidence that the parent is untrustworthy and undeserving?

Determinations of worthiness also affect whether additional financial sanctions are set into motion. Besides garnishing wages, states can freeze bank accounts, issue liens against property, and block the receipt of many public benefits. These sanctions can be applied by child support caseworkers. All support cases are expected to undergo regular review, so that when parents become delinquent with their payments caseworkers can search for funds. This can lead them to seize bank accounts and property. At times, it can even lead them to prison commissary accounts, which can be garnished in states like New York and Florida.[3] Several fathers from these states described having their prison accounts hit without warning. Since these accounts rarely had much money in them, they considered such garnishments gratuitous acts of meanness. Some, like New York City father Carlos, also pointed out the absurdity of what then transpired:

> My girl[friend] was the one to put the money in my [prison] account. One day I went to buy some shit and they told me there was nothing in my account. Fucking child support cleared it out.... So you know what I did? I just had my girl send me more money.... They took it out to give to her, I guess. So I had her put it right back.[4]

Financial sanctions can also be ordered and adjudicated by child support courts. Enforcement hearings often became fishing expeditions, with judges trying to ascertain all the resources a parent may have and might be hiding. They went through parents' budgets in detail to determine how much they spent and how they got by without regular employment. Judges also searched for hidden funds, trying to trap parents in lies. They could even order those associated with a parent, such as family members, partners, or coworkers, to testify to the resources at a parent's disposal. This was enormously invasive, especially when done in open court.[5] In one case, a Brooklyn magistrate demanded that a father bring his employer into court to prove he only had part-time work. When the father refused, arguing that it could jeopardize his employment, the judge took away his low-income order, which caused his monthly payment to more than double.

One northern Florida court, which I began to refer to as the "means-test court," took this one step further: it forced parents to sell their belongings as proof of their commitment as fathers. Judges had parents list everything of value they owned, from cars to work tools to electronics to jewelry to clothing. "What about those pants you have on? They are falling off your butt, but they don't look cheap" a judge noted to one father. Once the expensive objects were listed, court officials calculated how much money could be yielded by selling everything. What were these men willing to give up to be good fathers? Their cars? Their cell phones? Their jewelry? "That gold chain could pay a chunk [of the arrears]," Judge Clay proposed to a father. Once judges had computed how much their belongings were worth, they instructed fathers to sell their stuff and return to their next

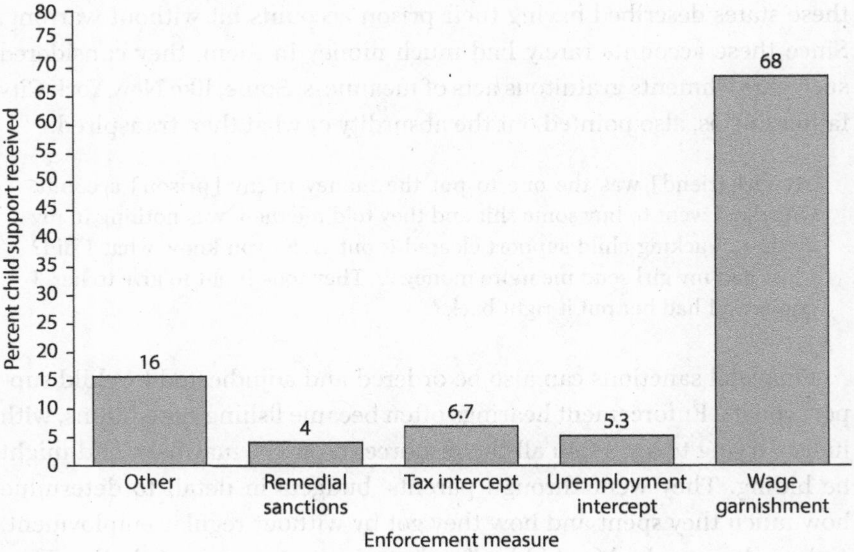

Figure 16. Child Support Received, by Enforcement Measure. SOURCES: Pirog and Ziol-Guest 2006; Turetsky and Waller 2020

court date with that amount of money in hand. If fathers balked, they were accused of being selfish or uncaring. Many were then threatened with the seizure of their belongings on the spot: "Maybe I should just give that chain over to her [the mother]," Judge Clay pressured. "I'll do it right here and now. 'Cause she's the one I'm getting this money for."

While the seizure of property and bank accounts are state-level civil actions, other financial sanctions are federal. These include the interception of tax refunds and social security benefits. Like wage garnishment, these interceptions are centrally administered and issued without warning. They often hit unexpectedly, to the shock of those reliant on state funds to make ends meet. Many parents planned to use unemployment compensation to get through rough economic periods, only to be denied assistance because of back arrears: "How do they want me to pay [support] when they take everything away?" a Miami father exclaimed in an interview. Then there was the father who was wheeled into court by his mother to complain about the sudden seizing of his disability pension.

Confined to a wheelchair after a serious accident at work, he relied on the pension to live—after the state garnished it, he and his elderly mother were left to subsist on her social security benefit alone.

As figure 16 shows, the support recovered from these intercepts is minimal: other research has revealed that 68 percent of support payments come from wage garnishment, while only 6.7 percent come from tax intercepts and 5.3 percent from unemployment intercepts.[6]

Remedial Sanctions

Next in the arsenal of enforcement tools are nonfinancial civil punishments, often called "remedial sanctions." These measures are designed to put pressure on parents to pay current and back support. They can involve the withdrawal of state-issued licenses and documents. At the federal level, this includes passport revocation, which happens when back support reaches $2,500. It also includes the suspension of state-issued professional licenses—from contractors' licenses to legal and medical licenses to hunting and fishing licenses. As with financial sanctions, these measures can be counterproductive. In interviews, fathers described being cut off from their families due to passport revocation. In court, they pointed out how the imperative to work stood in conflict with the withdrawal of professional licenses. In Florida, men complained about losing work as fisherman and longshoreman due to suspension. Fathers who had been licensed contractors discussed how much less they were able to make without their licenses. Then there was Alex, an aspiring soccer player who claimed to have been offered a spot on the Colombian national team but had to turn it down after his passport was suspended. As with most revocations, these usually happened suddenly and without warning—fathers learned about them when they got caught trying to use a suspended license or passport.

Of all remedial sanctions, the most dreaded was also the most common: the driver's license suspension. While all states have policies to revoke the driving privileges of indebted parents, those policies are applied in different ways. Map 6 reveals state policies on nonpayment triggers for license suspension. With such low thresholds, these suspensions are incredibly common: most of the Florida fathers I interviewed had their licenses

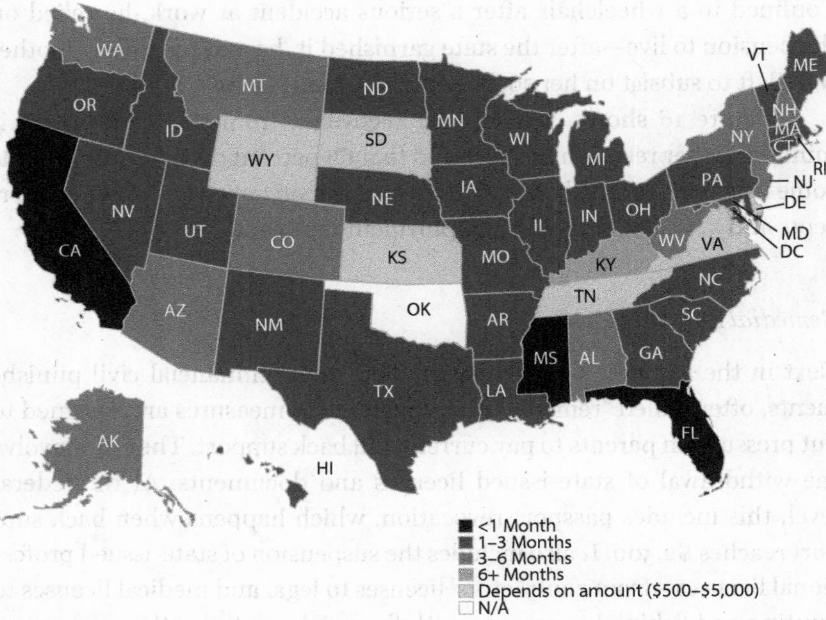

Map 6. State Policies on License Suspension. SOURCE: NCSL 2020a

suspended at some point. In California, support orders that remain delinquent for more than one month can be subjected to license suspension. This means that, almost by definition, all incarcerated fathers leave prison with suspended licenses. It also means they begin the reentry process unable to drive and must go to court immediately upon release to try and get their licenses reinstated. Despite their ubiquity, remedial sanctions account for a small percentage of child support collections.

While driver's license revocation is usually done centrally, imposed by the Department of Motor Vehicles, courts are involved in the process too. Judges can initiate a license suspension if one is not already in place. Courts can also order a suspension be lifted, which led to some of the most contentious court exchanges I observed. Here, too, parents highlighted the counterproductive effects of the measure, angrily pointing out how it impeded their ability to work: "Who is going to hire me when I can't drive?" Marco asked a Florida judge. Fathers claimed the suspension caused them to lose good jobs as cab drivers, truck drivers, and deliverymen. For instance, driving for Uber or Lyft can be important supplements to low-wage work. Quite often, parents used earnings from these second jobs to pay extra expenses, like child support. That option was gone once their licenses were revoked. As Miguel, a Florida father of three, explained in an interview:

> I had great work lined up driving a truck . . . 'cause I've been driving all my life. I did it in between regular gigs. But then they took away my license while I was on a long, out of state run. . . . I got pulled over on my way back here [Florida] and it was terrible. I had no idea I had lost my license. I was screwed. . . . I lost that job and can't get another now.

Parents also bemoaned all the time they spent taking inconvenient public transportation to work, time they could have spent working for wages. Indeed, quantitative data have confirmed their claims, showing that license suspension is associated with a significant decline in parents' wages and job loss.[7] This was especially true for fathers in areas of California and Florida with limited and inaccessible public transportation systems. In interviews, fathers provided precise accountings of how much more money they could make if they were able to drive. "I spend like three hours going to and from work," a Los Angeles father recounted. "If I worked that time, I'd pay $200 more and get caught up." Fathers also insisted that license suspension made it difficult to see their children, making them late to outings with their kids. "What about my kids?" a Miami father asked. "How would I get to see them? Where would I take them? Somewhere on the bus?"

Judges were usually not inclined to reinstate licenses. Instead, they tended to use revocation as a bargaining chip, dangling reinstatement in front of indebted fathers to get them to comply with their orders. Most of the time, they made license reinstatement contingent on the payment of back arrears. Judges also asked for one-time payments, called "purges," in exchange for parents' licenses. This was particularly common in Florida, where judges would offer to reinstate licenses after the payment of large amounts of cash, usually several thousand dollars. For fathers, these transactions could feel like bribes, with judges withholding driver's licenses until payment had been received. Other times judges had parents agree to attend retraining programs or conduct extensive job searches before lifting their license suspension. But if fathers could not or would not comply with the conditions of reinstatement, their suspensions continued.

When pressed, judges advanced two arguments to justify license revocation for child support nonpayment. Most common was an economic argument: they believed fathers who could afford to own and maintain a car could also afford to keep up with their child support. This argument was voiced most often in California, where judges went through parents' expense declarations and deleted transportation costs. As a Los Angeles judge once reasoned:

> Here's what I think: if you can afford to drive, you can afford to pay your child support. Because if you can afford gas, repairs, and insurance, then surely you can afford to support your kids. . . . I compute the cost of your car to be at least $300 every month. If you paid that to CSE, you'd be out of the red soon.

Then there were judges who used an abstract justification for license suspension, claiming it was a statement about reciprocal rights and responsibilities. As Brooklyn Judge Katz explained:

> Driving a motor vehicle is not a legal right. It is a privilege. It is something the state grants to citizens who are responsible. That is our contract. We grant the privilege but it is not inalienable. . . . So if you are not meeting your responsibilities, that privilege can be withdrawn. If you are not taking care of your end of the contract, it will be voided.

In Contempt

The final enforcement tool is perhaps the most serious: the contempt action, or violation order. As Florida's Judge Matthews always liked to remind fathers: "Child support is the one type of debt that you can go to jail for." This outcome has received considerable media attention, but that coverage has been short on detail and legal nuance. It frequently claims that this practice harkens back to the debtor's prison, which, although dramatic, is not entirely accurate. The legal basis here is different: imprisonment for debt was deemed unconstitutional in *Tate v. Short* (1971), but the Supreme Court held that debtors could be incarcerated for "willful" nonpayment. This reasoning was applied to the child support arena in the

2011 case *Turner v. Rogers*, which confirmed that a parent had to be shown to be willfully avoiding paying support to be imprisoned.

There are two main ways that debt can lead to imprisonment, which often get conflated. First, a parent can be deemed noncompliant with a court order (child support) and therefore held in contempt of court. Civil contempt is punishable by either immediate payment (also called a "purge") or up to 180 days in jail, while criminal contempt is a felony charge that can result in a prison sentence.[8] For formerly incarcerated parents, both forms can lead to a violation of parole and/or other conditions of release.[9] Second, a parent can be convicted of criminal nonsupport of a minor, which makes the legal sanction criminal since it is considered a crime against the state itself. All fifty states have criminal nonsupport statutes on the books, to be used when the court sees fit. The severity of the punishment ranges from misdemeanors with small fines and short jail terms to felonies with high fines and lengthy prison sentences.[10]

To prove civil or criminal contempt, courts must show that the child support order was willfully unpaid.[11] As a result, the definition of willfulness has undergone considerable debate—and the process to determine it varies by state and by court, in terms of both standards of proof and due process.[12] As was also decided in *Turner v. Rogers*, parents held in civil contempt are not entitled to the due process protections guaranteed in criminal proceedings, such as the right to counsel. This is true even though incarceration can result from a civil contempt order. Moreover, while *Turner v. Rogers* laid out a series of factors courts should consider in deciding on civil contempt, it gave them enormous room to decide when noncompliance becomes willful contempt.[13] Without clear guidelines or due process protections used in criminal proceedings, civil contempt hearings are exceedingly flexible and unpredictable.

This is where key battles of child support court occur: Is the parent willfully neglectful? Or is he just broke? This is also where negotiations over how to punish enter in, since courts can set conditions of remediation and allow parents to "purge" themselves of contempt. Courts can offer parents "deals" whereby they do not pursue contempt in exchange for an arrears payment. Or courts can decide to go straight for a contempt filing, especially if they dislike something a parent did. The stakes are high in these courtroom battles, for they can end with an arrest warrant or jail.

As Jacksonville Judge May explained when I asked how he decided who to send to jail:

> I can just feel if a guy's a deadbeat. I can see it in his eyes, in how he moves.... When I see it, there's no need to go through the motions. It's a waste of time.... I throw the book at them 'cause those guys give us country boys a bad name. They may fight me, argue with me, but I always come down real hard on them.

Or, as Brooklyn's Judge Patros responded to the same question:

> I never want to send them to jail. Who does this help? Not the child and not the family.... I want them to comply. If they don't comply, I have to send them up. In the most egregious cases, I can just tell a guy isn't ever going to pay so I send him right up.... I can just tell when it's willful...and when I need to elevate the case and put him in jail.

This judicial discretion continues to the next stage in the process: once contempt has been established, and an arrest warrant issued, it needs to be enforced. There are three main ways this happens. First, some courts can send parents directly to jail from court after they issue a ruling of civil contempt or of criminal nonpayment. This was the preferred method in Florida, especially in the north, where parents were routinely taken from the courthouse to jail, which was in an adjourning building. It was so common that court staff called it a "slow day" when only a few parents went to jail. "How many do we have back there?" Judge Matthews once asked, referring to the jail cell connected to his chambers. "Only two? We need to start fillin' it up today!" he remarked, only half-jokingly.

Second, warrants can be issued to parents not present in court, which are then served by the police. Most often, the arrest happened by chance: when parents were stopped for something else, police discovered the outstanding warrant. Police could also search for parents with warrants. Fathers told me that police often came to their homes or jobs with warrants, arresting them in front of families, bosses, coworkers. Here's how Judge Matthews instructed one mother to pursue a warrant for the father of her kids:

> Ma'am, you need to do a good, old fashioned stake out. Go park your car in front of his house. Watch him. Get to know his routine. When he comes and

> goes. . . . Then make your way down to the precinct and tell those nice policemen what you learned. You tell them where and when they can find him. Or, better yet, when you see him leave one day, follow him. Then call the cops and tell them to come get him. . . . This is on you now.

Finally, police and sheriff departments have been known to do large-scale sweeps—often called "deadbeat roundups"—where they set out to yield the most indebted parents possible. For instance, there are the Arizona raids, which send out more than seventy deputies to round up parents with child support warrants. Since it began in the early 2000s, this Arizona tradition has yielded more than eight hundred arrests.[14] And then there are New Jersey raids, which often yield more than a thousand fathers—a 2017 "Man Up and Pay" raid bringing in over fifteen hundred parents on outstanding warrants.[15] In some states these raids have become a Father's Day tradition, with sheriff departments sending out officers to track down indebted parents as they celebrate the day with their children.[16]

While these deadbeat roundups are media spectacles and seem to net lots of indebted parents, it remains unclear just how many parents become incarcerated for child support debt, be it through raids or other means. States and locales do not collect reliable information on their use of jail as an enforcement measure; those that do refuse to make it public. State child support offices that collect data on contempt actions rarely include how many of those actions were then filed by the court. Similarly, data from county jails and police departments are difficult to analyze, given the nature of the sentence. Most jail sentences are for civil contempt (as opposed to criminal nonpayment), which is a more complicated designation to track. Unless the reason for the contempt action clearly states it as related to child support, it is hard to ascertain whether the contempt action was for child support nonpayment or some other action.

With little reliable national-level data on imprisonment for child support debt, most of what is known here is based on guesstimates. Some researchers estimate that more than 50,000 parents are behind bars on any given day for child support.[17] Others estimate that one in seven fathers with support debt have served time for this debt.[18] Still others find that 5 percent of all fathers, and 15 percent of all African American fathers, had been jailed for child support.[19] The percentages seem to be even higher for parents with histories of incarceration—more than one-third of the fathers in my three-state interview sample reported serving time for child support debt.

There is also enormous variation across states in the use of jail as an enforcement measure. In some states, it is standard practice to incarcerate parents for nonpayment of support. In Florida, parents were routinely sent to jail: Over half of my Florida sample had done jail time for nonpayment or accumulated arrears. Most had done repeated stints in jail for contempt.[20] This is also the case in southern states.[21] States in the west and northeast tend to use incarceration less often: fewer than 20 percent of my respondents in California and New York reported going to jail for child support.[22] In New York City it was uncommon for a parent to go to jail merely for falling behind on an order, but jail could be used if nonpayment was accompanied by a large arrears balance. In fact, the Manhattan Detention Complex once had a special housing unit for men jailed for child support as well a program called "weekend warriors," which incarcerated indebted fathers only on the weekends and evenings so that they could work during the day. As Lamar, a Bronx father of two who had done several stints in the Tombs for child support, explained it:

> There's a whole section of the Tombs with just us in for child support. I don't know why they hold us separately, maybe so we don't get into more trouble. But I know all those guys real well 'cause we're always coming in and out together.... Most of us are poor, but there are some rappers in there too. And even some Orthodox Jewish guys. All of us went in 'cause of our arrears.... They keep sending us back, usually for ninety-day stints, because our debt just got bigger and bigger. The weekend warrior thing was their attempt to stop that.... To make us work on the outside, but then come back and do our time after work.

Moreover, even within states there is unevenness in the use of contempt. In New York and California, rates of contempt vary considerably by city and region. New York City rarely jails parents for nonpayment, while courts in upstate New York use jail more often and reportedly jail fathers for as little as a few hundred dollars in arrears.[23] California also has enormous variation. While the percentage of cases involving jail time is low in the state overall, there are several counties that rely on it quite heavily, such as Napa, Fresno, San Bernardino, and Riverside.[24]

The practice of jailing indebted fathers has also shifted over time. It was far more common in the 1990s and 2000s, even in states that now rarely use it. For instance, until the 2000s, California had one of the most punitive child support systems, routinely imprisoning indebted fathers. Indeed, the California fathers I interviewed who had been jailed for support served their time in the 1990s. In 2016, however, roughly 6,000 contempt cases were filed in the state, only a small percentage of its caseload of more than 1 million.[25] This shift was largely due to a change in control over the California child support system—before 2008, prosecutors oversaw the child support system and approached it as a law enforcement issue. After the California child support system became an independent entity, contempt warrants and jail time were used less often. California's Judge Robinson, who had been a child support prosecutor in the 1990s before becoming a judge, explained the change to me like this:

> Back then, all we were concerned about was getting big orders... the biggest orders we could get on the books. Lock them up if that's what it took. That was our goal, as prosecutors. In retrospect, maybe we were too narrow-minded.... Because once child support was taken out of prosecutors' hands, we started to see the bigger picture. Why make someone homeless or poor just to get a big order? Why send someone to jail to punish them for not paying? How does any of that help children?

In other states, the move away from custodial punishment for child support seemed to follow shifting political winds. In the late 2000s, state officials across the country began to question the cost-effectiveness of incarceration as a punishment for low-level offenses, including child support debt. Some of the push came from the federal government, with the national Office of Child Support Enforcement discouraging incarceration as an enforcement measure.[26] Many states then followed suit. New York is a good example of this: for decades, it sent thousands of parents to jail for nonpayment and debt. But it has scaled back now that officials have become convinced of the futility of jail as a punishment for debt. As fewer prosecutors sought custodial sentences, fewer judges granted them.[27] Bronx Judge Carlino summarized the shift in New York:

> We used to send fathers to jail all the time. It was standard practice five or ten years ago. But in the last few years, we've stopped.... State attorneys don't ask for it much anymore. If they don't ask for it, I don't usually offer

> it.... There is no point. It costs more to put them in jail than we could ever get back [in support] from these guys. Only when I see a really bad father who hasn't paid in years will I send him up [to Superior Court to be jailed].

So, even the most consequential of enforcement measures, imprisonment, is applied inconsistently. Decisions about when to apply financial sanctions, when to use remedial sanctions, and when to imprison remain variable. This discretion has left indebted parents feeling even more uncertain: one year they might be sent to jail, another year to a diversion program, another year they might be ignored altogether. This uncertainty becomes more trying when coupled with judicial swings related to *why* parents are punished. In theory, enforcement is supposed to sanction the nonpayment of child support. In reality, it has become a punishment for much more.

PUNISHING POVERTY: FROM BROOKLYN TO THE BRONX

Most punishments come with explanations. Whether doled out by a parent or a state official, they are usually accompanied by an account of what went wrong and how further punishment can be avoided. So it was with child support enforcement. When sanctioned, indebted parents were reminded of their failings. These reminders were so ubiquitous and harsh that it was unclear what the real punishment was: the enforcement measure or the lecture that came with it. "I don't understand why he can't just tell me his decision quick and then let me go," asked Arnold, a Brooklyn father of three. "He makes me stand there and listen to everything I've done wrong in my life.... Man, just tell me what you're doing to me and let me outta there."

Arnold was right: the judicial ritual was to offer the state's rendition of why parents were not paying support and then to issue the punishment. The most obvious reason for nonpayment was poverty. Court officials were well aware that most indebted parents had little or no income. So explanations turned to why this was the case. And the most common reason was that parents were not working hard enough to get out of poverty. This narrative prevailed in all the courts I studied. Even the most progressive judges in the most progressive locales insisted that parents had to work harder to rise out of poverty, although they also acknowledged how hard the rise would be. Since a parent's ability to rise from it all was linked to future enforcement, it sounded as if parents were being punished for more than nonpayment of support—they were also being punished for their poverty.

Given the ubiquity of this poverty narrative, it is fitting to analyze it in the megalopolis of child support enforcement: New York City. This system is so large and so spread out that its patterns seem amplified and exaggerated. The system fans out to all five boroughs, overseeing more than half a million support cases, 56 percent of which involve some sort of public assistance.[28] Each county runs its own child support courts, which rival other large cities' entire court systems in size. The New York system is tied together by a series of safeguards and protections, which makes it the most juridical of the court systems I studied. Proceedings begin with long speeches about the right to counsel and offers of case delays if defendants need legal advice. There are many actors in New York courts. In addition to the judge, there are lawyers for the state, the Office of Child Support Enforcement, and sometimes the parents. If a legal requirement remains unmet, cases end. Over 25 percent of the cases I observed got delayed because service rules were not followed. Even when both parents were present, judges postponed cases if service was not done properly.

New York child support courts are also more attuned to privacy. Unlike in other states, support proceedings are held in semiprivate courtrooms with judges calling in one case at a time. This means that cases feel less like public spectacles, without large audiences watching them. It also means that cases last a bit longer and have less of an assembly line feel to them. Parents ask more questions when they are not on public display and when supported by legal representatives. Connected to this, New York courts have a series of checks and balances that make them more attuned to due process protections. For instance, contempt cases follow a two-step process whereby support judges send contempt requests to a superior court judge, who can issue warrants. This makes it impossible for a parent to be sent directly from child support court to jail, since they have an additional step to go through. And New York requires defendants facing jail time to have legal representation, which can also slow the enforcement of a contempt warrant.

Despite these procedural protections, the substance of enforcement proceedings did not differ much in New York City. As in other cities, child support proceedings were marked by a poverty discourse. In New York, though, this discourse seemed to resound a bit louder than in other places. It also seemed to subsume more diversity into its explanatory frame. In New York courts, officials drew clear boundaries around parents' presumed failings: they were not working enough. This definition of the problem then gave rise to an obvious solution: parents had to work more. Of course, it was best if that work paid enough to cover child support. But the gainful employment imperative came later. Initially, parents just had to get a job.

Get a Job, Any Job

The first time I encountered this poverty discourse was on my very first day in court in the Bronx. The third case I observed involved an African American father and mother in a dispute over custody and child support payments. The father, Forrest, had been in and out of prison since 2007 and had not seen his daughter regularly. The mother, Lakisha, wanted to end his visitation. She also sought a contempt order for nonpayment of child support since he had not paid regularly for years while imprisoned. Both parents really wanted the judge to decide on the visitation issue, but Judge Mabel put it aside. "We need to first take care of the financial matters," she insisted. "Visitation can come later since the father has not seen the girl since 2006." The financial accounting then began, with the state prosecutor noting that Forrest had no reported income in the last year. "He's been out of prison two years, right?" Judge Mabel queried. "Why no work?" Forrest explained that he was looking, and had applied for several jobs, but nothing had come through. "Well, that just won't cut it," Judge Mabel declared. "You have responsibilities. . . . You can no longer shirk them. Unemployment is no excuse."

As Forrest listened to the lecture, he became agitated. Additional police officers were called into the room to stand directly behind him. This made him even more agitated. "Why are they here?" he complained while looking back at the officers. "I'm not doing anything." More questions followed from the judge: what was his plan for getting a job? Who was he living with? How was he being supported? Occasionally Lakisha interrupted:

"Yea, that's right, he's doin' nothing" or "You know it, he's not a real daddy." Eventually, Forrest erupted:

> You are all humiliating me. She makes me feel so low about myself, always.... Then I come here and I feel the same. Just like last time, you all keep humiliating me. I have no family, no relatives. I have been fighting to see my daughter for two years... since I got out [of prison]. I come here and all I get is humiliated.

As he continued to yell, the police dragged him out of the courtroom. Judge Mabel issued a one-month continuance to see if Forrest would find work. If not, she would pursue a contempt action.

Although few fathers responded like Forrest, this court dynamic became so familiar over the course of my fieldwork that it no longer seemed noteworthy. It was a standard child support ritual, played out day in and day out across New York City: a judge reprimanded an unemployed father for not working. The reprimands led the father to feel ashamed. The interaction eventually ended with the father leaving the courtroom defeated and often very angry. Whether or not the father's unemployment seemed understandable, the tactic was to question his diligence and desire to work. This was done for everyone in the courtroom to hear—lawyers, administrators, court officers, security guards, and other observers. All enforcement cases began with a recounting of parents' income and outstanding support debt. All read aloud. An unemployed status was always read with clear condemnation, as this exchange in Brooklyn indicates:

JUDGE BAXTER: So you have no income. And you have over $16,000 in arrears. True?

MR. MARSHALL: Yes, your honor, I think that is true. I have not been able to...

JUDGE BAXTER: I cannot hear you, speak up! Why are you whispering?

MR. MARSHALL: I am not, sir. I just wanted to say that I have not been able to find work since getting out [of jail] two years ago. I had one for a few weeks but lost it 'cause they were cutting back. I had no luck finding—

JUDGE BAXTER: I don't buy this! What is stopping you from getting a job? Any job? You are gonna tell me there is not one single job in all of the city? In this giant city, not one job? You are unemployed... for no good reason. So you need to get a job, any job, fast.

Some judges used condemnation to push fathers to work, assuming they just needed a judicial nudge to find a job. This was true even when court officials thought a parent was "legitimately" out of work—or when it was clear that the parent was actively seeking work. "It can be discouraging to keep looking for a job," a Bronx Judge explained to me one afternoon. "If I keep at them, they'll keep looking." Other judges seemed genuinely suspicious of all unemployed parents, insisting they could find work if they really wanted to. They drew on age-old stereotypes about the lazy, unmotivated poor to lecture parents about their unemployment. They mixed their condemnation with moral outrage and claims to be protecting women and children. As Brooklyn Judge Katz explained to an unemployed father who had called in for his hearing due to child care responsibilities—and whose two children we could hear crying in the background:

> Your order was modified to next to nothing a long time ago.... I am not going to keep it so low anymore because, sir, you need to get yourself a job. It's not a job to watch your new kids.... You need to care for the other ones who are already grown. That's your duty, as a father.... The only way you can do that is to get an income, from a real job.

When offering up their warnings, court officials rarely expressed an acknowledgment of the barriers confronting parents in their work search. They rarely related these parents' job search efforts to the realities of the New York City labor market, with its sharp division between low-wage service sector jobs and a shrinking sphere of well-paid unionized jobs. Their silence was peculiar, for it was partial: court officials often discussed these barriers among themselves during court breaks.[29] They talked about how hard it was to earn a living wage in the city, especially for men with little education or work experience.[30] In fact, many officials commuted from Long Island or New Jersey because they could not afford to live in the city. Yet when they chastised the unemployed, this awareness vanished. After observing this disparity for months, I asked Brooklyn Judge Patros about it. He responded:

> I know how hard it is to find work... to find any work these days. But I can't say that to them [parents]. They would use it as an excuse.... Everything is an excuse for them.... The fact is their kids have to eat and the only way for that to happen is for them to find work. Wherever, however, they need to work. I will not offer them an excuse for not caring.

This approach seemed to apply even more often to formerly incarcerated fathers, who frequently got the hardest line about the imperative to work. This was somewhat surprising given that court officials knew these parents faced unique obstacles. As fathers recounted how they had applied for job after job but never received a callback, the picture of discrimination became as clear as it was pervasive. Judges occasionally turned to me to ask about "ban the box" laws that ended the practice of forcing job applicants to reveal their criminal histories; one judge asked me about academic studies of labor market discrimination as it related to the formerly incarcerated.[31] But this awareness was offset by their sense that fathers with criminal records had gotten a "break" on child support while in prison. From Brooklyn to the Bronx, judges told these fathers it was finally time to pay up. Here, too, judges claimed that if they didn't get tough, fathers would have no incentive to find work. Yet in their zeal not to appear soft, they came across as disconnected from the reality of poverty. As Bronx Judge Moraga told a newly released father:

> You've been out [of prison] for over two weeks? And you don't have a job yet? Have you even tried to get one? Where? Show me the evidence.... After being away [in prison] for five years, now is the time for you to get responsible... to take care of your kids like you haven't been doing for all those years. No more delay.... Do it now.

The one concession I saw judges make to formerly incarcerated parents was the "program referral." New York City has several prison reentry programs that include workforce development and assistance. Before issuing enforcement measures, some judges referred parents to these programs for help with their job searches. Sociologist John Halushka has shown that these programs can play an important role inculcating "work wisdom," besides offering valuable employment networks of the kind formerly incarcerated parents often lack.[32] Indeed, some NYC fathers spoke about the job leads these programs gave them and the friendships and support systems they fostered.

At the same time, these programs had a clear social control function. Referrals to them were a way for courts to monitor parents. This is what sociologist Issa Kohler-Hausmann refers to as the "performative" capacity of courts—a technique for gauging who will abide by the rules.[33] As Kerwin Kaye reveals in his study of treatment programs, the line between services that rehabilitate and those that regulate can be impossible to discern.[34] Many parents viewed mandated programs as akin to punishment since they implied another set of eyes on them and new requirements to meet. "This is messed up," a Bronx father screamed as he stormed out of court after being referred to STEP, a local job readiness program. "Now I gotta do whatever they say too.... No one is tryin' to help me. They all just making new rules for me!"

No wonder he was angry: most of these programs can report back to the court, documenting participants' job searches and program compliance. While a good report from a program might help a parent's enforcement case, a bad one almost always led to the imposition of harsher enforcement measures. For instance, a court-appointed program counselor reported in this way to a Brooklyn judge about Marcus, an African American, formerly incarcerated father:

> When he was referred to us, he had $62,000 in arrears and no employment. We tried very hard to work with him.... But his job search diary was always incomplete and even falsified. He says he needs his license [restored] to start looking for work. We think this is an excuse.... He needs to show a good faith effort before any such privilege is restored.

These programs also widened the range of parental behavior under scrutiny. Designed to assist with job searches, they expanded their intervention to include anger management, substance abuse, and even hygiene. The same court-appointed counselor reported on another father:

> Mr. Rodriquez currently lives in a shelter and is working on and off.... He is mostly still supported by his family and friends. The real concern for us is he is not going to AA meetings. He says there are none around the shelter so I told him to look online for the nearest meeting. He said he has no internet access.... He is not taking care of himself... his basic needs. He is just not addressing his issues. He doesn't want to get cleaned up. He's not using now, but without going to meetings he will slip back.

Ungainfully Employed

When an indebted parent had no job, it was easy to blame unemployment for child support problems and the parent for joblessness. But the harsh reality was that many indebted parents did work yet were still unable to keep up with their support payments. This could have posed a challenge to the prevailing poverty discourse. However, state officials found a way around it: they blamed parents for working in jobs they deemed inadequate or unsustainable. They punished parents for not working enough or not securing full-time employment; they blamed parents for failing to find work that paid well or for doing work beneath their qualifications; and they accused parents of doing all of this voluntarily and intentionally. In effect, they berated parents for refusing to work their way out of poverty.

Hearings typically opened with this sort of berating, with judges reading aloud an accounting of the parent's wages and income: "Twenty hours a week at $12 an hour? Well, that's not gonna cut it now is it?" Parents were chastised as judges concluded there was no way their children could live on what they contributed: "You have been paying $50 a month [while in prison]. How do you think that helped your kids? What did it buy them? Now you need to make more of a contribution." Parents then faced detailed questions about why they were not doing more to get better jobs with better pay. Here, too, it was as if judges pretended to be unaware of men's employment options and the constraints of low-wage work. Officials might discuss the constraints among themselves, but this awareness evaporated once court proceedings began. While contentious exchanges were rare in Brooklyn, court interactions did on occasion get heated—as this exchange between Judge Patros and a Brooklyn father illustrates:

JUDGE PATROS: You don't think you need better work?

MR. CAMPOS: I wish I could find better work.

JUDGE PATROS: Well, you could if you really wanted to. You are having your material needs met, but what about your children?

MR. CAMPOS: No, sir, I am homeless. My needs are not being met. I sleep on couches, in shelters. . . . Your life is so easy! But you have no idea what I go through, what guys like me face out there. It's not like how you think. It's not easy!

JUDGE PATROS: Are you kidding me? Grow up, be a man. Why did you have a baby? Why did you have one if you can't support it? . . . If I don't see money by your next court date, you won't be homeless any longer . . . 'cause I'll find you a home for six months [in jail].

Just as unemployed parents had to prove to the court that they were diligently seeking work, employed parents had to prove they couldn't do more to get out of poverty. Those who had secured part-time work were called out for not trying to find full-time work and accused of lying about their search for better work. "You are gonna tell me all you can find are 20 hours [of work] in a 99 cent store?" Judge Martinez exclaimed to a Bronx father. "I find that very, very hard to believe." Courts then managed these parents by forcing them to keep job search diaries, that is, detailed accounts of all the jobs they had applied for with dates, locations, and contacts. If parents were unable or unwilling to keep up with the record-keeping, courts bombarded them with more demands, requiring them to submit financial affidavits, tax returns, W-2s, and pay stubs for additional years. It was punishment through paperwork, discipline through documents.

Court officials used bureaucratic punishments for everyone they believed to be intentionally underemployed, but they saved their highest level of scrutiny for parents they thought were hiding income. There were a handful of jobs that judges insisted were fronts for informal, unreported work. "I can't stand barbers," Judge Miranda once exclaimed in open court. "They hide all kinds of money, say they make nothing when they are pocketing so much." Or there was Judge Patros's obsession: "Whenever a guy tells me he's a cab driver, I want to scream," he once explained to me. "Those guys hide so much income and then come in here to cry poverty."

So they punished them through excessive paperwork. They set the requirements for record-keeping so high that even accountants would struggle meeting them. Parents were expected to keep extensive records of every financial transaction they made at work. They had to keep logs of every client and an accounting of each payment or tip received. If these documents did not seem to be recorded in real time, but put together for the sake of court, judges rejected them. Judges also had barbers and drivers bring in years of tax returns, which they then went over in enormous detail, looking for mistakes and omissions. They had parents complete complicated financial statements, often with affidavits from others, to verify their sources of income. And they gave parents little time to come up with these documents, insisting that they must be current on their record-keeping and accounting at a moment's notice. In one case, Judge Mabel became convinced an indebted father was hiding his tips as an Uber driver so he could make ends meet while he went back to college. Insisting that the father's tip money was higher, she refused to lift the suspension on his license, thus ending his supplemental income stream.

When doling out these punishments, judges often claimed to be acting on behalf of the "public." While increases in fathers' support orders were said to be in mothers' benefit, this was hard to sell in many cases, especially given that over 50 percent of New York cases involved at least some public assistance payback. Punishment for welfare debt tended to be framed as a way to stop fathers' financial irresponsibility from spilling onto the public. When applying a penalty, judges frequently launched into spirited defenses of payback policies. Drawing on the mythical "taxpayers" who wanted their money back, judges insisted it was their job to retrieve it. "Welfare is an advance the State of New York gives to you," Judge Miranda always explained to parents. "Think of child support as your payment to us . . . and your arrears are like the IOU note."

This argument was used quite often with formerly incarcerated parents, who were chastised for "double dipping" into public coffers: once to cover the costs of their criminal behavior and once for their family's public assistance. Judges reminded them how much taxpayers had spent on their incarceration and how unfair it was for them to care for their families too. While judges varied in the passion with which they made this argument, none questioned payback policies—not in court and not to me in private. As Judge Patros told a father: "Because of you, the mother of your children was forced to give up her right to child support. She had to go on public assistance. This made the welfare department responsible for your children. When this happens, everyone loses their rights . . . and you are obligated to pay back the government, not the mother of your children."

When faced with such arguments, some parents did push back. While I discuss fathers' responses in the next chapter, some men did call out court officials for punishing them for poverty. They pointed out how they were shamed for things they felt they had no control over. They tried to educate court officials about the realities of being poor with a criminal record and support payments. They tied together economic injustice and legal injustice. These exchanges were so similar they could appear to follow a script: judges or state attorneys would instruct parents to work themselves out of poverty and pay their support. Fathers would then explain all the impediments they faced. Judges would up the ante, threatening to come down harder if they did not stop with the excuses. Fathers would then launch a more pointed defense, using bolder arguments about how poverty was not a choice or a crime. This would go back and forth until either the judge ended the hearing or the father stormed out of the court in anger. As Lamar astutely explained in our interview:

> When we go to court, we are up against the myths of poverty. So I always have to explain it to those old white men in robes. What it's like to live in poverty. How hard it is to get a job. How impossible it is when you got a record.... They have no idea. They live in another world. We go [to court] to get them to see the realities of what we're confronting, every damn day of our lives. Until they do, ain't none of this is going to change. Ever.

PUNISHING FATHERHOOD: FROM NORTH TO SOUTH FLORIDA

"If you take me to jail, I won't be able to get my kids from school," Jay exclaimed to Judge May as the packed Florida courtroom looked on. "Today's my day to get them. If I'm not there, no one will pick them up. They'll be alone, waiting." Unfazed, Judge May launched into a lecture he repeated countless times that day:

> Well, you should of thought about them last month, or the month before, when you decided not to pay child support. Being a father is not a right. It is something you earn. Since you've been out of prison, you aren't paying child support. So I'm sending you to jail. You need to learn... what it means to be a real father.

Jay was then removed from the courtroom, in handcuffs, and told he would remain in jail until he came up with $1,000 to purge himself from contempt. The dozens of fathers looking on as they awaited their own cases froze. Some started to sweat, fidget, and shake their heads. "That's cold," one father says to another. "Tellin' that man he ain't a daddy if he don't pay. What law says that? What part of the constitution says that? It's messed up."

Although the Florida child support system is not as large as the New York state system, it is still formidable. Housed in the Department of Revenue, it handles roughly a million cases, less than half of which involve public assistance.[35] Florida ranks high among states with large child support debt, yet it lacks many of the legal safeguards of the New York system. Lawyers are few and far between in support proceedings, even in cases that end with incarceration. The only lawyers I saw on a regular basis in Florida were state attorneys acting on behalf of the Department of Revenue.[36] Procedural protections were also lacking in Florida, so much so that child support courts felt like a legal no-man's-land. For instance, rules for serving legal papers were very lax and unenforced. Unlike in New York, I never saw a case rescheduled due to service issues. Florida courts also merged different cases: proceedings that began as modification cases could quickly devolve into enforcement cases. And cases that began as enforcement hearings could quickly become contempt proceedings—as Jay would learn when what he thought was a simple modification request landed him in jail.

Florida support courts are completely public: cases are heard in open court, in front of large audiences of court staff and parents. They felt like public performances, where scripts had to be followed and speech patterns adhered to. The strict rules of demeanor and dress only added to their performative quality. As did all the onlookers, with up to one hundred observers evaluating the performances. "Oh, dang, that was stupid. Did you see how that guy talked to Matthews?" a Jacksonville father whispered to another. "This is not gonna end well." Many onlookers adjusted their performances after watching others. In parts of northern Florida, court officials held parents' driver's licenses and identity cards when they entered court, making them captive audiences unable to flee as they saw what was unfolding in front of them. "[So] they can't run away when they see how this works," bailiff Frank once explained to me when I asked about the practice.

Indeed, what parents saw unfold before them involved more than the enforcement of child support orders. As in New York City, Florida parents were scrutinized for their poverty. Yet Florida court officials coupled this with statements about the meaning of fatherhood. Again, while fatherhood was at issue in all the courts I observed, the no-man's-land quality of many Florida courts meant these lessons were relayed far more directly and overtly. What remained implicit in other states was explicit here, transmitted through public displays of celebration of the good and condemnation of the bad. The legal lesson about fatherhood was as clear as it was consistent: fatherhood was not a right, but had to be earned. The formula for how to earn it was equally clear: by paying child support regularly. Florida courts enforced a model of breadwinning that reduced men's parental contributions to the financial. And they insisted that these contributions be made through the state so that fathers' breadwinning could be managed and monitored.[37]

PRAISING THE PAYERS, HUMILIATING THE OTHERS

"Start the music!" Judge Ray exclaimed, half-jokingly. "This father here has kept current [with support] for ten years! He gets the Father-of-the Decade Award!" Another time, Ray began to laud a father even before he approached the bench or was sworn in: "Well, sir, I see here you have not missed a payment, even while you were in prison. . . . I must say, you impress me with your honorable devotion and responsibility." Such early praise was consequential, since what occurred in the first minutes of a support hearing could determine the remainder of the proceedings. In those first few minutes, state attorneys gave an accounting of parents' payment history, which led judges to decide which side of the good/bad divide they fell on. If the attorney reported that a father paid regularly and consistently, there were few follow-up questions about how often he saw his children or whether he had a relationship with them. Judges showered praise on the payers. "Thank you on behalf of the state of Florida," Judge Black gushed to a father he knew nothing about except that he kept current on his $515/month order. "It is rare that I see a parent with this kind of commitment . . . the kind of person, the father, you should be."

This was not empty praise. Fathers who paid their support were rewarded with a swift end to their cases. Once moved to the good side of the paternal divide, their cases became simple administrative issues and routinely closed. I observed this most often with license revocation. Florida set the suspension bar so low that fathers with otherwise spotless payment histories could be brought into court. For them, courts made corrections without delay, sometimes even with apologies. "Sir, we have wasted your time since you pay your support," Judge Vargas said to one father. "Sorry for the inconvenience when you do not deserve it." Or as Judge Matthews once explained to a father: "Those guys down in Tallahassee are like the Gestapo. They'll find you and get you. I wish I could stop them sometimes, like cases like yours when they go too far." Never mind that mothers occasionally protested the swift dismissals by raising other issues to be dealt with. Like the Miami mother who claimed her ex-husband never saw his kids. Or the Jacksonville mother who indicated there had been violence in the home and was concerned about visitation. As the hearings ended, they were both told to be grateful that "their men paid."

Far more common than the impeccable payers were fathers with spotty payment histories. For them, court officials saw their job as offering instructions on how to stay on track and, in doing so, how to become a good parent. The route to respectable fatherhood was clear: get a job, or several jobs if they aren't good ones; pay your support in full and on time; and eventually be redeemed as a committed parent. Judge Vargas laid out the route for this Miami father:

> Let's take this in steps. By next time, I want to see you add another job, even if it's at Burger King. Then I want payments to start coming in regularly. First at half [the order amount] then at the full amount. I will be watching you at every step. . . . You will report back to me every month. . . . You will build back my trust, one month at a time.

Anything that interfered with this route to redemption was to be ignored. For instance, many fathers complained that they were being asked to work so much that they rarely got to see their children. Others claimed they were leery to accept work that was far from their kids or that took them out of the state for long stretches for fear of losing touch with their kids. But the court's response was the same: they scolded these men for getting the order wrong. Access to their kids would come after they had shown themselves to be committed, dedicated fathers. Of course, that dedication could only be shown through financial payment.

This message was articulated with special force to formerly incarcerated fathers. Officials seemed to believe these men had lost their sense of parental responsibility while doing time. "The fun is over. You've had your years being selfish," Judge Ray explained to a father. "Now it's time to step up... to man up... and do the right thing." Again, the only way to "man up" was through money, by paying child support on time and in full every month. During these judicial lectures, I never heard them ask fathers if they had seen their kids while in prison; I never heard them ask whether fathers had written or talked to their children. The only type of prison contact raised was support payments: judges sometimes asked formerly incarcerated parents whether they had sent money home while incarcerated. This was a way to gauge the fathers' level of commitment to their children. As Hakim, a Miami father of three who had served a five-year sentence, explained in an interview:

> He [the judge] kept asking me if I sent money home when I was in Florida State [Correctional Institution]. How am I gonna do that?... Then they would ask if I ever used the collection unit from prison. Like how would I do that?... We gotta pay for stamps and for our calls. How would I get that together?

Hakim's comment points to another court imperative: all payments had to run through the state collection unit. Almost as important as *whether* a father paid support was *how* he paid it. It was not enough to get funds to families—those funds had to go through the state Office of Child Support Enforcement.[38] Ostensibly, this ensured there would be no disputes over payment amounts. But it also gave officials a way to monitor fathers. Even when fathers documented all direct payments to their families, courts scolded them. In some cases, judges refused to account for those payments. "I don't acknowledge money paid without department documentation," Judge Lansing once admonished a father. "You need to stop going behind our backs and pay the right way." There was something of an irony here given the court's imperative that fathers take family responsibility and stop relying on others. Yet to redeem themselves before the court, fathers had to show their compliance, by allowing the state to act as an intermediary with mothers.

The requirement to pay through the state may seem inconsequential, but in fact it presented real obstacles for some fathers. Undocumented fathers had a hard time with this requirement. Few of them had formal sector unemployment, so they were unable to adhere to the wage garnishments preferred by courts. What is more, many undocumented parents were leery of dealing with the OCSE and fearful of working with state authorities, given their legal vulnerability. Their wariness got them labeled noncompliant. "It is bizarre," Miami Judge Jones noted to me in an interview, shaking his head in wonder. "I am a judge but I have to order these [undocumented] parents to break the law by getting work.... And I punish them if they do not use [the state office, which] they can only do if they have on-the-books work."

A similar wariness characterized many African American fathers, who also preferred to make payments directly to their families.[39] Black fathers often shunned paying through state bureaucracies, insisting on providing for their children informally or giving support directly to their kids' mothers. In interviews, African American fathers explained that giving directly to their families was important to them. It was part of their own route to redemption—a way for them to show love and care through face-to-face interactions. This was particularly true for those who had been incarcerated for long periods and denied such contact for years. The problem was that this practice butted up against court requirements, leaving many in violation of court orders. They were then reprimanded, with courts coming down hard on them for "nonpayment."

In this way, just as fatherhood status could be conferred through courts' redemption rituals, it could also be lost. Men who were unable or unwilling to take the court's redemptive route were denied even a semblance of respect. As in New York courts, the assumption was that these men weren't paying because they didn't *want* to pay. Yet Florida courts took this one step further, connecting poverty to bad parenting and then punishing fathers for both. Once a father was placed on the bad side of the fatherhood divide, there were few constraints on what could be said or done to him. He was berated for being a failed father; he was criticized for thinking only about himself; and he was shamed for neglecting his children and forcing them into poverty. Most of all, he was treated as if he had no rights and no dignity. "You are a sorry, no good loser," Judge Matthews once proclaimed to a Jacksonville father, insisting he could not believe any woman "in her right mind" would have him. Then there was Judge Lansing, in a neighboring rural county, who instructed a father whom she called a "disgrace" to "pick up cans from the trash" if he needed to take care of his children.

Although hard to imagine, this treatment could get even harsher for fathers with large child support debt, many of whom were formally incarcerated. The size of a father's arrears became a barometer of his neglect as a parent. The larger his debt, the more degradation he experienced. The same court that showered praise on fathers who paid support shifted gears within minutes to humiliate those who did not. There seemed to be few limits on how low courts could go. As when Judge Matthews asked a Jacksonville mother if she was "drunk as a skunk" when she had a baby with such a "loser." Or when, in southern Florida, Judge Ray asked a father why "anyone would be with a man like [him]" since he was like "a disease." After watching a judge in a Jacksonville court subject a father to this kind of public humiliation, calling him a "disgusting scumbag," I asked him in chambers about his judicial approach. He responded: "Did you ever see those 'Scared Straight' shows? Well, that's what I do here. . . . I give it to them hard, real hard, so they won't ever want to come back to my court. So they will learn a lesson. Finally . . . and start paying their support."

When watching fathers treated like this, some mothers appeared shaken. Their faces expressed a mixture of shock, disbelief, and concern. As did their body language—many women squirmed and fidgeted as they watched these displays of paternal humiliation. They seemed to get nervous when listening to judges use them as justifications for such treatment. Yet they also seemed too frightened to say anything. Some of them did speak up, insisting that these men were otherwise good parents and pointing out how much time they spent with their kids. As one mother explained to Judge Matthews to stop him from berating her kids' father, who owed $36,000 in arrears: "He's having a hard time, since he has been out [of prison]. Please, this ain't gonna help him. . . . These names only hurt him." When the humiliation did not stop, some mothers asked that their cases be closed or proceedings finish. "I didn't come here for this," a St. Augustine mother explained to the court. "I didn't know this would happen. I want this whole thing stopped."

The court's paternal punishment sometimes had the unintended effect of bringing parents together. One morning in Miami, while pulling up to court, I noticed a couple fighting intensely in the parking lot. The woman was crying as she threw papers at the man. Once inside, they sat on opposite sides of the courtroom, glaring at each other. When their case was called, things got heated as Shantal, the mother, recounted how many months had gone by since Roberto had paid child support. They yelled back and forth until Judge Ray intervened: "It says here that Roberto owes over $30,000 in arrears. Is this correct?" Once confirmed, Ray hurled a series of names at Roberto, calling him a deadbeat and a "pathetic" breadwinner. As the names flew, Shantal got quiet. After fifteen minutes of insults, she broke her silence:

> Okay, but he is a good father. He may be a terrible husband . . . and terrible at payin' his bills . . . but he is a good father. He always takes the girls when he says. He's never late. He comes over to watch them when I need him to. . . . Even when it's not his day, he helps me out. He's a good daddy, for real. You don't see that, but it's real.

The hearing then concluded with no warrant issued, and Roberto and Shantal left court together.

LOVE DON'T BUY FOOD

Shantal's defense of Roberto raised a critical point about the court's definition of fatherhood: it excluded paternal caregiving and involvement. This was true in most of the child support courts I observed across the country: they left these important aspects of parenting out of the equation. But in Florida the exclusion was more extreme and more explicit. It ranged from an outright dismissal of men's caregiving to accusations that caregiving was an excuse for nonpayment. Some judges acknowledged that it was nice if fathers were present and involved in their kids' lives but added that this was irrelevant to court proceedings. Judges saw their role solely in financial terms—they were bill collectors. They thus defined fatherhood strictly in monetary terms and insisted that fathers put financial contributions before any other parenting activity. As Judge Black put it: "Please tell me what store accepts love as a payment for food. 'Cause I'm gonna head over there right after work and get me lots of food 'cause I got tons of love in my heart." This was how the Director of the Department of Revenue responded to my interview question about how the state might consider caregiving in the adjudication of arrears:

> Are you suggesting that we pay men for raising their kids? Giving them financial credit for child care? To stay at home and babysit? Are you serious? I wonder what my daddy would say about that. He grew up in the 1950s. He'd say this is the craziest idea. I know things have changed since then. But that's just crazy.

As his response indicates, the dismissal of fathers' roles as caregivers could turn into outrage at the suggestion that men's commitment to child-rearing be considered in court. Some court officials even used fathers' caregiving against them by suggesting it was an excuse for nonpayment. Particularly in northern Florida, men's claims to caregiving were frequently interpreted as attempts to get out of their "real" responsibilities. When given evidence of a father's involvement with their children, from visitation records to statements by custodial parents, judges could accuse them of trying to abdicate their financial obligations. They seemed almost offended by references to the time fathers spent with their kids. Judge Matthews could always be counted on to put the message pointedly and gracelessly:[40]

> I don't care what you do or don't know about [your kids]. I don't care how much you do or don't see them. . . . You need to learn what it means to be a real man. Real men don't rely on women. They don't ask women to care for them and their kids. Real fathers . . . they step up to the plate. They do right by their kids and provide for them. They get a J-O-B. . . . So stop hiding behind this "love" excuse.

This message about the "love excuse" differed markedly from the responsible fatherhood approach that has become a mainstay of state-sponsored fatherhood programs. While responsible fatherhood emphasizes men's wage-earning as key to what Jennifer Randles calls "marital masculinity," it also stresses men's caregiving.[41] The standardized curriculum of these programs includes a discussion of the need to be involved with children.[42] A few fathers mentioned this disconnect in our interviews, noting how prison programs stressed the importance of caregiving, which they were then punished for practicing in support court. But I only saw one father, Charles, try to insert this into court proceedings. Unfortunately, he did it with the least sympathetic of judges: "Why are you handing me this crap," Judge Matthews scoffed as he looked at the graduation certificate from a fatherhood program Charles gave him. "It has no bearing on this proceeding."

Many indebted fathers had an understanding of fatherhood that differed from both those articulated in state fatherhood programs and those imposed by court officials. They were more likely to define fatherhood in terms of their involvement in kids' lives—and to insist that being a father meant caring, loving, and paying attention to children. "Being a daddy is about being there" is a line I heard repeatedly. Few of these men had experienced this as kids, so they wanted to parent differently; they prioritized maintaining close bonds with their kids. Although they were not always able to achieve this, it remained an ideal they strived for. In fact, this ideal formed something of a discursive shield to protect fathers when confronted by angry support judges and dismissive attorneys. "No matter what they say, I'm not a deadbeat," Charles later declared to me in the elevator while leaving court. "I'm there for my kids. I remember that and I'm proud of it." Another Florida father put it this way:

> I'm always there, taking my kids every week. When they ask me for anything, I get it for them. 'Cause that's the kind of father I am. When they want something, I can't just tell them to go ask child support. No, I get it. I take care of them.... And that's what being a father means to me. Being there, always. I remember that all the time.

But such discursive protection only went so far. Courts had the power to back up their ideals with punishment. This was made particularly clear in the case of Ronald, an African American, formerly incarcerated father who was brought to court in Miami by Maria, the mother of his oldest son. Maria requested an increase in his support order to cover new child care expenses she had accrued by working extra hours at a grocery store. She explained that the increased hours came with a promotion, so she needed an extra $200/month. Ronald countered that he could not afford any additional expenses: since being released from prison, he had devoted himself to parenting his two smaller children, whom he was living with along with their mother. "Wait," Judge Jones interrupted. "You don't have a job? No work?" Ronald replied that he had work: he was caring for his children. "Being with my kids is my job right now."

Judge Jones let out a loud sigh. Before he could say anything, Ronald proposed an alternative: he could watch his oldest son while Maria worked her extra hours. Since he was already watching his other kids, everyone's needs could be met. To support the idea, he had his current partner submit a statement about his commitment as a father. He even got Maria to admit that he had taken good care of their son the previous summer. But Judge Jones would have none of it. "You need to get a J-O-B," he yelled. "We don't support househusbands here." They went back and forth, with Ronald insisting he had a job as a parent and another one would disrupt his current familial division of labor. In the end, Judge Jones did not just reject Ronald's proposal; he also ordered him to pay the extra $200 in child care expenses. "You will come in here next month with a real job. I will be watching you." As Ronald remarked as he left court, perfectly summarizing the punishment of fatherhood: "All the time I care for my kids and all the work I put into it. That means nothing. They just want me to pay. That's all that matters: money, money, money."

CREATING CRIMINALS

The enforcement assemblage that accompanies support debt is as vast as it is inescapable. It seizes everything from parents' wages to their property to their basic freedoms and liberties. It comes with a unique combination of civil and custodial punishments that is attached to no other form of debt; it blends fines, revocations, and confinement in a distinct mixture of penalties. Whether the debt is owed to custodial parents or the state, the enforcement of it allows for the withdrawal of the most fundamental of rights. Its punishments can last a lifetime and increase in severity over the life course. These punishments can swoop in at the most unexpected, inopportune moment to throw life into disarray long after the debt first accumulated.

This chapter has revealed that the child support enforcement assemblage is not only unique in its size and scope, but also in its unpredictability. At virtually every stage in the process, there is slippage in what is punished. In theory, enforcement should only target the repayment of debt. In reality, much more is policed, from poverty to fathering to breadwinning. These targets come together in the state's insistence that parents be "compliant" and align their behavior and commitments with those of the state. The compliance mandate goes far beyond the judicial discretion we have come to expect from legal proceedings. It actually acts as its own form of power. The unpredictability of enforcement keeps parents unstable and vulnerable. Unable to anticipate how state officials will react, parents can feel discombobulated. Unsure of what parts of their lives will be targeted, parents can feel sideswiped. Incapable of meeting state officials' ever-changing demands, parents can experience the enforcement process as criminalizing.

Indeed, both the scope and the inconsistency of the enforcement system made it difficult for indebted parents to manage. When confronted with the unpredictability of court, parents insisted the system was stacked against them. When the system seemed to invade all aspects of their lives, parents experienced it as inescapable. This was particularly true of formerly incarcerated parents, who received especially unforgiving treatment and were also the least knowledgeable about how to navigate the adjudication process. They were thus even more likely to see court as a trap, as a way to punish them for what remained outside their control. Like most people, indebted parents are more likely to cooperate with a system when it is perceived as fair and balanced. By extension, they are more likely to contest and resist a system seen as unjust.

In this way, the enforcement assemblage often created criminals where there were once only indebted parents. The creation of criminals was inherent in the system's design—the breadth, depth, and inconsistency of its control left few parents unscathed or unmarked. But this also emerged from fathers' response to this system. Many indebted parents ended up managing the enforcement system in ways that undermined their own and their families' well-being. Just as the accumulation of debt exacerbated cycles of poverty, the enforcement of debt created its own feedback loops of disadvantage. Together, these loops constructed their own prisons of debt. The next chapter explores how this happened.

4 The Imprisonment of Debt

Every weekday at around noon, a corrections van pulls up to the Miami Family Court and from it emerge five to ten men in bright orange prison jumpsuits. They are ushered into the courtroom by Jim, the burly court officer, and lined up in front of one of the three judges who handles the writs of habeas corpus. "So this is our yield from last night?" Judge Baker always asks. She calls each man to the bench and reads aloud a summary of his sins: an accounting of his child support debt. In these accounts, no one has a name and everyone is a computation. "There's $15,000 in arrears on a $160 bi-monthly order for two minors last paid in 2014 through a $500 purge." The men in jumpsuits then explain the numbers. Almost on script, each one chronicles how he cannot keep up with his support payments given the realities of poverty. All of them are out of work; many are homeless. Finally, the negotiations begin: How much can they pay to get out of jail? How much can they cobble together from friends or family? "How much do you want that orange jumpsuit off?" Judge Baker likes to ask. "Then show me the money!"

The men in orange are then taken to court offices in the back, sat in front of telephones, and told to start fundraising. Some give up before they even begin, claiming they have no one to call for help. So they are returned to jail cells to commence their sentence of anywhere from a few days to several months. Others begin their telethons, calling everyone and anyone they can think of to borrow money from: girlfriends, kin, friends, acquaintances, former bosses. "You gotta help me, cuz!" I overhear one man yelling into a phone. "I'm sittin' here, rotting in this place. They're gonna leave me in here forever.... I gotta get out." The lucky ones find someone, or usually a collection of someones, to contribute to their get-out-of-jail fund. The unlucky ones, who seem to be the overwhelming majority, end up joining the others back in their jail cells to begin what is always an unclear, unspecified sentence.

As I watched these spectacles day after day, it became clear that the child support enforcement apparatus had taken on a life of its own. Besides veering away from its stated mission of enforcing support orders by punishing fathers for poverty and failed breadwinning, its punitive assemblage had other far-reaching effects. Its enforcement measures sharpened the "hard edge" of what social scientists Haggerty and Ericson call the "surveillant assemblage"—modes of social control enacted through a combination of record-keeping, restriction, and custodial punishment.[1] As I showed in the previous chapter, the enforcement system has criminalized parents in the abstract sense by penalizing them for more than the nonpayment of child support. Yet it has also created criminals in a more concrete sense by entangling poverty and punishment in ways that complicate indebted parents' social integration. These complications are especially challenging for formerly incarcerated fathers struggling to stay out of prison, since they have created a series of fault lines they can fall through and land back in prison.

More specifically, the enforcement system poses three main challenges to this group of fathers. First, as fathers struggle to manage the realities of child support debt and enforcement, they develop financial survival strategies that, while seemingly rational and sensible, undermine them and their families. As they grapple with large wage garnishments, license suspensions, asset liens, and account seizures, fathers often feel pushed to go underground—thus cascading into what sociologist Sarah Brayne aptly terms "system avoidance" and disconnecting from important social institutions.[2] Second, the combination of massive debt and massive surveillance puts pressure on men's familial relationships, often to the breaking point. These familial breaks lead to the loss of resources and further dislodge men from vital support networks. Finally, some fathers become trapped in legal dynamics whereby their survival seems to require breaking laws. They are in a situation where legal transgression is necessary for system compliance and where they have to break some rules to abide by others. These challenges then affect fathers' social integration and eventual desistance from crime.

Those effects do not operate like the usual "spillover effects" of incarceration—they do not flow in a linear way from one institution to another but instead crisscross institutions. Nor do they simply "pile up" in fathers' lives in an additive way; instead, they work in circular ways, looping through different arenas of life. Fathers become entangled in processes similar to those of debt accumulation analyzed in chapter 2, which create their own feedback loops of disadvantage. Incarceration causes parents' debt to soar, while support enforcement deepens criminal justice involvement and worsens debt. The process is mutually reinforcing, leading to what I call the imprisonment of debt.

This chapter unpacks the financial, familial, and legal loops underlying the imprisonment of debt. It traces the emergence of a cycle whereby fathers' attempts to manage enforcement measures ultimately undercut the goals of those measures. In the process, indebted fathers begin to act like the parents the child support system is seeking to stamp out. As some fathers go underground to make ends meet, they seem duplicitous and "on the run." As others struggle to avoid becoming overreliant on family and kin, they seem detached and unreliable. As still others break laws out of perceived necessity, they seem hopelessly delinquent and transgressive. The system thus produces exactly the kind of subjects it most fears: men who retreat underground, violate rules, and commit crimes.

FINANCIAL LOOPS OF DEBT AND DESISTANCE

Despite all the talk in child support court about men's need to work, support enforcement can actually make it more difficult to find and maintain employment. Several quantitative studies have revealed a correlation between the size of a parent's support debt and a decline in employment—a correlation that is true for both low-income and formerly incarcerated

Table 2 Making Ends Meet with Child Support Debt

Average monthly wage (net)	$844*
Average arrears payment	–$100
Average child support payment	–$260
Remaining for living expenses	$484

*Based on the average yearly income of $10,128 reported by respondents, which is consistent with Western's (2006) wage estimates for formerly incarcerated men (converted to 2016 dollars). N = 125.

fathers.[3] These studies say little about the mechanisms underlying this pattern, yet those mechanisms are clear for indebted fathers. For them, it is not child support debt *per se* that complicates their employment. Instead, their sense of the unmanageability of debt and the practical obstacles to work lead many to conclude that they'll never get out of debt through formal employment.

It is no wonder they feel like this: the arrears of the fathers I studied far exceed their yearly income, averaging $36,500. Put another way, with a typical court-issued arrears payment of $100/month, it will take them more than thirty years to repay their debt. This is without accounting for the interest on their debt, which makes repayment almost impossible.[4] It is also without considering other legal debts, which can further reduce their monthly income. Table 2 reveals what the average formerly incarcerated father with support debt has left at the end of the month: $484.

Hidden within these numbers are a series of financial loops that lead fathers to question whether on-the-books employment is in their interest. The loops work like this: fathers struggle to make ends meet and find work amidst enforcement measures. After going round and round, still unable to make a living, some fathers retreat underground—a move that ends up undermining their ability to reintegrate and desist from crime.

Living in the Red

In the courts I observed, most fathers knew the drill: judges would scold them for not working, or not working enough; they would then defend themselves by claiming they couldn't find work. Depending on how many times they had been to court, fathers might be expected to bring props with them, such as job search diaries, completed job applications, or statements from work-training programs to substantiate their claims. While finding work was clearly a challenge, in our interviews a more complex story emerged. Many fathers revealed that the real obstacle was finding and keeping work that paid a livable wage. Living with child support debt made this more challenging: fathers who lived under the surveillance assemblage had a harder time finding work, keeping work, and making ends meet while working.

First was the challenge of finding decent work. Indebted fathers needed employment that paid enough to sustain themselves amidst mandatory wage garnishments. Since these fathers also had ongoing support cases (often more than one) and arrears, their wages could be garnished up to 65 percent. So minimum-wage work clearly wasn't going to cut it. "Even if I work full-time at Burger King like he [the judge] told me, I won't make enough to get by and stay current," explained Rick, a Jacksonville unemployed father of three with more than $50,000 in arrears. In their quest to find even those Burger King jobs, these fathers were disadvantaged. They had the mark of a criminal record, which research has shown continues to act as a scarlet letter for many employers. They also tended to lack the education and formal work experience that are increasingly needed for minimum-wage employment. Add to this the many restrictions and constraints of child support enforcement and the pool of potential work shrank even more.

For instance, indebted fathers underwent the many checks now involved in securing employment, from credit checks to background checks to license checks. Given that credit checks are used by roughly 30 percent of employers, particularly for low-wage service employment, the effect of child support debt could be disastrous.[5] Such debt not only lowers credit scores but can be reported as *child support* debt, with its enormous stigma.[6] Prisoner reentry programs claim employers are leery of hiring indebted fathers—for that reason, they help participants monitor their credit reports for any sign of child support debt. But since many indebted fathers are not connected to such programs, they have no idea how this mark on their credit can undermine their work search. The same is true of background checks: if a parent has been reincarcerated for child support debt or for civil contempt, it can come up on a background check. Here the effect on employers is even greater: indebted fathers often insisted that having an arrest warrant for child support come up on a background check was worse than an actual felony conviction. It put them in a marked category with moral connotations that were nearly impossible to escape.

Then there was the most common of these checks: the driver's license check, which has also become part of the standard background search for employment. Over and over again, fathers described losing jobs, sometimes lucrative jobs, because their licenses were not clean or had been revoked entirely. Some jobs were completely off limits to them. They were excluded from work as cab drivers, deliverymen, and truck drivers, which were some of the better-paid jobs available to them. They were excluded from the home care sector because those jobs frequently required an active driver's license or a clean driving record. Even some service-sector positions that did not involve driving became unavailable to them when employers discovered that their licenses had been suspended for child support debt.

The effects of license revocation were particularly serious in states like California and Florida given their limited public transportation systems—so much so that fathers in these states frequently claimed that employers would not even consider them because of their suspended licenses. Even in New York City, where one might not expect it to be a serious obstacle given the elaborate subway system, it became a central means to exclude indebted fathers from entire employment sectors. In fact, it was such a hurdle that several reentry and training programs in New York City created projects to work with employers to address the license issue. They tried to convince employers not to use a driver's license as a prerequisite for employment—or at least to consider child support suspensions differently from other types. A reentry counselor at Seedco, a large New York workforce development program, explained to me that the problem was employers' sense that a license suspension for child support reflected the parent's character, so that the stigma blocked many indebted fathers from work they were otherwise qualified for.

This leads to the second way that child support enforcement could impede employment: even if the lack of a license did not exclude them from work, fathers' inability to drive made it harder to keep their jobs.

According to the US Census, more than 75 percent of Americans drive to work.[7] With their licenses suspended, fathers were forced into especially long commutes to and from work—like Miguel, a Miami father whose daily commute to his two part-time jobs was over four hours. "If I could spend that time working, I would be paying off my debts faster," he wryly pointed out. After such long commutes, men would begin their shifts exhausted and drained. Like Barry, who had to leave at five a.m. to start his three-hour commute to his job at a barbershop that opened at eight a.m. Or Rafael, who crossed the large city of Miami via several buses every day to reach his part-time job at a Subway restaurant. These men were at the mercy of unreliable public transportation. When buses were delayed, they were late to work. "After too many times being late, they just laid me off," Fernando explained. "I don't blame 'em. . . . Buses are shit." And men like Fernando were not alone: a New Jersey study found that 42 percent of indebted fathers who had their driver's licenses revoked then lost their jobs.[8]

On top of this, support enforcement required continuous court appearances, which took parents from work, especially when they involved long commutes to court. And enforcement cases could stretch on for years, particularly for formerly incarcerated fathers with large arrears. During this time, courts stayed on them, issuing streams of court dates to monitor compliance. A key part of the required court performance was showing up on time and demonstrating conformity. But with every check-in, another workday was missed and another day's wages forgone. In most courts, work was not an acceptable excuse for missing a hearing. Hearings could be day-long events, with hours of waiting. So fathers were left to choose: miss work, lose wages, and risk job loss, or miss court and face court sanctions.

Sometimes child support enforcement intervened even more directly into fathers' work lives by literally following them to their jobs. State caseworkers and counselors were known to call employers to check in on parents' wages, work hours, and attendance. Fathers complained incessantly about this, insisting that the stigma of child support damaged them at work. "They're gonna make me lose my job," said John, a Miami father of three. "If they keep calling my boss, checking up on me, and reminding them that I got problems with child support, they'll get me fired." But the real damage happened to those arrested at work for child support. Several Florida fathers and one from New York recounted being taken to jail from work, with police showing up to their workplaces and arresting them in front of their bosses and coworkers. They were all summarily fired. As Louis, once a busboy at a nice Jacksonville restaurant, recalled:

> I loved that job. It was a real nice place, not like the shit I was used to.... Good tips. But one day the cops showed up [to the restaurant] looking for me. With a warrant. Can you imagine? They cuffed me right there... with everybody watching. I looked at my boss and he was red with anger... 'cause customers were seein' the whole thing. I knew right then I was gone. He wasn't gonna ever have me back no matter what I said or did.

While being taken to jail from work could certainly hurt fathers' employment, equally damaging was disappearing from work due to a sudden jail sentence for debt. "I really hate to mess up your work," Judge Matthews once remarked, cynically, to a formerly incarcerated father. "But I feel the need to take you to jail today." Many fathers recounted losing their jobs due to jail. The majority of fathers I interviewed who had served jail time for child support reported losing their jobs as a result of imprisonment. Since incarceration usually happened suddenly and unexpectedly, fathers' absences from work were without warning. Those disappearances left their employers in the lurch, which led to firings. Like the Jacksonville restaurant worker whose sandwich shop remained closed for the day after he was taken to jail and thus unable to show up for his opening shift. Then there was Willie, a twenty-year veteran of the Miami transit authority, who lost his stable, well-paid job after he was unexpectedly taken in on a child support warrant and served a ninety-day jail sentence that traumatized him:

> I'm an African American man who made it to forty [years old] without ever going to prison. That's success. But then one day they caught me jumping over the subway turnstile. The cop was like, "I'll let you go if your name is clean." But I knew it wasn't 'cause of my child support problems. So they ran my name and of course took me in. They left me there for three months 'cause I couldn't pay. It almost killed me, physically and spiritually. I got ill from a sickness I caught in there.... The way the guards treated us was like animals. I will never forget.... I still wake up at night, from nightmares about it.... And of course I lost my job after all that. It really messed me up.

Finally, besides making it harder to find and maintain work, support enforcement could make it more difficult for parents to survive while working. This was not only because mandatory wage garnishments left most men without enough to make ends meet, but also due to the enforcement measures that kicked in soon after support payments were missed. Formerly incarcerated fathers had a particularly hard time here: wage garnishments started as soon as work was found; driver's license revocations happened without delay; and support orders that had been modified due to incarceration rebounded to their original amount often within a month. The difficulties all of this raised for reentry was made particularly clear in a San Francisco case of a father recently released from prison after serving twenty years. Upon release, Darden had done everything right: he found a job and borrowed money from relatives to get his life back on track. Within months, he was called into court and ordered to begin paying off his $40,000 child support debt, all of which was owed to the state to repay foster care costs for his children. The court ordered a 40 percent wage garnishment, prompting this exchange:

DARDEN: Please, your honor, I have all these other debts . . . to family, to my aunt. If half my check is gone, I'll never make it.

JUDGE MORALES: I know, I know. You should be proud of yourself. You have a job and a place to live. But here's the thing: the citizens of California have been paying for your babies for a long time. They have paid a lot. . . . It is time for you to start paying them back.

DARDEN: I got a plan, really. I need to be able to get other things paid off . . . to use my money to settle myself . . . to not be strangled by half my check taken away.

Indeed, Darden raised one of the biggest obstacles arising from support enforcement: fixed wage garnishments could make parents more vulnerable by limiting their ability to move funds as needed. Being poor is a balancing act; it is a constant struggle to pay what's most urgent first and juggle all else. By tying their hands, and tying up their funds, wage garnishments could throw life out of balance. They left fathers unable to channel funds to deal with sudden emergencies, such as an eviction, a broken car, a health crisis, or a robbery. Several fathers also linked the inflexibility of garnishments to their childrearing, claiming that they restricted them from moving funds around for their kids. As one father, Arian, explained: "I just couldn't say no to my babies whenever they wanted something. Was I gonna say: 'Go get the money from the men down in Tallahasse?' Whenever I saw them, they asked for stuff. I could stop seeing them or I had to get them stuff . . . to feel like a daddy."

Of course, fixed payments are precisely what helps stabilize the finances of custodial parents. They allow mothers to manage their own balancing acts of poverty. They facilitate mothers' budgeting and ability to plan. They allow for all of this without the drama and disruption of court hearings. And many indebted fathers recognized this. They thus understood how wage garnishments on private orders benefited their families. But what about public orders? Were rigid wage garnishments essential for public orders and debt repayment? As Darden pointed out in our interview after his court hearing, did taxpayers really need to be paid back immediately? Did their needs supersede his need for time to get back on his feet and ultimately to help meet his children's needs? Or as LeRoy, a Florida father of two, asked: "Why would I work my ass off when it's all taken away and my kids see none of it? How can I be expected to give so much when I have so little . . . and so my kids get even less? This just makes no sense."

LeRoy was not alone in drawing this conclusion. After asking themselves similar questions, many fathers decided that their best route forward was to disconnect and go underground.

Going Underground

Moving off the grid, or "going offline" as some fathers put it, meant a variety of things. For many, it implied partial system avoidance: they kept one foot in formal institutions and one foot outside them. Some did this by splitting their work and having their employers report just enough to keep them below the mandatory reporting wage—so they could work additional hours off the books.[9] Or they worked one part-time job on the books, which they had garnished, and one off the books, which they lived off of. Or they got paid off the books for otherwise legitimate work, thus avoiding garnishments altogether.[10] These parents then paid the child support system what they could when they could without being held to the wage garnishments of formal employment. They gave their families informal, in kind support. Like Jimmy, a Florida father of two who got the landscaping company he worked for to pay him under the table after the state began to garnish his wages for public benefits received by his kids. Or Trevor, who insisted his kids got more money from him informally. "I like it this way," he explained. "I feel like a daddy when I can give them stuff... buy them stuff they need. It's not like that when I send a check to child support... Ain't no one seeing that. Or appreciating that."

For other parents, going underground meant living outside a few specific institutions they felt most threatened by. Financial institutions were high on the list: these men did all their economic transactions in cash. They had no bank accounts in their name and thus lived "unbanked."[11] They had no credit cards in their name. They allowed no financial records or paper trails to be kept. When they got paid for work, they found ways to stash away their funds—in others' bank accounts, in safe deposit boxes, or in hiding places at home. Cell phones posed an obstacle for them since they require a credit check or credit card to secure. So off-the-grid fathers used burner phones. Or they had friends or family add them to their cell phone plans. Or they put down large security deposits and paid much higher rates for prepaid phone contracts.

Some fathers went underground from the state specifically, disconnecting from as many state institutions and services as possible. They did not apply for any state benefits, like food stamps, unemployment compensation, or social security, even if they might have been eligible. They never filed tax returns. They did everything possible to avoid all police contact, ducking and running from them. They even stopped riding public transportation for fear of the police presence on it—and rumors about how transit police did warrant sweeps on subways and buses.[12] Some resigned themselves to never having a legitimate driver's license again. Given the numerous holds on their licenses and the large monetary purges they would have to come up with in order to get them back, they wrote off being able to drive legally. So they moved around via livery cabs and "dollar vans," which were unregulated and often unlicensed. Or they made informal arrangements with family and friends who could drive legally. Gene, an African American father in Miami who hadn't been able to drive during the six years since he was released from prison, described his transit routine like this:

> One of my homies could drive.... Legally, I mean. So I went everywhere with him. He came around in the morning, picked me and a few [others] up. And we'd do our shit.... We go wherever we needed to go.... Yea, it took a lot longer. 'Cause we'd stop five or ten times before we got to where I needed to go.... We took care of everybody's business.

Then there were fathers who seemed entirely submerged underground. They proudly described disconnecting from all the institutions they could. The goal was to sever ties with anybody that kept records on them, from financial to residential to driving to health records. Without employment records, there were no wages to garnish. Without tax records, there were no returns to intercept. Without a recorded address, there was nowhere to serve legal papers. Without banking records, there were no funds to freeze. Without asset records, there was no property to seize. Without driving records, there was no license for the DMV to suspend. Without health records, there was no way for their physical well-being to be monitored. As Amal, a father of three, proudly declared, "I'm off the grid, completely. No record of me anywhere."

While Amal may have felt proud to be living underground, he also faced serious risks by disconnecting from formal institutions. At a minimum, fathers like Amal risked angering support judges, who knew they were doing something to support themselves despite their claims to no income. The absence of all records on them made these fathers appear duplicitous. They seemed to be doing exactly what the courts most feared—escaping detection and accountability. Fathers' motivations for going underground were often quite different from this—most went off the grid to avoid state control, not to avoid supporting their kids. But that didn't matter: whatever their motivation, they seemed to be dodging their responsibilities and living lives of deception.

As a result, fathers' attempts to shield themselves from surveillance often backfired. They frequently found themselves exposed to more scrutiny. When state officials called them out on their behavior, these fathers covered up their indiscretions, which only compounded their problems. This is what happened to Chris, a Florida father of two who squirrelled away funds earned from off-the-books work to cover a deposit so that he could move into his own apartment—and who then lied about it in court so that the funds would not be garnished to repay his TANF arrears. It also happened to Tyrell, a California father of three who opened a bank account in someone else's name so that he could deposit part of his paycheck and save funds to buy a car—and who then lied about it in court so that the account was not seized. When Chris and Tyrell's indiscretions were eventually uncovered, judges just upped their scrutiny of them. They were now deemed noncompliant and untrustworthy, and state officials surveilled and punished them more.

Living underground could also prompt fathers to disconnect from institutions they needed to ensure their own well-being. Some institutional connections were necessary for fathers to stay out of the criminal justice system. Formerly incarcerated fathers could find themselves in violation of the rules governing their parole if they went too far underground. Parole monitored these men's ability to reintegrate—and to stay integrated—and system avoidance undermined this. Off-the-grid fathers could also breach the requirements of reentry and transitional housing programs, many of which required them to engage in formal employment to remain eligible for services. Several men recounted how their retreat to informal work cost them coveted spots in programs designed to integrate them into formal sector employment.

This disconnection made them more vulnerable in other ways. Those who were thrown into poverty suddenly because of job loss, eviction, or jail time found themselves without a safety net. Their disconnections made them ineligible for all kinds of state benefits. Without employment records, they were ineligible for unemployment compensation. Those who had been injured on the job or became disabled could be ineligible for benefits. In fact, several fathers I interviewed seemed to have clear disability cases, but their claims were rejected because of incomplete records and spotty histories of formal employment. Without tax returns, these fathers found themselves ineligible for low-income housing or subsidized housing programs. Without bank accounts, they could not save funds safely, and remaining unbanked made them more vulnerable to robbery on the street or at home. Forced to stash away funds wherever possible, they could have their savings stolen or used up by others in need. Without credit to fall back on in an emergency, they were at the mercy of predatory lenders to make ends meet. All of this made these fathers' reintegration and desistance from crime harder to sustain.

The risk of going off-the-grid was especially high for those who had slipped back into their old networks. The reality was that few fathers could exist without any support systems. When they fell out of formal ones, they frequently fell into informal networks. "I started hanging with my old associates," admitted Ralph, a white Oakland father of two. "I was crazy 'cause I knew better, but they were all I had." In turning to their "old associates," fathers like Ralph exposed themselves to further danger. Reconnecting with these associates could be disastrous for fathers who, if caught, were in violation of the terms of parole, halfway houses, or reentry programs. Many of them had noncontact rules as part of their parole, which barred them from interacting with others with felony convictions. Hanging with those associates, and being exposed to all they did, could jeopardize it all. Ralph described how the debt/desistance feedback loop made getting out of poverty and staying out of jail all the more difficult:

> I got paroled down to the central valley and it was bad. I mean, I had an okay set-up at first, since my mom's boyfriend gave me a place to live.... But then I started associating with all my old associates. Just a bad scene.... And then they started fucking with me. They'd come over to my place and do all kinda shit they knew would get me sent back.... It got really bad. When I got picked up for something they set me up on, I lost it all. My place to live, my girlfriend, everything.... Then a judge... found a way to parole me up here [in Oakland] to get me away from the negative influences down there.... Life is still real hard, but being up here lets me see my kids.

Other fathers discovered that something so seemingly trivial as driving with the wrong group of associates could set this feedback loop into motion. Recall Gene, the Florida father discussed earlier, who, when faced with a suspended license, began to use his homeboys as a taxi service to drive him around while they took care of their business. It turns out that some of the business they took care of wasn't legal. One day, the police pulled them over for a broken headlight and, after finding drugs in the car, arrested everyone. Gene insisted he wasn't involved: "I wasn't so stupid to hang with that shit," he exclaimed to me. "I had just got out of prison...

didn't want to go back for a ride." But they were all accused of conspiracy to distribute. Even though everyone agreed that Gene was just in the wrong car at the wrong time, he had prior criminal convictions and thus faced serious prison time, which he ultimately served. When he left prison after that second stint, the likelihood of finding future employment had diminished even more. And the size of his child support debt had doubled and his driver's license remained suspended. He was right back on the debt/desistance feedback loop.

Of course, these financial loops also made paying child support more difficult. When fathers lost jobs without recourse or protection, many stopped paying their child support. When their savings were stolen without a safety net to catch them, many slipped further behind on their payments. When they were hit with an eviction without funds or credit to sustain them, they fell deeper into arrears. As the enforcement measures were upped and new sanctions were applied to them, the loops of disadvantage seemed all the more inescapable. And it was women and children who ultimately suffered from these loops. They received less money less reliably, which made their lives more vulnerable, insecure, and unstable. Again, while nonpayment might not have been the motivation for going underground, it was often the outcome. It was also an outcome that ended up chipping away at perhaps the most important network of all: familial connections.

FAMILIAL LOOPS OF INTERDEPENDENCE AND OVERDEPENDENCE

The importance of familial networks to reintegration after prison is well-established in both quantitative and qualitative research. Social science has consistently revealed that family networks are critical to men's well-being, especially to those with criminal records.[13] For instance, familial connections emerge as key resources in Bruce Western's comprehensive analysis of prisoner reentry.[14] They are similarly vital in Meghan Comfort's research on partnership during and after prison—her work shows how families serve as the "front line" of reentry as men depend on them for economic, emotional, and social support.[15] Although neither Western nor Comfort focuses on fathers with child support debt specifically, the hardship they describe is familiar to many indebted fathers. Also familiar is the essential role that family can play in indebted fathers' ability to cope with post-prison vulnerabilities.

While there is a clear correlation between familial support and reintegration, the mechanisms underlying it remain elusive. The assumption is that kin and family networks form a safety net for formerly incarcerated men, creating a buffer to shield them from the vicissitudes of reentry. The fathers I interviewed found this to be true; they spoke of their families as a foundation upon which to stand. Yet familial support often flowed in a reciprocal way: it ran from their families to them and then back from them to their families. In fact, the most effective familial support seemed to involve mutual reliance and interdependence, with fathers feeling reliant on others and relied upon by others. This reciprocity gave fathers the sense that others counted on them. It served as an incentive not to veer off track or skid backwards.

Such reciprocal relationships were precisely what support enforcement could complicate. Indebted fathers' familial relations were fragile. Given how much they had weathered, from incarceration to poverty to abandonment to neglect, they were threadbare and overextended. As fathers repeatedly turned to family networks for help dealing with the restrictions, revocations, and incarcerations of child support enforcement, they could seem like drains on those networks. Connections that may have started out as reciprocal could become lopsided; relationships that had been interdependent could begin to feel dependent. This created its own set of feedback loops, with some fathers responding to their sense of dependence by disconnecting. Those disappearing acts ended up undermining fathers and disadvantaging them further in their struggle to reintegrate.

"It feels good to be needed"

It was the end of a long day in a courtroom on the outskirts of Jacksonville, and everyone just wanted to go home—including Jim Harvey, the father in the final case of the day. "My uncle is waiting for me to fix him his food," he noted as he approached the bench. "So I gotta hurry." Rushing Judge Matthews was never advisable. "This will take as long as I say," Matthews retorted. Sitting back in his chair, Matthews slowly read through the case file and took long pauses to make Mr. Harvey nervous. He ridiculed Mr. Harvey for his twenty-thousand-dollar debt on public and private orders for his two teenage sons. He derided Mr. Harvey for paying little on his debt since his release from prison a year earlier. He scoffed at Mr. Harvey for not presenting any employment records. "I'm thinking you are one sorry man, a real loser," Matthews concluded. "I'm thinking you need a bit of time in jail . . . to think about your deadbeat ways and how to change them."

Hearing these words, Mr. Harvey began to panic. And then to plead. He wasn't working because he was caring for his elderly, incapacitated uncle. In exchange for a room in his uncle's house and shared meals, he did everything for the man. It was an arrangement he had informed his caseworker about so the court knew the situation. If he went to jail, there would be no one to care for his uncle. The old man depended on him. He had promised to be there for his uncle no matter what, and so far he had kept his promise. "But who'll care for him if I'm not there?" His question hung in the courtroom air, unanswered, for a minute or two. Until Matthews punctured the silence: "Excuses, excuses. You need to get yourself a real J-O-B. Stop acting like a nurse and take care of your sons. Their mama needs the money you owe her . . . You will have time to think about how [to do this] now." As bailiff Frank led him off to a jail cell, Mr. Harvey continued to plead, "Who's gonna make his dinner tonight? Who's gonna get him ready for bed?"

Although I later learned that Mr. Harvey used his one phone call from jail to call an elder care agency to assist his uncle for the time he spent incarcerated, his experience exemplified a common loop entangling indebted fathers: familial cycles in which mutual dependencies were established, only to be derailed by an unexpected enforcement measure. There were many fathers like Mr. Harvey who, in the face of terrible job markets and limited employment options, integrated into family networks to form reciprocal relations of support. While these fathers needed a lot of support, it turns out they also had something to give. They had valuable resources that their familial networks often lacked. By providing these scarce resources, indebted fathers could help support their networks while being supported by them.

Perhaps the most important resource these men had to give was caregiving. Although often referred to with the more gender-neutral term "time," fathers stitched together reciprocal relations of care that helped sustain family members. Like Jim, some of these men exchanged their time and labor with elderly relatives, acting as home health aides, cooks, and companions for those in need. Particularly in rural areas where there was an absence of reliable and affordable elder care, they helped aunts, uncles, parents, and grandparents maintain themselves. In exchange, their relatives helped fathers sustain themselves—providing a place to live or paying them a small salary. "I live with my grandma to help her out," Mateo, a Los Angeles father, explained. "I got all the time in the world... and she needs me. She [has] no one and her social security won't cover a [nursing] home."

Even more common than elder care was childcare, with fathers acting as day care providers for their family networks. Sometimes they did this for their biological kids, if they had been able to maintain a good relationship with their mothers. Like Ronnie, who, despite being homeless, was able to help out his kids' mother by relocating to a nearby shelter in order to take the kids to and from school every day. Or like Arnold, who stepped in when his kids' mother started using drugs again, staying at their apartment for days at a time to watch the kids when she disappeared on benders. Then there was Joe, whose ex-wife agreed to forgive all the arrears owed to her in exchange for his help caring for their four kids after school and during summers. Yet courts frowned on these arrangements, for they left men without reportable income. Never mind that they could be advantageous for women and children—some judges disparaged these men in court, calling them "househusbands" and "Mr. Moms." Indeed, in Joe's case it took several court hearings to get his support debt forgiven. The court actually advised his ex-wife against it and required her to undergo a waiting period before issuing the debt modification.

Fathers also provided childcare to siblings, aunts, uncles, and cousins, which they exchanged for housing, food, transportation, and wages. One of the most memorable examples of this was Reggie, an African American father I spent weeks trying to track down. Referred to me by a Miami reentry organization, Reggie was a no-show for several of our appointments. I was about to give up on interviewing him when he offered to meet me early Saturday morning at the city children's hospital. When he arrived at the cafeteria, he was accompanied by a posse of nearly a dozen small children, who ranged in age from three to twelve. He then explained why he had been so hard to reach: a month after he was released from prison, his young nephew suffered a seizure and was placed in intensive care. Because the boy's mother had to continue to work, she asked Reggie to stay at the hospital while she took the night shift. As he proudly explained:

> I was the one who was there when he became conscious. . . . We saw him moving a lot so he had his breathing tube removed. He spoke his first words. To me. If I wasn't there, ain't no one would have been there for him . . . just the hospital people. I'm pretty sure he wouldn't have said nothing if it had just been them there and no family.

As Reggie described the situation to me, he kept one eye out for his young troop, which played at the adjourning table.[16] "That's my brother's two kids," he said, pointing to the two littlest kids. "Then all those next to them are their cousins from their mama's side." The final two kids were his biological son and daughter, who had different mothers but considered themselves siblings because he always took care of them together. As we finished our interview, he gathered up the crew to head to his nephew's hospital room. "I am so glad I can be here for them," Reggie explained, pointing to the kids. "As well as my sister. . . . 'Cause she helped me out after I got out of Baker [prison] with nowhere to go. . . . We count on each other."

Like Reggie, many fathers appreciated feeling needed and taking care of others. They liked that they could be relied on; it made them feel responsible to come through for others. It also made them feel competent and confident that they were trusted to take care of their children. Since confidence can beget confidence, having others believe in them made fathers more secure about their abilities. They began to see a clearer path to doing right and doing good. Their familial interdependencies also made them aware of the cost of veering off course: others counted on them, so they didn't want to let anyone down. As Damon, a Brooklyn father of three who was taking care of a cousin's kids since his release from prison, put it: "I spent so much of my life fucking up. . . . It feels good to be needed."

Besides providing carework, fathers contributed material resources to their networks. They described quite elaborate exchange relationships in which all kinds of resources were pooled through all kinds of familial partnerships. Reminiscent of Carol Stack's classic account in *All Our Kin*, fathers formed barter relationships to sustain themselves.[17] They partnered up with someone who had an apartment, in exchange for cooking all the food. They partnered up with someone who had a state pension, which could be combined with their own SSI to make ends meet. They partnered up with someone who had a car and a valid driver's license, who they offered a place to stay in return. And caregiving could also be sprinkled through all of these partnerships to equalize a seemingly lopsided exchange. Like Omar, who lived with his female cousin after his long prison term, and who performed a complex exchange of home repairs, cooking, cleaning, and childcare. Or Jackson, whose sister became his chauffeur in exchange for a small percentage of his wages, which she then used to move from her Section 8 apartment into a safer neighborhood—an apartment where she often allowed Jackson to stay when in need.

Familial interdependencies could involve emotional support. Here, too, fathers needed support and also developed relationships in which they provided it. Many indebted fathers had overcome addiction and could thus be a benefit to those with similar issues. Men who had gotten clean in prison often shared survival strategies and took family members to AA and NA meetings. One father had an app on his phone that listed meetings in the area. "I'm taking my sister to meetings all the time," he explained as he showed me how the app worked. Fathers also supported those grappling with mental health problems. Depression ran rampant among these men—close to half of them admitted to struggling with it.[18] They looked to family to cope with emotional struggles, but they also reciprocated, helping family members deal with their issues. "I know the signs," Damon said in reference to his cousin. "I know when she's going down 'cause I've been there." Or as Ronaldo described turning his ten-year plight with HIV into a valuable lesson for loved ones: "I told them if I could admit to this [being HIV positive], then they could stand up to their problems... and get the help they need. It's not that hard once you admit it."

Disappearing Acts

These familial interdependencies were sustaining for indebted fathers and helped them stay afloat. They also helped men feel like they were not simply draining their families. Yet these relationships could also be quite unstable. The ups and downs of poverty and scarcity took a toll on them. When the punishments of child support enforcement hit, they could strike like lightning bolts. When that lightning jolted these relationships, they at times fell apart.

Child support enforcement could throw these relationships off balance. Indebted fathers' lives often seemed like an obstacle course, with various hurdles to jump or avoid altogether. When courts levied unexpected punishments, those hurdles got higher. This might result from a sudden increase in the amount fathers owed on current or past support orders. It might result from the sudden revocation of a driver's license. It might result from the unanticipated seizing of assets or bank accounts. Or it might result from the issuing of a large financial purge to avoid reincarceration. All of these enforcement actions forced fathers to come up with extra resources, often urgently—like when they lost their driver's license but still had to get to work the very next day. Or when their bank account was frozen but they still needed to pay rent. Or when they had to come up with thousands of dollars to pay a purge and avoid jail.

Quite often, family networks were the only place they could turn to meet these sudden needs. Several fathers described feeling bad about always asking for money from family, particularly at the last minute. They worried they had become burdens on those networks and were overusing these relationships. They also felt uncomfortable about changing the terms of relationships they had worked so hard to establish. For instance, many of their familial interdependencies involved the complex bartering of time, care, and help. But child support enforcement usually required a sudden influx of cash, which was quite scarce in these networks. As Eddie, a Miami father of two, put it:

> It was like $40 here, $40 there. I was always askin' them for something. I just felt like such a burden on everyone. My people aren't people with a lot of extra cash. So all those $40 loans added up . . . and I got worried they'd want to run when they saw me coming or calling . . . Like I was gonna always be hittin' them up for something.

What's more, support enforcement could unexpectedly dislodge men from their reciprocal relations, leaving them unable to fulfill their end of the exchange. Indebted fathers were always being hauled into court, sometimes as often as a few times a month, for ongoing enforcement. Managing these court dates could be difficult, especially since hearings could be delayed or postponed at a whim, leaving fathers suddenly unable to fulfill an obligation. In court, I often observed men plead with court bailiffs to call their cases early so they could leave for familial responsibilities. "I gotta go pick my sister's kids up at daycare," an Oakland man whispered to the bailiff after waiting hours for his case to be called. Unsympathetic, the bailiff just reiterated what the man already knew: he could leave court and face the legal ramifications of being a no-show or he could leave his nephews waiting. Ultimately, he took the gamble and left court at lunch, more concerned about the consequences of leaving two small kids alone.[19]

The worst scenario was the one faced by Mr. Harvey, the father described earlier whose court hearing unexpectedly ended with jail time. This left Mr. Harvey unable to fulfill his responsibilities to his elderly uncle, which was something that happened to other men caring for their kids or their parents. Mr. Harvey's first phone call to get backup care for his uncle was typical: many fathers called family members from jail to get coverage for those relying on them. Since these were likely the same family members that men would eventually turn to for the funds to get out of jail, they worried about becoming burdens on their family networks. Indeed, ongoing, low-level criminal justice interventions have been shown to destabilize families in unique ways, forcing family members into what sociologist Meghan Comfort calls a "20-hour-a-day" job overseeing and assisting loved ones' cycles of arrest and jail.[20]

Besides destabilizing their family networks, fathers feared they could be a threat to them. Some men were nervous about exposing their family to heightened surveillance. They feared that their own criminalization could spill onto others. And their fears were not unfounded. Bringing a partner or family member to court was a risky proposition, especially in Florida, where companions could be drawn into court proceedings. They were asked to vouch for what men were saying; they were questioned about their own resources; and they were accused of lying, as if they were guilty by association. Fathers also worried about support enforcement bleeding into law enforcement and entrapping family or friends. Many fathers experienced the "deadbeat raids" so notorious across the country. Since police often showed up at fathers' homes or family gatherings, others could be swept into the law enforcement net. Even if others weren't arrested, the experience of a police roundup could cause reverberating anxiety.

While most of these threats remained challenges to be grappled with, for some fathers they led to breaks from family networks. These breaks could be initiated by family members, who, after one too many unfulfilled promises, just walked away. But these breaks also originated with fathers themselves. Feeling like a drain on familial well-being had emotional effects, from guilt to fear to anger. These feelings could make fathers leery of remaining in familial relationships they perceived as overly dependent. A few fathers spoke of how their child support problems led to embarrassment and disconnection. They felt guilty when they failed to fulfill their responsibilities to family members who counted on them; they were ashamed to act in ways that confirmed the worst suspicions of them. The humiliation of court stung even more when observed by family members from whom they sought approval.

These feelings could prompt fathers to disappear from those networks altogether. Here, too, some fathers were brutally honest about how the cycle worked. Embarrassed by their failure to meet others' expectations, they retreated from loved ones. They were frustrated with themselves, with the court, and with child support authorities, so they lashed out, exhibiting destructive and self-defeating behavior that only increased the likelihood of expulsion from the family. They lost control and became belligerent in court, screaming at judges in ways that even the most sympathetic officials had to punish. In private, they exhibited more anger and thus alienated those they needed the most. Once again, such responses then looped back to worsen their problems through the loss of social support and connection. At worst, fathers became more isolated and more vulnerable to skidding backwards.

These familial loops could be mutually reinforcing. The more vulnerable fathers became, the more likely they were to retreat underground and disconnect from family; the more they disconnected, the more isolated they felt; the more they felt isolated, the more fathers could feel compelled to stretch or break the system's rules to survive—and the less they felt was at stake in doing so. These loops crisscrossed and intersected, ultimately leading some indebted fathers to even more transgressive behavior.

LEGAL LOOPS OF TRANSGRESSION AND COMPLIANCE

The financial and familial loops experienced by so many indebted fathers could lead indirectly to criminal justice involvement, leaving them with what they thought was no other option to survive than a return to crime. But there were other, more direct routes to criminal justice entanglements. Managing the sanctions and restrictions on their lives could be its own form of imprisonment. The imperatives of the child support and legal systems could be contradictory; the demands placed on parents could seem inconsistent. This led to a situation where compliance in one arena seemed to require transgression in another. Or where fulfilling one set of demands meant neglecting another. Fathers discussed several examples of these contradictory pulls, but the most common were the legal loops created by the revocation of their driver's licenses and contempt of court actions.

Besides making the earning of a livable wage more challenging, license revocations created legal loops that made indebted fathers feel compelled to break the law to meet judicial demands.[21] Fathers knew that persistent unemployment would cause the enforcement apparatus to come down hard on them, but they also needed to drive to work. Many jobs required a driver's license; others were so remote that they could only be reached by car. Since much low-wage work has been pushed out of urban centers into "urban suburban" spaces, it has become hard to reach without a car or reliable public transportation. Since many fathers lived in urban areas where they had family and other support services, the work available to them required a commute. Add to this their need to double or triple up on jobs to make ends meet and commuting without a car was impossible. If the second or third job was in a distant "urban suburban" area, there was often not enough time in between shifts to get from one job to another without a car.

Some fathers dealt with these contradictory pulls by prioritizing work over the law: they drove on suspended licenses. Given the risk, they usually did this as a last resort. Like after a judge came down particularly hard on them for their unemployment, promising to make their life especially difficult. Or after a judge demanded that they get another job or risk being held in contempt of court for nonpayment. Or after they finally saw a way out of their cycle of debt and poverty with the offer of a better-paid job with more hours, but the job necessitated driving. In a few cases, fathers filed a court request to have their licenses reinstated and waited out the decision. But in most cases, indebted fathers decided on their own. They weighed their options, ultimately opting to break a criminal law in order to remain compliant with child support law. As Marcus, a Miami father of two, explained:

> It just makes no sense. He [the judge] yells at me to work, work, work. But then they take my license away. I haven't had a license in seven years. Who's gonna hire me if I can't drive? If I'm always late getting to work 'cause of the buses? I lost so many jobs 'cause of this [lack of a license].... Sometimes I just take the risk [of driving].... Been lucky so far.

Another thing that could tip the scale toward breaking the law and driving illegally was children. Here, too, the system's demands seemed contradictory: fathers knew that both the court and mothers expected consistent visitation from them, but it could be difficult to maintain without a driver's license, especially if children lived far from them. Or if their work schedules left only a small window of time in between their shifts to spend with their children. Here, too, fathers felt damned if they did and damned if they didn't. If they didn't drive, they missed spending valuable time with their kids. But if they drove, they risked racking up an arrest and possible felony conviction, which could mean an even longer separation from their kids.

This was the dilemma facing Marty, a Los Angeles father who had recently obtained custody of his two children from their mother, who was homeless and using drugs. His young daughter lived with him while his son lived in a facility close to San Diego. Visiting his son regularly was critical to maintaining custody and to his son's well-being. But going to see him took more than five hours each way by bus. If he got a ride, or drove himself on a suspended license, he could make the trip in half the time and thus spend more of the day with his son. As Marty explained it: "When we go by bus, we spend more time getting down there than being there. It's all day, but I don't even get to spend much time with him. 'Cause I don't got a car, we need to stay in the facility with him. I can't take him out anywhere. It sucks, but we still do it."

Given these conflicting demands, fathers like Marty often felt justified when they broke down and got in the driver's seat. Over and over, they insisted they were just doing what was necessary to fulfill their work and family obligations. But the risks were very real; fathers could land in serious trouble. In some jurisdictions, driving on a suspended license carries jail time and can thus have cascading effects. If caught, driving without a license could lead to a parole violation. It could be a breach of the terms of their reentry program and thus undermine their ability to stay out of jail. It could create legal loops whereby men met their work and family obligations only to worsen their legal problems. And it was yet another way that fathers' vulnerability in one arena exacerbated their vulnerability in another.

Michael's trajectory into and out of jail was an especially good example of these legal loops. When I interviewed him in Miami, he was still recovering from a jail sentence he had served for driving on a suspended license. He had been jailed for child support before, but the last one really got to him. Prior to it, things had been going well. He had secured a good job in a restaurant kitchen and a second job cleaning the parking lot of a nearby shopping mall. Together, these two jobs yielded enough for him to begin to pay off his support arrears while also making regular payments on his current order. Both jobs were near his new apartment, so he could walk or take the bus to work. But then he made a mistake. His kids had been complaining about how many of their belongings had been lost after a previous eviction, and he didn't have the money to replace them. So in an attempt to salvage some of his old belongings and repurpose them for his kids, he took what he thought would be a quick road trip:

> I knew I wasn't supposed to drive.... But then my family in South Carolina was fixin' to move and told me to come get all my stuff. I couldn't let all that stuff go. So I went. I drove. And wouldn't you know it, I got caught up in a police road block? It was over. They took me in, threw the book at me.... Left me in jail for weeks. I lost my jobs, fell behind in my rent.... Everything got worse from then on. I had to hustle again to get myself back on my feet.... It took years.

Driving on a suspended license was a minor offense that could have major consequences. But fathers also described serious criminal misconduct. This was most common for those facing contempt of court and the threat of jail time. Before holding a parent in contempt, most judges gave them a chance to "purge" their way out by paying large sums of money as a condition of remediation. These purges were issued in one of three ways. First, once contempt was filed and a warrant issued, parents could be picked up by law enforcement, brought to court, and ordered to pay up to be released. Or parents could avoid the warrant process altogether by paying the purge amount in court once it was issued. Finally, parents could negotiate with judges to set a fixed amount of time, usually a week or two, for them to come up with the purge payment.

The actual amount of these purges varied quite dramatically. Indeed, they often seemed to be issued at judicial whim. Since there were few fixed guidelines structuring them, they could range from a few hundred to several thousand dollars; the average I observed hovered around $1,000. So although purges were supposed to be set at a reasonable amount to allow parents to pay them and show a good faith effort, they were out of reach of most parents. In fact, they could be set at such absurdly high amounts that they seemed more like punishment than remediation. For fathers who earned the minimum wage and barely made ends meet, a $1,000 purge was several times their weekly salary. To an unemployed, homeless man, that amount was simply unobtainable.

Instead of feeling like a way out, purges could so entangle fathers in debt and punishment that crime seemed like their only route out.[22] This happened in two primary ways. First, ignoring the purge usually resulted in an arrest warrant, which could lead to a parole violation and jail time. In cases of criminal contempt, this resulted in charges of new crimes, which could also cause the revocation of parole and imprisonment. Those who found themselves unable to pay the purge often tried to avoid it—but their avoidance tactics made them seem like callous lawbreakers. They didn't return to court for follow-up hearings; they didn't respond to letters from local child support offices; and they were steadfast in their avoidance of all state officials and law enforcement authorities. Most did so sheepishly, embarrassed and scared of getting caught, but a few fathers dealt with the threat of contempt with defiance. They tended to be fathers who owed their debt to the state and who insisted that serving jail time for public debt was an injustice.[23] For instance, Randolph, a white father of two from Napa who had spent years chased by state authorities for a series of arrest warrants issued for his public debt, justified his defiance this way:

> Think about how crazy this is: they spent thousands and thousands of dollars to track me down for not paying [the purge]. Now they are sending me to jail, where they will spend tens of thousands of dollars to lock me up.... And all for money I am told I owe them, the government. You can't make this shit up.... So I'll keep fighting... and telling how rotten this system is.

Then there were parents who dealt with the threat of contempt in the opposite way: the possibility of returning to jail or prison so terrified them that they were willing to do anything to purge themselves of contempt. Even if it meant committing new crimes. When issuing purges, some judges seemed unaware of the enormity of what they were asking. But others were acutely aware of the impossibility of the purge and even cognizant of how purges could push parents back into crime. Indeed, several Florida judges referred to crime when they set these purges: "I don't care how you get the money," Judge Matthews said after issuing a purge. "Go rob a bank if you have to. Just come back with the money...." Or as Judge May once told a father after issuing a $2,000 purge: "You aren't even a good criminal. If you were, you wouldn't be in this predicament.... So become a better criminal or get yourself a bunch of new jobs."

This is precisely what some fathers did. With no other way to come up with so much money so quickly, they got the purge money illegally. They returned to selling drugs, even if only temporarily, to make enough to get out of the red. They did burglaries to get the cash they needed to pay the purge. As with driver's license revocations, some fathers said they felt justified in breaking the law to comply with their court order. They insisted that they were simply doing what was necessary to fulfill one set of demands, even if it meant breaking the law. Here's how Jesse, a white thirty-year-old father of three who had been rearrested for robbery to pay off a child support purge, explained his cost/benefit analysis:

> I think about it like this. I can get incarcerated now for not paying what he [the judge] ordered. If I go back to court without the money, I know I'm going away.... Or I could "find a way" to get the money. My way. Maybe I

won't get caught. Maybe I will. But at least there's uncertainty there. It's a gamble. Sometimes I win. This time, I lost.

Other fathers seemed much more conflicted about their decision to return to crime. They described feeling so trapped they could imagine no other way out. Perhaps the most open and honest of all the fathers who admitted to returning to crime to pay their purge was James, the Jacksonville father berated by Judge May for being a "bad criminal." As we sat down in a Burger King the day after the $2,000 purge was issued, he was still shaken. He admitted that he once considered killing himself after one of Judge May's tirades. Humiliated, he became depressed after each and every court appearance. "It's like they bring me in every week, or every month, to have a go at me." He could not even recall how many times he had been held in contempt and jailed for the $32,000 he owed in back support. After trying several times to "go legit," he recently decided to return to drug dealing to get himself out of the immediate threat of yet another reincarceration. At the time of our interview, he was still dealing, and he realized all the risks it entailed. But what he feared in the long term was offset by the relief he experienced in the short term. He finally had a way out of the legal loops he had been cycling through for years. "I'll start paying now," he proclaimed. "They have to stop messin' with me."

LOOPING THROUGH PUNISHMENT AND DEBT

One of the most perverse effects of systems of social control is that they tend to produce the precise behaviors they are designed to regulate. Perverse yet exceedingly common: from excessive policing to punitive corrections, state control often escalates what it aims to eradicate. The child support enforcement system is no different. When the proclamations of state officials like Judge Matthews and Judge May are juxtaposed with the responses of fathers like Jesse and James, it is clear the system has produced the subjects it most fears—indebted fathers who feel they must transgress in order to survive and who disconnect from those they so desperately need.

This chapter has traced how fathers' responses to the enforcement system complicated their social reintegration and desistance from crime. It has revealed how this system undermines fathers by creating a series of loops through which disadvantage worsens and deepens. These loops push fathers underground, thus making them more vulnerable to financial hardship. These loops disconnect fathers from familial bonds, thus straining already fraught and overburdened relationships. And these loops force fathers to choose between adhering to one set of state demands and breaking others, thus putting them at greater risk of reincarceration.

These loops are also the central way that child support and criminal justice sanctions become intertwined. They hasten some fathers' slide backwards and onto criminal trajectories. Rather than working through linear collateral consequences, these slides are being produced by institutional entanglements that crisscross time and space. Yet the mechanisms underlying these loops have too often remained hidden. Most attention has been on their outcomes—or how fathers act out, disconnect, and need to become more compliant. By stepping back and untangling these loops, this analysis has exposed how enforcement can become its own prison. In the process, enforcement strikes at the heart of what could protect the well-being of fathers and their families: relations of care and interdependence.

Despite these outcomes, there has been little discussion of how the enforcement system might be reformed or transformed. The accumulation of debt has prompted some state officials and lawmakers to think more seriously about policies of debt relief, but there has been little movement to reconsider the form and focus of enforcement. There is no clear mandate from the 2016 Federal Final Rule about how states should rethink enforcement; there have been few state-level discussions about reforming the punitive response to debt. In fact, this is one area where I found state officials most resistant to change—even those officials who are responsive to other areas of reform balked when the issue of reforming punishment came up.[24] Except for rumblings in a few locales about the counterproductive effects of driver's license suspension and reincarceration, the enforcement piece has escaped serious analysis and scrutiny.[25]

As I have shown throughout this chapter, state officials and politicians avoid reforms to enforcement at great peril. Debt accumulation and enforcement are intricately linked: as debt worsens, enforcement is amped up. As enforcement is heightened, institutional loops become entangled. And as entanglements deepen, debt worsens further—thus reigniting the cycles. As they remain hidden, these cycles perpetuate the self-fulfilling quality of punishment. They also blind us to how much is lost when fathers cannot socially reintegrate and when reciprocal parental relationships are undermined. The next two chapters turn to those relationships, exploring how men grapple with the system of debt accumulation and enforcement in their lives as fathers.

PART III Indebted Fatherhood

As I circled the county Sheriff's Department complex for the third time, I double-checked the address of my destination: one of Northern Florida's largest prisoner reentry programs, where those convicted of felonies in the Jacksonville area must register soon after their release from prison. As I pulled into the parking lot, I questioned the symbolism of locating a reentry program within a large law enforcement complex. Wouldn't this be the last place someone would want to go after doing time? I entered the office, and more trappings of law enforcement surrounded me—metal detectors and police pat downs, usually reserved for courts and police precincts, were required of everyone. Then there was the sign taped to the entrance door, handwritten in capital letters:

YOU ARE ENTERING AN AREA WHERE THERE ARE CONVICTED FELONS!
INCLUDING CONVICTED SEX OFFENDERS!
USE JUDGMENT WHEN ENTERING!

As the large steel door opened, I was hit by the heavy smell of stale cigarette smoke. The room was jam-packed with men, who all looked up at me as I entered, clearly perplexed and puzzled. From the corner of the room, a small group of men elbowed their way over to me. "You're here for the interviews, right?" one asked. I nodded, and he continued. "I'm Sonny. Is it okay if I go first? 'Cause I gotta get home soon for my kids." We exited the room to even more bewildered stares and retreated to a quiet office. As we walked, I noticed Sonny limping. Lifting up his pant leg, he pointed to the heavy ankle monitor weighing down his leg. "Sorry I'm so slow," he explained. "I'm not used to it yet. It might go off while we talk. Sometimes it goes off when I sleep or play with my kids. Just ignore it."

Sonny began our interview by describing himself as a former "gangster" who was "not always a good guy." Within minutes, he also revealed himself to be quite open and reflective—and struggling. Having spent ten years in prison, he had recently returned to his family and felt overwhelmed. After living in a small cell, often alone in solitary confinement, he now lived with fourteen people in one house. His three kids craved time with him; his partner craved financial assistance from him. Tears started to fill in his eyes as he discussed how much he wanted to make up for lost time with his kids. In prison, he had dreamt about this—of finally being the parent his kids needed. But he didn't have the space to do it. Then there were all the letters from child support and all the money they insisted he owed. The pressure was getting to him. He had panic attacks; he had heart palpitations. Over the course of two hours, we stopped the interview several times not because his ankle monitor went off, but because he had to regain his composure and ability to speak. "Society has this mark on me so it feels like they don't want me back," he explained, sobbing. "But I know I have a role to play in the world, as a father. Man, I know my kids need me. That's what I need to make it."

That day in the Jacksonville area was my first stop on a journey across several states to interview formerly incarcerated men about their lives as fathers—a journey that stretched over three years and took me from Florida to New York to California to talk for hundreds of hours with fathers. Sonny was the first father I interviewed, and his pain startled me. I assumed his willingness to express his feelings so openly was unusual. In the years ahead, I became less startled by such pain. In fact, I came to expect it: fathers were often emotional, particularly when discussing their kids. In retrospect, this should not have surprised me—after all, they had been away from their children, some for long periods, and bottled up feelings of loss while in prison. Still, their emotions do surprise largely because of misguided assumptions about them. Frequently portrayed as hard or insensitive, they are not thought to have complex emotional lives. They are not perceived as caring parents. They are not imagined as committed fathers invested in correcting past mistakes. Unaccustomed to being addressed as fathers, these men often broke down.

Until now, my focus has been on how the child support and criminal justice systems became entangled to push millions of fathers into debt and how fathers then managed the loops of debt accumulation and enforcement. In part 3, I turn to how men coped and responded as parents. These fathers expressed strikingly similar struggles—all of their post-prison transitions were perilous. In fact, few enjoyed the kind of time the term "transition" connotes: without delay, they were hit with all sorts of demands. Fathers who were lucky enough to return to families confronted high expectations from those awaiting their return. Their partners had had to make ends meet without them for far too long, so they wanted to contribute. Their kids had been growing up without them, so they wanted to be present. Fathers wanted to meet all these expectations; they felt like they owed everyone and wanted to come through. And they wanted it to happen without delay. Those without family demands faced other, equally urgent pushes: state parole boards, reentry programs, and transitional services required them to find housing and work. They had little time to recuperate or retool.

Child support added to their sense of urgency. Within weeks, fathers received The Letter, which outlined how much they owed in back child support and how quickly the clock was ticking and interest accruing. Although these fathers insisted that child support was of course their obligation, they questioned the timing. In most states, child support orders spring back to their original amount thirty days after release from prison, leaving parents little time to get back on their feet. This caused fathers' anxiety to spike even higher. While child support officials and judges insisted that this anxiety pushed men to get to work faster and to start paying back child support from the outset, it was the source of enormous stress. "They actin' like I was on vacation," Sonny exclaimed. "Like kicking back and not paying. I was in PRISON, man."

These fathers also spoke vividly about how difficult it was to be a parent behind bars. They discussed their sadness about being disconnected from their children's lives. Emotions were especially fraught for men who had been away for long periods of time and had missed most of their kids' upbringing. Many fathers fantasized about glorious reunions with their kids, but were rarely prepared for the range of emotions their kids expressed. Kids had all sorts of reactions to them: some were angry, some felt neglected, some were attention-starved, and some were withdrawn. No matter what the reaction, their kids needed to be cared for. "I had to earn my space as a parent," Sonny explained. This provoked its own feelings, challenging men's sense of self and identity as parents. Many were simply unprepared for it. No one had told these men they also needed time to heal; no one had instructed them on how to cope with their emotional needs.

Here, too, the urgency of child support debt complicated the transition. With debt accruing and enforcement measures mounting, fathers had little time to regroup. Again, this was the point: to get them into a job, any job, without delay so they could begin to repay. The imperative to work was backed up by looming sanctions, which put competing and conflicting demands on men: courts required them to pay while their kids wanted them to play. Since their kids' demands often expressed themselves as requests for things they had done without for so long, fathers felt stuck. "At one point, I had to choose between buying the Air Jordans my kid wanted or pay the court to keep them off my back," Sonny told me. "Guess who won?"

Most of the men I met expressed this combination of peril and pain. This was true regardless of where they lived, how many kids they had, or how much time they had served in prison. Close to all of them thought child support was an obligation fathers must meet, and their inability to do so only added to their sense of failure. But their responses to this peril and pain differed; their ability to navigate this difficult terrain diverged. So instead of treating these fathers as one group, which I have more or less done up until now, part 3 analyzes differences among them. Some men responded to the constraints of indebted fatherhood in heroic and almost superhuman ways, meeting the many demands on them while caring for their kids in consistent and reliable ways. Then there were those who responded the opposite way: already unresponsive or ambivalent parents, these constraints only prompted them to act in the most stereotypically neglectful ways. In between these groups was the vast majority of fathers—men who had the best parental intentions but who had found themselves entangled in debt and punishment. These men cycled through their kids' lives, fluctuating between feeling committed as parents and overwhelmed as indebted fathers.

The next two chapters chart these divergent paths through indebted fatherhood. Chapter 5 examines two groups of fathers who parent at the extremes: those who behaved like paternal superheroes and those who acted like iconic "deadbeats." Chapter 6 then explores how most fathers actually existed someplace between those extremes, parenting in cyclical ways and forcing their families to withstand the ups and downs of their caregiving. Throughout this analysis, I point to key factors shaping fathers' trajectories, arguing that they have less to do with individual resilience and more to do with men's access to critical social resources. These two chapters, then, add a twist to the empirical narrative I have told until this point. Until now, state institutions have appeared as a force coming down to constrain fathers through punishment and debt. A more complex image of the state will emerge here: one that is both constraining and potentially enabling. Through interactions with the state, men constructed and performed fatherhood, whether by striving to emulate or by rejecting state definitions of good parenting. Through these interactions some fathers were able to carve out valuable resources, using the state to develop into the kind of fathers they wanted to be.

5 The Good, the Bad, and the Dead Broke

The plight of poor, disadvantaged men has been of interest to social scientists for decades. Yet as researchers revealed how poor men struggle for respect amidst discrimination, fatherhood rarely entered the picture.[1] In work on poor women, motherhood always emerges as a controlling image; understandings of the role of fatherhood in the lives of poor men have always been less clear.[2] Social scientists have done extraordinary work to debunk the myth of the "unwed mother"; far less has been done with the stereotypical portrait of her partner—the iconic deadbeat dad.

Over the past several years, however, researchers have begun to focus on disadvantaged men as fathers. Their work has gone a long way toward illuminating the many economic and cultural constraints on men's parenting.[3] From structural economic shifts, to limited paid employment, to wage depression, to educational barriers, disadvantaged men face serious material challenges to achieving their parenting ideals.[4] These same challenges undermine their ability to meet the breadwinning ideal that so many others hold them up to. Social scientists have also exposed the social and community pressures facing poor men as fathers.[5] From the bravado of hegemonic masculinity to the condemnation of the deadbeat, the paternal expectations facing these fathers are as contradictory as they are unattainable.[6] These pressures can make men vulnerable and insecure about becoming the fathers they want to be—which, as sociologist Alfred Young points out, can make men even less inclined to express their paternal struggles and more inclined to withdraw from them.[7] Together, these challenges have led some to conclude that poor men confront a "perfect storm of adverse effects" on their fathering.[8] And this storm is particularly rough on men of color, who have been hit hardest by structural economic shifts, the punitive grasp of mass incarceration, and the controlling image of the deadbeat.[9]

The linkages among economic disadvantage, cultural constraints, and racialized parental tropes are clear, but one link remains less so: how state policies affect men's parenting. Here, too, we have a far better sense of how state imperatives affect poor women and mothers and the social, familial, and community support they need as parents.[10] With fathers, though, it can seem difficult to view their parental behavior as constrained by state policy and to recognize how welfare reform and mass incarceration constrain fathers too. The weight of state imperatives on fathers remains underestimated; their autonomy is overestimated. This can feed stereotypical portrayals of their paternal practices as reflecting only personal choice and resilience.[11]

This overemphasis on men's personal autonomy and resilience is perhaps clearest in "responsible fatherhood" programming, which has been the main governmental response to the challenges of fatherhood. From Bush's 2002 Healthy Marriage Initiative to Obama's 2011 Fatherhood, Marriage and Family Innovation Fund, the approach has been to enhance what Jennifer Randles calls "marital masculinity" and men's motivation to be breadwinners in a changing social landscape.[12] State programs have followed suit, using public funds to encourage men to adjust their paternal behavior. Such programs have marked a shift away from the discourse of the deadbeat but have replaced it with a focus on teaching men to be responsible. Yet, as Black and Keyes so astutely put it, responsible fatherhood is "not simply an individual choice; it is also a socially and institutionally constituted process."[13] This fatherhood programming is not unlike the personal responsibility push that poor women got a decade earlier with PRWORA—here, too, the target is men's behavior as opposed to the policies shaping their lives as fathers.[14]

As previous chapters have made clear, state policies have enormous consequences for fathers who live at the intersection of the criminal justice and child support systems. For them, fatherhood is doubly mediated by the state. The accumulation and enforcement of debt create a common set of mutually reinforcing constraints on their lives. So how do men cope, as parents? Cultural stereotypes lead us to believe there is just one response, that of the absentee deadbeat. Yet I uncovered a variety of responses along a continuum—with those who act as paternal heroes at one end and those who act as iconic deadbeats on the other.[15] This chapter examines fathers at both ends of that continuum, beginning with those who defy all odds to meet their fatherhood ideals and ending with those who seem to reject parenting out of a mixture of anger and pain. These responses were not random or simply the result of individual choice. Instead, they were socially structured and produced, resulting from men's differential access to social, familial, and state resources. Understanding exactly what prompts some men to check in and others to check out as parents thus helps illuminate the challenges of indebted fathers.

It also offers an important conceptual lesson. From their accounts, fathers reveal their complex relationship with the state. It can be one of constraint, as state policies confine their parenting through debt and punishment, but there is more to the relationship than this. Just as fathers engage in boundary work with one another, often mobilizing morally loaded categories to stigmatize one another, they define themselves through the state. Through interactions with state actors, men become motivated or repelled as parents. Through encounters with state constructs of "good" and "bad" fathers, men experience pride in their ability to meet those standards or anger at their inability to do so. Through negotiations with state agencies, men gain coveted parental resources or find themselves resourceless. Thus, the way men conceptualize, conduct, and judge themselves as fathers has an enormous amount to do with state policy and practice.

FATHERING AGAINST THE ODDS

"I don't care what anyone says, I'm not a deadbeat," Mario exclaimed, pounding his fist on our table at a Brooklyn Starbucks. "Since I've been out, I'm showing everyone I'm not like that. I take care of my kids." Mario's sentiment was echoed by many fathers I spoke to. Determined to correct for past mistakes, they wanted to do right by their children, even if they were not always able to. In fact, those who did so consistently were clearly the exceptions, constituting around 20 percent of the hundreds of fathers I encountered through interviews and court observations. The constraints in which these men were enmeshed propelled them to work even harder as parents. As Mario put it, the "problems getting in the way" motivated him to "up his game" as a father.

Some men upped their game in ways that were clearly recognizable and distinguishable. Committed to the category of the "good father," they struggled to model their behavior around it. They were exemplars of how to handle the perils of life at the intersection of the criminal justice and child support systems. Some of these incredibly committed fathers could be found in unexpected places: in homeless shelters and other impoverished environments, men stepped up to transcend the constraints and do right by their kids. In doing so, these men exposed the hurdles facing disadvantaged men as fathers and the pride felt in overcoming them.

The Superheroes

Stereotypes are pernicious for their ability to shape the behavior of those who mirror them as well as those who defy them. So it was with the specter of the deadbeat: it loomed so large for indebted fathers that even those who transcended it for themselves often unintentionally helped to ensnarl others. Fathers who transcended were held out as models by legal authorities. They were the ones who proved that the seemingly impossible was possible. They came to court on time, with all their documents in order. They remained in good standing with parole officers and reentry programs. They never missed court dates. They never missed visits with their kids. And they rarely missed child support payments. "I accrued $53,000 in child support while I was in prison," explained Daniel, a Brooklyn father of four. "But it's not an issue. I gotta pay it, that's for my daughters. I don't have the money to dish out, but I have no choice and I just find a way 'cause that's what they need." Daniel's ability to "find a way" to do it thus haunted other men in the system. "I just had a father in here who's working four jobs and mows lawns on the weekends," Judge Patros scolded a father facing contempt. "Don't tell me you can't do it."

Indeed, these fathers seemed almost Herculean in their ability to weather the storm of debt and punishment. They attacked the storm head on, the way experienced surfers ride the highest waves that come at them. These fathers defied the odds to meet their competing and conflicting obligations. Except for the lucky few with unionized employment, these men worked two or three low-wage jobs. Most worked in the service sector, so one job was never enough. They used wages from one job to pay their child support debt and those from the second and third to sustain themselves. They seemed to devote every waking minute to making money. Like thirty-eight-year-old Barry, who worked from nine to two in a barbershop and from five to eleven as a busboy in a restaurant and whose commute via four buses across Miami added more than three hours to his daily grind. Or Manuel, a father of two whose three service-sector jobs took him to three NYC boroughs each day—and then back to a fourth at night, where he slept in a room he rented. Or Sebastian, a Sacramento father who, despite being homeless for nearly six months after his release from prison, kept current on his child support. "I never missed a payment," he proudly recounted. "They can say a lot of shit about me, but not that.... I'm no deadbeat."

While managing their multiple jobs, these men juggled all the requirements of criminal justice supervision. They had mandatory appointments with parole officers. They had compulsory programs and classes to attend, from job readiness to anger management to substance abuse to domestic violence. They had mandated community service and internships to finish. These obligations have led sociologist John Halushka to call these men "professionally poor," referring to how managing the infrastructure of poverty can become a full-time job.[16] Yet these men met all of the demands of that infrastructure, almost seamlessly.

What's more, they accomplished this while remaining within the boundaries of the law. They worked legally, on the books. When they came to court, they had formal employment to impress judges and wage garnishments to prove their payment histories. "I thought a lot about going back to selling [drugs] to pay down my bill," Mason admitted. "It would be easier.... But I didn't. Then things got better." These men found ways to avoid driving on suspended licenses, thus bypassing the risk of re-arrest. "I lost four or five jobs 'cause I didn't have a clean license," Roman explained. "I almost got to the point where I was gonna lie about it." Instead, men like Roman stuck it out on public transportation, going to and from work with a carefully choreographed transportation route. The unreliability of buses and subways only added to everything they had to manage. This is how Lewis, a Brooklyn father of three, described his daily routine:

> My days start at like eleven p.m. and it ain't over until like seven p.m. the next evening, with the transportation and everything. So I've really been beat. [I work] at Pathmark in Atlantic Center, but the internship place is all the way uptown, almost in the Bronx. Then I leave from the Bronx to come to the other job.... I spend like five hours on the train.

When men like Lewis stumbled, they employed legal survival strategies to get back on their feet. They took on extra hours at work. They found additional jobs. They tapped their familial and friendship networks to find additional ways to earn money. Like Junior, who started to babysit for his baby mama's two other kids: since one was autistic, and the other had ADHD, she was having trouble finding someone to care for them while she worked the early shift as a home health aide. So Junior stepped in after he lost his morning job as a warehouse cleaner. The arrangement also gave him extra time with his own son, which was an added bonus. Others moved in with family or friends to get them through tough periods. They moved into shelters to survive bouts of unemployment. Or they took in roommates to keep living expenses low. One man, Jamal, had all of these living arrangements, moving from transitional housing to family to rented rooms—and then back to family—all in the two years since his release from Rikers. His perpetual movement allowed him to keep up with his arrears payments *and* his support order.

All the while, men like Jamal showed enormous commitment to their children. In between their long commutes to multiple jobs, they made time for their kids. Some insisted on seeing their kids every day, even if it meant getting up extremely early to take them to school or returning home late so they could end their days with visits. Like Roman, who organized his subway commute to his second job so he could see his kids after school and take them to dinner. Others condensed all their work into six days so they always spent one day a week with their kids. "We go to the park, play, eat out," Justin described. "Those days sustain me." Others made a point to call their kids several times a day. Like the Brooklyn father, Diovan, who called his young children each night during his dinner break to read bedtime stories and say goodnight.

Even though money was extremely tight for these fathers, a number of them described setting aside special "daddy funds," which they used on their kids as expressions of love. Some months it was only a few dollars, in which case they would buy their kids small gifts or trinkets. "I always make sure I have a dollar in my pocket in the summer... for the ice cream truck. That's our thing," a Bronx father explained. Other months they saved up more and bought their kids special toys and coveted sneakers or took them to amusement parks. These men often opposed their use of daddy funds with their obligatory child support. They separated the two in ways reminiscent of Vivianna Zelizer's separation of finance and intimacy—one stash was imbued with love and care, while the other symbolized duty and indebtedness.[17]

Amidst descriptions of their strategizing and problem-solving, these men beamed with pride as they recounted details of their kids' lives. The specificity with which they discussed their children was indicative of their devotion. They listed kids' personality traits like a trained psychologist. They knew about the ups and downs of friendships. They knew about kids' hobbies, from what instruments they played to what sports teams they liked. Here's how Tyler described his kids and the time they spent together:

> My son likes me to read to him, to get him to learn more words. I like to take him outside too. He just finished a baseball program. McKenzie, not so much. She likes it when I run in the sprinklers with her. Trying to get her to count now and the abc's.... My son, too, I'm trying to get him to get the reading and writing down as well.... I do this thing where I write two or three words and I read them all. I ask him which one fits in a sentence best. Like how he might say something. And he'll choose one and I'll say if it sounds correct. He loves that.... Then he writes the correct word in the blank line. We do that all the time. And he likes to cook with me after that, after we're done.

Fathers like Tyler often recounted the details of their kids' lives by using props: from pictures of their kids playing sports or hanging with friends to videos of them performing or acting silly. Then there were all the Facebook posts of kids demonstrating a unique talent or expressing love for them. "Every time I spend time with my girl, I just feel good," Jose, a Bronx father, concluded after showing me dozens of pictures of them from his cell phone. "Being around her... listening to her... I just feel good." As Jerry, a Miami father of two, explained: "We guys get real emotion[al] when it comes to our kids. Whenever I need to stay positive, I think of them. When I think I can't go on, I call them. Or I look at their faces on my phone. I remember all our good times. And all this shit I go through is worth it."

These fathers spoke at length about everything they did to address their kids' emotional needs. They took the time to educate themselves about the toll their absence had taken on their children and invested time to help heal these wounds. They tried to understand how parental absence could adversely affect children; they took fatherhood classes to learn how to deal with the resulting emotions and behaviors; they went to counselors with their children to address their feelings of loss, neglect, and anger; and they attended church groups and met with their pastors to come up with ideas for how to encourage children to express their feelings. Lamar, a Bronx father, even made a series of videos so his two sons could express their pain and anger toward him in ways they could not do directly. As he described it:

> Those videos were real hard to do. Hearing my sons get mad at me and telling me how messed up they were 'cause of my mistakes.... But they were part of the healing for us. It made me listen to them. To cry with them.... It gave them the space to tell me things they [were] holding in. On camera, they could say things to me that they couldn't say straight up.... Now we have those videos to look back on and to show to others. So others can learn from them.

When child support judges used these men as models in court, they made their lives look easy—as if managing everything coming at them was just a matter of personal commitment. Yet when I looked inside their actual lives, it became clear why only a minority of men could juggle what they did: it was exceedingly hard. It was also clear that their ability to do so was largely dependent on support systems. While these fathers could seem superhuman, they were able to manage the matrix of indebted fatherhood with some interventions. In large part, these were the same interventions that eased the reentry process overall: social and familial support. But for those who made the transition while living at the intersection of criminal justice and child support, these supports became all the more essential, especially those coming from state and public programs.

For some fathers, the key support came from a reentry program. These state programs provided them with concrete skills to help them with their job searches. They assisted with child support orders and debt. They gave men access to mentors, many of them themselves formerly incarcerated, to provide advice and encouragement. When I asked Sonny to tell me about the best father he had known, he didn't hesitate: "Mr. Burns, the office head at Gulf Coast [reentry program]. I never had no other fathers, no Dads. But Mr. Burns was that for me. He watched over me. He checked on me. He gave me advice.... I call him when I get upset or think I might slip up. He's the best." As Sonny indicates, these programs offered guidance on how to navigate the reentry process as well as legal advice about their criminal and child support cases.

Spots in good state programs were hard to come by. As John Halushka has shown in his study of the plight of the professionally poor, these programs guard their coveted connections for a select few—they are not usually for men with the messy entanglements of incarceration and debt.[18] Yet when fathers did secure spots in state programs, they could be transformative. This was especially true for men incarcerated for long periods of time and released without support systems. Ali, a Bronx father, had been incarcerated for nineteen years and paroled to an area where he no longer had family or friends. But, as he once joked, he had the "good fortune to find Fortune"—a large reentry program with resources and networks. Ali was unusual in his determination, having obtained both a high school diploma and a college degree while in prison. When he was referred to Fortune upon release, he ran with it: he used them to secure a job as a mentor in a state-funded project and a small apartment in Fortune's transitional housing complex. He also worked with their legal department to modify the massive child support debt he had accrued for the decade of public assistance his daughter received. Then, with the encouragement and mentoring of Lamar, he reached out to his daughter and began to form a relationship with her. As he explained, his "new start in life" allowed him to reconnect with her: "I would have never had the courage to contact her if my life wasn't together. Now I can proudly go to her and see her. I can show her I got my shit together.... I don't have my head down anymore. And that's all thanks to this program."

Then there was Tyrice, a mentee of Ali's, who credited Ali with his own transformation from (in his words) "gang banger to stable suit." Tyrice had a long gang history, which started in his early teens when his father went to prison and his mother passed away. "I had nothing to live for," Tyrice explained. So he sold drugs and fought. He fought a lot—on the streets, in school, in jail. Eventually, he picked up a two-year sentence for assault, which he served at Rikers. "I fought every single day of that sentence," he recalled. "The CO knew I was a Blood.... He could see from my marks [tattoos]. He wanted to fuck with me, so he put me in another block.... And I fought every single day I was in. There was not a day without a fight." Tyrice pointed to the scars covering those parts of his body not colored with tattoos to prove he was not exaggerating.

When he came out of Rikers, he was determined to change. Referred to one of Ali's groups, Tyrice knew he had struck gold. They hit it off, and Ali mentored him almost like an AA sponsor. They spoke every day. Whenever Tyrice felt a pull back to his old ways, Ali stepped in to deter him. Together, they set out a path for him: a job working with a state program for youth transitioning out of gangs and an apartment away from his old neighborhood. Ali also introduced him to his own mentor, a professor who worked with Tyrice to get him enrolled in college classes. A key part of the path Ali laid out for Tyrice involved reconnecting with his seven-year-old son. So, despite a contentious relationship with his son's mother, Tyrice took his son every single weekend. He devoted himself to being the kind of father he hadn't known until late in his life. As Tyrice explained when I asked him who was the best father he had ever known: "My mentors, man. They taught me everything.... Mostly, they taught me to be a father myself. What it means to be present. To show up. To be a role model. 'Cause they were all those things for me. Without them, I'd still be in Rikers. I'd still be fightin' every day. Without them, I'd probably be dead."

For other fathers, the necessary support came from family members. To be more precise, it came from female kin who helped stabilize them after prison. As described in previous chapters, these relationships can be difficult to sustain given all the pressures on them. But for those who did manage them, familial interdependencies were invaluable. Female kin provided a safe, secure home base from which men could put their lives back together. Having a place to live gave these fathers the time to find employment, even if it meant spending extra time in work readiness and retraining programs. These home environments were conducive to childrearing, which also made it more likely that men spent time with their children. Because female kin frequently served as the familial link to men's children during incarceration, it was natural to extend the link after prison. Since these women already knew their children so well, they could advise fathers about how to reconnect with them. They knew about kids' hobbies, interests, and problems and what fathers could do to address them all. As well as how to smooth over conflicts with the kids' mothers in order to keep their relationships as stable as possible.

Quite frequently, this meant paying fathers' child support until they were able to do so. It was not uncommon for female kin to take on men's child support payments as they transitioned from prison. They did this to keep men out of legal trouble and outside the enforcement assemblage outlined in previous chapters. "I am sure she's tired of payin' my order," a Miami father of three once explained to a judge who asked how he paid his child support with no job. "But her doing it keeps things cool with everyone." Or as Juan, a Los Angeles father of two, described his mother's help: "She is my everything. She is the reason I am still here today. And why my kids are with me. I thank the Lord every day for her."

In addition to female kin, female partners were key to these men's fatherhood formula. As has been shown continually in research on prisoner reentry, female partners are essential to men's reintegration after prison, helping keep them afloat through battles with poverty, unemployment, addiction, and depression.[19] So it was for formerly incarcerated fathers. But for these men, it was not just any partner: it was best if she was a partner with some financial stability. This stability could come from a secure job with benefits. Or from secure state assistance, such as a disability pension, social security benefits, public housing, or a Section 8 voucher. All of these resources provided much-needed material support, cushioning fathers so they avoided reverting back to illegal strategies to manage their material entanglements.

Such material stability was all the better if it came with emotional stability—ways of grounding men so that they were not overtaken by the waves of fatherhood. Perhaps one of the best examples of this was Malcolm, an Oakland father of two who had been incarcerated for more than a decade. While in prison, one of his cellmates introduced Malcolm to his sister, Melinda, who was getting her Ph.D. at the time. They became close and eventually married during his incarceration. Malcolm attributes his ability to survive prison to Melinda. Her support became even more essential upon his release: she not only helped him deal with the practicalities of reentry but also helped him stay balanced. "She gives me perspective," Malcolm beamed. "She knows what I'm going through, so I can go to her when things seem like too much. . . . And she makes me laugh all the time." As Diovan, a New York father who had spent much of his life going in and out of prison on drug charges, described his partner: "My significant other . . . she's been great support to me. She encourages me . . . not to pick up [drugs] no matter what happens in my life today. And that helps me. It gives me encouragement. Doing the right thing is important to me. . . . I don't want to go back to that life. She's depending on me to get my life together. To be a responsible man and father."

Or as Kingston described his wife, who had stayed with him during and after his long sentence and raised their son, who had been conceived while on a conjugal visit:

> Now, my wife. My god, she's everything, everything to me. She stayed with me. Now she does this, does that. She open[s] up bank accounts for me. Everything. Now all I want to do is get a job and help her. She don't need my help, she's strong as shit. But I just finally want to show her that I'm a man too, I can help her too.

The gender politics of placing so much responsibility on the shoulders of women is complicated. This burden has taken an unquestionable and unrecognized toll on women. It is a toll that has yet to be tallied up as women cover many of the costs of mass incarceration and sort out the challenges of post-prison fatherhood. Yet the harsh reality remains: finding women to assist with reentry is transformative.[20] None of the superhero fathers I met were making it on their own; few were doing it without some kind of female support. In a world where caregiving is privatized, men's ability to be supportive and nurturant fathers depended on access to female support and nurturance. Without them, the need for state resources became all the more pressing.

Fathering by Wraparound Team

It was a hot July afternoon in Los Angeles, and I had come to South Central to interview Benito, a father of two young boys. As I buzzed his building's intercom for the third time, I peered into the interior courtyard encased in layers of gates and bars, thinking about how similar it was to the community-based prison for mothers I had researched years earlier.[21] Just as I was about to give up, Benito came rushing through the first set of doors, accompanied by a woman in a suit. Large and muscular, Benito apologized nervously for scheduling our interview for the time of his "maintenance" meeting. "Well, luckily you didn't need much maintenance today," the woman in the suit commented while exiting. "But I'll be back tomorrow."

As we entered his building, we walked by a group of kids playing soccer in the courtyard. "They're mine," Benito said, pointing to the two youngest boys. Through several more metal doors and security gates, we reached his apartment. Toys were strewn throughout, and kids' clothing and diapers covered the well-worn, institutional-style furniture. Benito explained how proud he was to have his own place and to give a home to his boys. He also knew how fortunate he was to have this chance. It was rare for fathers like him, with histories of substance abuse and long rap sheets, to have the opportunity to parent. But his transgressions actually paled in comparison to those of his sons' mother: also plagued with addiction problems, she had hooked up with a notorious drug dealer who abused both boys. One day the abuse turned to torture when the boyfriend took a cigarette to the youngest boy's genitals. The incident was horrific enough to make it onto the local news. The mother and boyfriend went to jail and the boys to foster care.

The news about his son reached Benito in prison while he was preparing to be paroled. At that moment, he realized he couldn't continue his disappearing acts and absentee routine:

> I went to the [prison] counselor and was like "I don't want my kids to go to foster care. What do I gotta do?" I was ready to do anything. She's like "You gotta drug test in the next thirty minutes. If you're clean, we can try to get

them back." So I went down and I drug tested. Then they said, "Start enrolling in services right now." So in the next week I was released and enrolled in all these services.

With this, Benito and his sons became enmeshed in an array of case management services. Realizing how vulnerable Benito was as a father, city officials found space for him in this transitional housing complex, which had child welfare and child care services on site. They put him on public assistance and food stamps. His days were spent weaving his way through a labyrinth of mandatory meetings and appointments. After getting the boys to school, Benito devoted himself to his own services. To keep his boys, Benito had to comply with a series of mental health requirements: mandated individual counseling for PTSD; required AA meetings with his sponsor; frequent drug testing; compulsory domestic violence counseling; and obligatory meetings at Project Fatherhood, a not-for-profit group for disadvantaged fathers. After school came all the boys' services: individual counseling and family counseling together. "Then we're doing that counseling where the lady you saw comes and we play," Benito described. "It's called PTS or something. To be real, I can't keep track of all the names of everything."

So there was Benito, only a few months out of prison, and fathering on his own. Or, more precisely, fathering amidst a constant stream of women in suits, who were both monitoring him and assisting him. Benito calls this collection of services his "family maintenance." But he also considers himself to be parenting "on his own." He attends meeting after meeting and gets his sons to everything required of them. The only thing he does for himself is to lift weights, which he claims keeps him strong for his new life as a father. Actually, Benito considers fathering his job now. As he explained to his former employer:

> He [former boss] was getting mad. He'd say "don't all these social workers understand you have a job to do?" Finally, I told him this *was* my job. He got it. He was like, "You know, you need to go take care of your kids. I'll find someone else. Call me when you can." Now I'm taking care of my kids . . . It's my job.

Benito also realizes this new job is full-time and requires lots of "family maintenance." He wants to get it right this time and believes he needs all those women in suits to do it. "I'm gonna continue to do their services forever if I can," he concludes. "Even when it's not required. 'Cause it doesn't mean there's not pain any more. I'll keep helping my kids."

When we think about "good fathers," men like Benito rarely come to mind. Given his long criminal record and large child support debt, on paper he seems like the stereotypical image of the "deadbeat." In reality, Benito was an unquestionably caring, committed parent. He was parenting under the worst possible conditions—in poverty and with extremely traumatized kids. Yet he had stepped up as best he could to help his kids navigate the many pitfalls in their lives.

Benito was not alone here. I encountered many fathers who parented under the most untenable circumstances but remained committed caretakers: men who were homeless and lived in shelters or drug rehab facilities yet persevered as fathers. A group of these fathers even formed a support network through Project Fatherhood, a Los Angeles public program that Benito credits with keeping him sane. Their stories reveal what it takes out of these men to sustain their parenting—and what kind of state support they need to plug into to sustain themselves.

For instance, there was Rico, a thirty-three-year-old Latino father of three. Rico was also blind, having lost his eyesight, and almost his life, in a gang-related shooting when he was sixteen years old. Like so many other men, Rico revealed a past of poverty, violence, and addiction. Also like so many others, his past showed on his body. "I may be blind, man, but I know how I look," Rico joked within minutes of meeting me. "All the tattoos and shit. Like a gangbanger, I know. I used to be in the streets, doing bad things. But not [any] more." He spent years getting to this point, securely off the street. Those years were punctuated by a very tumultuous relationship with his sons' mother, who was also a former gang member with a history of substance abuse. They both had severe anger problems that, when combined with drug use, led to vicious fights and numerous stints in prison. After one stint, Rico discovered his kids had landed in foster care, which motivated him to change:[22]

> One day one of the foster mothers told me a story. He [his son] was sharpening a pencil, and she asked him what he was doing. He said he [was] sharpening a pencil so she asked why? He put the pencil to his neck and

> goes, "I don't want to live no more. My dad doesn't love me." That's what people were telling him. They would tell him, yeah, your dad doesn't love you no more. That's why he gave you to us. And he's going to go to prison for life. . . . So that day when I left him [at the foster home], he was hugging me tight. He wouldn't let go, wouldn't let me go.

That was Rico's moment of epiphany, when he realized his lifestyle was hurting his kids. "I said to myself, 'That's it. No more. I need to do good for him.'" He went on a mission to get his kids out of foster care and released to his care. First, this meant showing his commitment and visiting them at least twice a week. And that meant a day-long commute across Los Angeles:

> At first, I used a disabled taxi to see my kids. But that got expensive since all three of them were in three separate foster homes. My daughter and my baby son, over there in an agency in South [LA]. My older son on the other side. So I started using the taxi and bus. I would leave from here at eight in the morning to take the taxi to Union Station. Wait at Union Station until I caught my Metrolink that would take two hours, to take me to Palmdale. Then catch a taxi from there to the other agency. Saw my kids for an hour. Then the Metrolink to the other agency to see my son for two hours. Then go back to Metrolink, take a taxi back to the metro. Then the metro wouldn't come till 6:00. From 6:00 to 8:00, I would get to Union Station at 8:00 or 8:15, wait there for my taxi to pick me up and take me home. I would get home at 8:45.

He did this trek twice a week, while also returning to school. With the help of a social worker, he found a nearby school for the blind and eventually graduated with an Associates Degree. "I got good at computer classes," he explained. "So good that I got accepted for another school, a BEP program, Business Enterprise Program." He was planning to take the entrance exam when he discovered that two of his kids would be released to his care. His social worker then told him to take some time off from school to be a full-time parent to his kids, which is what he was doing at the time of our interview. Like Benito, he devoted himself to parenting and to organizing the many aspects of their care. Indeed, one of the most moving aspects of Rico's account was how attentive he was to his kids' needs: he told detailed stories of their distress and everything he was doing to help them heal. He was most concerned about his eldest son who, at six years old, had experienced enormous trauma. "I have him in lots and lots of therapy," Rico explained. "Because he went through a lot, you know? Terrible stuff. He's the oldest one, he saw the most." With their mother incarcerated, it was up to Rico to do it on his own, more or less.

Like Benito, Rico relied on a collection of state services and service providers to parent. For Rico it was a team of helpers, which he referred to as his "wraparound team." Part of the team assisted him as a blind man: they found him an apartment that accepted his disability rent subsidy. They helped him pay for its upkeep and for a cleaner once a month. His disability pension, while small, kept him afloat. He had subsidized transportation and vouchers for what he called the "disabled taxi." He also got legal assistance that led to the temporary suspension of his child support payments while his kids were in his care. The other part of his wraparound team was there to help his children as "at risk" youth. They included state counselors, therapists, and child welfare workers, who all dealt with different parts of the children's lives. They also helped the children get to school, receive tutoring after school, and go to camp in the summer. It was this combination of state funds and services for both Rico and his kids that made their life possible. All the pieces were critical to holding his fatherhood puzzle together.

Then there was Marty, a big, boisterous white father of two living in East Los Angeles. Although Marty was only in his mid-thirties, decades of drug abuse made him look much older—as did the other signs of his hard-knock life. As soon as we sat down in a Subway shop, Marty mentioned the film. "Have you seen it?" he proudly asked. "The director got real famous after she made it. . . . It's all about me and my wife." Marty beamed as he pulled up the film trailer on his phone. Never mind that it was actually a documentary chronicling the despair of addiction, especially for those with children. This was Los Angeles, after all: what mattered most was that someone made a film about him.

But the film did not capture what was perhaps Marty's most major accomplishment: after decades of drug use, he got clean. It took years of going in and out of public rehab programs. It also took leaving the mother of his kids, a woman he still loved but who was still addicted to drugs and alcohol. "I realized it was her or the kids," he explained to me with tears in his eyes. "She wasn't gonna quit. The kids were taken all the time by others.... First her family and then CPS." When the latter got involved and took his two kids to foster care, he arrived at his moment of awakening. He claims he couldn't bear the thought of his daughter and son, who had been diagnosed with special needs, growing up in institutions. "That was not gonna happen to my kids," he exclaimed. "I was gonna stop the shit... for them."

Two years clean, Marty was raising his daughter, Mandy, on his own. A precocious and sassy ten-year-old, Mandy had a slew of her own issues. Born addicted to crack, she had physical delays and challenges. Marty devoted his life to getting her through them. She also had learning disabilities, for which she needed tutoring and therapy. He took her to all of these sessions. They were partners and went everywhere together. "The only time I'm not with her is when she's in school," he explained with pride. "But I pick her up every single day." In fact, they were even together during our interview. Mandy insisted on being there, eating her Subway sandwich and playing on Marty's phone while half-listening to our conversation. Occasionally, she chimed in with comments like "Yeah, that was terrible" or "I remember when that happened, it was awful."

When Marty went to the bathroom, Mandy pulled her chair next to mine to put in her two cents. Perhaps fearful that I was a social welfare official in disguise, she made a few things clear:

> My Dad is the best. He does everything for me.... Before I lived with him, things were really terrible. Sometimes I was with my grandparents but they were so mean. Sometimes I lived with people I didn't even know.... I don't want to go back to that, not ever. Please, I will do anything to stay with my dad 'cause he really loves me the most.

Unlike Benito and Rico, Marty did not have a vast support team to rely on. Instead, he cobbled together all available state resources. He received public assistance, disability benefits, and food stamps. He rented out a spare bedroom in his apartment to acquaintances. "But only if they are safe," he assured me. "I'm not gonna let some pervert into our place." Like Rico, he was able to negotiate a "break" from paying off his child support debt. Perhaps most importantly, he had secured placement in a residential program for his autistic son. Putting him in a residential facility was a heartbreaking decision, but Marty realized that his ability to care for Mandy rested on the placement. It allowed him to focus on raising her and addressing her issues. Since state funding covered the program costs, it freed up just enough money for him to make ends meet. Marty insisted on seeing his son every week, which involved a four-hour commute via a series of buses to reach the boy's facility. This was their Sunday routine, which Marty and Mandy did together.

There are many other fathers like Benito, Rico, and Marty—men living in the most difficult of conditions but who did their best to overcome them. Like Eduardo, a sole father who came to our interview with his three-month-old son, who had been born addicted to drugs. This prompted Eduardo to quit his job and become a full-time parent until his son's health stabilized. Or Randy who, despite his homelessness, made his way to state-subsidized family counseling three times a week. While their situations were all different, one crucial thing united them: all of these men lacked the familial support systems that other superhero fathers had. They did not have female kin to support them. None of them had female partners to rely on. Actually, it was the absence of women in their lives that gave them the opportunity to parent full-time. These fathers were permitted to step in and caregive because their kids' mothers could not; they were offered state services because of the missing women in their lives. They thus depended on public support to grapple with their kids' problems. All of the individual will and resilience could not solve those problems. They needed actual resources. That's where the women in suits came in.

As a metaphor, the women in suits point to an interesting twist in state politics of the family. In many ways, these women act parallel to the paternalism the state has expressed toward man-less women for decades—a paternalism that led some scholars to deem the state patriarchal and male-dominated.[23] The female wraparound team signifies a reversal of roles. Instead of intervening to replace fathers or husbands, they stepped in to sustain women-less men who are caring for extremely vulnerable children. As has been the case for sole mothers for decades, this assistance is always double-edged. It weaves together support and surveillance, as Mandy's comments in defense of her father made clear. Yet these state services also fill a real void for fathers. Despite public stereotypes about their need to take individual responsibility, what these fathers really needed was a wraparound team to form around them. Despite calls for them to "man up" and make better choices, what these fathers really depended on was access to family maintenance to prop them up.

Just as these men reveal the paternal success that can come with public services and support, another group of fathers exposed what can happen without such support.

UNAPOLOGETICALLY ABSENT

Social scientists who conduct research with disadvantaged groups often confront a dilemma: fearing that our research might feed stereotypes of those we study, we can be tempted to downplay their unseemly qualities. Ethnographers are at particular risk here since we often get to know those we study in all of their complexity—from the good to the not-so-good aspects of their lives. So we can find ourselves trying to debunk myths about them and emphasizing their good intentions amidst what seems like bad behavior. Or we can find ourselves unwittingly censoring what we reveal to avoid undermining our subjects' struggles for respect. Yet doing so is a disservice to everyone. It leaves us with empirically inaccurate accounts, besides holding our subjects to an idealized model of goodness that few can meet in reality.[24]

I grappled with these issues as I contemplated how to write about the men at the other end of the fatherhood continuum: those who acted as undependable and uncommitted parents. I stress "acted like" because I am leery of categorizing them as a *type* of father based on limited observations of their actions. That said, they clearly exhibited neglectful parental behavior. They are the fathers we hear so much about in the media. The male equivalent of the iconic welfare cheat, they are the specter that haunts all men in the child support system. When child support judges "trap" one, they hold him up like a hunting trophy. They are the men for whom all the criminal justice and child support punishments are designed. They have long rap sheets and even longer child support enforcement files. They have many kids from multiple women, few of whom they see regularly. Yet they are a minority of the men caught in the system, representing at most 10 percent of the thousands of men I encountered in court and in interviews. Analyzing their parenting, or lack thereof, provides a window onto the underside of indebted fatherhood.

While there is no typical absentee father, those who acted in this way rarely looked like the images plastered around in "most wanted" posters. This was true in at least two ways. First, these fathers tended to be slightly better off financially. They were not well-off, but neither were they destitute. They usually had some form of work, albeit low-paid, which meant they had some material resources. Indeed, it seems it was their material resources that fueled their sense of entitlement and indignation, as well as their perpetual insistence that their rights were being ignored and violated. Their financial standing also meant they were usually ineligible for public assistance and thus did not have access to wraparound services of the sort that benefited fathers like Benito and Rico. This further triggered their resentment and sense of victimization.

This leads to the second way they defied the stereotypical image: these fathers were more likely to be white. While the majority of fathers I interviewed and observed were men of color, that was less true of this group.[25] This is not to say there was a causal connection between race and parental neglect, or that white fathers were somehow more neglectful.[26] That said, fewer black fathers claimed to have checked out of parenting entirely or had withdrawn completely from their kids' lives. Fewer black fathers expressed the indignation and entitlement to their children that underlaid the rage of this group of men. Even fewer black fathers expressed the kind of rights talk linking finances, control, and access that was so characteristic of men at this end of the parenting continuum.

Indeed, these fathers were a small yet loudly vituperative bunch. They all felt angry and wronged. While those who behaved as paternal superheroes used the good/bad father distinction to model their parenting, these fathers seemed repelled by it. In court, they acted in the most belligerent and adversarial ways. In fact, it could take months, even years, to get them into court at all. In New York, where the rules for serving legal papers are rigidly enforced, it seemed impossible to hold them accountable. They slipped out of sight when court servers showed up; they changed addresses without notification; and they left jobs to avoid paying child support. When they did end up in court, these men appeared noncompliant, even cynical, toward the entire process. Some refused to provide basic information about their income or family life. Others defiantly ignored the maze of rules swirling around them, expressing rage when any sanction was imposed on them. None of this behavior freed these men from the power of the state systems they lived under. These fathers accumulated debts and arrest warrants, which only made them go missing for longer periods of time and deepened their anger and rage.

While all these fathers had plenty of anger to spread around, the targets varied. That said, their two main targets were "the system," as embodied in state officials and judges, and women. In other words, their rage was aimed at precisely those figures the previous group of fathers looked to for support. And while superhero fathers harnessed familial and state resources to support their children, these fathers ended up letting their anger at those same figures detract from, or spill into, relationships with their children.

"Fight the Power"

Given the breadth and depth of child support enforcement, it should not be surprising that many fathers insisted the system was out to get them. While they weren't quite sure what constituted the system, they were positive it was against them. The system was thus a metaphor for all forms of state power they encountered, from caseworkers to support magistrates to policy-makers to the local police to prison officials. Indeed, men referenced all of these state actors when discussing the system. Quite often, it had taken something from them—their wages had been garnished unexpectedly, their bank accounts had been seized, liens had been placed on their assets, licenses had been revoked, or arrest warrants had been issued for them. Sudden enforcement actions like these knocked them off the ledge and provoked their rage. This anger then prompted them to become noncompliant with all aspects of "the system" and to withdraw from everything related to their child support cases, even their children.

If "the system" became a metaphor for injustice, then judges became a symbol of the system. Fathers put a face on it all, and it was the face staring them down each time they went to court. Moreover, because child support judges and magistrates often "own" a case, fathers usually saw the same official over the course of their case history. This could mean years of interaction. In interviews, these men spent hours describing to me the litany of things done to them by state authorities. Some of their claims were outlandish. Like the Bronx father who insisted his judge had come down extra-hard on him because he was sleeping with his ex-wife: "I could see how they were looking at each other [in court]," he explained. Then there was the Miami father who arrived to our interview with a bursting file folder, full of "documentation" of how his child support judge was out to get him. He pulled out motions that were denied and warrants that were issued a decade earlier, all as evidence that his judge had it out for him.

Yet it wasn't that outlandish for fathers to feel like judges were against them. They didn't have to make up such stories: they had real experiences of humiliation to draw on. These were the fathers that some judges called the nasty names: from scumbags to liars to losers to trash to deadbeats. They were the ones who faced the most extreme interrogations into their priorities, their finances, and their lives. They were the ones who had their worth and dignity questioned at every step and in every court interaction. So just as these fathers used judges to justify their anger, judges used these men to justify all the punitive enforcement. As a California state attorney explained to me when I asked about his expansive use of contempt filings, "They are there to get the really bad fathers on the right path. I use them to force the terrible ones to step up and become responsible . . . and it works about 10% of the time."

Anger toward judges could also be fueled by repeated enforcement actions that knocked them off the ledge one too many times. These men recounted a series of hits that they believed proved judges were out to get them. Like the time one father was "tricked" into coming to court with the promise of a modification, only to be confronted with a contempt charge. Or the time a judge told another father a certain amount would be garnished from his wages, only to have twice the amount withdrawn, forcing him to wait months for a hearing to contest the garnishment, and meanwhile he lost his car, his housing, and his financial stability. Or the time a judge promised a father that his driver's license would be reinstated following a purge payment, yet months after making the payment he was arrested for driving on a suspended license. While it was hard to assess the accuracy of their accounts, men used them to prove that the system was against them. Their rage was guided by a deep sense that judges were engaging in a coordinated effort to destroy them.

Although most indebted fathers agreed that child support judges treated them unfairly, these fathers used such injustice to justify their withdrawal. They withdrew in several ways. First, they did everything possible to withdraw from the court process. They opted to fight fire with fire: they stopped paying support, stopped complying with everything asked of them, and stopped coming to court. For them, public degradation was the last straw, so they disappeared from the process. They did everything possible to duck out and avoid being caught in the punitive net. And thus began a cycle over the course of which these men's behavior seemed to confirm the court's worst expectations of them. That same cycle undermined any chance they might have had to extract the state resources they needed to ease their plight as parents. Instead of prompting fathers to "step up," the judicial punishment prompted them to go underground.

Fathers' angry tirades often pointed to real systemic injustices, from how much their arrears had increased, to how modifications were impossible to secure, to how counterproductive it was to revoke their driver's licenses. But these fathers used the injustice to enter into a battle with the system. They were engaged in a power struggle that seemed to justify their disappearing acts. Never mind that they would eventually get caught, and dragged back into court, having further angered the judges they had tried to evade. They saw themselves as "standing up" for their dignity. Or, as one Miami father sang while he waited for his case to be called: "Fight the power. . . . Fight the powers that be," his rendition of the Public Enemy anthem of the 1990s.

These judicial encounters often seemed like masculinity matches, with both sides refusing to yield. Fathers behaved in the most angry, belligerent ways: fighting with court officials, calling judges names, and refusing to cooperate with court protocol. Judges countered with their own anger and retribution. Realizing their authority was being challenged, they hit back as hard as they could. Of course, these were unequal power struggles, with judges pulling out their large arsenal of reprimands, fines, restrictions, revocations, and jail time. Yet fathers countered with their ability to disappear, which only seemed to deepen the power struggle.

Sometimes these power struggles went on for years. Take Carlos, a fifty-two-year-old Bronx father of five whose battle with one family court judge lasted so long it defied all rhyme or reason. It began shortly after Carlos was released from prison: having served a twenty-seven-year sentence that began in the early 1980s, he came out with a large child support debt for one of his kids. He was hauled into court and put on a payment plan to pay off his arrears before he had even gotten a job. He quickly fell behind on his payments, which brought him back to court. After each court exchange, the judge upped the purge. Then the warrants started coming, and he was arrested and put in jail on a sixty-day child support hold. But that didn't clear his record: over the next year, he accumulated more bench warrants for everything from failure to pay to missing court dates. "I thought the whole thing was cleared with my sixty-day bid," he explained. "But, no, that fucking judge was out to get me." With his debt and warrants accumulating, Carlos's sense of injustice mounted. As did his commitment to system avoidance: he stopped responding to correspondence from child support, and stopped attending hearings.

Eventually, his case had been referred to the sheriff's department. He claimed they set out to apprehend him, tracking his whereabouts and showing up to his apartment at all hours. This ratcheted up the game of cat and mouse, with Carlos taunting the law as flagrantly as he could while law enforcement upped their pressure on him. Carlos described incidents when he'd climb down fire escapes or race down crowded Bronx streets on his bicycle to allude capture. With each escape, he felt energized and victorious—like he had won one against "the system." As he put it: "It's no longer about me and the baby mama. I don't care about her anymore.... This is about me and that judge. He sends the cops out to find me... okay. He threatens me with jail all the time... okay. They'll put me on their 'most wanted list'... okay. And I'll waste their time and all their fucking resources."

When they caught Carlos for the last time, he claimed that more than a dozen cops surrounded his apartment building and snatched him as he snuck out a basement window. "My neighbors thought I committed murder or something," he recalled. "I was like, no, all this for child support." That capture landed him in The Tombs on another sixty-day hold. At over $600 night, it cost New York more than $36,000 to jail him—more than Carlos's remaining child support debt.

When I asked Carlos how often he saw his kids amidst this chase, he sheepishly admitted it had been a long time. With so much energy devoted to evading the law, he had let "other things" slide. He followed up with a justification: "But they [his kids] are older now, they don't need me as much.... And, anyway, that's the judge's fault." With this admission, Carlos pointed to the real cost of these battles with the system: they had become more important than parenting. The power trip had become all-consuming, blinding him to all else, perhaps even his kids' needs. In some cases, these battles even became a way for fathers to dismiss their failure to care for their children. Insisting that judges used kids as collateral, they rationalized their neglect; claiming that the system made them "pay to play," they justified their retreat from parenting. As Ray, a Jacksonville father who hadn't paid support in years, put it: "It seems like I'm expected to pay to see my kids. I have to pay admission for a visit.... They are my kids. I'm not gonna pay to see them. If that's the game, I just won't play... even if that means not seeing [them]."

At their most honest moments, men like Ray and Carlos admitted that their withdrawal came from years of withstanding what they perceived as humiliation by state officials. Exasperated by their inability to keep up with the obligations issued by child support officers and the punishments doled out by judges, they disconnected. Unable to extract the public support they might have needed, they withdrew in anger. Their rage thus emerged from a toxic combination of frustration and humiliation, which overlaid any commitment they once might have had to their parental responsibilities. In this way, while these fathers clearly rejected the state's dichotomous categorization of their fathering, they had nothing to replace it with. They experienced the state as a constraint, and nothing more; they saw no hope of harnessing it for help. So they retreated.

This retreat was made clear to me one afternoon by Fred, a big, burly San Bernardino father of two. After a long day in court, which involved hours of waiting and a heated exchange with the judge over his failure to pay off his arrears, Fred explained to me that he had been tricked into coming to court. He had refused to show up for hearings for months until his caseworker offered him a modification if he came to court. When he arrived, he learned of the bait and switch: he faced a contempt charge instead of a modification agreement. He saw this as further evidence that the system was in cahoots to destroy him. Enraged, he explained:

> You can only beat someone down so many times before they die. You can only lie to someone so many times before they disappear. . . . This system has taken everything out of me. I did try to do the right thing. For years. Now I just say "fuck it." They lied to get me here. . . . I'll never make that mistake again. I will never come back. Catch me if you can.

"She put me on child support"

The faceless quality of the child support system led some fathers to battle with judges. But there was another, more personal face they *could* put on it: their children's mothers. The complex system of state policies and legal sanctions facing men had them searching for someone to blame, which often led them to women. This displacement was partly a byproduct of the way some courts worked. By placing mothers on one side and fathers on the other, the adversarial dynamic was built into these court proceedings. Child support officials were supposedly neutral intermediaries, yet they rarely disguised their goal of getting custodial parents the most money possible. The same was true of judges, who often made no secret which side they were on. Many made long, impassioned speeches about how their role was to protect women. So it is not surprising that the "system" and women became blurred in some men's heads.

The anger this tapped into was often surprising and shocking. Emotions can run high in family court cases. When relationships dissolve, what is left is often a toxic mixture of anger, resentment, and bitterness. The animosity only deepens when feelings of abandonment are real and recent, as they usually are with formerly incarcerated parents. When finances are involved, and when money can act as a stand-in for emotional losses, the situation can become even more heated. And when serious punishments are being doled out in the process, it is easy for things to boil over and for parents to call each other names, make threats, and storm out in fits of rage. The effects of the legal tumult can be as long-lasting as they are consequential.

In the process, men's expressions of rage could turn into raw misogyny.

They mobilized all sorts of stereotypes to buttress their anger toward women. The brutality voiced by this group of fathers could be chilling. The name-calling could get extreme, with men often using terms like ho, whore, and bitch to refer to their kids' mothers. Underlying their rage was an insistence that these women were the source of their legal and financial problems. "She put me on child support," was a common refrain among these fathers. They offered long accounts of how women used the child support system against them, as revenge for everything from infidelity to deceit to jealousy. They insisted that women harnessed state officials and policies to control and reprimand them. In their view, women could somehow use the system however they wanted, pulling the levers and moving the pieces to meet their vindictive ends. This supposed manipulation then justified men's refusal to participate in the entire process.

Such accusations seemed far-fetched and outlandish. They were obviously inaccurate in cases of public debt since, with public assistance payback, women had no say over the process. In order to receive benefits for their children, they had to relinquish their rights to child support and enable the state to claim it. Either fathers didn't know the rules guiding public orders or they didn't care to know. In court, when fathers made conspiratorial claims about the collusion of state officials and women, they were rarely corrected. Instead of using the moment to educate fathers about how the law worked, court officials usually said nothing. Instead of diffusing the anger between parents, many of them let it fester. So fathers continued to insist on their conspiracies while mothers felt unjustly accused, which only exacerbated the conflict between them. State officials required mothers to turn over their right to child support in exchange for public assistance, while men attributed all state actions to mothers. It was a classic case of blaming the victim.

In our interviews, these fathers showed themselves to be completely unaware of how child support actually worked. Unlike court officials, who could leave men misinformed, I asked follow-up questions of fathers: How were child support orders initiated? Who decided when to pursue a case? Who got the funds? Almost without fail, fathers demonstrated a complete lack of understanding of the system. What's more, when answering my questions, they often doubled down on their accusations. "Oh, it was all their mama," Randall exclaimed when describing how a child support order was issued against him while he was in prison. "She was pissed when she heard other [women] visited me.... She was getting back at me." Even after it became clear that his kids' mother had gone on public assistance while Randall was incarcerated, he refused to relent. "I don't care, I know it was her. She was behind it all the way."

As these fathers blamed mothers, they often drew on controlling images of women. The trope of the welfare queen loomed large in their accounts, as they described women who refused to work, swindled the public, and lived high off the system. Over and over again, fathers insisted that it was possible to live well from a combination of public assistance and child support, refusing to acknowledge that one form of support negated the other.[27] They offered up impossible scenarios of women who gamed the system, had multiple kids from different men, and manipulated them all to gain vast amounts of child support and public aid. These scenarios were often coupled with accusations that women were stealing from them, lying to them, and covering up their sources of income. Then there were the claims about how women misused child support funds for their own personal luxuries. As Peter, a Los Angeles father of three, recounted:

> I see her in new clothes every time.... Her nails done. She's got fancy shoes and bags and all. Even a new car last year. Where's all that money coming from? That's what I want to know. She's certainly not using my money for my kids. I want to buy stuff for them directly 'cause I don't trust her to spend anything on them.... She takes it all for herself.

As Peter's comment indicates, fathers frequently used misrepresentations of women to rationalize their own refusal to pay child support. In effect, they used one set of stereotypes to buttress another: the mythological welfare cheat made them act like stereotypical deadbeats. Women's lying, cheating, and stealing became justifications for men's withdrawal from the child support process. In fact, it could even underlie their system avoidance altogether. As one father exclaimed to his girlfriend, as they left a Los Angeles child support hearing: "That bitch thinks she can get me, but I'm smarter.... Smarter than this whole system. I'll go underground.... They'll never find me. I'll never come back here. I'm done with this shit. [They] won't get no money from me, I swear."

It was not just the legal process these men exited from: they also seemed to withdraw from their kids' lives. Their anger and animosity toward women often spilled into relationships with their kids. Such reactions were quite typical of this group of indebted fathers and involved some extremely painful tirades as fathers ranted about children they clearly had no connection to. They unapologetically admitted to knowing next to nothing about their children—not where they lived or how their lives were going. Some conflated their kids and mothers, using "they" to describe both groups. So "they" were manipulative and scheming; "they" only cared about what "they" could get from others; "they" only cared about money. Other fathers insisted that mothers had turned their kids against them, spreading lies about them and teaching their kids to disrespect them. This was particularly true of fathers whose relationships had soured during long prison sentences—and who thus explained away their feelings of loss through anger and blame. "She learned that shit from her mama," a Jacksonville father declared to me when explaining why his daughter refused to see him. "Both of them. . . . They don't have any respect for me."

Given such narratives, these fathers felt justified in neglecting their children. They ignored them. They didn't return phone calls. They blocked them on social media. They stopped attempting to see them. They disappeared from their lives. They formed new families and had new children, without making gestures to include their existing kids in those families. And they insisted that fathering was a perpetual battle with the courts, with mothers, and with children. They saw no way out of those battles. In fact, they claimed to have little interest in seeking the resources or support they might have needed to parent. They just opted out of it all.

Indeed, this was the one thing fathers in this group shared: they were unapologetically absent. While some blamed judges and others blamed women, they all seemed self-righteous in their abandonment. As I discuss in the next chapter, many other indebted fathers also had periods of withdrawal and cycles of disengagement from their children's lives. What made this group of fathers distinct was how indignant they were about their disengagement. It was never clear whether they had always been hostile and disengaged parents or whether their experiences as indebted fathers had hardened them to act as such. Ultimately, it didn't much matter: the child support system provided them with the excuse they needed to behave in ways that were both self-defeating and extremely harmful to their families and children.

THE STATE OF FATHERHOOD

Listening to these fathers echo damaging mythologies of women and justifying their neglect of children, it is hard not to assign personal blame. Or to attribute their behavior to individual choices. The same applies to those who acted as parental superheroes: it is difficult not to view their individual strength and perseverance as all that motivated their committed caregiving. Although there are always individual aspects to behavior, these men's parenting was too patterned to reflect only their personal biographies and backgrounds. In this chapter, I have stepped back from such individualization to expose those patterns. Men's trajectories through indebted fatherhood were also socially structured and produced. They resulted largely from men's differential access to familial and state resources. Those who could harness these resources were able to model their behavior to align with common conceptions of "good" fathering. Their model behavior then afforded them more public and familial resources to support their children. Be it assistance from a state program or a family member—or help from women in suits or a female partner—support begets support. Yet for men who saw these resources as unavailable, models of good fathering became unobtainable and untenable. Their resulting anger then detracted from, or even spilled into, relationships with their children.

For those fathering at the extremes, there was an either/or quality to their parental trajectories. Either men had resources or they did not. Those with resources tended to rely on either private help or public support. In fact, access to one form of support often precluded the other. It was the absence of women that prompted the state to step in; it was womenless men who could parent by public wraparound team. And it was the lack of public programs that made men rely increasingly on individual women. This is yet another way in which the plight of indebted fathers mirrors that of poor women. State policy has always structured disadvantaged mothers' dependencies by tying them to domestic relationships or public programs. Indeed, the history of welfare policy can be read in terms of the private and public dependencies it facilitated.[28] Perhaps what has emerged for poor fathers replicates this dynamic, as their ability to parent also depends on differential access to private and public resources. Perhaps this access is also tied up with state constructions of what good and bad fathering entails.

In this way, there is a larger lesson to be drawn from men's fathering at the extremes. While pointing to the social basis of their parenting in no way absolves them of responsibility, it does expand that responsibility outward. For fathers, it points to the importance of the social context of their parenting and the need to seek out support for it, which some may not be inclined to appreciate. It suggests that fathers recognize the very real dangers of trying to parent without this social support—and that they should be wary of the individualizing narratives of personal resilience that too often distract from the need for social support. And it indicates how fathers can find possibilities in what appears to be an all-encompassing state system of constraints.

For those of us trying to understand the plight of indebted fathers, these experiences may make us more attuned to the extraordinary social accomplishment of those men who defy all the odds and harness the resources to care for their children as they see fit. It can motivate us to fight to keep those resources available, particularly when they seem to be vanishing amidst ongoing welfare retrenchment and state cutbacks. It can also make us more responsive to just how painful it is when those resources are lost or absent altogether—and how this pain may underlie the rage and destructive survival strategies some fathers revert to. Indeed, these lessons become even clearer as we move from men who father at the extremes to the majority of fathers, who parent in more cyclical ways. As I discuss in the next chapter, cyclical fathers not only show that social resources matter but also reveal how and why those resources matter so much for indebted parents.

6 Cycical Parenting

“Well, I am very impressed,” Judge Matthews announces as he reads through the large case file before him. Those words are so rarely uttered by Matthews that they prompt everyone in the courtroom to look up in wonder. Standing before Matthews is Willie Jenks, a thirty-something African American father of three. Willie nervously sways from side to side as Matthews continues reading. “Looks like you’ve got it together.... Your job at Home Depot is full-time now. You took on landscaping work on weekends. Your support is coming in on time. Looks good to me, son. I’m proud of you.” As Willie stops fidgeting and stands up a little taller, the state lawyer chimes in with her own praise, noting that Willie even overpaid on his current support order a few times in the past few months. “This is what we like to see,” Matthews concludes. “A father who takes his responsibilities seriously and meets his obligations.”

As Willie leaves the courtroom, I follow him in the hopes of landing an interview with one of the rare fathers able to elicit praise from Matthews. Since his hearing went better than expected, and his girlfriend wasn’t due to pick him up for an hour, Willie agrees to an interview. “My license is still suspended so I gotta wait for her to come,” he notes. “I’m gonna ask for that [license] back next time.” This surprises me given his seemingly superhero status. "Shit, no," he corrects me. "I've been through hell with them [the court]." Willie then recounts the ups and downs of his child support case, from the times he failed to pay, faced the insults doled out by Matthews, had his bank accounts seized, and served time in jail for nonpayment. His life has only recently been on the upswing, with a new girlfriend and a full-time job at Home Depot. "Man," he concludes, "if you had been here a few months ago, it would've been a different scene."

Willie's comment was an epiphany for me: besides warning me of the danger of categorizing fathers too quickly based on limited observations, it exposed the cyclical nature of so many men's experiences with child support and, indeed, with fathering. Most of the men I encountered rode the waves of fatherhood. At any moment, they could be on an upswing or a downswing, depending on how other parts of their lives were going. In court, attention usually went to those who fathered at the extremes—those who acted as parental superheroes or as absentee dads. But only a minority of these fathers lived consistently at those extremes. Instead, the vast majority fluctuated between them, at times tackling it all and at other times failing at most everything. Most of the time they muddled through in the middle. Just as their child support entanglements operated in circular ways to form feedback loops of disadvantage, so did their parenting: they looped in and out of sight and into and out of children's lives.

I am certainly not the first to notice these waves. Ask any of the mothers connected to these fathers and they are likely to complain about men's ups and downs. Other social scientists have also written about this inconsistency, using different terms to connote the waves of their parenting, from "serial fatherhood" to the "father-go-round" to "daddy-b-gone."[1] Some researchers connect fathering waves to economic waves, by stressing the material underpinnings of men's parenting, while others emphasize their social-psychological and relational roots.[2] They have described how the pleasure of fatherhood can draw men to parenting and offer them a motivation to change, while unrealistic expectations can push them away from their parental roles. They have also explored how men's search for self-esteem and redemption leads them to engage as parents, while their inability to meet others' expectations can steer them away.[3] And they have shown how dominant masculine ideals lead men to feel the need to contribute as parents, while their sense of failure can make them unable to follow through.[4] So while accounts of the father-go-round expose tensions in men's lives as fathers, those struggles are often related to the personal attributes, modes of masculinity, or economic vicissitudes that constrain men from meeting their obligations.

Without question, men's fathering is bound up with struggles around intimacy, self-respect, and masculinity. Yet the state can also underlie these struggles. And men's emotional responses to those struggles can themselves be bound up with larger state processes. While men like Willie may have grappled with fidelity and maturity, his movement into and out of his kids' lives was driven by factors that were not simply personal or social-psychological. Nor were they merely economic. His cyclical parenting also related to how he managed the state constraints that had been placed on his life. He cycled down when his ability to see his children was undermined by the revocation of his driver's license. Or when a stint in jail suddenly cost him his apartment and the wages he relied on to support his kids. These cycles also relate to his harnessing of social resources and support. He cycled up when his girlfriend's ability to drive lessened his embarrassment at not being able to. Or when his shame at having his bank account seized was lessened by a new job that gave him money to spend on his kids and pay their mother support.

In this way, like those men who fathered at the extremes, cyclical fathers' familial relationships were also shaped by state institutions. Their cycles into and out of their children's lives were shaped in part by public policies and provisions. By probing those cycles, this chapter offers a clearer sense of the role played by social resources. While the previous chapter established that social and state support matters to indebted fathers' parenting, this one delves into *why* they matter so much. It explores men's cycles upward, exposing how state actions can give men the confidence and wherewithal to reengage in their children's lives. It then examines men's cycles downward, showing how they are often propelled by new circumstances that create external and internal obstacles to parenting. Although cyclical fathers' lives were far messier than those of "good" or "bad" fathers, they were also patterned: when fathers found resources to bolster and give value to their caregiving, they cycled up. But if all they encountered was blame for what they lacked and failed to provide, they got derailed, and crashed as parents. The first part of this chapter analyzes these cycles and the difficulties fathers had getting off the parental roller coaster.

No matter what the particular motor, these roller coasters had serious consequences for men's families. The cycles fathers rode up and down led to real familial turmoil and exacerbated the distrust that plagued their relationships with women and children. The distrust that mothers feel toward cyclical fathers is well-documented and is made worse by social institutions that foster a sense of powerlessness, suspicion, and neglect in women.[5] Their male partners encounter something similar: as they move through the criminal justice, child support, and court systems, they experience a profound sense of disrespect, injustice, and insult that can become tied up with their identities as fathers. State institutions and policies are thus woven into the fabric of their lives, resulting in cycles of push and pull in their parental relationships. The second part of this chapter charts how cyclical fathering affects women and children and how it often undermines precisely those relationships proven to be essential for familial well-being.

THE WAVES OF INDEBTED FATHERHOOD

In previous chapters, I described indebted fathers' material lives as a tsunami. A similar metaphor applies to their lives as parents: these fathers hit storms so turbulent that even the most financially secure and emotionally stable parent would have a hard time weathering them. While some fathers parented through these storms undeterred, and others jumped ship as soon as they encountered rough waters, the overwhelming majority struggled to stay afloat amidst them. These fathers flowed into and out of their kids' lives, recalling the many times they went missing and the pain those cycles caused. If fathers who acted like heroes were the most inspiring, and those who acted like deadbeats the most cantankerous, cyclical fathers were the most emotional. They often broke down in interviews, crying as they discussed how they missed so much of their kids' upbringing and all the times they disappeared from their kids' lives.

More than any of the fathers I interviewed, these men's lives seemed to be a constant struggle. Staying above water and out of jail was a challenge.

The back and forth of their legal and economic struggles was reflected in the back and forth of their childrearing. While all of these fathers insisted that "doing right" by their kids was important to them, they were having a hard time doing the right thing consistently or reliably. So while the stories underlying the lives of the close to one hundred cyclical fathers I interviewed—and of the hundreds more I observed in court—were all different, there were patterns in what set their cycles off. There were convergences in what lifted them up, pushed them down, and gave their cycles momentum. The impetus upwards came from an opening, however small, that would enable them to care for their children, which then gave them the confidence to follow through. Conversely, downward cycles were triggered by sudden and unexpected hits that shook their sense of worth as caregivers, sending them into a tailspin that undermined their consistency as parents.

On the Upswing and Catching a Break

Interviewing men in the kind of turmoil experienced by indebted fathers could present challenges. These fathers' accounts were not always linear; they jumped around in time and place no matter how hard I tried to keep them on track. They were not always consistent; they frequently mixed up people and places as they accounted for important events in their lives. They were not always believable. Emotionally charged, their accounts could include exaggerations and embellishments. Yet there were also commonalities among their narratives, from the timing of their upswings to the events that triggered an upturn in parenting.

The first set of commonalities involved the timing of men's upswings. As they recounted their good memories as fathers, men usually noted how they involved some sort of opening that gave them new access to their children. They described how positive periods were preceded by the opportunity to parent in a more consistent way. For some, this opportunity took the form of getting back on track with their child support. Once out of the red, they would resurface in their kids' lives with optimism. For others, it was something like having a driver's license reinstated, which could prompt fathers to ask to see their kids. Or it could be an opening afforded by a new housing arrangement that felt child-friendly. All of these opportunities prompted fathers to reach out to their children. "I saw them [his kids] at this family bbq at my cousin's," explained Jonah, who had gone years without seeing his teenage children. "We got to talkin' and things just got better from then on."

Of all the events that triggered an upward parenting cycle, the most common was the end of incarceration. Being released from prison or jail often prompted men to rethink their familial relationships. While incarcerated, most prisoners create long lists of things they anticipate doing post-release: they pine for their first steps outside prison gates, their first meal, their first drink, and their first night with a partner. For these fathers, seeing their kids was high up on this list. Most of them came out of prison ready and eager to reunite with their children. For those who had spent long periods in prison, the time away could provoke a reassessment of their parenting practices. Unlike other familial relationships, which tended to be fraught and riddled with anger or suspicion, their kids held hope and promise. Fathers imbued these relationships with enormous possibility and optimism. They pledged to become better parents; they committed to righting the wrongs with their children. And they came up with all sorts of plans to actualize these changes, some more realistic than others.[6]

The specificity with which fathers recalled the post-release reunions with their children was indicative of their significance. Men remembered exactly when and where they occurred, even what they wore. They remembered what their kids' faces looked like when they saw them for the first time. They recounted what it felt like to hold them. They recalled what they talked about and how their kids' voices sounded. Fathers built up high expectations for these reunions. Rick, a Florida father of three who was incarcerated for seven years, beamed as he recalled:

> That was the best day of my life. Went to a cookout at my cousin's.... Drove over right from Baker [prison]. My kids saw me pull up. They ran to the car, jumpin' all over it till I got out.... They all hugged me at the same time. I think I fell to the ground. They were so big. I remember thinking, "These ain't my kids," 'cause they felt so big when they hugged me.... We spent the day eating and talking and catching up.... The best day of my life.

Clearly, these reunions gave fathers like Rick a parenting high. Yet their ability to turn that high into sustained parental practices depended on other factors. Some factors were practical. Again, fathers were rarely at a loss for plans, but those plans could be unachievable. Catching a break and finding resources to implement their plans were the difference between a momentary upswing and a sustained period of parenting. The state was an important resource here: those fathers who caught a break by getting a new job, an apartment, or the ability to drive often did so by connecting to a state program. It might be a public reentry program that provided coveted job retraining, job placement, or child support assistance. Or a state caseworker who took a special interest in them and their well-being. Or even an occasional judge who stepped in to offer realistic advice as fathers tried to realize their plans to change. As Ralph, a California father of two young adults who had served over fifteen years in prison, explained:

> I was having a hard time... living in the central valley and struggling. There was this one judge down there who helped me. Found a way to parole me up here [in Oakland] to get me away from the negative influences down there.... Even helped me get housing up here, at a Volunteers for America.... Life is still real hard, but being up here lets me see my kids. I'm getting back on track now, so I can be there for them. Hope it's not too late.

For cyclical fathers, finding a stable partner could also fall into the "catching a break" category. This was true for all the expected reasons: female partners could ground indebted fathers materially, socially, and emotionally and thus trigger an upswing in their parenting. Indeed, this is precisely how Jorge, a Miami father of three, talked about his new girlfriend. Jorge moved in with her soon after being released from prison and credited her for "changing everything." In addition to having a Section 8 rental subsidy and a disability pension, she was in recovery, so they supported each other's commitment to staying clean. Although it took a while, they started to fulfill their financial obligations: he kept up with his support payments and started to pay down his debt; he had the liens on their bank accounts lifted and his driver's license reinstated. As things started to look hopeful, Jorge channeled his optimism into his parenting and started to get back on track with his kids, parenting the way he had always wanted to.

When it came to fathering, though, forming new relationships could be tricky. These partnerships could cut into the limited time fathers had for their children. They could provoke a range of emotions in children's mothers, from anger to distress to jealousy. These emotions could evolve into what fathers referred to as "baby mama drama," especially if men failed to handle the tensions carefully and sympathetically. All of this could be emotionally draining, further distracting from fathers' ability to care for their children and families. So although proceeding down this path was fraught, it could also trigger an upswing in men's parenting.

This is what happened to Manny, a Miami father who had served several years in prison for drug dealing and moved in with his new partner, Miranda, within a month of his release. When we met, Manny's year-long struggle to find work had finally ended; he had landed a job as a bouncer at a nightclub. The job was far from ideal for a former drug dealer, given all of the partying it exposed him to. It was also challenging since he worked from five p.m. to three a.m. every day, which cut into the time he spent with his ten-year-old son. This only added to the anger and distrust his son's mother felt toward Manny, which further complicated an already difficult situation. Then there was the new baby he and Miranda just had, whom Manny wanted to spend time with, and whom Miranda insisted he help care for when he was not working.

As we sat on the floor of the bedroom they shared with their newborn son, in a house owned and occupied by Miranda's parents, Manny was feeling both hopeful and woeful. With dark circles under his eyes, Manny explained his mixed emotions and the difficulties he had managing it all. Even so, he insisted that connecting to Miranda had given him a lifeline and improved his parenting. The relationship not only provided him with rent-free housing in her parents' small house but also gave him stable support—someone to care about and who believed in him. Indeed, Miranda seemed exceptionally compassionate and supportive. Much younger than Manny, she acted as the caregiver during our interview, alternating between holding the baby and caressing Manny's arm when he got upset. She also helped him avoid the temptations at his work, calling him at regular intervals throughout the night to remind him to stay clean. This support allowed Manny to start paying back his mounting child support debt, which offset some of the anger his ex-partner felt about his new relationship. Since his older son liked to come over and play with the baby, he used the new family to bond with him. As Manny described:

> Most of all, I regret so much not being there for him [older son]. I missed so much of his life, I feel so terrible.... Sometimes, when I think about it, I panic and my heart races. From all the guilt. I'm just trying to be better now.... I bring him here now to be with the baby. I'm hands on with both of them. My ex tells me it's too late, but I know it's not. She [Miranda] reminds me it's never too late.

As Manny's account indicates, catching a parenting "break" included more than practical help. In fact, when fathers discussed them, the practical benefits were usually secondary. Far more important were how these breaks affected men's confidence in their parenting and the value others ascribed to their parenting. These two factors—confidence and value—seemed to be the real triggers for parental upswings. This is not entirely surprising: most of these men had heard about their failings as parents for years, from state officials and judges and custodial parents. So when they encountered boosts to their confidence and value as fathers, they felt emboldened to follow through. They began to insist they had the ability and the right to be caregivers. The acts that prompted such realizations could be big or small, and they could come from people they didn't know or those they were extremely close to.

The big gestures had predictable effects on men's confidence as fathers. When men found supportive partners who encouraged their parenting in ongoing ways, they reported that their self-assurance soared. This is what Miranda did for Manny. It was also what Malcolm, an Oakland father, got from his partner. After serving years in prison, he came out uncertain about his value as a father. But he was also committed to his kids, insisting that they needed him to be present and supportive. His partner helped with his confidence: she talked to him about his insecurity, accompanied him to church services on fathering, and made room for his children in their life. Her support was a major factor in Malcolm's renewed connection to his kids:

> I know how to be a good daddy.... I did all the things I needed when I was in prison. I was there for my kids, when I was away. Since getting out, life can get hard. I kinda lost focus... got myself distracted from my kids. But she [his partner] helps me get back to what's important. She reminds me that I am a great daddy and I know how to do this.

Gaining access to a good reentry program could have similar effects. Fathers frequently claimed to get a major boost from the resources provided by such programs. Their casework services offered fathers help managing the legal demands of indebted fatherhood and thus the hope of more space for their parenting. Job training programs provided fathers with help finding work that paid a living wage, which boosted their confidence that they could sustain a renewed focus on parenting. This was what happened to Alex, a father of two, when he got Gulf Coast, a Miami reentry program, to get him into their coveted work program and to pay for his training as a forklift operator. Suddenly the possibility of future union employment came into view, with all its benefits and security. Yet what he found so important about this opportunity was its message about his worth and importance, both as a potential worker and as a parent: "They believed in me.... It wasn't just a bunch of empty promises... about how great it was that I cared about my kids. They got me into a program, put the money in to get me training. That said something to me. They believed in me."

Such confidence could also come from small acts than might seem inconsequential. Yet fathers talked about them as quite meaningful. Encountering one person in a sea of faceless bureaucrats who recognized and valued them was momentous. As was finding someone in these enormous state systems who reached out to confirm their parenting struggles. Again, it could be a child support official who spent a bit more time helping them navigate through the maze of rules and regulations guiding their orders. Or a caseworker who offered a sympathetic ear instead of lecturing them about their failings. Or a child support judge who engaged in a small act of recognition. For instance, California's Judge Robinson regularly provided fathers with these glimmers of hope. She began her hearings by thanking both parents for coming to court and trying their best to care for their children. She asked both parents what they needed to meet their parenting ideals and listened intently to their answers. As she explained to me: "My job is *child* support, which means community support. Which means parenting support. I work with them. I have them come back. I want them to come back so it's important that the court experience is not a terrible one for them."

Indeed, one good interaction with an official like Judge Robinson could alter a father's course. In her court, fathers stood up a little taller and lifted their heads a bit higher, emboldened by how she listened. "She made me hopeful that maybe someone in power would get it," a father explained after an appearance in her courtroom. Other fathers who did not have access to a Judge Robinson recounted how consequential it was when they encountered state officials who "got it." When they felt heard, they felt more confident as parents; when they felt respected, they felt their caregiving was appreciated. All of this could trigger a surge in fathers' commitment as parents, with some riding these highs back into their kids' lives—resurfacing and reengaging with their children, even after long absences. As Gerard, a Florida father of six, put it:

> People think it's all about the money. But it ain't. My kids raised me and they taught me they need *me* and not the money I might bring. It's mostly about the time and the care and the nurturing we give. When I can remember that, I am a good parent. When other people can see that too . . . and respect it and not take it away from me . . . then I'm a really good parent. That don't happen much, but when the system lets me be one [a good parent] and doesn't take me away, I'm good.

While state officials could provide the validation needed to trigger an upswing, it was also powerful when it came from children. Over and over again, fathers revealed that gestures from their kids were the parenting opening they most hoped for. The smallest gesture could be interpreted as an opening, like an Instagram post, a voice mail, or a text. Given the layers of guilt and regret that encased these relationships, fathers proceeded with trepidation and nervously questioned their role in their kids' lives. As Kendrick, a Bronx father, described seeing his daughter after years:

> I was nervous. I didn't know what to expect. . . . In my mind, I imagined things to be like it was before I left. She still smiling, I can still talk to her. But it wasn't like that. She sat in front of me, we were eating at the food court. I'm watching this little girl, watching her eat and not say a word. . . . I didn't know what to do. I was lost. I was really, really lost as a parent. I was so nervous.

Many fathers described testing the waters with their kids to see if they were open to reconnecting. Birthdays and Father's Day offered excuses for these tests, with fathers sheepishly reaching out to children. If they got a response, fathers' confidence could surge to launch them through the opening and back into their kids' lives. Jermaine, another Bronx father, explained his elation at his son's openness to getting together after years of no contact: "He would not see me for so long. He was so angry, really mad at me. But I did not give up. Then one day he just said yes. That he would see me.... I was shocked but it was like the heavens opened up. And light came shining down on me." Then there was Lee's description of how he used Facebook to test the waters with his daughter:

> I didn't know if she missed me... if she even cared for me. When I got out [of prison], I first posted something on Facebook to let everyone know I was out.... But really it was for her... so she knew I was out. We started communicating [through Facebook], liking posts and things. We always liked the same things.... So we started talking on there. Then by text. Then in person.

Yet just as these exchanges with their kids could be especially reaffirming, they could also be uniquely devastating. Fathers often placed so much significance on them that they could not withstand the weight. Just as a small gesture could strengthen a connection, an equally small act could make it slip away. Rahem, a Brooklyn father of two, expressed this precarity and the slide from a parenting upswing to a downswing: "I feel most proud when my kids say I love you. I feel most calm when I'm around them. But then I feel the worst when I can't care for them... in the ways a daddy needs to.... The guilt just overwhelms me. And I just can't be around them when I'm like that."

On the Downswing and Breaking Apart

Indebted fathers were accustomed to managing state punishment. They always seemed on the cusp of being taken down by its waves or its undertow. Just as there were patterns in fathers' ability to withstand the pull, there were commonalties in what submerged them. Like fathers on the upswing, those on the downswing did not always go under because of the size of the waves: many fathers managed the big hits, like job loss or reincarceration, with their parental relationships intact. But other waves had disastrous consequences for them. And this seemed related to the timing of the waves and their effects on men's sense of themselves as parents.

First and foremost, waves that hit all at once seemed more devastating. Social scientist Marie Gottschalk writes that the civic and economic turmoil experienced by formerly incarcerated men tends to be revealed incrementally, over time; as they attempt to reintegrate into social life, gain employment, or vote, the depth of their marginality becomes apparent.[7] When it comes to those who are also indebted fathers, problems tended to strike suddenly and in clusters. It often started with The Letter—that is, official notification of how much fathers owed in back child support and how quickly those orders needed to be repaid. Some fathers were unaware they had child support orders accruing while in prison, so these letters hit them hard. Others were unprepared for how much their debt had grown and how it was going to mean seized bank accounts, suspended driver's licenses, and large wage garnishments. Then there were the court dates, where they came face to face with the condemnation that accompanied their status as indebted fathers.

In addition to their reentry hits, indebted fathers experienced troubles in clumps. State control tends to exact its punishments in clusters, with the revoking of driver's licenses, garnishing of tax returns, and issuing of property liens happening in one fell swoop. Having appeared on the state's radar screen, fathers can be hit with a slew of enforcement measures at once. This timing only confounded fathers' struggles, linking the constraints of debt to the constraints of enforcement. It also made the entangled nature of their troubles all the more apparent. Fathers often discussed how unnerved they became when the constraints on their lives worked together to undermine their ability to reintegrate and how paralyzed they felt experiencing it at once. This paralysis could trigger a downward parenting cycle.

Overwhelmed, fathers claimed to be unable to cope with parenting challenges along with everything else confronting them. The issue was partly logistical: Under pressure to get out from under debt, these fathers took on whatever work came to them. For those who went the legal route, this meant working longer hours, adding new jobs whenever they could, or taking the least desirable shifts. All of this then made it hard for fathers to see their kids. They were working in the evenings and on the weekends, when kids were out of school. Many fathers had become too overwhelmed to be present, which made them feel guilty. They mourned the loss of quality time with their kids and not being present at important stages in their lives. As Gerard described it: "All the birthdays I missed. All the football games I didn't see. All the trips to the park I missed…I missed so much from their lives. 'Cause of my stupid shit. 'Cause of my mistakes. I didn't man up. 'Cause I got lost in my shit, they suffered."

In addition to this clustering of troubles, downward cycles were generated by unexpected difficulties. Many of the waves that cyclical fathers rode came at them when they least expected it. When troubles came by surprise, fathers were left reeling; when they were hit while their guard was down, they felt discombobulated. Fathers gave many examples of how this happened. They might go to court for what they thought was a simple support order review, only to discover it was in fact an enforcement hearing that landed them in jail. Or they might think making partial payments on their support order would suffice, only to get slammed with the sudden freezing of a bank account that left them without any money. Or they might get pulled over on a simple traffic stop, only to discover that they were driving on a suspended license. The lack of anticipation could be worse than the punishment itself.

It was Rodney, an older Miami father of three, who first made me aware of how a sudden onslaught of trouble could be especially debilitating. While most cyclical fathers led tumultuous lives, Rodney's was different, in terms of both how hard he struggled and how reflective he was about it. Within minutes of meeting me, Rodney rattled off a long list of tragedies that marked his life, any one of which would have sent others reeling, from the loss of his parents in a robbery, to his own incarceration for drugs, to an early heart attack, to the loss of two of his sons to gun violence. After every tragic event, he rebounded and managed to stay close to his surviving kids. But the last hit he experienced shook him. He wasn't even sure why. Things had been going well: living with a new partner, Rita, in a small house outside Miami, he had a stable job and the future looked brighter. Then Rita got into a bad car accident and, while driving back from the hospital, Rodney was pulled over for driving on a suspended license. He went to jail for a few days. When he got out, he fell into a deep depression. He started having panic attacks, he stopped sleeping, he missed work, and he went on anti-anxiety medication. Then he began to miss visits with his kids. His inability to understand his depression just made it worse.

When we spoke, Rodney claimed to be in the midst of a "doom and gloom" period. Like so many men and women living on the margins, he had few safety nets. He was one crisis, one health problem, one failed relationship, one car accident, or one arrest away from falling apart. "I dread waking up some days," Rodney confided. "To face the sense that the next terrible thing was just around the corner. . . . It could hit me at any time." The fear that he could meet this terrible thing even when life was on an upswing paralyzed him. The result was a pervasive sense of dread. Like other men, Rodney insisted it was only a matter of time before everything fell apart again. "You go through so much," he continued. "And then one day it's just too much. There's no obvious reason why . . . but you just break apart." By the end of our interview, Rodney had began to assure himself that he'd pull through this tumultuous period. But he was also sure he'd lost his kids in this round, having disappeared from their lives one too many times.

Rodney's account of his gloom-and-doom period points to a pattern that other cyclical fathers described as well: crises that hit during moments of upswing could be the most devastating, especially for their parenting. They often described their lives as climbing up a mountain, so that when they were hit while on an ascent, they slid all the way down in despair. Even though they were on track and making progress, it seemed impossible to get back up the mountain. Their hopelessness only deepened their desperation about the future. These men knew that even if they worked hard to stay current on their child support and arrears payments, they were looking at twenty to thirty years of extreme hardship before they were out of the red. So if a crisis hit precisely when they thought they were on an upswing, they saw no way out of poverty. The gloom and doom that Rodney described soon followed.

This gloom and doom underpinned many men's cyclical parenting. Exasperated, they lost perspective and their lives veered out of control. Fearful of another hit, they retreated. And this could mean retreating from their kids. As they felt pulled under by their woes, they pulled away as parents. In these downward parenting cycles, fathers faded out as parents. They saw their kids less frequently; they missed their scheduled visitations. Feeling pulled in different directions, most fathers were aware that their parenting suffered. In interviews, fathers could recount exactly how and when they slipped as parents. As Daniel, a NYC father, recalled:

> My children used to believe in me. My word was important to them. At this point, I lost that.... I lied [to them], that's what I'm good at and they're not happy with me. For them, my word is nothing.... My word used to be everything to them. I was a great dad and they would always speak to me. Even for a while when I was away. But then it changed, it changed a lot. They don't speak to me now.

Why would these life crises affect men's relationships with their kids? In addition to the logistical challenges of repeatedly climbing out of the hole, these crises had emotional reverberations that came to propel fathers' parenting cycles. Here it is important to recall how these men defined fatherhood: most of them insisted that "good daddies" were those who showed children love, attention, and care.[8] When they could not provide these things, because of their time in prison or the entanglements of their lives, they felt like failures. In contrast to popular stereotypes, most cyclical fathers blamed themselves for their downswings: they insisted that the missed visits, missed phone calls, and missed support payments were their fault. This created a vicious cycle: their guilt and regret led to avoidance and neglect, which led to more shame and more cyclical parenting. Aware that they were on a "father-go-round," they felt worse about themselves at each and every go-round.

As important as the timing of these blows was what they could trigger in fathers: they touched off a sense of failure and chipped away at their confidence as parents. Their ongoing derailments then left them feeling broken. Some dealt with this by self-medicating with drugs or alcohol. But this only made them less reliable and more likely to miss visits with their kids. In court, cyclical fathers usually looked beaten down. They often gave testimonies in soft, almost inaudible voices, with their heads bowed down. As Charlie, a Florida father facing civil contempt, explained to Judge Black: "Yes, your honor, I did go six months without seeing my kids. I could not bear to tell them, again, that I had been locked up. I was ashamed. I told them it wouldn't happen again, but then it did.... But now I'm over that. I'm gonna get back on track.... Give me a chance, just one more chance."

When their lives seemed to be falling apart, these fathers tried to hide from view; they didn't want others to know, least of all their children. While cyclical disappearances exasperated everyone, from mothers to judges to caseworkers to kids, they often seemed motivated by a desire to save face. What seemed like neglect could be a misguided attempt to buffer kids and protect them from the burden of their own turmoil. "I don't want them to see me like this," explained Joel, a homeless father who hadn't seen his kids since he lost his apartment. "What will they think of me when they look at me like this? With nowhere to live?" Diovan, a NYC father of two, explained this cycle and its effect on his confidence as a father:

> I ain't never been around as a father because of the things I have been through. I made bad decisions as a kid that led me to incarceration.... And I kind of feel sad because as a young man growing up, having a kid was overwhelming to me. I was confused which led me to alcohol. I got depressed which led me to cocaine and marijuana. Which led me to incarceration. Through that experience, I felt bad, growing up as a young man who did not know his son very well. Every man should know to be there for their son.... But I wasn't always. I really don't know how to be a father.... I feel I never will know how.

Some fathers then began to question their own value as caregivers. While on an upswing, cyclical fathers felt respected for their parenting and their nurturing. This seemed to evaporate when they were on a downward spiral, as they began to ask themselves if they were of any significance to their kids. The pressure to stand up for their version of fathering in the face of state punishment could be crushing, leading men like Jason, a Jacksonville father, to question whether his son would be better without him. "Maybe his life is best if I'm no longer in it," he reasoned. "There are many ways to be supportive as a father... and maybe the support he needs is for me to disappear. At least for now stop pushing for a relationship and let him move on?"

Fathers like Jason frequently told themselves that their withdrawal was only temporary. They promised they would get off the father-go-round and end the parenting cycles once they stabilized—after catching up on debt payments, securing better work with better hours, having their driver's license reinstated, or returning from jail. They seemed to have every intention of making it back, and some of them did. But many others did not. Never finding that calm after the storm, some fathers were unable to end the parenting cycle. When one problem got resolved, another emerged; after they were out of one snag, they got entangled in another. They kept pulling back from their kids, and the cycle would start again.

In trying to figure out how to manage these downswings and the feelings that triggered them, cyclical fathers had few role models to follow. Only the lucky few had someone in their life whom they identified with as a father—a relative or an acquaintance who could guide them in grappling with their problems.[9] Instead, most men had fathers who had also disappeared when things got tough. This put them at a real disadvantage: they wanted to parent differently but had no concrete sense of how to manage adversity as fathers. Perhaps this lack of role models made them more attuned to, and affected by, the public models used to evaluate them. Perhaps it made them all the more vulnerable to downward spirals when public officials accused them of failing to meet their parental standards and models of "good" fathering. Perhaps, as a result, they ended up replicating the cyclical model they were most familiar with, despite their best intentions to avoid it. As Ricardo, a Brooklyn father of two, explained:

> I never had a role model. I never had a father. He was never around.... So I was gonna be different, man. I was gonna love my kids and shower them with attention. Go to every school thing, sports thing. But here I am, the same as my dad. Locked up, I missed it all. Now I'm workin' all the time to keep up with [child support]. I still never see them.

In fact, one of the most telling moments of my interviews with these fathers came at the end, when I asked about the best father they knew. The question was almost always met with silence. It was a painful silence, with men searching for someone, for anyone, they could say was a model for them. They sat thinking for long periods, wracking their brains and going through everyone they knew. Not their own fathers, who were usually absent. Not any of the fathers in their extended family, who were rarely involved. Not any of the fathers they knew in the community, who were few and far between. Not even any fathers in popular culture, who rarely encountered the challenges they faced. "I mean, maybe once I would have said Cosby," Rodney joked. "But now, well, probably not." Rather than a real example, many fathers answered my question by describing what such a role model *would* have looked like if they actually had one: "He would have been kind and caring, but also tough," Carlos imagined. "He would have spent lots of time with me, always being there for me, really doing just the simple things. Just being there, showing love and being a model for how I would like need to act in life." Then there was Manuel, a Bronx father who put his own spin on the role model question:

> I tell my son that he's my role model. I tell him he's my idol. "How's that? But you're older than me" [he says back]. I tell him it doesn't make no difference. I fucked up in life. I gotta correct my life by correcting you. If you follow my footsteps, I didn't do a good job. I put that in his head. So when I see him doin' things I never did, I say, "Yes, my son, you're doin' the right thing."

CYCLICAL FATHERING AND FAMILIAL DISTRUST

"Bring the mother in," Judge Maddox announces. "Because Mr. Roger is coming up on the screen now." It is video day in NYC family court, and fathers are being streamed in from across the state to receive official notification of their new child support orders. "This is an unusual case since the wife is actually here," Maddox notes to me as a woman enters the courtroom and sits behind the video screen. Then Maddox checks herself, asking the couple if they are indeed married. "Yea, been married for fifteen years," Mr. Roger interjects from his prison cell in Sing Sing. As usual, the actual hearing lasts only a few minutes, with the court informing Mr. Roger that a child support case has been initiated in his name to cover the public benefits received by his children. He agrees to the order, with no questions asked.

Just as Judge Maddox is about to cut off the video stream, she stops suddenly and turns to the mother. "Wait, would you like to see him?" she asks. "I mean, he's right here, would you like to come around to the other side and say hello?" The woman nervously rises in her seat, unsure of what to do or where to go. As the bailiff pulls her around to the front camera, her husband starts whispering to her: he tells her how much he misses her and how much he thinks about their kids. Clearly uncomfortable, she looks down as her husband continues to talk. Judge Maddox tells them to wrap up, so the woman says her first words: "You know, today is my birthday and yet another year that you forgot to . . ." Before she can finish her sentence, Mr. Roger starts apologizing. "Oh, baby, I didn't forget. Dang, I was fixin' to call you later, when I got phone time. Really, I wanted it to be private, I swear, baby." Shaking her head in disbelief, with her eyes filling up with tears, the woman rushes out of the courtroom without saying another word.

In preceding chapters, I have been reluctant to discuss the women and children enmeshed in the child support system. This is not because their experiences are unimportant to the dynamics of indebted fatherhood. Just the opposite: their experiences are so important that they deserve their own in-depth analysis. Amidst the archive of books, articles, and reports written on child support, too little is known about how women relate to this system and think it can help them.[10] This is especially true of poor women. Instead, policy-makers extrapolate from what is known about middle-class women, whose voices tend to get the attention of politicians and state officials working on this issue. Or they simply assume to know what impoverished women need, frequently reducing their concerns to material issues of payment. Since few state actors stop to ask these women about their needs, they are rarely heard in the child support process.

Since I did not interview the women and children involved in support cases, I have not been able to relay their voices either.[11] Yet I observed thousands of women in child support courts across the country, catching many glimpses of their actions. Since judges rarely asked women to speak at these hearings, their body language was often the only way they could express themselves in these environments. Through facial expressions and bodily gestures, women exhibited a range of responses, from anger to frustration to hurt to empathy. This was echoed in my conversations with them during court breaks. But even those exchanges were short, rushed, and partial. My perspective was even more partial when it came to children, who were not allowed in courtrooms.[12] So I got even fewer glimpses of their behavior, limited to those occasions when fathers brought them to our interviews. Yet here, too, it was possible to read between the lines: as I listened to fathers describe their parenting cycles, I gleaned a sense of the toll these cycles took on their families.

Indeed, the toll seemed to be great. Despite my limited view, it was clear that men's cyclical parenting created deep suspicion and distrust in those around them. Even when others understood and sympathized with men's struggles, they had trouble trusting them. Having lived through all their ups and downs, they proceeded with caution. When fathers were on an upswing, others didn't believe it would last. When they were on a downswing, others didn't believe it would end. Their pessimism was well-earned: they had experienced too many missed visits and unmet promises to get their hopes up that anything would change. Their distrust then made it hard, if not impossible, for fathers to acquire the confidence they might have needed to launch into an upswing or combat a downswing. This deepened everyone's sense of misgiving and mistrust.

Gender Distrust

In his early work on disadvantaged single mothers, sociologist Frank Furstenberg analyzed the gender distrust expressed by so many women—their sense that men are unreliable, inconsistent, and thus not to be trusted.[13] These feelings of distrust can lead men to feel resentful and disrespected and ultimately to act in distrustful ways. The interpersonal dynamics of distrust can take on a life of their own, leading to unsustainable relationships and parental absence. More recently, sociologist Judith Levine has added a broader institutional context to gender distrust, revealing how it extends beyond personal relationships and into the public arena.[14] In their interactions with employers and caseworkers, disadvantaged women are vulnerable to ongoing neglect and disrespect, which leads to a generalized sense of distrust. Levine argues that such distrust can actually become a form of social and interpersonal power, as the withholding of trust can offer the semblance of control in an otherwise powerless life. This is particularly true in women's relationships with the fathers of their children, which, as Levine claims, frequently ricochet back and forth amidst layers of mistrust and control.

This gender distrust is further complicated by the racial and class injustice that marks parents' lives. Trust is hard to establish amidst experiences of hardship, abandonment, and violence—so much so that distrust can seem like a necessary survival strategy.[15] Add state punishment to the mix and the dynamics can get even more explosive. Women can feel caught between a rock and a hard place: state officials demand their cooperation in public surveillance and control, while fathers blame them if they comply. The faceless quality of state punishment only adds to the mother blame, as women too often become the personification of those injustices. This makes the formation of trusting connections seem even more out of reach. As bell hooks has characterized it, histories of pain and abandonment find ways of replicating themselves in intimate relationships.[16] And as men and women unwittingly reenact those histories, they remain divided by the fear, rejection, and anger they conjure up.

The many layers of gender distrust separating disadvantaged mothers and fathers come into sharp view in the child support arena. As judges and state caseworkers force mothers to participate in punitive enforcement practices, fathers' anger toward them builds. The private and public aspects of gender distrust frequently collide in this legal arena, making court dynamics particularly explosive. Hurt and betrayal frequently accompany the end of a relationship, and child support adds money to the mix. Money can act as a replacement for complex emotions and experiences. Money can also seem like a way to address parents' corresponding sense of suspicion and mistrust, as if fixing a child support order is akin to fixing histories of distrust. State officials often play on this by equating familial well-being with child support payments. So a father's failure to comply with a support order gets interpreted as profoundly disrespectful to the mother, and his failure to pay is read as an attack on her dignity and worth, instead of as a sign of his poverty and inability to get out of debt.

Child support can therefore exacerbate gender distrust and undermine parental connection. This can happen in several ways. First, instead of diffusing these conflicts, state institutions often appropriated them, further entangling gender, race, and class in unproductive ways. Court officials regularly used the struggles between parents to enforce their version of compliance—with a Florida judge once instructing a mother to "find yourself a rich guy next time" and to "stop being with these poor losers who do you wrong." In this way, they drew on mothers' anger toward men to buttress public tropes of them as careless deadbeats. Yet, since many mothers had themselves been stigmatized by controlling stereotypes of their own parenting, they were likely aware of how damaging these images of fathers could be. Mothers also came to this legal arena suspicious of state officials' promises to look out for them.[17] Thus, mothers could seem quite conflicted as the personal betrayal by fathers that they felt collided with men's public humiliation in court. As they listened to white male judges berate impoverished men of color for abandoning their families, many mothers nervously looked down; some were brought to tears. Judge Matthews once lectured a mother who wanted to forgive the arrears owed to her by her children's father, and her eyes welled up with tears:

> He has SEVEN orders, ma'am. Only some of them are for your kids. You say he don't have the money to pay? You say you wanna let the scoundrel go because he can't pay? If you let him off the hook, he'll keep doin' this again.... The only thing they understand is threat.... You lettin' him off would send all the wrong messages.

Although mothers like this one rarely had the opportunity to respond to such lectures, they seemed distraught by how state officials characterized and used their family lives. Judges repeatedly told them their lives had been destroyed by male abandonment; state lawyers represented them as marked by neglect and desertion. While this was certainly true for some mothers, they were never asked to weigh in on such constructions. They were not asked to confirm the representations in court, which denied them the ability to account for their own histories. On the rare occasions when they had an opening to speak, mothers could seem paralyzed—unsure of what to say or how to proceed in these state spaces. As Matthews continued, his questions to this mother seemed more rhetorical and condescending: "I know what it's like when your man disappears for years and leaves you to hold up everything. Right? You feel wronged, true? But if you don't stand up to him, you'll be walked all over all the time. You know that, right? He'll keep doin' it, right?"

Then there was California Judge McKay, known for her "get tough" approach, who once claimed to "side" with a mother whose ex-husband had $200,000 in support debt from his time in prison:

> I don't care if he's paying now. I don't care if we take 50 percent of his wages at Home Depot.... That doesn't even cover the interest [on his debt]. So he needs to find more work, better work. I don't care if DCSS advises us to be patient. Enough with patience, right? For you, I'm going to issue a warrant for his arrest. I'm so sick [of] fathers who leave it all to women like you.... Hopefully, he will comply now, with this warrant on him.

Of course, some mothers agreed with these punishments and constructions. There were those who mobilized these constructs in their own battles with fathers, calling men everything from irresponsible deadbeats to scumbags. And many mothers received important help through the child support process, especially those left to raise their children alone without the support they were entitled to. Some mothers seemed to appreciate public confirmation of all they had endured. Having struggled for so long, they appreciated the recognition of their sacrifices. They wanted fathers held accountable for their parental failures, even if it meant humiliating them in court. So they nodded when judges called fathers out, prodding them along with the occasional "That's right" or "You tell him." They interjected examples of men's neglectful behavior. As a Napa mother explained after a warrant was issued for her kids' father: "Finally, someone is holding him [the father] accountable. I mean, he keeps disappearing. Making promises, but never meeting them. He gambles away the money, then says he's poor and can't afford anything. He's always a no-show so he just gets away with it. But now she [the judge] is gonna get him. Finally."

For every woman who wanted punishment amped up, there were others who seemed uncomfortable with it.[18] This was particularly true when it came to incarcerated fathers: when imprisonment was the reason for men's absence, mothers seemed leery of cooperating with further punishment. Some didn't show up for hearings; others didn't participate in those hearings when present. In fact, a surprising number of mothers withdrew their cases entirely or dropped key demands.[19] Those owed arrears often waived them; those entitled to large support orders often agreed to lower amounts. Some mothers came to court to support fathers in their requests for order modification or arrears settlements. For instance, there was the NYC couple who came to court to contest the father's mandatory arrears payment: they had begun to live together again and insisted that the payment made it impossible to make ends meet. Judges could get frustrated when this happened, as it undermined the claim that they were acting on behalf of women and children. This was especially true for public assistance orders; with these, state officials demanded mothers' participation and threatened to withdraw assistance for noncompliance.[20]

Since mothers had more control over the child support owed to them, courts could not make such demands. Women had the power to change or dismiss these orders, but not before state officials tried to convince them otherwise. Judges often lectured women about the risks of changing their orders or proceeding without protection. Here, too, they drew on the distrust these mothers already had toward fathers, subjecting them to speeches about the danger of trusting men to abide by "private settlements." One Brooklyn judge even had a mother undergo a waiting period before agreeing to drop her case. "Don't be manipulated by them scoundrels," Judge Matthews once cautioned. "They'll tell you whatever you want to hear right now, but then go back to their old deadbeat ways as soon as the case goes away."

Indeed, when mothers expressed frustration, it usually centered on men's cyclical parenting. Men's disappearing acts and up/down parenting seemed especially troubling to them. In court, mothers expressed a variety of concerns about this cyclical parenting. Most often, they were troubled by fathers' erratic involvement with their kids. They insisted that men's tendency to move in and out of kids' lives was disruptive, confusing, and self-serving. This made them hopeless as co-parents, unable to be counted on when help was needed. Mothers felt they had to do it all yet were then accused of shutting fathers out. As a Los Angeles mother explained to a judge when her kids' father failed to show up for their hearing: "Of course he's a no show. He's been a no show his whole life . . . and for our kids' whole life. [He] didn't show up for birthdays. For games. For school events. For meetings with teachers. It was always me. Why should I expect him to be any different here [in court]?" Or as a Brooklyn mother once summarized the situation to me as she walked out of her support hearing: "Why can't he just do what he says? Why can't he just pay what he supposed to pay? Be where he's supposed to be? Why does he act like a baby? He thinks the world needs to take care of him. Why can't he just stop making mistakes and getting locked up?"

While this unpredictability disturbed some mothers, it was predictability that seemed to anger others. "Whenever there's a good time, he's here," an Oakland mother explained to the state lawyer during her hearing. "Parties, cookouts . . . he shows up. But never for the hard stuff." Mothers explained that men made time for the fun aspects of childrearing, from sports games to birthdays to holiday celebrations. Then, like clockwork, fathers disappeared when it came to the difficult parts. They were nowhere to be found if children had learning or behavioral problems at school. Or if they had medical issues that required inconvenient doctors' appointments. Or if their kids got into trouble with the law. In these instances, men seemed to be missing in action. "They ain't never there when you need 'em and always there when you don't," a Jacksonville mother whispered to me as we watched a father get berated by Judge Matthews at his hearing.

Mothers also complained about the cyclical nature of men's financial contributions. As with their visitations, fathers' payments could be unpredictable or all too predictable. On the unpredictable side, mothers reported that they never knew when they would receive child support. They went months receiving nothing, only to be shocked when a payment came in. This made budgeting nearly impossible, since being poor is a balancing act and not getting funds on time disturbed the balance. Yet other mothers claimed the timing of fathers' payments was quite predictable: when payday came around, fathers emerged. Feeling flush, they took their children out to eat and bought them toys, clothes, and so on. "He acts like Santa when he gets him [his son] the [sneakers] he wants." But then the support would evaporate, and men would go underground. No matter how often they asked for support, it never seemed to be forthcoming when needed.

Many mothers, then, seemed less troubled by the amount of fathers' financial support than by its erratic nature. As fathers told their stories of their financial waves, mothers would just glare at them. "Really?" a Los Angeles mother blurted out as she listened to her kids' father explain why he had stopped paying support for two months because he ran out of money. "Do you think I'm livin' high, like I don't struggle every damn day?" Some mothers claimed to be willing to accept lower payments if they came in consistently. Many of them preferred wage garnishments for this reason: garnished payments came in at the same time of the month, which allowed them to plan. Similarly, while mothers understood why fathers worked off the books, particularly if they had large public arrears payments, this left their families in financial uncertainty. For their part, fathers saw women's insistence on consistency as a test to prove their reliability or as a way to control their finances. So the struggle continued, ultimately undermining the reciprocity that co-parenting requires.

Parental Distrust

State child support programs characterize their mission as one of child protection. They often produce glossy information materials, covered with images of smiling children, that they plaster all over their websites. Yet in the day-to-day practices of child support adjudication, children are missing. They are literally absent: most courts bar them from support hearings. They are also figuratively absent: of the dozens of courtrooms I observed, only two judges regularly used children's names. Instead of being referred to by name, kids emerged as computations or order amounts. "So there is $15,000 in arrears on a $160 bimonthly order for two minors last paid in 2014," Miami Judge Baker proclaimed. Sometimes parents insisted on using children's names, trying to puncture the impersonal quality of the exchange. "You mean my two kids, Bobby and Angela?" the father responded to Judge Baker. But it rarely worked: "Yes, if they are the two minors in question," Judge Baker replied.

Moreover, in court, state officials rarely asked about the kids they purported to be protecting and serving. They rarely queried parents about how their kids were doing or how they were surviving familial separation. They avoided questions about how often kids saw noncustodial parents—unless they were related to the child support order in question. Those parents who raised such questions were often shut down and told that child support proceedings were only about setting and enforcing financial orders. The limitations of this were best exemplified in public assistance cases, which were still called "child support" cases even though children saw little of the money collected from these orders. State officials offered the most contorted of explanations to justify why it was still "child" support to require that parents direct the limited funds available to them to repay the state instead of their families. As California Judge McKay explained to a father who was paying over $2,000 each month in current and back support, less than half of which went to his actual children:

> When you pay the money it is for your children, but it goes to the taxpayers. She [the mother] has no rights here—as long as she gets welfare, she will see none of this money. You can incentivize her getting off [assistance]. But your children see it [money] because taxpayers have fronted it. Taxpayers have the rights here . . . rights for you to pay them back for their contributions to *your* children.

Social scientists know very little about how children fare in this system of indebted fatherhood. Because of the complexities of research with children, they are rarely interviewed. Most of what is known about them comes from statistical portrayals of their lives or others' representations of them, both of which have limitations. Although quantitative accounts of their life trajectories are enormously important, revealing the effects of parental imprisonment and child support enforcement on child poverty, education, and criminal justice involvement, they do little to explain how kids understand the cyclical parenting they experience.[21] For this, we rely on how others represent kids' lives and needs. Yet such constructions tend to reflect the perspective of those who create them. Parents frequently project their own needs onto their kids, especially when they are embroiled in contentious court dynamics. Even the most committed of caseworkers can let their own agendas and interests seep into their representations of kids' needs.

My analysis reflects this partiality. Even more than their mothers, children were hard to see or hear from in this research. They were missing from court and usually absent from my interviews with their fathers. When they did come to interviews, they tended to be with the most committed and engaged fathers. Although these children said little during our encounters, when they did speak it was enormously revealing: they indicated how much they appreciated fathers for the small acts and everyday practices. It was not the grand gestures or the big purchases they appreciated. It was the little things they did day in and day out. As Mandy noted to me in our few minutes alone while her father went to the bathroom during his interview:

> He does everything for me, like everything. He cooks, he cleans, he takes me to school, he's there when I come out. He tickles me when I'm sad to make me happy and laugh. He takes me to eat, McDonald's is my favorite. So we go there all the time. He lets me order large fries when I've been good and done all my homework. . . . He's the best.

In these exchanges, children often revealed clues about what was important to them about their fathers: the time they spent, the commitment they showed, and the connection they maintained. Just spending time with their fathers could be rewarding. Or, as the group of kids that Reggie brought with him to our interview revealed, just sitting next to him was so coveted that they alternated who sat by his side during our two-hour interview. Then there was ten-year-old Jimmy, who came with his father to our interview all decked out in his football gear and proudly announced that his father "never missed a game" in his two-year-long football career.

Fathers echoed these priorities. Their memories of the good times with their kids suggested that children placed significance on the small parenting acts: like the times they showed up for events and were present at celebrations. Or all the letters they sent from prison, which many kids stored away. Or all the times fathers took them to and from school and insisted on not being late. Or all the times they called to say goodnight. Or all the special meals they made for them—the barbeque ribs, the pasta, or the pancakes fathers cooked when their kids were with them. Kingston, the Brooklyn father who had spent most of his son's life in prison, described what his son likes to do:

> We go to the movies, hang out in the park, eat and talk. He always says to me, "Let's spend time, let's talk, let's be together." I think a father should be reliable like that... and try to help your son by being a good example. Answer all his questions. Always tell him that he's your idol. He's your role model. Most of all, though, just spend time.

Marco, a Jacksonville father, pulled up his son's Facebook page for me: "He has all these pictures of us doing nothing. Like sittin' around, chillin', watching TV. Like dumb stuff. I'm like what about all the big stuff? Why don't you post about us going to the [amusement park]? Why you posting stupid shit?"

Given their prioritizing of fathers' time, it is likely that kids felt the loss when fathers stopped giving it. Or when they offered it inconsistently. Some fathers were reluctant to admit to this, denying that the cycles of debt and punishment affected their kids. As Mike, a Brooklyn father, put it, with a bit of irritation in his voice: "I can separate the love from the debt." Yet we know from quantitative data that support debt is associated with less involvement with children.[22] We also know from fathers that their cycles caused parenting waves. So even if they separated debt from love, fathers revealed mistakes they made with their kids. Those mistakes must have caused some kids to become distrustful in their relationships with their fathers.

The mistakes that seemed most damaging and consequential were related to time. The issue of time was very fraught for fathers: as they served "their time" in prison, they had lost "their time" with their kids. Thus, time had special currency for them. They knew they could never get that time back; they knew the effects of its loss could reverberate for years. Many also knew how important time was to connecting and bonding with children. Perhaps for the same reasons, time might have taken on special significance for children.[23] Fathers described how incarceration was hardest on their kids because it meant they could not be present at key moments in their lives. They recounted phone calls in which children cried for them to come to celebrations and events; they read letters in which their kids wrote about being upset by not having a father to play with or confide in. As Mike recounted the importance of time for his young daughter:

> This is no lie: every letter from her to this day I have, from when I was in prison.... I saved everything. Every letter and every puzzle that she made when she was a baby.... One day, I'm going to go over all that stuff with her.... There was a lot of pain in it. She used to cry. Whenever they brought her up to see me, she would just hold on to me. She wouldn't let me go. When she knew our time was done, she grabbed me and never let me go.... That's the most hurting moments I experienced with her. When our time was over.

Time also took on significance upon their release from prison. When fathers came and went again after their release, their kids surely felt it. When they were on a downswing, and did not show up for visitations or planned events, their kids surely felt it. Although some children did express their feelings of disappointment to their fathers during incarceration, the loss might have felt worse after prison, since they could no longer blame prison for their fathers' absence. It was no longer outside their fathers' control. Fathers seemed aware of this, realizing that their broken promises and disappearing acts hit their kids hard. And since many indebted fathers believed that all they had to offer kids was time, their failure to provide it made them feel like failures.

It is quite possible that the more fathers' disappearing acts happened, the more distrust built up in kids. It is also imaginable that this buildup made it increasingly difficult for children to forgive and forget their fathers' downswings. Yet it is also possible that kids were more forgiving of fathers' mistakes—certainly more so than their mothers. According to men's accounts, kids were more likely to give them additional chances and to reengage despite their anger and hurt. Children were also more open to connecting with their fathers when they resurfaced even after long absences. This forgiveness could provide fathers the kind of boost they needed to trigger a parenting upswing and to become more consistent caregivers.

While forgiveness could be reaffirming for fathers, it remains unclear what toll it took on children. From what is known about child development, it is inconceivable that children were left feeling safe and nurtured amidst fathers' absences. Yet there are many unanswered questions about those feelings. So it seems appropriate to conclude by simply asking questions like these: How did children understand fathers' parenting waves? Did they blame themselves for the disappearances? Did they turn their feelings inward, fearing they were unworthy of parental attention? Or did they turn them outward, as calls for attention and care? Were they able to voice their disappointment and sadness to their fathers? And were their fathers able to hear them?

And how do these experiences affect children who may one day decide to become parents themselves? Will their own caregiving be shaped by the cyclical parenting they encountered as kids? Or will they form the parental models that so eluded their own fathers? This dilemma was articulated quite powerfully by Tyrice, a young African American father who realized he had taken the replication route while sitting in a jail cell once occupied by his own father. This epiphany gave him the will to change:

> I had done time in the same exact cell as my father. An officer told me that. She came to me and was like "are you related to [——]?" I'm like, yea, that's my dad. She told me that my dad was in the same cell as me before…

> offered to show me the papers. It was crazy. Man, when I realized that it hit me. This is why I gotta be the father to my son. There will be no third generation of us in that cell. That shit's gonna end with me.

BREAKING THE CYCLES

Tyrice's image of himself sitting in his jail cell and committing to a different model of fatherhood captures the multiple confinements of so many indebted fathers' lives: the physical confinement of incarceration, the financial confinement of debt, and the emotional confinement of cyclical parenting. Like other aspects of their lives, these confinements were interconnected, with each set of constraints intersecting with others. Doing time in prison took away time as parents; devoting less time to children created gaps in their caregiving; lacking confidence in their parental role prompted disconnection; and withdrawing from families exacerbated gender and parental distrust, which could worsen their parenting cycles. As I have shown in this chapter, a common set of factors enabled fathers to end their cycles and their downswings. But for a father like Tyrice to actualize his will to change, he would need social resources that boosted his confidence and facilitated his caretaking. Those resources could come from a reentry program, a sympathetic judge, a stable partner, or a loving child. With those resources, his chances of making good on his promise to break the parenting cycles would be strong.

Without them, Tyrice was more likely to inherit those cycles and pass the father-go-round to his own son. He was also more likely to parent in ways that made his son's mother increasingly distrustful and suspicious. In her analysis of gender distrust, sociologist Judith Levine concludes by asking what kinds of public policies could enhance poor women's trust of those in their lives—and suggests that policies that enhance cooperation, protection, and procedural justice are good starting places.[24] My analysis contributes to her list if we flip the question around, asking instead what kinds of state policies deepen gender distrust. And the policies of indebted fatherhood rank high on the list. In this way, the two parts of this chapter are connected: debt accumulation and enforcement end up undermining familial well-being not only because of the financial burden they exact, but also because of the kind of fathering they can lead to. Despite state officials' insistence on protecting women and children, their institutional practices can breed the cyclical parenting that makes trusting, reciprocal relationships more difficult to maintain.

The experiences of cyclical fathers make it clear that disrupting these patterns requires looking beyond the personal constraints on their fathering and placing less emphasis on how unrealistic these fathers may seem—even when their behavior seems to mirror such characterization. Just as with the mothers these men frequently leave wanting, fathers' experiences reflect social dislocation and disadvantage. As with mothers, these fathers' lives cannot be separated from the structural currents that run through them. While it is important to remember that those currents do leave emotional and psychological scars, it is equally important to recognize the role of state institutions in this scarring. Doing so points to public policy and legislative reforms that might nurture and stabilize men's parenting. I turn to these policy reforms in the concluding chapter.

Conclusion

REFORMING DEBT, REIMAGINING FATHERHOOD

Over the past forty years, few social experiments have been as costly to the United States as mass incarceration. Although most estimates of its financial toll tend to stop with the $90 billion spent annually on federal and state corrections, the actual cost is surely much higher.[1] Social scientists have thus started to propose more expansive and creative computations of the financial toll mass incarceration has taken on individuals, families, and communities.[2] One particularly inventive calculation adds over twenty additional costs to the formula, from the lost wages and earnings of the incarcerated, to the eviction and health care expenses of families, to the costs of child welfare and the criminogenic effects of prison on communities.[3] Together, these costs add up to $1 trillion a year. Of all these expenses, the burden on families and communities is the greatest, exceeding that on state budgets more than fourfold.

The huge and widespread costs of mass incarceration have awakened many to the need for reform. Indeed, criminal justice reform now enjoys broad support from an extraordinarily diverse collection of politicians, policy-makers, and activists.[4] It has, of course, been a central component of the Black Lives Matter movement, and some of the most inventive and encompassing reform ideas have come from its activists. Yet justice reform has also gained traction among political conservatives, from Newt Gingrich to Bernie Kerik to the Koch brothers, as well as from a host of wealthy businesspeople, media moguls, and celebrities.[5] From such a broad swath of advocates has come an equally broad array of reform proposals. While many of these reforms center on cost reductions, others take on the underlying causes of mass incarceration, engaging in the larger project of decarceration through reforms to policing, sentencing laws, the bail system, and penal practices. Some have even attempted to address the burdens shouldered by families and communities by targeting the school-to-prison pipeline, criminal justice fees, underfunded reentry programs, and housing insecurity.[6]

Amidst these broad conversations about the form and focus of criminal justice reform, a few issues have been notably absent. Child support is one of them. Calculations of the true cost of mass incarceration rarely include child support debt. Few proposals for criminal justice reform attempt to address it, be it at the federal or the state level.[7] This is a peculiar omission, given that upwards of 30 percent of incarcerated men leave prison with child support debt, unprepared to weather the storm awaiting them. Many of them do realize just how vulnerable they are to these storms: surveys of formerly incarcerated parents indicate that they rank child support as one of their most pressing problems, with more than 85 percent reporting that they need assistance with their support orders and 30 percent ranking it among their most pressing needs.[8] Clearly, child support belongs in ongoing discussions of criminal justice reform. If a central goal of reform is to address the challenges of reentry and the link between incarceration and familial disadvantage, there are few better places to start than with child support—and with the cycles of punishment and debt brought on by it.

To be sure, these cycles are far less familiar than other criminal justice inequities. As a recent series of *New York Times* articles devoted to child support noted, Americans have little knowledge about how the child support system actually operates.[9] Even fewer have any idea how it works for disadvantaged parents or for those with criminal records. So while ignorance is certainly part of the reason for the silence on the need for reform, I would go a bit further: even for those who are informed about the perils that come with child support debt and enforcement, there is still an untouchable quality to parents experiencing them. While the accusation of being "soft on crime" may not have the political salience it once did, appearing to be soft on deadbeats still does. The politics of the deadbeat is almost a third rail of criminal justice reform, one that even the most reform-minded politicians and lawmakers try their best to avoid. That includes those who reject straightforward reforms to this debt for fear they will end up rewarding parental irresponsibility and neglect.[10] And those who fail to defend the basic rights of indebted parents to due process protections and legal representation. And those who refuse to include the indebted in the most urgent of state safety nets, even in times of national emergency.[11] Moral indignation surrounds this debt and those who have it, based largely on myths about how it accrues and falsehoods about who it harms. Such indignation is then reflected in the general silence about how support debt undermines social reintegration, economic security, and the well-being of families.

This book has challenged those mythologies and fallacies. It has done so in several ways. First, it has confronted misconceptions about who indebted parents are, showing that most of them are poor and many are struggling to make ends meet while rebuilding their lives after prison. It has exposed precisely how their debt accumulates and how federal, state, and local policies work in unison to cause parental debt to rise to unmanageable levels. It has also tracked the institutional processes that underlie this tsunami of debt, from the crushing effects of public assistance payback provisions to restrictive modification policies to default support orders to the undertow of interest charges. Together, these processes have generated a system in which poverty and incarceration, as opposed to neglect and desertion, lead to massive debt. I referred to this as the *debt of imprisonment* to capture how the physical confinement of prison leads to the financial confinement of debt.

Second, this book has challenged misconceptions about how support debt is enforced. On the one hand, it has revealed just how harshly parental debt is punished and how this penalization ends up targeting more than the nonpayment of child support—it has become a way to criminalize poverty and to impugn men's parental and work practices. This criminalization then creates feedback loops of disadvantage, from financial loops that can lure fathers off the grid, to familial loops that can dislodge them from support networks, to legal loops that can land them back in jail. These loops end with the *imprisonment of debt*, a term I used to characterize how the support debt can become its own prison. Making it all the more confining are the ways debt accumulation and debt enforcement become entangled so as to exacerbate each other. As the confinement of debt leads to increased punishment, and heightened punishment then leads to increased debt, the system can seem inescapable. In the end, the system can create criminals—both literally and figuratively—where there were once only indebted parents.

This leads to the book's third set of challenges: it has questioned many of the mythologies swirling around poor men's lives as fathers. It has exposed the effects of these institutional entanglements on men's ability to caregive consistently and reliably. It has done so by highlighting both the possibilities and the limitations of men's commitments as parents. Some men were able to remain consistent parents despite all the turmoil, and in doing so, they revealed what an extraordinary accomplishment it is to be a loving, caring parent amidst so much dislocation and violence. Other men crumbled under the pressure, retreating to the most stereotypically negligent parental behavior. Yet the majority of fathers inhabited the zone in between, engaging in what I referred to as cyclical parenting—at times showing up and being present for their families, at other times derailing and disappearing from their lives. These cycles only deepened the distrust that mothers and children harbored toward them, which further depleted fathers' ability to care for their children and undermined familial well-being.

In covering this territory, I made an argument about the central role of state policy and practice in shaping the livelihoods of disadvantaged fathers. As I noted throughout, social scientists have tended to view poor men's parenting at the very micro or the very macro levels: as reflective of either men's individual, personal attributes or of large-scale, structural shifts in the economy. While both levels illuminate key aspects of their parenting, they are partial. Most glaringly, they omit the critical role of concrete state policies and institutions in men's conceptions of themselves as fathers. Moreover, when researchers do examine the state arena, they tend to portray it in either/or terms, using metaphors of the state's complete withdrawal and abandonment or of its oversurveillance and excessive control. Such portrayals can leave us without an understanding of how state policies can be both constraining and enabling. They obscure the ways men's interactions with state institutions can give them coveted parental resources or leave them frustratingly resourceless.

These portrayals also leave us wanting when it comes to imagining how to move forward. If the barriers to men's parenting were simply individual, the response would be to teach them resilience and responsibility. But that does little to address the institutional entanglements that trap so many. At the other end, if we focus solely on how men's parenting is bound up in large socioeconomic structures and barriers, then change seems overly abstract, as if broad societal shifts must occur before reform can come. The arena of state policy and law lies in between these poles, and the cycles of debt and punishment underlying men's struggles are indeed propelled by such concrete provisions. It follows that concrete reforms are possible that would help disrupt these seemingly never-ending cycles. When social scientists retreat from a serious analysis of legal and policy reform, we end up ceding that terrain to policy-makers and miss the chance to use our unique insights into social life and institutional processes to propose inventive reforms. We then wonder why reforms often fail to address the institutional obstacles to men's parenting. A sociologically inspired policy analysis of indebted fatherhood, and of reform in general, is decidedly necessary.

The kinds of policy reforms I am proposing will not be simple or uncontroversial. Quite the opposite: it will require insight and imagination to address the inequities operating across policy and legal arenas and stretching from the federal to the state to the local levels. These reforms will also require movement along two registers, with policy changes occurring alongside shifts in perception. Without critical changes in how men with criminal records are perceived as fathers, even the most straightforward legislative reforms will remain difficult to secure and limited in scope. But this is exactly why a social scientific perspective is so crucial to the reform process: by drawing on existing research on child support policy, and infusing it with a sensitivity to the lived experiences of indebted parents and their families, we can begin to uncover new ways to transform policy and to guide criminal justice reform more broadly.[12]

UNTANGLING PUNISHMENT AND DEBT

Throughout this book, I have shown how fathers who live at the intersection of the child support and criminal justice systems are uniquely positioned. Their intersectionality makes them doubly indebted: as they serve their debt to society in prison, they accrue new debts as parents. They struggle both as low-income, noncustodial fathers and as reentering citizens. Yet their needs cannot be reduced to those of either group. Because their debts become entangled across systems to form feedback loops of disadvantage, reforms aimed solely at fathers with support debt or solely at those with criminal justice exposure may not capture their most pressing challenges.

The most meaningful reforms would emerge if we blended changes targeted at child support with those targeted at criminal justice. As I have argued in this book, two broad processes create the webs of inequity in fathers' lives: the debt of imprisonment and the imprisonment of debt. These webs are woven together by threads stretching across state spaces and institutions. Yet those threads can be untangled and unwoven. This disentangling could begin with a suite of reforms to address what captures parents, with one set of reforms addressing the accumulation of debt and another the punitive costs of being indebted.

Settling the Debt of Imprisonment at the Federal Level

Perhaps more than any other process, the accumulation of debt is what ensnares incarcerated parents. This debt builds on itself rapidly and exponentially; it sets into motion other disruptions in parents' lives; and it propels their cyclical parenting. So any reform plan must start with how these parents amass debt in the first place. Since this debt accumulates during and after prison, reforms must address both stages of accrual. Three reforms would go a long way in doing this: *the creation of a consistent definition of incarceration as involuntary unemployment*, which would allow for clear modification guidelines across states; *the end of public assistance payback for institutionalized parents*, which would cut the balance of their debt by at least half; and *an exception from the Bradley Amendment for incarcerated parents*, which would pave the way for more consistent debt relief programs after prison.[13]

This suite of reforms must be accomplished primarily at the federal level. Although the federal government often insists that child support is a state issue and tries to punt the issue, the federal role in the formulation of child support policy is long-standing. As outlined in chapter 1, there is a long history of federal involvement in this arena, from legislation regulating order calculations, to laws forbidding retroactive modification, to policies mandating public assistance payback, to laws dictating enforcement measures. The feds create the framework within which individual states operate; they have strong oversight powers. The most recent example of this federal involvement was the 2016 Final Rule's recommendations, which inched support policy closer to meaningful reform and urged states to address the debt of imprisonment. Yet those recommendations moved policy by only a few inches when it needed to move miles. So while the Final Rule was a start, it needs to be extended and enhanced.

One of the most important aspects of the Final Rule was its insistence that states put in place policies to address incarcerated parents' child support. This requirement essentially invalidated state definitions of incarceration as "voluntary unemployment" then prevailing in at least one-third of states, which deemed prisoners ineligible for order modification. The difference between maps 2 and 3 evidences this shift. But while the Final Rule mandated eligibility, it did little to ensure accessibility. The next step is thus to create guidelines for order modifications for institutionalized parents. The federal government mandated formulas for the setting of support orders decades ago; it should now do the same with orders for parents unable to earn wages due to institutionalization. Such guidelines could help even out judicial discretion over modifications and ensure they were accessible to imprisoned and indebted parents.

Such reform would be even more transformative if it went further, mandating that prisoners receive modifications through the administrative order suspension during incarceration. As I discussed in chapter 2, a handful of states have "incarceration orders" in place, particularly for public assistance orders. Although incarceration orders are in no way a panacea, since they are often undermined by bureaucratic barriers and a lack of institutional cooperation, they remain the best way to stop the debt of imprisonment from accruing in the first place. Especially when coupled with extensive outreach to parents, these orders can lead to a significant decline in incarcerated parents' arrears as well as an increase in support payments after prison.[14] In short, suspending the support orders of incarcerated parents is an effective first step in reducing the debt of imprisonment.

This leads to the second step to reform debt accumulation: waiving public assistance payback for institutionalized parents. As I demonstrated in chapter 1, these payback policies were quietly inserted into welfare reform provisions in the 1980s and 1990s. Without much public awareness or fanfare, their expansive reach contributed to the massive rise in child support debt during those decades. So even as TANF caseloads declined dramatically in the 2000s, the policy of charging welfare as child support continued. Over half the parents in the child support system have families that are receiving public assistance, or received it in the past. This explains why, at the national level, as much as 30 percent of child support debt is still owed to the government as a form of cost recovery for a variety of state benefits—and why in some states, like California, the percentage is well over 50 percent.[15]

In an ideal world, these payback policies would be rescinded for all low-income parents, for they undermine the basic ethos of public assistance as a form of collective social support. And they end up harming the poorest of children, given that these are the children who lose the support their parents do pay, since it goes to the government.[16] So while payback policies should be lifted for *all* parents, doing so for incarcerated parents would acknowledge the unique constraints on their ability to earn income.[17] It would also be a recognition that this debt is almost entirely uncollectible. Public debt places enormous economic pressure on reentering parents but does very little to relieve the fiscal burden on the state.

Then there is the issue of social justice: it takes a uniquely mean-spirited state to incarcerate so many parents and then to hold them financially responsible for the poverty their families are thrown into. During my research, some of the most egregious examples of inequity arose when judges enforced the public debt of incarcerated fathers. Like when a San Francisco judge told newly released Darden that half of his wages from a job he had just secured would be garnished to offset foster care costs. Or when Judge Matthews threw a Jacksonville father in jail because of his public debt, causing him to lose his apartment and the one job that had kept him afloat.

Concretely, this reform could be achieved by waiving payback policies for incarcerated parents or by passing through 100 percent of their payments to families. As I analyzed in chapter 1, states differ in the percentage of child support passed through to families in public assistance cases. Evaluation research on state pilot programs that eliminated government payback show how effective ending them is: it increased the frequency and amount of child support paid, reduced parents' overall debt, and expanded the resources available to children.[18] These effects were especially pronounced for low-income parents of color and incarcerated parents.[19] However, while state experiments are promising, this reform would need to be implemented at the federal level for it to be significant. Without a change in federal law, there will continue to be a hodgepodge of payback provisions across the country, with states with higher arrears likely to be the last to reform.[20] Indeed, several lawmakers and policy-makers have begun to consider the federal repeal of public assistance payback.[21] While their recommendations do not target incarcerated parents *per se*, the effects on these parents' lives would be transformative.

Finally, guaranteed incarceration orders and an end to public assistance payback would help slow the accumulation of debt for incarcerated parents but would do little to address the needs of those already saddled with debt. For a variety of reasons, some parents will continue to fall through the cracks and amass debt while in prison. In chapter 2, I set out various reasons why this happens—incarcerated parents lack knowledge about their orders, they are unable to advocate for themselves while in prison, and they cannot access the resources needed to adjudicate support orders from behind bars. States need to acknowledge that barriers to access will inevitably leave some parents with enormous support debt after prison.[22] So there needs to be a clear, consistent, and accessible mechanism for post-prison adjudication and debt relief. And this will require an exemption for incarcerated parents from the Bradley Amendment's bar on retroactive debt forgiveness.

As with the rescinding of public assistance payback, the Bradley Amendment should be reconsidered for all indebted parents. Several legal scholars have begun to make this case, arguing that Bradley is one of the primary causes of the debt bubble in which so many poor parents are trapped.[23] As I outlined in chapter 1, Bradley emerged in a very different era, when support judges may have been overly lenient toward some fathers and inclined to wipe out their arrears. But this is rarely the case now: if anything, the pendulum has swung so far in the other direction that few poor fathers receive fair treatment. Nowhere is this clearer than with incarcerated parents—judges come down exceptionally hard on them. Rethinking Bradley for incarcerated parents would recognize the unique constraints on their ability to manage their orders while institutionalized and the barriers they face in curtailing the debt of imprisonment. This could pave the way for more consistent debt relief programs to kick in when other modification methods have failed.

Indeed, over the past several years, there has been considerable interest among states and locales in debt relief programs for low-income and incarcerated parents, and these programs have proliferated across the country.[24] These programs vary in size and scope, with some focusing on all indebted parents and others on those who meet specific eligibility criteria (employment, arrears levels). Most programs offer reductions in debt if parents agree to follow a repayment plan, such as paying a percentage of the debt in a specified amount of time, or paying one lump sum at the outset in exchange for the forgiveness of the remainder of the debt. Like other policy pilots, debt relief programs tend to mix incarcerated and non-incarcerated parents together in their evaluation studies, so their effects on each group are not always clear. That said, the best evaluation research on these programs finds debt forgiveness to be associated with lower parental debt, more consistent support payments, and improved familial relationships.[25] Some have found reduced parental stress and improved relationships with children.[26]

To appreciate how these reforms might have changed the life trajectory of an indebted parent, recall Mr. Garcia, the Los Angeles father highlighted in the introduction to part 1. With the largest and longest-running debt in this study, Mr. Garcia owed over $500,000 on an order dating back to the 1970s. If California had incarceration orders when his debt began, it would not have soared during the times Mr. Garcia was in prison. If public assistance orders had been waived for institutionalized parents, a large part of his debt would never have accrued. If incarcerated parents had been exempt from the Bradley Amendment, he could have negotiated his debt to a more manageable level. If debt forgiveness had been more widely available, Mr. Garcia could have compromised some of his debt and thus saved his sons from making payments on it to keep their father out of jail. When Mr. Garcia was in court in 2016, had the state lawyer not foreclosed the possibility of reducing his debt, in part by citing Bradley, more could have been done to right the wrongs of Mr. Garcia's case thirty years after it began.

The debt of imprisonment can create inescapable financial confinement, yet it is possible to ease the internment with targeted reforms at the federal level.[27] But following through on reform will require a shift away from using child support to shame the indebted. And this will require more accurate representations of who indebted parents are and how debt affects their caregiving. No one benefits when fathers accumulate uncollectible and unmodifiable debt while incarcerated. No one benefits when they are tapped dry by public assistance payback upon release—not their children, not their children's mothers, and not the state itself.

Escaping the Imprisonment of Debt at the State Level

Reforms to debt accumulation raise the issue of what is reasonable and repayable for incarcerated parents; reforms to the enforcement apparatus raise the issue of the very purpose of debt. I grappled with this issue throughout this book, but especially in part 2: What is the goal of child support debt? Is it a way to ensure that families get financial support? Or is it a punishment for parents who failed in some way? As I outlined in chapter 3, the child support system has broadened and deepened its punitive reach over the past forty years, expanding its enforcement apparatus to include more and more punishments that reach further and further into parents' lives. And over this same period, debt has soared to unparalleled levels. As I argued in chapter 4, punitive measures did not work to get families the child support they needed; instead, they created their own prison, one with especially high costs for parents with criminal records.

Thus, as with the reform of debt accumulation, changes to the enforcement system necessitate a shift in logic. Instead of continuing to hit indebted parents with bigger and bigger sticks, enforcement could be reoriented to help them meet their support obligations and manage their debt. This would require less punishment and more help with post-prison reentry, a shift in approach that might make this set of reforms even more challenging to implement. Yet unlike reforms to the debt of imprisonment, which would require federal changes in legal definitions as well as congressional repeals of existing policies, reforms to enforcement would occur mostly at the state level. Here, too, a multipronged approach is needed: an expansion of assistance to parents coupled with the dismantling of punitive measures that take the biggest toll on incarcerated parents.

Perhaps the most straightforward way to reform the enforcement system would be to expand the assistance offered to indebted parents as they grapple with their support orders. Such help is particularly pressing for formerly incarcerated parents, who, as already noted, are well aware they are in dire need of such assistance. They need support not only to make sense of their orders but also to navigate and stay current on them. Here, too, some guidance can come from evaluation research on pilot programs that offer such assistance. This research suggests that child support assistance is most effective when it encompasses two components. First, it needs to be as proactive and service-oriented as possible. It should come in before fathers reach the point of no return or have become so entangled in debt and punishment that they see no way out. Second, support services are more effective when located in reentry programs, as opposed to child support offices alone.[28] The fear and stigma associated with support enforcement cause many parents to resist programs based in child support offices—too many fathers flee these programs, perceiving them as only adding to their surveillance and control.[29] Coordinating child support with reentry services is a promising way to avoid this.[30]

This leads to the second prong of this reform: dismantling key parts of the enforcement system in response to the unique risks facing incarcerated parents. The enforcement assemblage is a one-size-punishes-all system, with enforcement measures hitting parents irrespective of their particular challenges. Yet those measures have vastly different effects on different groups of parents. Nowhere is this clearer than for incarcerated parents, for whom everything from interest charges to license revocation to contempt of court has especially profound effects. The enforcement system could be made more responsive to the reentry challenges of these parents through distinct tracks of enforcement that kick in at different moments for different groups.

As I analyzed in chapter 3, there are three main pillars of child support enforcement: financial, remedial, and custodial. Of these, it is financial sanctions that actually lead to the most support retrieval, with wage garnishments constituting most of this recovered support. Because few incarcerated parents have wages to garnish, other financial sanctions tend to hit them harder. The best example of this is the interest charges levied on support debt, which have uniquely devastating effects on institutionalized parents since they are unable to pay down their debt while in prison. Despite this, states continue to compute regular, compound interest on support debt at high rates. These interest charges are a main engine of debt accumulation; they also act as an enforcement measure. They are designed to punish indebted parents through the threat of soaring debt. Again, although most of this debt is uncollectible, states continue to charge compound interest on it. For instance, in California over $4 billion is owed in interest on public assistance debt—that is close to 25 percent of all support debt.[31]

The reform path here is quite clear: if interest charges on institutionalized parents' support debt were waived, two problems could be addressed with one action. The amassing of arrears would slow, and their punitive effects would be muted. The main rationale for charging interest on support debt is to push parents to prioritize their arrears over other debt. But this logic is difficult to sustain for incarcerated parents, who rarely *choose* to withhold payment—most *cannot* pay while in prison. With wages averaging less than a dollar an hour, incarcerated parents aren't paying any of their other debts either. Charging interest on a debt that cannot be repaid seems gratuitously punitive since it worsens reentry outcomes.[32] When support payments, arrears, and interest are deducted from post-prison wages, most parents are left in severe financial hardship with little chance to pay off their debt.

Similar hardships emerge from remedial sanctions. Here, too, many enforcement measures pose particular difficulties for incarcerated parents, from state license revocations to asset liens to bank account seizures. Yet the most consequential of these has to be the driver's license revocation, which all states use to punish the nonpayment of as little as a few hundred dollars. The low threshold for license revocation basically ensures that close to all indebted parents leave prison with suspended licenses. As I showed in chapter 4, these suspensions then impede parents' employment while placing them in considerable legal peril. While this is true for all indebted parents, suspensions are even more damaging for those with criminal records since they face added challenges finding and maintaining work. Moreover, driving on a suspended driver's license can have a domino effect for these parents, since it can complicate parole. Thus, license suspension contributes in unique ways to the imprisonment of debt. And it can be easily addressed by ending the practice for child support debt. The ability of parents to remain mobile, to transport themselves to work, and to see their children must not depend on the financial means to pay off an outstanding debt.

Nor should other basic freedoms and liberties be rescinded simply because parents are unable to pay back support. This leads to the final enforcement pillar: the use of criminal and civil contempt to reincarcerate parents for nonpayment of support. It is hard to imagine a more consequential punishment for indebted parents in general and for the formerly incarcerated in particular. Images of nineteenth-century debtors' prisons come to mind when courts send citizens to jail for indefinite periods of time simply because of their failure to pay a debt. Those historic parallels may have been what prompted the Obama administration to include this practice in the 2016 Final Rule, suggesting that states establish procedures for the issuing of contempt orders and ensure that they use them within constitutional limits. But since the Final Rule did not mandate any meaningful oversight, it remains unclear whether it led to many changes. Given the on-the-ground realities of support courts, more serious reform is needed to address the enormous discretion and inequality in courts' use of jail to punish indebted parents.

It is curious and perplexing that so little is known about the use of a legal practice with such far-reaching consequences. Almost no systematic empirical research has been conducted on contempt actions, so basic questions remain about their use across time, place, and group, as well as about their short- and long-term effects. That said, even from the little that *is* known about contempt orders, it is hard to see any effective way to reform that stops short of the obvious: banning the use of jail for support debt. This is true for at least two reasons. First, we know that the current "ability to pay" standard is inadequate, for judges often conflate the ability to pay with the ability to work. So any indebted parent can face a contempt order if a judge so desires. Some legal scholars have begun to argue for using Thirteenth Amendment jurisprudence to challenge incarceration as a form of support enforcement precisely because courts use employability as the standard for contempt.[33]

Second, punishments as weighty as the denial of one's liberty should always abide by due process protections and guarantees of legal representation, both of which are missing from this arena of law. The disruptive capacity of incarceration is too great to be the outcome of judicial whim, yet judges act on their whims with shocking frequency in some child support courts—particularly those in Florida and in rural areas across the country. Moreover, custodial punishments derail parents from the reentry process like few other enforcement measures.[34] They set into motion cascading effects that undermine parents' reintegration. They have serious economic consequences, causing parents to lose employment, wages, housing, and overall stability. They disrupt familial networks, interrupting intimate relationships of care, reciprocity, and interdependence. And they have profound legal ramifications, complicating parents' desistance from crime and ability to stay out of prison. Given the lack of evidence to indicate that contempt actions yield anything positive to counteract their devastating effects, it is difficult to imagine why banning them would not surface as the centerpiece of any child support reform.

Together, these three reforms suggest that while there is no simple escape from the imprisonment of debt, it is possible to forge a path out of it. At a minimum, these reforms could protect indebted parents from encroachments on their basic rights and liberties. Yet they might also facilitate the reintegration process. If we return to Ronnie Jones, the Jacksonville father this book began with who spent years dodging law enforcement out of fear of reincarceration, these reforms could have been transformative. Without interest charges on his public debt, he might have paid it off before his debt ballooned to an unfathomable amount. Without the revocation of his driver's license and liens on his bank account, he might have stabilized his finances and stayed current on his support order. Without the repeated rearrests, he might have been able to keep his jobs, his housing, and his family's trust. And without the perpetual threat of being thrown back in jail, he might have come out from life underground and cared for his children with the parental dignity and respect that he so desired.

BEYOND THE BREADWINNER

Yet for any of this to happen, men like Ronnie would have to be viewed as worthy of respect and dignity. Herein lies perhaps the greatest challenge to reform: the little social value given to these men's fathering. Years of observing child support courts across the county have convinced me that this is probably the biggest hurdle of all. The profound stigmatization faced by indebted parents, and especially those with criminal records, distorts public perceptions and representations of them. There are few state arenas where such stigmatization is expressed as blatantly as in child support courts. Parents often face judges who relay their disdain for them without filters. They frequently confront state lawyers who echo that disdain as they mobilize enforcement measures to exact the harshest of punishments. And they regularly encounter state caseworkers who insist that their inability to manage child support is a sign of their lack of parental commitment. These state practices are held together by a conception of fatherhood that is as ubiquitous as it is disconnected from the reality of these men's lives.

The old, stale breadwinner model of fatherhood is rarely encountered in other public arenas. But it is alive and well in child support courts, where paternal responsibility is relentlessly monetarized and the caregiving role of fathers is too often denied. That model finds form in all the judicial lectures about what "daddies do," from Judge Matthews's proclamations that "love don't buy food" to Judge Ray's lauding of fathers who "man up and pay." It is expressed in the praise showered on fathers who exhibit little more than an ability to pay support when ordered. It surfaces through all the times judges overlook worrisome parental behavior, from missed visits with children to indications of family violence, simply because the father pays consistently. It even creeps into policy experts' evaluations that assess policy reforms solely for their effect on support payments, irrespective of other familial outcomes.

As with other normative models, this conception of fatherhood reveals itself most clearly when applied to those who do not adhere to it. Clearly and unforgivingly, the full weight of the system comes down on these indebted parents. Using what Judge Black calls "scared straight tactics," some state officials treat these parents with unrestrained fear and loathing. Like those who launch into lectures about the causes and consequences of men's bad fathering, from Judge Baxter's condemnations of the unemployed for failing to work their way out of poverty, to Judge Jones's threats to punish "househusbands" who prioritize caregiving, to Judge Matthews's insistence that nonpayment is a disease to be eradicated. Couple this with the way some state officials express condemnation—through name calling and violations of privacy and basic rights. These dehumanizing practices vary in degree across states and court systems, but they rarely vary in kind; indebted parents, as a whole, are treated with little respect for their value as caregivers.

Without question, any attempt to reform the child support system must target court practices that allow for such humiliation. Leaving indebted parents feeling ashamed and despondent does no one any good, least of all the families this system purports to serve. Indeed, some social scientists have begun to focus on how routine legal hearings turn into spectacles of stigmatization and how to overhaul them so they acknowledge that most fathers want to care for their children.[35] While these changes should be at the forefront of reform, they will do little good unless there is a corresponding challenge to the model of fathering underlying these judicial practices and tirades. Without a shift in understandings of fathers' caregiving, the impulse to shame will remain. In much the same way that advocates of criminal justice reform had to first humanize and thereby make visible the men and women that mass incarceration had taken from their communities, indebted parents' caregiving should to be acknowledged, visualized, and validated.

It is precisely this kind of social recognition that so many indebted fathers find missing in the current child support system. This absence is often what troubles them most, even more than the debt and punishment they accumulate. As we consider how to move beyond the breadwinner model of fathering, we could take some advice from fathers themselves. In interviews, these men were eager to suggest ways the system could change. Their ideas were often quite creative, from the creation of caregiver credits to enable them to pay down their debt while spending time with their children, to the creation of public childcare programs for debt forgiveness, to formulas to compute in-kind support as forms of debt repayment. Yet what struck me most about their ideas was the conception of fathering that guided them and how their model was premised on a broad understanding of who needs care and who can provide it. Their expansive model of fathering implied three moves to redefine and highlight their caregiving.

First, these fathers asked that state institutions focus less on what they cannot do and cannot achieve. They asked not to be portrayed as failed fathers, labor market rejects, and broken work machines. They asked that state law stop holding them up to parenting ideals that reduce fatherhood to breadwinning. In effect, they asked that they stop being pushed into, and punished through, precisely the fatherhood standards they are least able to meet. Indeed, these fatherhood standards are unobtainable, and often undesirable, for many middle-class and privileged men as well. Yet disadvantaged fathers with the mark of a criminal record continue to be held to them.[36] The cruel irony of shifting masculinities is that men's ability to redefine their identities as workers and as parents can be a mark of class privilege—it is an ability that often comes last to those who most need it.[37] Instead of moving beyond this outdated model, state officials reassert it and require paid work from indebted fathers in ways reminiscent of forced labor.[38]

Second, fathers asked that state institutions focus more on what they do provide and contribute to their families. This point was echoed by fathers across the parenting spectrum, from the good to the bad to the dead broke. Fathers relayed this every day in courts across the country, with the most contentious court exchanges involving clashes over conceptions of fatherhood. As fathers insisted that parenthood meant paying attention to and caring for children, courts blamed them for trying to escape their real duties. As fathers asserted their own parental commitments, courts threatened to punish them. As fathers put forth a new "package deal" that stressed their role as caretakers, courts insisted on the old deal of breadwinning fatherhood. And while time-budget surveys do reveal that disadvantaged fathers, particularly men of color, provide more carework than other groups of men, state officials refused to budge in their insistence that earning money made a man—and paying child support made a father.[39] Despite losing the battle, many men continued to insist that caregiving defined them as fathers.

Yet fathers are not the only ones to value these contributions: when asked, their families often express how much they need fathers' support. Their children emphasize the attention they get from their dads. Referring to them as "all the little things," kids savor the meals they eat, the games they play, and the books they read together. Recall Mandy's account of how her dad does everything for her: how he cooks, takes her to school, makes her laugh, and keeps her happy. Or recall the pride with which Jimmy announced that his dad hadn't missed a game in his two-year football career. Even children's mothers, who can be understandably ambivalent and distrustful of fathers, often see them as playing important roles in kids' lives.[40] They frequently tried to contextualize men's struggles to judges and suggest the need for father involvement. This is not to say that mothers don't need financial assistance—of course they do. But they also acknowledge the care that indebted fathers want to give and their efforts to provide it.

Thus, in addition to highlighting the caregiving of so many indebted fathers, we need a more expansive understanding of who benefits from their care. This was not something these fathers asked for explicitly, but it emerged from their own experiences with fathers. At several points, I have noted the painful silence that followed my questions about the best fathers these men had known. When fathers did offer a response, their answers rarely included their biological fathers. Instead, they mentioned male kin: grandfathers, uncles, or cousins whom they felt fathered by. They named male mentors who guided them and men in the community whom they modeled themselves after. Their responses suggested a paternal parallel to the "other mothering" so essential to African American women's parenting—a mothering born out of the need to relieve biological mothers and later became the backbone of community care and activism.[41] Often downplayed with disadvantaged men, or assumed to have vanished long ago, indebted parents spoke of a social fatherhood through which they were cared for by others.

Recognizing the work that men put into parenting others could be enormously validating for them and transformative for public perceptions of them. Recall Sonny, the Jacksonville father who credited the head of a reentry program with fathering him through his post-prison transition. Or think of Ali, the New York City man who found a father figure in an older man, Lamar, who supported him as he put his life together after a long prison stay. And how Ali then paid it forward in his care for Tyrice, the young Bronx father who credited him with his own ability to "show up" for his son. Although they struggled to maintain their expansive fathering practices in a state system that actively discouraged them, they found meaning in these connections. I also saw glimmers of social fatherhood enacted by these men, when Reggie brought his crew of a dozen little kids to the Miami hospital where his nephew was in a coma and held vigil for days while his biological parents worked. Or when Junior volunteered to take care of his son and their mother's two other kids, both with special needs, while she worked. Or when Ronnie woke early every morning to walk his children to school, along with a group of neighborhood kids, smiling while thinking of himself as a big duck leading a flock of little ducklings.

By making these practices visible and recognizing their social value, it might be possible to consider the fathers who perform them as socially valuable. Instead of shutting them down, state institutions might begin to find new avenues for men to pursue their fathering and open up possibilities for their caregiving. State officials might then begin to see beyond the size of their debts and to visualize the scope of their paternal involvement. This might then encourage all of us to see the potential in their contributions and commitments as parents. Once this occurs, we might begin to unravel the entangled system of punishment and debt and bridge the yawning chasm that separates state policy and law from the lives they govern.

APPENDIX About the Research

The idea for this project came to me many years ago when I was giving a talk at NYU Law School on my previous book, *Offending Women*, and discussing how the penal state familializes women by using their roles as mothers as a form of social control. After the talk, someone asked me a question about how the penal state familializes men and whether their treatment differed from that of women. As I so often did when I got this question about men, I launched into a discussion about how the state did not treat men as men—and certainly did not familialize them. Just the opposite, I claimed: men's roles as parents were ignored and denied by the penal state, both during and after incarceration. But as I was making the argument that time, I began to question it: did I really *know* that the state disregarded men as fathers? Was the penal state's failure to address men as fathers during prison the same as negating their roles entirely?

Little did I know that these questions would linger, leading me on an almost decade-long journey that would evolve into a large, multi-method, multi-state, multi-system research project. From the start, I knew that the study would have to be multi-method. Since I was interested in how criminal justice and child support had become linked through both policy and practice, the study would have to include ethnographic observation.

But because I also wanted to know how fathers experienced these interconnections, the project would need an interview component as well. I also had a sense that these interviews would be complicated, both for the fathers I spoke to and for me—a feminist researcher who had spent her career studying women.

While all of this pointed to a complex research design, there were several things I didn't realize in the early stages of the project—issues that made the research even more complicated than I initially imagined. Most importantly, I underestimated the extent of state variation in this arena. The United States is very much a collection of fifty state systems, each with its own criminal justice, welfare, and legal institutions. Still, I had no idea just how much variation I would encounter in these systems. States differed in the size of their indebted populations and in key aspects of their child support systems. They had different approaches to setting, modifying, and enforcing support orders, both in general and for incarcerated parents. What was possible in one state was often unimaginable in another. Moreover, because I was interested in the links between criminal justice and child support policy, I had to remain attentive to these differences both within and across policy arenas, which made state variation doubly complex and significant.

Quite early on, then, this multi-method study became a multi-state project. Before I could select my case study states, I had to do an enormous amount of background research. Because I needed my cases to capture a diverse population of indebted parents while also including key dimensions of policy variation, I approached the case selection quite systematically. I devoted months to a comprehensive analysis of national patterns in child support debt and policy. As these policies seemed to be perpetually changing, my analysis needed continual updating. For this, I relied on student research assistants to track policy developments over time and across states, using data from the Office of Child Support Enforcement (OCSE) and Departments of Child Support Services (DCSSs). These policy updates were used to construct state maps of the policy landscape. These maps also guided my case selection, leading me to locate my research in three large states—New York, California, and Florida. Together, these states accounted for a large percentage of the nation's child support arrears, even while taking different approaches to debt accumulation and enforcement.

This is especially true of their policies on order modification, use of custodial sanctions, and assessment of interest charges—three policy areas that were critical to my analysis.

Even after I selected the states of my research, variation continued to surface. Within each state there was enormous variation in court systems and legal practices. These divergences were not simply the result of judicial whim or discretion; they also reflected systemic differences in how courts operated. The differences between northern and southern Florida were just as pronounced as those between northern and southern California. Rural and urban differences were so profound that they could trump all other variation. And within NYC, cross-borough differences were considerable. This prompted me to base my court observations in at least two locales in each state: the Jacksonville and Miami areas in Florida, Brooklyn and the Bronx in New York City, Los Angeles and the Bay Area in California. At all sites, I conducted the observations myself and tried to cover the complete slate of judges and magistrates, which in some places meant observing more than a dozen judges several times. It also meant that the research was now located across even more state terrains, focused on child support and criminal justice policies at the federal and state levels as well as on the practices of child support courts.

As the research evolved, its scope became broader. It began to encompass many moving parts at different empirical and analytical levels. By the time the data collection was over, I had been engaged in five years of research (2014–18). That included three years of ethnographic research in support courts, where I observed 1,200 distinct child support cases and conducted 145 qualitative interviews with formerly incarcerated fathers with support debt. The fathers came from the states of my research, equally divided among them. In particular:

In Florida: I observed 410 child support cases through ethnographic work in nine courtrooms in the areas around Jacksonville and Miami-Dade Counties. I also carried out fifty in-depth interviews with formerly incarcerated fathers with child support debt in these regions.

In New York: I observed 365 support cases through fieldwork in twelve courtrooms in Brooklyn, Manhattan, and the Bronx. I also carried out fifty interviews with formerly incarcerated fathers with child support debt across New York City.

In California: I observed 435 child support cases through fieldwork in eleven courtrooms in the areas around Los Angeles, San Bernardino, San Francisco, Napa, Alameda, and Contra Costa Counties. I also carried out forty-five interviews with indebted fathers in Los Angeles and the Bay Area.

From afar, this may seem like an unmanageable amount of data. Reflecting back on these totals, they even seem a bit unwieldy to me. Yet they rarely felt unmanageable at the time. In part, this was because I often approached the research in stages, trying to complete the data collection and analysis of each case study state before moving on to the next. Although this did not always work as I was frequently pulled back to states for important interviews and observations. In addition, my ability to move among research methods, state spaces, and analytical levels was both the challenge and the advantage of this project. Figuring out how to hold together the many moving parts, while grappling with the obstacles that emerged in each part, made the research exciting, enriching, and trying all at once. Several methodological issues did surface in the process, and I discuss two of the more consequential ones here: the power dynamics of observing in court and the emotional dynamics of interviewing indebted parents.[1]

SILENCE AND POWER IN COURT: THE ETHNOGRAPHY

As I have done in all my past research projects, I began this one ethnographically, since my early experiences in the field have often been predictive of future areas of analysis. So it was here: as I ventured into child support courts, I was immediately struck by the dynamics of power and punishment. Even my ability to enter the spaces was indicative of these dynamics. Like most courts, child support hearings are supposed to be open to the public. While most of them are, there is a caveat to their openness: judges and magistrates can remove anyone they like from "their" courtrooms. Many judges interpret this right as extending to observers as well and require those who enter their courts to be vetted. For those with cases, this vetting happens by court administrators prior to the start of court day. But for observers, the vetting could happen at any point. So I got used to explaining my presence. Sometimes this happened in advance—several Florida courts required that I submit written requests to judges before entering court. Many courts also put constraints on my observations: besides banning all electronic devices, they required that I omit all personal, identitifying information from my notes. Some also asked me to use pseudonyms or to keep things "off the record." Other judges ignored me for weeks, only to turn to me suddenly one day in open court to demand that I explain why I was there. When this occurred, I felt the panic that so many parents must have experienced: Was I going to be reprimanded? Tossed out? Humiliated?

This permission-granting revealed a lot about these state spaces: while it was always clear where the power lay, it was totally unclear how it would be used. As discussed in chapter 2, judicial power was often wielded so unpredictably that it could seem arbitrary and at times abusive. This was true despite all the rules that guided support hearings. These courts were tightly scripted and controlled spaces. The protocols were clear, interactions were curtailed, and behavior was regulated. In some Florida courts, men and women had to sit on separate sides of the courtroom and deviations were not allowed—not even for me, a researcher without a case. In one Jacksonville court, days began with a lecture on how parents should talk and walk while in the presence of the judge, with the bailiff, Frank, warning that "Jerry Springer behavior" would result in an immediate expulsion from court.

Of all the court protocols, perhaps the most consistent across locales was the insistence on silence. There was to be no talking before, during, or after one's case was called. Parents were allowed to speak only when spoken to by court officials. Otherwise, they had to sit in silence. No cell phones or computers were allowed. Court officers policed the space, surveilling the silence and calling out violations of it. All of this only added to the courts' performative quality and made them seem like judicial theaters. It also made my ethnographic work uniquely challenging. On the continuum of participant and observer, I was forced into the farthest end of observation. Sitting in silence, I was left to follow facial expressions, to track bodily movements, and to listen intently to the smallest of utterances. And to write everything down, verbatim. The one silver lining to these courts of silence was that I could take copious notes of the words being said in them.

Still, maintaining silence for hours on end was not easy. It became almost unbearable given what was often being said by those who could speak in these spaces. Child support courts can be sites of extreme humiliation. I learned this on my very first day in the field in the Bronx, when the third case I observed involved a recently incarcerated father who was called names and eventually dragged out of court by the police. I learned something similar on my first day in court in Florida, when, upon exiting the elevator, I heard Judge Matthews screaming at a father so loudly that his voice resounded through the closed courtroom door and echoed all the way down the hall. Such treatment stunned me day after day. Even by the end of the fieldwork, after I had spent years observing, I had not become numb to it. It never got easy to observe the humiliation in silence. For the better part of three years, I would leave court during breaks to run around the block and release the tension. Or I'd call friends and family to unload on them, as if simply giving voice to what was occurring in these spaces relieved the pressure of silence.

If *I* was having such reactions, I could only imagine what the targets of this punishment were experiencing. While I was anxious to hear from them, I quickly realized that court was not the right environment to do it in. Not only was I forbidden from talking to parents during hearings, but when I tried to approach them during breaks they often shut down. Parents seemed so concerned with their cases that they were in no place to reflect on their experiences. What's more, distrust ran so deep among these parents that many refused to believe I was not a court officer out to expose them. The suspicion was so pervasive that I even abandoned my initial plan to recruit parents for interviews during their court appearances. The trust I needed for our interviews would be impossible to secure if I was associated with court, even indirectly.

This is where my ability to move among research methods and units of analysis proved helpful. Once I realized I needed to speak to parents in an environment where they felt safe, I stopped trying to pursue conversations with them in court and focused on observing their actions and their responses to court dynamics. This is not to say I remained mute while in court—I'm too committed an ethnographer for that. In order to make the court research as interactive and as ethnographic as possible, I struck up conversations with friends and family members who accompanied parents to court. I became friendly with the court officers, speaking at length to bailiffs, guards, and police officers. I spent time with state attorneys, asking them about details of cases and their approaches to specific legal issues. When possible, I chatted with custodial parents who were open to talking, asking them about their children and their experiences with child support.

My attempts to move away from the observer end of the ethnographic continuum were more successful in some states. The structure of many support courts inhibited interaction. For instance, in Florida it was nearly impossible to be interactive since courtrooms tended to be large, with strictly enforced protocols. On the other hand, New York City courts were more private, with a few cases called into a courtroom at a time. This meant there was more discussion among court staff before and after cases were heard, as well as among parents while they waited outside the courtroom for their cases to be called. As a result, I interacted quite a bit in these courts and got to know several state lawyers, so that they often whispered points to me during hearings and offered clarifications during court breaks. While this also occurred in several California locales, there was more variation in that state's court system. In some parts of the Bay Area and Los Angeles, courts were interactive and open to dialogue. But in other regions, like parts of Napa County and the Central Valley, courts felt far more scripted and thus less dialogical and interactive.

This leads to the judges and magistrates. For many reasons, it can be quite challenging for ethnographers to work in spaces so heavily defined and dominated by one person. When one person wields so much control, it can be difficult for researchers to negotiate the resulting power relations. While I had dealt with similar dynamics before as a young researcher, it was more difficult to do so now. Despite my attempts to come off as non-threatening, I seemed to provoke more concern among those in power. There seemed to be more at stake in my observations, more at risk in my note-taking.

That said, judges had a range of responses to me—and I had a range of relationships with them. Some judges completely ignored me, leaving me to do my observations with no mention of who I was or what I was doing there. Other judges highlighted my presence whenever possible, continually referring to the "professor watching us" during court proceedings. One

Florida judge insisted that I sit in the jury box, on display for everyone to see, during the court day (and making me extremely uncomfortable, to say the least). Other judges seemed to perform for me, exerting their power with a bit more aplomb after they learned I was a researcher. Other judges tried to impress me, constantly referring to how many cases they had presided over or how many fathers they had sent to jail—like the Brooklyn judge who regaled me with how much back-support "he" had secured for mothers during his time on the bench. Other judges tried to educate me, turning to me to explain their judicial logic or reasoning behind a decision. Still others tried to draw me into their work, talking to me after cases and taking me back to chambers to elaborate on sensitive legal issues they did not want to discuss in open court. Indeed, confidentiality was important to many of these legal authorities, which both surprised and intrigued me.

In many ways, judges' responses to being observed mirrored their judicial approach. Those judges who were most punitive with parents also seemed to be the most uncomfortable with my presence. This prompted them to highlight my presence or to perform for me, which could feel like further exertions of power. By contrast, judges who were more progressive—or sensitive to the political complexities of their cases—tended to take a more educative approach to me. But no matter how they ran their courtrooms or responded to being researched, all judges dominated in their spaces. They remained the central forces in court, so their voices resounded through my ethnography. Even the most reformist judges established environments where they were the arbiters of who could speak and what could be said. Thankfully, I was able to carve out alternative spaces where other voices could also be heard.

LISTENING DEEPLY: THE INTERVIEWS

Given the silence of child support courts, I realized early on that the interviews would take on a particularly important role in this project. While I often do interviews in my research, I usually use them as supplements to ethnographic research. But this project had to be different: listening to indebted parents was more essential here because of my inability to hear them in court and the more general unwillingness to listen to them. As

Gerson and Damaske remind us, in-depth interviews do more than illuminate the arena of thought and reflection; they also allow us to gain perspective on the hypothetical and on routes not taken.[2] Indeed, I wanted the interviews for this project to cover all these aspects. I wanted parents to tell their stories in their own words—and to feel heard.

But I also realized this would be very challenging. From the start, simply finding indebted parents to interview was daunting since they often try to maintain a low profile. Given how enmeshed these parents were in multiple state systems, I knew I could utilize state institutions to locate them. But I also knew I could not limit my sample to state programs, for that would skew it toward parents integrated into state services and support networks. Moreover, because recruiting only through criminal justice or child support institutions would skew my sample, I worked hard to recruit an equal percentage of indebted parents from both systems. In the end, I recruited through close to twenty different agencies and penal facilities, some of which I also worked hard to gain the cooperation of.[3] On the criminal justice side, I utilized agencies ranging from state Departments of Corrections to reentry programs to legal aid offices and probation services. On the child support side, I used agencies ranging from state Departments of Child Support Services to fatherhood programs to local support groups. I worked hard to maintain this recruitment strategy across all three states and the locales within them. I also worked hard to manage the different constraints these agencies placed on my work: some forbade me from recording on the premises, which is a common restriction in penal facilities; others asked that I use pseudonyms when referring to their agencies in order to protect program participants' confidentiality; and still others requested that I use their actual agency names in order to make their institution's work visible. So the constraints placed on this part of the research varied. Fortunately, this sampling procedure also resulted in a varied and diverse sample of fathers. Table 3 includes their demographic breakdown.

Even with the assistance of such a wide range of agencies, it took an enormous amount of work to reach indebted parents. Many parents cycled in and out of prison; others were busy navigating work and family demands. So I had to keep calling and following up. When I reached them, it was frequently a struggle to nail down a time and place for the

Table 3 Respondent Demographic Breakdown		
Sample characteristics	*Number N = 145*	*%*
Marital status		
Never married	77	53
Divorced/separated	54	37
Married	14	10
Race*		
Black	52	41
White	37	30
Latino/Hispanic	34	27
Native American	1	1
Asian	1	1
Number of children		
One	14	10
Two to three	64	43
Four or more	68	46
Resides with		
Alone	36	25
Partner	29	20
Relatives	26	18
Roommate/friends	17	12
Homeless	37	25
Reported income		
None	44	30
Less than $10,000	64	44
$10,000–$20,000	24	16
$20,000–$40,000	8	5
$50,000 or more	6	4
Time in prison		
Less than 1 year	14	10
2–5 years	58	40
5–10 years	45	31
More than 10 years	28	19
Incarcerated for child support		
Yes	52	36
No	93	64

*N = 125 for data on respondents' racial identification.

interview. The hurdles were not just logistical: many parents were wary of me and my intentions. Given how heavily surveilled their lives were, I understood that. I spent a lot of time assuring them I was not a court officer or caseworker in disguise. I also had to convince them that I wanted to hear their experiences and would listen without judgement. And that I would protect the information they shared. For this, it helped to have a trusted confidant or service agency to vouch for me. But even with this, I was often met with suspicion. "I googled you and see you're on their side," a Napa father once greeted me. After I explained I had no connection to court, he corrected me. "No, I saw that you write a lot about women . . . so you're on their side?" The layers of suspicion were many.

Negotiating those layers was often a process. With some fathers, I had to work hard to secure their trust before asking them to talk to me about such sensitive parts of their lives. And for some, this meant agreeing not to record our interview. Most of these fathers pressed me from the start about who would have access to their information. Even with my repeated guarantees of confidentiality, they remained wary. Here, too, I understood the reluctance: these fathers were under so much scrutiny and surveillance, they worried that something they said to me could come back to haunt them. Since I wanted them to feel safe with me, I sometimes had to forgo the recording of them. While I understood this, it presented real challenges for my data collection: it meant I had to stop several times during interviews to write down direct quotes. It also forced me to get quite creative with the data analysis—writing long memos after each interview, which then got coded and analyzed.

For most of the fathers I interviewed, their suspicions dissipated when the interview actually began. In fact, most of them opened up quickly and seemed to appreciate being heard—with some even agreeing to be recorded midway through the interview. These fathers were not used to being listened to, especially on the topics I asked about. We discussed everything from their time in prison, to their child support history, to their experiences in court, to their lives as fathers—all topics these men were rarely asked about. Instead of ignoring their identities as parents, I probed them. Instead of denying the effects of prison on their parenting, I asked about them. And instead of shutting down the emotions this raised, we talked through them. There was a lot of ground to be covered here, and it often led us into rough terrain. The toughest parts of the interview always seemed to come when we ventured into fathers' experiences as incarcerated parents and their feelings of regret. Or into memories of their own fathers and their fears of replicating the losses they experienced as children.

When confronting these difficult topics, few fathers held back. The interviews frequently went very long, sometimes stretching on for several hours. Once fathers realized I was there to listen, the floodgates often opened. Of course, not all fathers opened up; some came to our interviews with walls up and kept them up throughout. But the overwhelming majority of men came across as honest and candid. They were open about their experience in prison and the pain it involved. They were open about their court experiences and the range of emotions they provoked, from anger and rage to embarrassment and humiliation. Some even brought case files and court correspondence with them to buttress their claims about being mistreated and disrespected. Most of all, though, fathers wanted to talk about their families and children. Here, too, they seemed disarmingly honest as they revealed the good and the bad aspects of family life. They recounted all the times they came through for loved ones, as well as the times they hurt and neglected them. They recalled all the things they did to support their families, as well as the familial conflicts their actions caused. They remembered all the pleasures and joys of fatherhood, as well as the guilt and remorse they struggled to manage.

As they recounted all of this, fathers could get very emotional. And these emotions had to be grappled with. Quite often, fathers broke down in tears—which I was both unprepared for and continually surprised by. While I expected these men to have complex and rich emotional lives, I was astonished by how willingly they gave me access to those parts of themselves. Initially, I found myself overthinking these dynamics and struggling to develop special interview strategies to grapple with the emotional outpouring. Yet over and over again, these fathers taught me there was comfort in the simple act of being heard. So although I would never exaggerate the effects of one interview, many fathers sent follow-up texts and phone calls to thank me for listening and for acknowledging them as parents.

There were, however, a few fathers who got so emotional and so angry that it was hard for them to contain their rage. When they got worked up, their anger could spill over into all aspects of the interview. Some of them then became dismissive of subsequent interview questions, while others insisted on saying extremely hurtful things about their families and children. It was never clear how to interpret these outbursts. Or how to respond during interviews when fathers went down this route. Particularly because it was then very challenging to get them back on track and set boundaries around the interview exchange.

Indeed, the struggle to maintain boundaries while conducting emotional interviews was ongoing. Far more common than fathers who were unable to contain their anger were those simply in a lot of pain. And who often sought confirmation of this pain from me. These men asked me to corroborate their feelings of regret and sense of injustice; they asked me to support their childrearing approaches. I understood their desire for confirmation. As discussed throughout this book, many fathers lacked the support needed to weather the financial and emotional storms in their lives. They were uncertain about how to proceed through those storms. They rarely felt respected or acknowledged as parents. So they sought reassurance wherever they might find it—which could prompt them to ask me for it. Because of all the dangers, both ethical and methodological, of being a source of approval and support, I struggled to avoid getting pulled into this role while also remaining responsive to and respectful of all they faced in their lives.

Despite my best attempts to avoid it, some fathers tried to pull me into their personal lives by insisting that I run interference with their kids' mothers. "You get it," one Miami father once explained to me. "I need you to talk to her... to explain where I'm coming from... 'cause she'll listen to you." Even after I made it clear that this was not an appropriate role for a researcher, a few fathers contacted their kids' mothers and family members to ask them to talk to me. Then there was the Sacramento father who secretly texted the mother of his kids my phone number during our interview, instructing her to call me immediately. Imagine how confused we both were when I answered the call, just minutes after the interview concluded, only to realize how inappropriate it was for us to be speaking to each other about such personal matters. In all of these cases, I had to walk a fine line between maintaining fathers' trust and remaining a responsible researcher. Walking that line was often hard.

As I walked that line, there is no doubt that my own social position and background mattered. They mattered a lot. The social differences of gender, race, class, and generation separating me from these fathers were as clear as they were vast. At times, I made them vaster by awkwardly trying to bridge them—like when I caught myself using more swear words than usual in interviews (which is saying a lot since my speech is already littered with curse words). While there are many excellent methodological reflections on how to negotiate such differences, I was continually reminded that good human relations and social skills go a long way here. As does an acknowledgment of one's positionality and an ongoing commitment to remain as reflexive as possible—all of which I insisted on throughout the research process.

At the same time, it is also important to remember that social differences can be productive. There were times when fathers seemed to speak more candidly with me perhaps *because of* our differences—because I was a woman, and also a parent, whose background was so different from theirs. This first occurred to me when I reviewed the transcripts of interviews done by John Halushka, the only research assistant I trusted to conduct parts of the research. John was an exceptional interviewer and in the midst of doing research on the reentry experiences of this group of men. While his interviews revealed a great deal about men's lives, they were far less emotional than the ones I did, even though we used the exact same interview guide. From the transcripts, I sensed fathers' wariness with a male interviewer. Questions that almost always provoked emotional responses in my interviews did not seem to provoke the same emotions when John asked them. It was as if the social distance separating us allowed some fathers to let their guard down and drop a stance they may have felt compelled to maintain with other men.

There were other, more direct ways that our differences proved beneficial. Recognizing that I knew a considerable amount about support policy and law, many fathers requested legal assistance from me. And while I maintained boundaries around my involvement in their personal lives, I was more open to requests for help with state institutions. As this book has made clear, indebted fathers are at a real disadvantage navigating the complex world of child support; only a minority receive assistance with their support cases or debt modification. During our interviews, as these men recounted misunderstandings about how policy and law worked, it was difficult for me not to assist them or encourage them to rethink a legal approach I knew would be a losing one. At the same time, I didn't want the interviews to turn into legal advice sessions. So I started coming to interviews with referrals to legal aid offices and reentry programs. Only when a parent was in extreme legal jeopardy did I stay after the interview to offer advice. In a few cases, I also agreed to help fathers make sense of court paperwork and prepare legal appeals.

Of course, I never came close to meeting the needs these fathers had—nor would it have been appropriate for me to try. It was in the process of assisting them that I began to grasp the enormous obstacles they faced in managing cycles of debt and punishment. Those insights contributed to my analysis in important ways, cluing me in to the legal mazes and institutional loops parents often got stuck in. They also pushed me to get involved in policy reform work once the data collection was complete. That is, the more I learned about these systemic inequities, the more I began to seek broader ways to address them. And the experiences of indebted parents showed me where to target efforts to make a difference: from collaborating with California Department of Corrections to build bridges with child support, to joining forces with several reform groups to pass legislative reforms to California's public assistance payback and interest policies, to collaborating with the Department of Justice and National Institute of Justice to propose federal reforms in this area.[4] This policy reform work was motivated by the concrete experiences of the indebted parents in this research.

And this leads me back to how I began this methodological discussion: how this project allowed me to move among many dimensions and how such movement enriched the overall analysis. Just as I moved between methods and across states, I also moved from research to policy in ways that offered insight into the politics of reform and indebted fatherhood more broadly. In fact, this policy work is what led to many of the conclusions I end the book with—from the specific reforms needed at the federal, state, and local levels to the need for a sociologically inspired approach to reform. It was also my foray into policy work that sensitized me to just how challenging it will be to bring about these changes: from the deep suspicion that follows indebted fathers to the deep denial of their important role as caregivers, the obstacles are many. So while it remains unclear whether child support reform will find its way onto the criminal justice reform agenda, it *is* clear that such integration must occur for the cycles of punishment and debt experienced by so many disadvantaged families to come to an end.

Notes

INTRODUCTION

1. For more on the Stroup case and his eventual death in jail, see Hudes, "Absent but Beloved: America's 'Most Wanted Deadbeat Dad' Dies While Serving Sentence," *Calgary Herald*, 20 June 2019, https://calgaryherald.com/news/local-news/absent-but-loved-americas-most-wanted-deadbeat-dad-dies-while-serving-sentence.

2. For more on the case of Walter Scott, see Hager 2015a, as well as Robles and Dewan, "Skip Child Support. Go to Jail. Lose Job. Repeat," *New York Times*, 20 April 2015, https://www.nytimes.com/2015/04/20/us/skip-child-support-go-to-jail-lose-job-repeat.html.

3. Sorensen, Sousa, and Schaner 2007. For more on the income breakdown of those who owe child support debt, see Putze 2017; and Turetsky and Waller 2020.

4. For more on this research, see the Methodological Appendix. Briefly, this fieldwork was conducted in the three case study states and in two locales in each state—the areas of Jacksonville and Miami, Brooklyn and the Bronx, and Los Angeles and the Bay Area. In these areas, I observed the processes and practices of support adjudication. I conducted all the court observations myself, usually in three-month intervals. All judges granted me access to their courtrooms, while also placing some constraints on how I could collect and report my observations. Although courtrooms varied in organization and degree of privacy, I observed the complete slate of judges and magistrates, which in some locales meant observing

more than a dozen judges several times. Because some judges made access to their court contingent on robust protocols to protect confidentiality, I agreed to use pseudonyms when referencing them. Even for those who did not explicitly request this, the use of pseudonyms helped all legal officials feel that their courtrooms were not under direct scrutiny or evaluation—perhaps making them less inclined to adjust their behavior accordingly.

5. The interviews ran for one to three hours and were recorded (when respondents granted permission) and transcribed. I recruited equal numbers of fathers through the criminal justice and child support systems, sampling a similar percentage from prisoner re-entry programs, offender registration offices, child support programs, and legal aid offices. This resulted in a diverse sample of fathers—table 3 includes the demographic breakdown. To protect fathers' privacy and the sensitive information many of them shared with me, I use pseudonyms to refer to them and their family members.

6. This state debt is discussed in detail in chapter 1. Put simply, public assistance payback mandates that the cost of everything from TANF to Medicaid be calculated as child support and repaid to the state itself. For more on the history of these mandates, see Turetsky and Waller 2020.

7. Carson 2020.

8. For more on the relationship between criminal justice and the institutions of health care, see Lara-Millan 2014 and Comfort et al. 2016; for more on education, see Rios 2011 and Morris 2018; for more on family and kin, see Braman 2004; Arditti 2012; and Western et al. 2015; and for social services, see Miller 2014; Stuart 2016; and Schept 2016.

9. See Lara-Millan and Gonzalez van Cleve 2017.

10. The scholarship on collateral consequences and reentry is massive. For a few comprehensive reviews, see Visher and Travis 2003; Wakefield and Uggen 2010; Harding, Wyse, Dobson, and Morenoff 2014; Morenoff and Harding 2014; Harding et al. 2016; Bersani and Doherty 2018; Kirk and Wakefield 2018; and Phelps 2020.

11. See LeBaron and Roberts 2010; Comfort 2008, 2016; and Solinger et al. 2010.

12. See Nurse 2002; Schnittker and John 2007; Schnittker, Massoglia, and Uggen 2011; Wildeman and Mueller 2012; and Comfort 2016.

13. On childhood disadvantage, see Geller et al. 2009, 2012; Wildeman 2009; Wakefield and Wildeman 2013; on familial instability, see Turney 2015; Apel 2016; and Harding et al. 2016; and on parental depression see Turney, Schnitter, and Wildeman 2012.

14. For an excellent overview of these effects, see Chondry and Smith 2018; as well as Wildeman 2009; Arditti 2012; Hagan and Foster 2012; Wakefield and Wildeman 2013; and Wakefield, Lee, and Wildeman 2016.

15. Kohler-Hausmann 2018.

16. For more on the fines and fees, see Harris, Evans, and Beckett 2010; Beckett and Harris 2011; Martin, Smith, and Still 2017; Martin et al. 2018; and Financial Justice Project 2020.

17. Martin 2018.

18. Harris, Evans, and Beckett 2010; Harris 2016; Martin, Smith, and Still 2017. For an analysis of child support debt as a "collateral consequence" of incarceration, see Turetsky and Waller 2020.

19. This is in contrast to the logic at work in the use of fines and fees in Europe, where they have become an alternative to the incapacitation of prison. In the United States, they are added to the incapacitation and a lingering consequence of it. For more on European approaches, see Kantorowicz-Reznichenko 2015; and Martin et al. 2018.

20. Turetsky and Waller 2020: 120.

21. Zelizer 2012.

22. Zelizer 2010, 2005.

23. See Fourcade and Healy 2007; Healy 2006; Polletta and Tufall 2014; Wherry 2012; and Wherry, Seefeldt, and Alvarez 2019.

24. For a fascinating study of how this occurs with distant creditors and debt settlement, see Polletta and Tufall 2014, 2016.

25. For a copy of the bill to create this registry, see Tom Lackey, "Lackey Bill Would Put Child Support Evaders on Blast," http://lackeyforassembly.com/lackey-bill-put-child-support-evaders-blast.

26. And these fathers were not alone here—while research on indebted fathers is quite limited, others also find that fathers insist child support is their parental responsibility and obligation. See Vogel 2020b for another example of fathers' views on the importance of child support.

27. For two examples of this, one old and one recent, see Moynihan 1965; and Mead 2011.

28. Liebow 1967; Anderson 1978; and Dunier 1999.

29. This is true of the best prison ethnographies, such as Irwin 1987; Rhodes 2004; and Sykes 2007.

30. For a recent and particularly comprehensive and insightful account of this, see Black and Keyes 2021. See also Randles 2013, 2020; Young 2016; and Battle 2019.

31. See Holzer 2009; Smeeding, Garfinkel, and Mincy 2011; Burton et al. 2016; and Harding et al. 2016.

32. See Austin 1996; Roy 2005, 2006; Berger and Langton 2011; Marsiglio and Roy 2012; and Mincy, Jethwani, and Klempin 2015.

33. See Mincy and Sorensen 1998; Sum et al. 2011; Miller and Mincy 2012; and Harding et al. 2016.

34. See Nelson 2004; Roy 2005, 2006; and Young 2011, 2016.

35. See Young 2004; Harding 2010; Rios 2011; and Smeeding, Garfinkel, and Mincy 2011.

36. See Clayton, Mincy, and Blankenhorn 2003; Edin, Nelson, and Paranal 2004; Nelson 2004; and Mincy, Jethwani, and Klempin 2015.

37. Edin and Nelson 2013. For more on the "package deal," see Townsend 2002.

38. Hobson and Morgan 2002: 3. For notable exceptions, see Black and Keyes 2021. And for legal analyses of fatherhood, see Maldonado 2006; Cammett 2011; and Brito 2020.

39. See Martinson and Nightingale 2008; Randles 2013, 2020; and Mincy, Jethwani, and Klempin 2015.

40. The literature here is massive. For some of the best overviews of this work, see Visher and Travis 2003; Clear 2007; Pager 2003, 2007; Wakefield and Uggen 2010; Rios 2011; Morenoff and Harding 2014; Western et al. 2015; and Western 2018.

41. Sorensen, Sousa, and Schaner 2007.

42. See Blankenhorn 1995; and Bennett 2001. Or as Mead (2011: 18) put it succinctly: "Young black men will often refuse to work for 'chump change' even if it means not working at all. Or they accept jobs but then find them unrewarding or abusive, so they leave in a huff or are fired."

43. For examples of these deleterious effects, see Hays 2004; Reese 2005; Haney 2013; and Edin and Shaefer 2015.

44. This is not to say that child support *per se* fails to help mothers. As I discuss throughout this book, there are many positive aspects to the child support system: child support is the second largest source of income for poor families (after wages) and has contributed to the large increase in paternity establishment. My point here is about the criminalization of child support.

45. For more on the feminist politics of the crisis of care, see Fraser 2016.

CHAPTER 1. MAKING MEN PAY

1. This phrase was the title of an influential book on child support from the late 1970s. In *Making Fathers Pay*, law professor David Chambers (1979) made the case for getting tough on fathers who failed to pay support—which helped pave the way not only for automatic wage garnishments but also for the use of incarceration as a punishment for child support debt.

2. Sorensen, Sousa, and Schaner 2007; Putze 2017. As Turetsky and Waller (2020) have shown, two-thirds of indebted parents live below the poverty line and three-quarters of their families receive some sort of public assistance.

3. Of these parents, 60 percent had no reported income at all, while 16 percent had a reported income of less than $10,000. For more on these breakdowns, see Arthur 2018.

4. It would be impossible to summarize the vast array of work on the history

of child support policy. For comprehensive overviews, see Pirog and Ziol-Guest 2006; Garfinkel, Meyer, and McLanahan 2001; Cancian, Meyer, and Ha 2011a; and Mincy, Jethwani, and Klempin 2015.

5. This should not be confused with orders that fall outside the state's purview altogether—or the nearly 40 percent of support orders that are worked out between parents without state oversight. In this way, my terminology differs from that used by many others in this field: I use the private/public distinction to connote distinctions within the Title IV-D program regarding whom the debt is owed to and who is in control of the support. For more on these distinctions, see Roberts 2000; Freeman and Waldfogel 2001; Cancian, Meyer, and Casper 2008; and Solomon-Fears 2016.

6. Over 80 percent of all custodial parents are mothers, and closer to 90 percent of custodial parents with open child support cases are mothers. See Grall 2020 for these data.

7. For more on the early child support system, and local-level variations, see Garfinkel 1992; Garfinkel, Meyer and McLanahan 2001.

8. Sorensen and Halpern 1999.

9. For more on these shifting rationales, see Krause 1989; Minow 2001.

10. For more on the role and functions of OCSE offices, see US Department of Health and Human Services 2018.

11. Cited in Cammett 2014.

12. Casper Weinberger, Memo to President Gerald Ford, quoted in Doar 2017.

13. Yet they did so temporarily, for three years, as a way to get the legislation passed. For more on these politics, see Cassetty 1978; Garfinkel 1992; and Garfinkel, Meyer, and McLanahan 2001.

14. There is a long history of intrusions into the lives of poor women, especially mothers of color. See Roberts 1993, 1997; Gordon 1994; Quadagno 1994; Brito 2000; Cammett 2011, 2014; and Abramovitz 2017.

15. Memo from President Gerald Ford, quoted in Doar 2017.

16. For more on the breakdown on AFDC and non-AFDC families, see Krause 1989: 6–7; Cammett 2011: 138; and Pirog and Ziol-Guest 2006: 951.

17. For instance, despite the federal mandate regarding paternity establishment, by the late 1970s only 20 percent of eligible support cases had paternity established. Some claim this was because the window to establish paternity was very small; true or not, it was also due to considerable avoidance and foot dragging on the part of many states. For more on the early politics of paternity testing, see Garfinkel, Meyer, and McLanahan 2001; and Pirog and Ziol-Guest 2006.

18. For instance, a 1979 study of one district court in Denver found child support orders ranging from 6 percent to 52 percent of an obligor's income for one child and from 6 percent to 42 percent of an obligor's income for two children. See Yee 1979.

19. For more on the history and politics of welfare pass-throughs, see Legler

1996; Wheaton and Russell 2004; Cancian, Meyer, and Caspar 2008; and Hahn, Edin, and Abrahams 2018. For more on current pass-throughs, see map 1 as well as Turetsky and Waller 2020.

20. For more on these models, see US Department of Health and Human Services 2002; NWLC 2002; and NCSL 2013.

21. "Senator Bradley's Welfare Zinger," *New York Times*, 26 June 1988, www.nytimes.com/1988/06/27/opinion/senator-bradley-s-welfare-zinger.html.

22. Some legal scholars have argued these provisions were potentially in violation of parts of the US constitution, including: the Fourteenth Amendment's equal protection clause—in addition to the Eighth, Ninth, and Tenth Amendment protections against excessive fines, cruel and unusual punishment, and states' rights. For legal analyses of Bradley, see Krause 1989; Cammett 2011, 2014; and Brito 2012, 2019. And for a legal advocate's perspective, see Southern Center for Human Rights 2013.

23. With this clause, Bradley was also possibly in violation of the Fifth Amendment's due process protections. But despite all of the potential constitutional issues raised in Bradley, there have been few legal challenges to it. One unsuccessful challenge was *Bowes et al. v. Reno et al.*, No. 00-12557-NG (D. Mass., which was dismissed 22 October 2001). Yet as Cammett (2011) discusses, there have been other challenges to Bradley's inflexibility. Advocates for its repeal often cite extreme examples of noncustodial parents, such as the father held hostage in Kuwait for five months and unable to notify the court of his inability to pay support, or the father who was falsely incarcerated for murder and later exonerated—only to be arrested for nonpayment of child support. For more on these challenges, see Weimer 2000. And for media accounts of these egregious cases, see *Seattle Times*, December 16, 1990, http://community.seattletimes.nwsource.com/archive/?date=19901216&slug=1109727; *Washington Times*, November 21, 2002, http://web.archive.org/web/20050413100236/http://militaryparents.org/dt_gs_families_and_the.php.

24. For more on the use of these arguments in discussions over Bradley, see Patterson 2008b; and Cammett 2011.

25. For more on these broader justice reforms, see Garland 2001; and Gottschalk 2006, 2016.

26. 132 CONG. REC. S5303-04 (daily edition, 5 May 1986, statement of Sen. Bradley).

27. Reagan made these comments as early as 1983 in his "Remarks on Signing the National Child Support Enforcement Month Proclamation" and then in his 1986 Fathers' Day Proclamation.

28. For an account of feminist arguments here, see NWLC 2002.

29. Bartfeld and Meyer 1999.

30. For Schlafly's blaming of feminists, see Schlafly 2006, 2009.

31. For more on recent advocacy to repeal or modify Bradley, see González 2011.

32. Daniel P. Moynihan, "Congressional Records—The Family Support Act of 1988 Is Underway," Congressional Records, Congress of the United States of America, 3 October 1990, http://congressional.proquest.com:80/congressional/docview/t17.d18.c4760ea30d00013d?accountid=12768.

33. The FSA enacted other changes as well: it allowed states to "pass through" $50 of the collected support to the family when the payment was made on time; it set mandatory order reviews for every four years; and it facilitated the garnishment of NCPs of unemployment compensation by providing federal records to states seeking to withhold this compensation. US Congressional Research Service, *The Family Support Act of 1988: How It Changes the Aid to Families with Dependent Children (AFDC) and Child Support Enforcement programs*, 80-702EPW, 7 November 1988.

34. For more on these changes in caseloads, collections, and debt, see Pirog and Ziol-Guest 2006.

35. For overviews of this massive literature, from very different perspectives, see Blank 1997; Handler and Hasenfeld 1997; Harris 1997; Gilens 1999; Corcoran et al. 2000; Weaver 2000; O'Connor 2001; Reese 2005; and Soss, Fording, and Schram 2011.

36. For overviews of how PRWORA affected child support, see Legler 1996; Brito 2000; Curran and Abrams 2000; Garfinkel, Meyer, and McLanahan 2001; OIG 2000; Roberts 2000; and Cancian, Meyer, and Casper 2008.

37. To be more specific, these two sets of costs are charged differently to NCPs. Support owed to the state as TANF repayment does not correspond to the actual amount of money paid out for public assistance—it is calculated as a percentage of income the NCP owes under the state's child support guidelines. By contrast, states calculate debt for other public benefits at their full cost—for instance, the amount owed for Medicaid is calculated based on the amount of money paid out by the state. Overall, thirty-nine states authorized the collection of Medicaid pregnancy and birthing costs. This repayment added an additional $3,000 to $7,000 to an NCP's child support debt. The difference in these amounts lies in state variation in medical costs and the type of birth—with an uncomplicated birth billed at $3,100 and a C-section at $6,700. For more on these repayment rates and practices, see NWLC 2002; May and Roulet 2005; and Brito 2012.

38. For more on how these retroactive calculations are made, see OIG 2000.

39. Although, about ten years later, the majority of states reinstituted pass-throughs, at least in part because they saw compliance decline when NCP families got none of the money repaid as support. See Cancian, Meyer, and Roff 2007 for more on pass-through trends and PRWORA.

40. There was also support from high-profile democratic leaders, such as President Clinton and HHS Secretary Donna Shalala, as well as the Democratic Governors' Association. For examples of their support, see US House of Representatives 1996.

41. For more on Ellwood's views of welfare and PRWORA more broadly, see Ellwood 1996.

42. For some of this early work, see Krause 1989; Garfinkel, McLanahan, and Robbins 1994; Edin 1995; Legler 1996; Sorensen 1997; and Mincy and Sorensen 1998.

43. For an analysis of Hillary Clinton's support for the PRWORA as an example of neoliberal feminism, see Perry 2016.

44. In fact, when reviewing the congressional record from the period, I discovered there were many more policy experts and social scientists influential in this debate than feminists—although many later came to disassociate themselves from PRWORA. So while leaders from the Children's Defense Fund and National Women's Law Center may have supported PRWORA, it is a stretch to call them major players in its construction. For more on PRWORA politics, see Beatty et al. 1997; Blank 1998; Bryner 1998; Camissa 1998; Solow 1998; Mink 1999; and Gordon 2001.

45. For more on the feminist politics of reform and PRWORA, see Fraser and Gordon 1994; Mink 1995, 1998, 1999; Orloff 2006; Hays 2004; Reese 2005; and Gustafson 2011.

46. Jennifer B. Dunn, Republican House Member from Washington, Congressional Daily Edition, "Welfare Reform Bill: New Methods of Collecting from Deadbeat Parents," 104th Congress, 1st Session, 21 March 1995.

47. For more on the criminalization of the deadbeat in this period, see Hansen 1999; Cammett 2011, 2014; and Brito 2012.

48. Bill Clinton, "Remarks Made to the Citizens of Denver," 18 July 1996, in Hansen 1999.

49. H.R. 3811, cited as the Deadbeat Parents Punishment Act of 1998.

50. Senator Herbert Kohl, Congressional Record Senate Bill S12667, "Deadbeat Parents Punishment Act of 1997," 13 November 1997.

51. To be fair, the Obama administration did initiate some child support reforms throughout the 2010s, particularly at the end of his second term. But there were few substantive changes in policy trajectories. Instead, the punitive discourse of the deadbeat began to be coupled with the discourse of responsible fatherhood—and with the federal government proposing ways to turn the former into the latter. See Randles 2013; and Battle 2018.

52. OCSE 2015. As Turetsky and Waller (2020) show, most of this debt remains uncollectible—with $23 billion collected in 2018, a small percentage of the $115 billion owed.

53. OCSE 2017a.

54. Pirog and Ziol-Guest 2006.

55. Sorensen et al. 2003.

56. For a map of where states came out on imputing income, see the map included on my author's website (www.Lynne-Haney.com).

57. For an overview of all the Final Rule covered, see OCSE 2017b.

58. For instance, the threshold levels ranged from $400 per month in Colorado to $421 in Mississippi to $531 in Massachusetts—which means these orders were only available to the extremely impoverished. In other states they were set closer to the poverty level, for example, in California ($1,000), Montana ($893), and Idaho ($800). For a full list of state breakdowns, see OIG 2000: 21.

59. For a map on state policies on low-income orders, see my author's website (www.Lynne-Haney.com).

60. For orders between parents, these front-end costs can include everything from case processing fees to lawyers' fees to paternity testing to birth-related medical costs. For a breakdown of which states charge what, see OIG 2000: 7–10; and NCSL 2013.

61. More specifically, retroactive support for public assistance was standardized with the 2005 Deficit Reduction Act, which gave states until October 2009 to stop charging retroactive support in public assistance cases. By the late 2010s, the majority of public assistance payback was for families no longer receiving assistance. See OCSE 2014; and Turetsky and Waller 2020.

62. For more on pilot programs and evaluation studies of pass-through programs, see Sorensen and Hill 2004; Cassetty 2002; Legler and Turetsky 2006; Cancian, Meyer, and Caspar 2008; Lippold, Nichols, and Sorensen 2013; Financial Justice Project 2019; and Turetsky and Waller 2020.

63. Of course, this does not mean there was a corresponding decline in the overall debt owed to the state, given that all government-owed debt that accumulated prior to this remains unpaid and continues to grow at high interest rates.

64. Indeed, according to 2017 data, fewer than half of custodial parents received the full amount of their orders—24 percent received partial payments and 30 percent received no payments (Grall 2020).

65. See Turetsky and Waller 2020 for more on past public assistance charges.

66. Sorensen 2004: 314.

67. The breakdown of who gets what from public assistance payback is shocking: nationally, most of the funds received are kept by the state to cover everything from TANF costs to child support enforcement. In California, the distribution is particularly imbalanced: of the $368 million collected in public debt in 2017, $176 million went to the federal government as reimbursement, while $168 million went to the state and $23 million to counties. Several groups are thus pushing for a 100 percent pass-through of payments. See Financial Justice Project 2019; and Turetsky and Waller 2020.

68. For a state-by-state overview of policies on modification in general, see OCSE 2012.

69. It is interesting that there is no universal standard here. For instance, in *The State of Oregon v. Vargas*, the California Supreme court ruled that because incarcerated parents involuntarily have no opportunity to work, their orders should

be set at $0. But for decades there has been enormous variation in how this is implemented, with some states adopting the Vargas stance and others ruling that because criminal behavior was "voluntary," so was their unemployment. For more on this logic, see Turetsky 2008; and Meyer and Warren 2011. This variation was a motivator for the 2016 Final Rule, which only partly addressed the issue of state variation.

70. Many of these states only recently moved into this category, having defined incarceration as voluntary for decades. So in these states, there are hundreds of thousands of parents with debt that accumulated before such modifications were possible.

71. Of course, caseworkers can, and often do, find ways to reduce private arrears informally, essentially institutionalizing debt compromises in secret. A study by the National Women's Law Center found that many participants claimed that local child support offices offered retroactive debt forgiveness on the down-low, particularly for state debt. As one said, "It's an attempt to institutionalize without anyone finding out." NWLC 2002: 32.

72. The 2007 numbers came from a study by the Office of Inspector General; the more recent data are from OCSE reviews. See OIG 2007; OCSE 2011, 2018.

73. More specifically, Florida allowed incarcerated parents to petition to hold orders in abeyance until released. Upon release, a judge would review the underlying order and set a "reasonable" schedule for the repayment of arrears. But as I describe in the next chapter, few fathers knew about this option—and even fewer were able to get a judge to lower the debt upon release.

74. These interest charges are in addition to the fees that accompany support orders: processing fees, court fees, paternity testing, and income-withholding fees—none of which are waived for the incarcerated. See Anderson 2009 for more on these charges.

75. For more on these estimates, see Sorensen 2004; and Turetsky 2007.

76. As Spencer-Suarez (2021) has shown, this is also an argument made by state caseworkers, who claim to want "their money back" from indebted parents.

77. For more on poverty rates for women, children, and female-headed households, see Corcoran et al. 2000; and Edin and Shaefer 2015.

CHAPTER 2. THE DEBT OF IMPRISONMENT

1. See Sorensen, Sousa, and Schaner 2007; Putze 2017.

2. For a particularly insightful account of this confluence of shifts and their effects on disadvantaged fathers, see Black and Keyes 2021.

3. Carson 2020.

4. See Western and Petit 2010. For more on children with incarcerated parents, see Geller, Garfinkel, and Western 2011; Wakefield and Wildeman 2013; Geller, Jaeger, and Pace 2016; and Wakefield, Lee, and Wildeman 2016.

5. The numbers are even higher for African American children, who are six times more likely to experience parental incarceration. By the age of fourteen, over 25 percent of African American children will have had an incarcerated parent—and 10 percent have a parent who is currently incarcerated. See Western and Wildeman 2009.

6. On the number of parents in prison, see NCSL 2019b and Carson 2020. For estimates of those with child support cases, see Griswold et al. 2004; Turetsky 2007; Cancian 2017; McLeod and Gottlieb 2018; and NCSL 2019b.

7. A few state-level studies conducted in the early 2000s estimated the percentage of prisoners with open support orders to be 22 percent to 26 percent, which puts the number closer to 350,000. Because they were done in low-arrears states (Massachusetts and Colorado), their numbers are not generalizable. See Griswold and Pearson 2003; Griswold, Pearson, and Davis 2001; and Justice 2007.

8. Recent data suggest that even this estimate may be too low. A study of 1,482 incarcerated fathers in five states found that 60 percent had at least one verifiable support case. If generalizable to all states, the size of this population moves closer to 1 million. See Mellgren et al. 2017.

9. For these data, see OCSE 2006; Levingston and Turetsky 2007; Ha et al. 2008; and Arthur 2018. In addition, a 2018 Federal Demonstration Project found the numbers to be even higher: based on a study of 10,000 parents in the child support systems of eight states, two-thirds reported histories of incarceration. See Turetsky and Waller (2020) for more on this Demonstration Project.

10. See Putze 2017.

11. That said, one recent national-level study has indicated that parents with the mark of a criminal record accrue an average of three times more support debt by the time their children are fourteen years old than parents without histories of incarceration. And the disparity only grows as their children get older. See Turetsky and Waller 2020.

12. For this average see NCSL 2019b. Another reason it is so hard to estimate this debt is that most of the studies of it are dated. Many were done in the early 2000s, and much has happened since then to suggest that accumulated debt has increased significantly. For these earlier studies, see Griswold, Pearson, and Davis 2001; Thoennes 2002; Pearson 2004; Pearson, Thoennes, and Davis 2003; Griswold and Pearson 2005; and McLean and Thompson 2007.

13. The higher average among my respondents points to yet another reason why estimating average debt is so complicated: it is highly contingent on the states included in estimates. There is enormous state variation in how support debt accumulates overall and for incarcerated parents—particularly given modification laws and interest rates. My research is based in three high-arrears states (Florida, California, and New York), which affects my respondents' debt size significantly.

14. For more on the average child support debt of low-income fathers overall, see OIG 2000; and Turner and Waller 2017.

15. Maruna 2011.

16. Of course, these experiences are not equally distributed among the population: certain groups get drawn into these judicial ceremonies and subjected to their condemnations more often than others. This makes courts a critical source of and site for social inequality. For instance, journalist Amy Bach (2009) has revealed in rich ethnographic detail how these inequalities surface and are maintained. From the uneven distribution of legal resources to unreasonable expectations of legal authorities, courts proceed in ways that solidify hierarchies of power and privilege. See also Clair (2020) for a fascinating ethnographic account of the racial and class inequalities of contemporary US courts.

17. Child support courts vary in the degree to which they are in fact public. The majority are open to the public—with large audiences given access to all the legal proceedings, even those with quite sensitive information. This was the case in Florida and California, where courtrooms filled up in the beginning of a court session with several dozen parents awaiting their cases. Yet some courts limit the number of observers, bringing only small groups of parents into the courtroom so as to maintain some semblance of privacy. Moreover, some courts are headed up by judges and others by magistrates. In order to maintain the confidentiality of those I observed, I refer to both groups as "judges," which was, in fact, how most court staff and all parents referred to them as well.

18. In one of the only analyses of the judicial variation in child support courts, Brito (2020) categorizes the judicial approaches—differentiating between what she calls navigators, bureaucrats, zealots, and reformers. These categories are defined according to judges' overall perception of cases and their role in them as well as their orientation to enforcement. While I encountered all four varieties in my research, zealots were most common (especially in Florida courts), while navigators stood out for the ambivalence with which they implemented punitive enforcement (especially in California courts).

19. The one location I never saw this occur was in New York City, where the rules of service and notification were always abided by. This was true even in cases where one of the parents seemed unlocatable. Still, overlooking service requirements was just one of the many violations in due process that characterized child support courts across the country—many of which did occur in New York courts as well.

20. See Haney and Link 2017.

21. Sorensen et al. 2003. Furthermore, a more recent study found that in 18 percent of all support cases, orders were set with no income information from the non-custodial parent (Financial Justice Project 2018). Yet other studies have revealed the cascading economic effects of failure to appear for low-income NCPs (Murphy 2005; Brito 2019). Although none of these studies controlled for incarceration, my court observations across all three states suggest that many default orders involved parental imprisonment.

22. This sense of helplessness and hopelessness may contribute to fathers' inability to pay these orders back. Public assistance orders are the least understood by all fathers and especially institutionalized fathers (Mellgram et al. 2017). Other research indicates that fathers are more likely to pay back support if their obligations are manageable (Meyer, Ha, and Hu 2008)—with the "sweet spot" being around 20 percent of parents' income, after which compliance declines (Turetsky and Waller 2020: 130).

23. Edin and Nelson 2013.

24. They were not alone: a report by the Marshall Project indicated that most incarcerated fathers who wrote letters about their child support got no response from state authorities. See Hager 2015b.

25. Hager 2015b.

26. Other research indicates that mothers were not supportive of public assistance payback—perhaps in part because it stripped them of their own right to support and they realized it would lead to less support. For more on custodial parents' views of assistance payback, see Financial Justice Project 2018; and Hahn el al. 2019.

27. When I concluded my New York fieldwork in 2017, they had just begun the process of moving these cases back to the boroughs—which, according to one judge, was because Manhattan had become too overwhelmed handling all of the public assistance cases.

28. For the precise budget breakdowns and variation over time, see figures 9 and 10.

29. There was an irony to this man's use of such a defense, given the racist and antisemitic roots of the "sovereign citizen" movement. See SPLC, "Sovereign Citizens Movement," www.splcenter.org/fighting-hate/extremist-files/ideology/sovereign-citizens-movement.

30. As Allan Newcomber, an incarcerated father interviewed by the Marshall Project, put it: "Everyone in the penitentiaries was getting the letters." Newcomber saw his support debt rise to more than $68,000 while he was incarcerated in a Missouri prison. See Hager 2015b: 7.

31. Hager 2015b: 4.

32. For an overview of where states came out on designating incarceration as "voluntary unemployment," see maps 2 and 3.

33. Roman and Link 2015.

34. The percentage in my sample is lower most likely because it includes Florida (which Roman and Link's does not). That state has made it virtually impossible for incarcerated parents to have orders modified and has been slow to adopt and implement the changes mandated in the Final Rule.

35. For more on their lack of awareness of their own support orders, see Mellgren et al. 2017.

36. For more on their lack of understanding of modification rules and eligi-

bility, see Pearson 2004; Patterson 2008a; Roman and Link 2015; and Spencer-Suarez 2021.

37. For more on all of the factors that go into their inability to put together a complete modification case, see Cammett 2011; Meyer and Warren 2011; and Haney 2018.

38. In fact, the percentage of parents who claimed such assistance was their highest priority was as high as those who claimed to need job training. See Roman and Link 2017.

39. This is what could very well happen in those one third of states that the Final Rule mandated introduce some modification policy for incarcerated parents—they will have a policy on the books that few parents know about.

40. According to a former OCSE secretary, the common federal interpretation of Bradley is to allow forgiveness of public debt—although this is not followed consistently across states. See Turetsky and Waller (2020: 136) for more on the federal take on Bradley.

41. For more on New York policies like the Arrears Cap Initiative, see NYCHRA 2021.

42. This also made it difficult for me to assess which cases actually involved incarceration. For instance, while I only observed three New York fathers use incarceration as the basis for a modification request, it is quite likely that many more had their orders modified because of incarceration—they just did not "come out" as formerly incarcerated in open court.

43. To be eligible for an incarceration order, a parent had to be incarcerated for more than ninety days and have no other sources of income—and not have any domestic violence convictions. The $0 order would then be issued within 180 days from the date of the request. Until the modification was granted, the incarcerated parent owed all unpaid child support plus 10 percent interest.

44. These efforts were spearheaded by an especially committed local child support director who took it upon herself to link DCSS offices with CDCR. She even made the videos distributed across CDCR facilities. And she wrote and distributed information sheets to be given to prisoners at intake. For an example of some of the materials she produced, see California Support Information for Incarcerated Parents, "California's Child Support Program," https://csdaca.org/wp-content/uploads/2016/07/incarcerated-parent.pdf.

45. While these internal data were never made public, I was collaborating with DCSS at the time on a project on their incarcerated caseload—so they shared the information with me, somewhat perplexed by the findings that so few of those parents eligible for modifications actually received them. I was also quite involved in the legislative process with AB 1091, which would have made the administrative granting of incarceration orders permanent in California.

46. While this might seem quite straightforward, it was actually complicated to facilitate. In 2018, I was asked to collaborate with CDCR to construct a notifi-

cation project across the California prison system to enable parents to apply for these modifications. We struggled to implement even the most seemingly simple steps. It was unclear how to best reach prisoners with support orders; indeed, it was even unclear in which county they should file their requests. While we eventually created an application procedure, it remained at the discretion of individual correctional facilities to introduce and implement it. And that process remains ongoing.

47. There were several reasons given for why such an interface was impossible to create, with issues of privacy issues cited most often—on both the DCSS and the CDCR sides. Indeed, this inability to connect the systems was one reason why a 2019 report by the National Council of State Legislatures (NCSL) called this one of the most urgent child support reforms needed. For more on what other states are doing to access incarcerated parents, see Aharpour et al. 2020.

48. States have also begun to ramp up their prison outreach to enable administrative orders. For an overview of how states address this outreach, see Aharpour et al. 2020.

49. See map 5 for those states that currently do not charge interest on support debt.

50. For an overview of state debt relief programs, see map 4.

51. For two of the more elaborate analyses of these effects, see Financial Justice Project 2018; and Hahn, Edin, and Abrahams 2018.

52. For more on these findings, see Pearson and Davis 2002; Heinrich, Burkhardt, and Shager 2011; Pearson, Thoennes, and Kaunelis 2012; Hahn, Edin, and Abrahams 2018; and Haney and Mercier 2021.

53. For more on rates of repayment overall, see Solomon-Fears 2016.

54. See Financial Justice Project 2019.

55. See Sorensen et al. 2003.

56. In particular, resistance to the Rules from Republicans in Congress was fierce, with House Speaker Paul Ryan and Senator Orrin Hatch introducing legislation to block the Rules. For more on the politics of the Final Rule, see Hager 2016; and NCSL 2017; as well as primary source documents collected here: Govinfo, https://www.govinfo.gov/app/details/FR-2016-12-20/2016-29598.

57. Other policy experts expressed similar concerns, with Ron Haskins claiming that debt relief could "undermine the child support concept," which he and other conservative thinkers hold so dear. See Hager 2016: 2.

CHAPTER 3. PUNISHING PARENTS, CREATING CRIMINALS

1. Mincy, Jethwani, and Klempin 2015: 39.

2. Importantly, the support order itself is rarely suspended—so parents' debt continues to accrue even if they are no longer being subjected to enforcement measures.

3. Although the garnishing of prison accounts was never reported by parents in California, policy-makers admitted to me that they were indeed considering it. The state Child Support Director explained to me that she was contemplating a policy to garnish prison wages, particularly for the tiny group of incarcerated parents who are fortunate enough to make livable wages while in prison.

4. Unfortunately, it was Carlos's girlfriend who got the short end of the stick here: his arrears were owed to the state, for public assistance payback. So she was unlikely to see any of the garnished money she had "returned" to him.

5. Judges and state attorneys would read aloud detailed accounts of exactly how much parents made and from what sources—provoking embarrassment and humiliation in some. State authorities would also announce parents' expenditures, even when they were quite personal (therapy bills). And then there were judges who grilled parents about their monthly costs—or for spending money on items they saw as unnecessary and frivolous (such as clothing, car payments, cell phones, restaurants, etc.).

6. For more on these breakdowns, see Turetsky and Waller 2020.

7. See Cadigan and Kirk 2020. License suspension is also associated with lower rates of support payment—see Meyer, Cancian, and Waring 2020 for these payment effects.

8. For more on these different contempt actions, see Patterson 2008a; Cammett 2011; Solomon-Fears, Smith, and Berry 2012; and NCSL 2019b.

9. Parents held in contempt can find themselves in violation of the rules dictating their participation in various reentry programs or transitional housing—both of which often require clean records and no new arrests. Moreover, in many states and locales, staying current on child support is a condition of parole, which places indebted parents at risk of a parole violation. For more on these risks, see Cook 2015; and Turetsky and Waller 2020.

10. For a map of state punishments for criminal non-support, see my author's website www.Lynne-Haney.com.

11. Some states have clear standards for assessing intent and willfulness, while others leave this largely to judicial discretion. Some states have clear due process standards, requiring full and unambiguous notification of the accusation of contempt, while others apply lax standards for notification. The same applies to the guarantee of legal representation: some states guarantee it, since contempt filings can lead to incarceration, while others do not.

12. Under the Fourteenth Amendment, punitive proceedings (such as criminal prosecutions and criminal contempt proceedings) must feature certain due process protections that are not mandated in civil contempt proceedings. States are split regarding whether there is a right to appointed counsel in a child support contempt case—some require it (New York), while others do not (Florida). Indeed, in *Turner v. Rogers*, the US Supreme Court ruled that the due process clause did not mandate legal counsel in support proceedings, even when imprisonment was

possible. For more on how states come out on these dimensions, see OCSE 2006, 2007; Solomon-Fears, Smith, and Berry 2012; and NCSL 2019.

13. The Final Rule requires states to implement procedures to ensure standards set out by Turner. It also urges states to establish clear criteria for the use of contempt actions, including case screening for ability to pay, assessments of purge amounts, and information about the standards for proving ability to pay. Yet it remains unclear how many reforms have been implemented. For more on contempt and the Final Rule, see NCSL 2019; and Aharpour et al. 2020.

14. For more on Arizona tradition, see "Sheriff's Deputies Round Up 'Deadbeat' Parents," *azfamily.com*, www.azfamily.com/story/31217449/sheriffs-deputies-round-up-deadbeat-parents.

15. For more on this New Jersey tradition, see "New Jersey Rounds Up 1,221 Deadbeat Parents," *NewJersey 101.5*, http://nj1015.com/nj-rounds-up-1221-deadbeat-parents-owing-25-4m-and-theyre-about-to-arrest-more.

16. For more on this fathers' day tradition, see my editorial "Fathers' Day Raids on Deadbeats," https://www.latimes.com/opinion/op-ed/la-oe-haney-fathers-day-child-support-20180615-story.html; "MCSO Celebrates Father's Day," *azcentral.com*, www.azcentral.com/story/news/local/phoenix/2014/06/14/dead-beat-dad-round-up/10532081; and "Child Support Deadbeats Rounded Up in New Jersey," *philadelphia.cbslocal.com*, http://philadelphia.cbslocal.com/2017/04/11/deadbeats-rounded-up-nj.

17. Solomon-Fears, Smith, and Berry 2012; Galbi 2015.

18. See May and Roulet 2005; Cook and Noyles 2011; and NCSL 2019.

19. Most of these estimates are based on state and local-level studies with samples either of parents with incarceration histories or of those in jail with support debt. See Zatz 2016; Cozzolino 2018; and Zatz and Stoll 2020.

20. Unfortunately, very few of them could tell me which form of contempt they had been incarcerated for—which is itself indicative of how difficult it is to track the use of jail as an enforcement tool. In some cases, their sentence length clued me in to which form of contempt it was, since civil contempt usually comes with no more than a few weeks of jail time—although this varies when a purge is involved. Criminal nonpayment tends to carry a longer sentence.

21. That is, data from the Fragile Families survey show Texas and Tennessee as the two sample states with the highest contempt rates. See Cozzolino 2018.

22. This was also reflected in Cozzolino's (2018) quantitative data on indebted parents from several states (and not just formerly incarcerated fathers).

23. Mincy, Jethwani, and Klempin, 2015: 64.

24. CDCSS 2017.

25. CDCSS 2017.

26. In large part, this was due to Vicki Turetsky being at the helm of the agency from 2009 to 2016. By the end of her tenure, OCSE had even distributed a powerful information sheet with graphics to outline the cost/benefit analysis of incar-

ceration for debt, showing the cost of jail versus the benefits of employment for indebted NCPs. Since her departure, the momentum on this issue has been lost, as has the push for states to implement key aspects of the Final Rule.

27. See NYC Independent Budget Office 2015.

28. For breakdowns of case types, see NYC Independent Budget Office 2015.

29. In her study of child support workers, Vogel (2020a) uncovered a similar front-stage/back-stage tension, with staff voicing their awareness of the systemic inequities confronting indebted parents in interviews even while regulating parents through those same systemic mandates in their work.

30. For more on the socioeconomic shifts that hit this group of fathers especially hard, see Holzer 2009; Berger and Langton 2011; Smeeding, Garfinkel, and Mincy 2011; Mincy, Jethwani, and Klempin, 2015; and Black and Keyes 2021.

31. This was an interesting dynamic: judges often seemed both uncomfortable with my presence and solicitous of advice from me. This was especially true in NYC courts, perhaps because their semiprivate quality meant that the number of people in the courtroom was much smaller than in courts in other areas. So judges "felt" my presence more. It may also have been a reflection of NYC judges' familiarity with NYU. Some of them had even gone to law school there, so perhaps they were more sensitive to being observed by a professor from their alma mater.

32. Halushka 2016. See also Mincy, Jethwani, and Klempin, 2015; Western et al. 2015; and Western 2018.

33. Kohler-Hausman 2018.

34. Kaye 2019.

35. For more on the Florida system, see FOCSA 2012, 2017. When it comes to public assistance cases, it is important to note that most cases are for *past* assistance, given that only 15 percent of the current caseload involves public assistance. This is because Florida's welfare system is now a shell of what it once was, with benefit eligibility narrowed and levels cut dramatically since the 2000s.

36. In fact, in many Florida counties, these lawyers completely ran the show: they presented the cases to start the proceedings and largely dictated how judges would rule. Since very few parents had their own lawyers, the state attorneys were often the only ones with the legal knowledge to guide the hearings. And when parents' lawyers were there, they frequently complained about the unchecked power of state attorneys: "Who is leading this court?" one Miami lawyer once queried during a hearing. "Is the judge in control here, or you [the state attorney]?"

37. In the same way that the poverty discourse did not only characterize the New York City system, this definition of fatherhood was not unique to Florida. Indeed, it was applied in most of the courts I studied, from LA to NYC. Yet it was deployed more explicitly and more inflexibly in Florida, which led to more intense courtroom exchanges.

38. Several states—including California, Michigan, New Jersey, and Washington—have entered into agreements with 7-Eleven stores to put kiosks on the

premises so that child support payments can be deposited to accounts. At the time of my research, Florida had not yet approved these kiosks; it continued to require that support payments be made to central dispersement centers.

39. For more on these racial differences, see Maldonado 2006; and Pate 2016.

40. Which is somewhat ironic, given that Judge Matthews had been married five different times and frequently discussed how many children he had from these different marriages. He hardly seemed like a model of spousal or parental commitment.

41. Randles 2013.

42. Curran and Abrams 2000: 670. For more on these fatherhood programs, see also Roy 2006; Martinson and Nightingale 2008; Young 2004, 2016; and National Fatherhood Initiative 2018.

CHAPTER 4. THE IMPRISONMENT OF DEBT

1. Haggerty and Ericson 2000: 611.

2. Brayne 2014.

3. Most of these studies have found that support obligations negatively influence employment and are associated with fewer average weeks in the formal economy—see Turetsky 2007; Miller and Mincy 2012; and Turner and Waller 2017. Yet, as Cancian, Heinrich, and Chung (2009) have found, this effect seems contingent on income level, with low-income parents working less in the formal economy if they have support obligations and higher-income parents working more. And the effect is even greater for those with debt, especially public debt, and for incarcerated parents. For more on the latter groups, see Cammett 2011; Garfinkel and Nepomnyaschy 2010; Noyles, Cancian, and Cuesta 2012; Cancian 2013; Link and Roman 2017; and Pleggenkuhle 2018. And for an overview of all this research, see Haney and Mercier 2021.

4. Since, with interest, this debt balloons to over $400,000 in the same period. For an example of how this occurs, see figure 12.

5. For more on how child support and debt affects credit scores, see Paperno 2016; and Kiviat 2017.

6. For an example of how a record of child support debt can be interpreted as especially stigmatizing, see Pleggenkuhle 2018.

7. See Turetsky and Waller 2020.

8. Financial Justice Project 2019.

9. As with most else, states have different minimum levels above which employer reporting must occur. Although these minimums are often quite low, hovering around $500 in earnings, fathers rarely made more than twice that—making it possible for them to split their wages to avoid reporting.

10. Indeed, quantitative research has shown connections among child support

obligations, debt, and informal employment, with the first two pushing more fathers to engage in the latter. This did not reflect fathers' desire to avoid paying any support at all; in fact, the men I interviewed had a more strategic assessment of where their earnings had the most influence. They claimed that providing assistance directly to their families was advantageous to everyone, especially in public assistance cases. See Turetsky 2007; Cancian, Heinrich, and Chung 2009; Miller and Mincy 2012; and Pleggenkuhle 2018 for more on these arguments.

11. In fact, there are islands of the unbanked across the United States, and the Bronx is one of the largest of those islands—close to 50 percent of residents in the borough are reportedly unbanked. Compare this to the national rate of 7.7 percent. For more on patterns of the unbanked, see Spencer-Suarez 2021.

12. I found little evidence to confirm such sweeps. Yet many fathers mentioned them in interviews, so even if they were urban myths, they did deter some men from taking public transportation.

13. For instance, recent research has found that 92 percent of formerly incarcerated people receive financial assistance and support from family members. See Visher et al. 2010; and Liu and Visher 2021. For other research on the link between family support and criminal justice involvement, see Braman 2004; Bales and Mears 2008; Berg and Huebner 2010; Sampson 2011; Wakefield, Lee, and Wildeman 2016; and Western et al. 2015.

14. Western 2018.

15. See Comfort 2007, 2008, 2012, 2018.

16. This was a moment when interviewer and interviewee connected: I had dragged my young son to the interview, so our kids played together at the table—and we bonded over our caretaking demands.

17. Stack 1974.

18. The prevalence of depression was surprising to me. It emerged from background questions I asked fathers about their health, which some interpreted as mental health. Many fathers then discussed serous battles with depression and their use of medication to treat it. Similar levels of depression were reported in a large national study of parents with child support debt, with 25 percent of these parents reporting major depression. See Turetsky and Waller 2020.

19. A recent quantitative study found similar tensions facing indebted fathers. Drawing on a sample of 1,017 noncustodial fathers from the Fragile Families Survey, Turner and Waller (2017) found a clear relationship between debt and parenting, with child support debt associated with less paternal involvement with children—that is, significantly less contact with children, less engagement with their children's daily activities, and less frequent in-kind support to them.

20. Comfort 2018. See also Liu and Visher 2021.

21. For other research on these loops, see Cadigan and Kirk 2020; and Emory et al. 2020.

22. In a recent quantitative study, Zatz and Stoll (2020) found that the mere

threat of incarceration was correlated with a decline in fathers' wages and well-being. They also discovered the effect of the carceral threat to be stronger and more damaging than the threat of financial sanctions. For a similar study on financial sanctions (using the same dataset), see Cadigan and Kirk 2020.

23. This was an argument used by fathers who *knew* their debt was owed to the state itself. Yet only a small minority of men I interviewed actually knew who their debt was owed to. Most assumed it was owed to custodial parents, but when pressed they admitted they didn't actually know. Since many of their families had been on public assistance, it is likely that their arrears were owed to both the state and mothers. But the fact that they had no idea about this is most telling.

24. In my policy work on this issue, I have encountered the most resistance in the area of enforcement—especially around contempt actions. And when I have tried to discuss the contempt data I collected from California counties, I have been met with enormous suspicion from some county support directors.

25. That said, the Final Rule did include recommendations to curtail the use of contempt actions. Also, a 2019 NCSL brief advised against jail as an enforcement measure. In addition, a high-level government panel tasked with proposing reforms for the child support system included enforcement in its recommendations (Hahn, Edin, and Abrahams 2018).

CHAPTER 5. THE GOOD, THE BAD, AND THE DEAD BROKE

1. For examples of this classic research, see Liebow 1967; Anderson 1978; and Dunier 1999.

2. For work on how motherhood is used in the controlling images of poor women, see Collins 1990; Roberts 2002; Katz-Rothman 2005; and Gustafson 2011.

3. For comprehensive overviews of the research on low-income fathers, see Nelson 2004; Berger and Langton 2011; Mincy, Jethwani, and Klempin 2015; and Black and Keyes 2021.

4. See Holzer 2009; Smeeding, Garfinkel, and Mincy 2011; Sum et al. 2011; Miller and Mincy 2012; Burton et al. 2016; and Harding et al. 2016.

5. See Austin 1996; Roy 2005, 2006; Berger and Langton 2011; Marsiglio and Roy 2012; and Mincy, Jethwani, and Klempin 2015.

6. See Young 2004; Harding 2010; and Rios 2011.

7. Young 2016.

8. Smeeding, Garfinkel, and Mincy 2011: 13.

9. For a particularly masterful account of how all of these forces come together to undermine the fathering of poor men of color, see Black and Keyes 2021.

10. The vast literature on gender and the welfare state has revealed the social basis of motherhood and helped conceptualize motherhood as a social relationship. For instance, see Koven and Michel 1993; Orloff 1993, 1996; Gordon 1994; Mink 1995; and Hays 1996. Gender scholars have also exposed how the dynamics

of punishment can saddle mothers with unmeetable obligations that derail their caretaking. See Enos 2001; Solinger 2005; and Flavin 2009.

11. See, for example, Blankenhorn 1995; Bennett 2001; and Mead 2011.

12. Randles 2013, 2020.

13. Black and Keyes 2021: 189.

14. For exceptions to this focus, see Hobson and Morgan 2002; Orloff and Monson 2002; Nurse 2002; Haney and March 2003; and Fernandez-Kelly 2015.

15. For a variety of reasons, I am leery of branding some men "good" or "bad" fathers. While some exhibited laudable behaviors and others decidedly not, I did not assume that such behaviors defined them as parents. As I discuss in the next chapter, many fathers rode waves of parenting that led them up and down as parents. To avoid such essentializing, I prefer to use more precise language to capture what I actually observed: men acting in ways that reflected cultural standards of good and bad fathering.

16. Halushka 2017, 2020.

17. Zelizer 2005.

18. Halushka 2016, 2020.

19. See Visher and Travis 2003; Comfort 2008, 2016; Visher et al. 2010; Visher 2013; Western et al. 2015; Wakefield, Lee, and Wildeman 2016; and Western 2018.

20. What makes this reality so harsh is that these are precisely the men for whom finding and maintaining a female partner is most challenging. They often find themselves at the bottom of the dating pool due to all the issues and complications that come with their status as indebted fathers. For more on women's calculations of this, see Edin and Kefalas 2005.

21. Haney 2008.

22. Other social scientists have written about how men position fatherhood as a form of redemption, claiming it as a turning point or a route out of their tumultuous lives. See Edin, Nelson, and Paranal 2004; Nelson 2004; and Edin and Nelson 2013.

23. See McIntosh 1978; and Mackinnon 1989.

24. This argument was articulated most forcefully by Loic Wacquant in a contentious exchange about the politics of ethnographic representation. Regrettably, that debate turned caustic; it did, however, raise critical arguments that ethnographers continue to grapple with, especially those of us working with marginalized groups. See Wacquant 2002.

25. I cannot give precise breakdowns here since I did not quantify or code all of my observations of paternal behavior by race. But of those men I interviewed who were unapologetically absent and neglectful, only four were men of color. Black and Keyes (2021: 119) found a similar pattern among the disadvantaged men they studied—in the site of their research with more white fathers, they found men to be more resentful, entitled, and angry (particularly at women).

26. That said, a national-level time-budget study conducted by the Centers for Disease Control (2013) found that black fathers were more likely to have fed, cooked for, bathed, and dressed their children than white or Hispanic fathers. And they were much more likely to have played with and read to their children.

27. Because custodial parents on public assistance must forgo child support payments, it is impossible for mothers to "double dip" by receiving both public assistance and child support, as some fathers have claimed. For more on the effects of public assistance payback and increasing the pass-through amounts given to families, see chapter 1 as well as the Financial Justice Project 2019.

28. For an example of this reading of welfare history, see Fraser and Gordon 1994. And for an empirical account of the state's use of public and private dependencies, see Haney 1996, 2008.

CHAPTER 6. CYCLICAL PARENTING

1. For discussions of patterns of men's fathering, as well as some of the terms used to describe it, see Young 2004, 2016; Edin and Kefalas 2005; Roy 2006; Harding 2010; Edin and Nelson 2013; Randles 2013, 2020; Mincy, Jethwani, and Klempin 2015; and Black and Keyes 2021.

2. For analyses of the parental implications of economic marginality, see Roy 2005; Holzer 2009; Smeeding, Garfinkel, and Mincy 2011; Sum et al. 2011; Berger and Langton 2011; and Black and Keyes 2021.

3. For particularly powerful accounts of these pushes and pulls, see Edin, Nelson, and Paranal 2004; Nelson 2004; and Edin and Nelson 2013.

4. See Rios 2011; Burton, Burton, and Austin 2016; and Young 2011, 2016.

5. See Furstenberg 2001; Edin, England, and Linnenberg 2003; Carlson, McLanahan, and England 2004; Edin and Kefalas 2005; Estacion and Cherlin 2010; and Levine 2013.

6. For a revealing account of how incarcerated men use fatherhood to counter the emotional distance and violence of prison, see Curtis 2019.

7. Gottschalk 2016.

8. In this way, men often used the term "daddy" (as opposed to "father") to connote their loving bonds with children. For more on the distinction between "fathers" and "daddies"—as well as the ways it intersects with state policy and discourse—see Haney and March 2003.

9. In their study of disadvantaged fathers, Black and Keyes also found a total absence of paternal role models. They were actually able to quantify it, claiming that two-thirds of the men in their study had absent fathers themselves. See Black and Keyes 2021: 241.

10. When women's experiences with child support are discussed, they usually emerge in analyses of other topics—such as female poverty, fertility decision-making, or relationship turmoil. See, for example, Sorensen and Hill 2004; Edin

and Kefalas 2005; Cancian, Meyer, and Casper 2008; Cancian, Meyer, and Ha 2011a; and Edin and Nelson 2013.

11. And this presents real limitations for my analysis here. Because I would never assume to know their perspectives on the child support system, I can only offer partial views of their actions and reactions in court—and how those reactions suggest an ambivalence toward the process.

12. Even small children were banned from courtrooms. Most courts had child care centers where parents could leave their children while awaiting their hearings. In California there was only one judge who allowed children to come to court, and that was if the child care center closed before parents' cases were heard. Otherwise, children were entirely absent from the process.

13. Furstenberg 2001.

14. Levine 2013. For a more recent analysis of gender distrust among impoverished women and men, see Black and Keyes 2021, esp. chapter 8.

15. For one of the best analyses of this cycle of distrust, abandonment, and survival, see Edin and Kefalas 2005. And for an exceptionally thoughtful account of the ambivalence that can then mark these intimate relationships, see Mpondo-Dika 2021.

16. bell hooks 2004. See esp. chapter 4 on the replication and abandonment involved in patterns of male violence.

17. As Levine (2013) shows, low-income women are often as distrustful of state caseworkers as they are of the men in their lives. Their experiences with state actors have taught them not to believe the many promises they make—or their claims to have women's best interests in mind. So it is likely that many women entered these legal spaces with multiple forms of distrust and suspicion intersecting to shape their behavior in court.

18. Indeed, many custodial mothers resist involvement with the system. One quantitative study based on data from the Current Population Survey demonstrated that 89 percent of the mothers who did not have a formal child support order were motivated by "objective constraints"—which included reasons such as the "fathers already provided what they could" and the "fathers could not afford to pay child support." See Huang and Pouncy 2005: 555. For a discussion of how support enforcement can undermine sole parent households, see Wimberly 2000.

19. Although child support offices do not keep reliable data on the percentage of custodial parents who drop their support cases (if they are able to), I would estimate that 10 to 15 percent of the mothers I observed did try to pull their cases back when fathers had been incarcerated—by reducing either the order amount, the arrears' settlement, or the case entirely.

20. This withdrawal of assistance was built into the 1996 PRWORA that mandated custodial parents' involvement in child support collections. By threatening to deny assistance to mothers deemed noncompliant, PRWORA forced them

into the enforcement process—thus exacerbating tensions between mothers and indebted fathers.

21. For a few of the best examples of this vast quantitative scholarship, see Geller et al. 2009, 2011, 2012, 2016; Turney 2015; Wildeman 2009; and Wakefield and Wildeman 2013.

22. Turner and Waller 2017.

23. For more on the effects of parental incarceration on children—and especially this issue of lost time—see Arditti 2018; Wakefield, Lee, and Wildeman 2016; Chondry and Smith 2018; Kotova 2018; and Oldrup 2018.

24. Levine 2013. For more on the politics of trust, see also Cook 2001; Heimer 2001; and Cook, Hardin, and Levi 2005.

CONCLUSION

1. Many estimates of the yearly cost of corrections put it at around $80 billion, but since that number does not account for expenses such as pension obligations, health care benefits for correctional staff, and health care provided to prisoners, the actual amount spent on corrections is closer to $90 billion. For these different estimates, see Wakefield, Lee, and Wildeman 2016; and Heinrichson and Delaney 2012.

2. Those estimating these costs are keenly aware of empirical slippage here, given how difficult it is to disentangle the costs of incarceration from the costs of poverty. For examples of these methodological complexities, see Wakefield and Wildeman 2013; and Western 2006, 2018.

3. See McLaughlin et al. 2016.

4. For more on the expansive politics here, see Dagan and Teles 2014, 2016; National Research Council Committee on Law and Justice 2014; Travis 2014; Aviram 2015; Green 2015; Phelps 2016; and Phelps and Pager 2016. For excellent overviews of research of criminal justice reform, see Beckett 2018; and Sabol and Baumann 2020.

5. For an example of these strange bedfellows, see Chettiar and Raghaven 2019, a collection of speeches and statements by lawmakers, activists, and celebrities on criminal justice reform.

6. For some of these expansive reform proposals targeted at families and communities, see DeVuono-Powell et al. 2015; and Lewis and Lockwood 2019.

7. When child support does surface, it is lumped into discussion of criminal justice fines and fees. Yet these forms of debt are not reducible to each other: child support is a larger financial burden and also touches off parental identities as caretakers in ways criminal justice debt does not.

8. Roman and Link 2015, 2017.

9. See Robles and Dewan, "Skip Child Support. Go to Jail. Lose Job. Repeat," *New York Times*, 20 April 2015, https://www.nytimes.com/2015/04/20/us/skip-child

-support-go-to-jail-lose-job-repeat.html; and Martin, "Child Support vs. Deadbeat States." *New York Times*, 10 September, https://www.nytimes.com/2019/09/10/opinion/child-support-states.html?referringSource=articleShare.

10. For example, see my discussion of the fate of California's SB337 and AB 1092 in chapter 1. And for more on Governor Newsom's veto of them, see Cal Matters, "Newsom Vetoed Two Bills," https://calmatters.org/california-divide/2019/10/newsom-vetoes-two-bills-aimed-at-reforming-child-support-payback-system.

11. In perhaps the most stunning example of this, the 2020 CARE Act, created to provide urgent aid during the coronavirus pandemic, included provisions that denied stimulus checks to those with child support debt. They also seized pandemic state benefits and put them toward accrued arrearages. See OCSE 2020, 2021.

12. For an even more detailed and comprehensive overview of what such reforms should entail at the federal, state, and local levels, see Haney and Mercier 2021.

13. Also important would be policy reforms to make the setting of child support orders more reasonable and responsive to parents' incomes—since research has shown connections among order amount, compliance, and debt. See Meyer, Ha, and Hu 2008; and Takayesu 2011 for more on these connections. Indeed, the reform of order setting was one of the central policy recommendations of a high-profile government panel of policy experts. See Hahn, Edin, and Abrahams 2018. While such changes are important for all low-income parents, my focus here is on those reforms most consequential for incarcerated and formerly incarcerated parents.

14. For instance, in one of the most original policy evaluations of incarceration orders, Maria Cancian and her colleagues examined Milwaukee's Prison Project, which targeted more than 20,000 child support cases involving incarcerated parents. This study is unusual as it was the first to use a "natural experiment" within a state to assess proactive suspensions. See Noyles, Cancian, and Cuesta 2012; Noyles et al. 2017; and Cancian 2017. For other quantitative analyses, see Griswold, Pearson, and Davis 2001; and Roman and Link 2015.

15. Since this is a national average, it obscures the enormous variation in what is owed to the government in different states. For more on state percentages, see chapter 1.

16. Turetsky and Waller 2020: 123.

17. While the end of public assistance payback is being considered in a few states for all poor parents, to my knowledge it has yet to be proposed for institutionalized parents specifically. For more on these proposals, see Hahn, Edin, and Abrahams 2018; and Financial Justice Project 2019.

18. For examples of these evaluation studies, see Sorensen and Hill 2004; Cassetty 2002; Legler and Turetsky 2006; Cancian, Meyer, and Caspar 2008; and Lippold, Nichols, and Sorensen 2013.

19. See Financial Justice Project 2019.

20. In particular, the federal government can rescind the requirement that welfare funds recouped by states be distributed back to it. To use the California example: in 2017, the state recouped $368 million in TANF payback, but nearly half ($176 million) went to the federal government. The remaining percentage went to state and local governments, as well as to families through small pass-throughs. If the fed relinquished its payback amount, ending public assistance payback would become economically feasible for more states. For California calculations, see Financial Justice Project 2019, n5.

21. See Hahn et al. 2019; Hahn, Edin, and Abrahams 2018; and Turetsky and Waller 2020.

22. The federal government and APSE recently compiled a policy brief of all the strategies states are taking to increase their prison outreach. See Aharpour et al. 2020.

23. See Cammett 2011; and Brito 2012, 2019.

24. See OIG 2007. For an overview of states with forgiveness programs, see my author's book website www.Lynne-Haney.com.

25. See Pearson, Thoennes, and Kaunelis 2012. Besides evaluating the positive effects of debt relief, research has shown the effect of not compromising parental debt: large child support debt correlates with a decrease in support payments. This is true of both formal and informal support. See Emory et al. 2020 for recent data on these associations.

26. Hahn et al. 2019.

27. A few policy analysts have gone even further, proposing reforms modeled after what is done in parts of Europe, where child support is always expressed as a fixed percentage of a parent's income and where publicly financed child support benefits cover families with a parent without income. See Garkfinkel and Nepomnyaschy 2010. Cancian and Meyer (2018) have proposed a guaranteed family support policy, one in which all children are guaranteed a fixed amount of support and all parents have a set maximum obligation. When there is a gap between the two, or when a parent cannot pay his or her part (as in cases of incarceration) public resources would bridge the gap.

28. See Roman and Link 2015, 2017.

29. This is another reason for the low participation and compliance rates—if not framed properly, these programs provoke suspicion and are perceived as further punishment. This is true even of programs that attempt to offer debt relief, which many indebted parents think are sting operations designed to catch them. For more on such suspicions, see Vogel 2020a, 2020b.

30. Pilot studies from a variety of states reveal that robust support assistance programs can lead to increases in employment rates, wages, and the amount/frequency of child support payments. See Pearson, Thoennes, and Davis 2003; Pearson 2004; Griswold and Pearson 2005; Schroeder and Doughty 2009; Schroeder

and Kahn 2011; Roman and Link 2015; Link and Roman 2017; Cancian 2017; McLeod and Gottlieb 2018; Brito 2019; and Georgia Department of Human Services 2019.

31. Financial Justice Project 2019.

32. See Sorensen, Sousa, and Schaner 2007; and Brito 2019.

33. Zatz 2016, 2021.

34. For examples of this, see Pearson 2004; Patterson 2008a; Cammett 2011; Cook and Noyes 2011; Spjeldnes, Yamatani, and Davis 2015; and NCSL 2019.

35. For two examples of this focus on court practices, see Battle 2019; and Brito 2020. And for an example of this call for change in support adjudication, see Hahn, Edin, and Abrahams 2018.

36. As many social scientists have argued, these are no longer the standards that middle-class or privileged men are held to, so holding poor men up to them seems especially cruel. For more on middle-class men's fathering ideals, see Gerson 1994; Faludi 1999; and Marsiglio and Roy 2012. And for public opinion research on the breadwinning model of fatherhood and parenting patterns, see Pew Research Center 2019.

37. See bell hooks 2004 for more on the class politics of shifting masculinities.

38. Zatz and Stoll 2020.

39. See CDC 2013.

40. England and Edin 2007.

41. Decades ago, in 1990, feminist sociologist Patricia Hill Collins first theorized the power and importance of other mothering for African American women's upbringing and politics. See also Stanlie 1993 for more on its link to community activism.

APPENDIX

1. For a more elaborate and extended methodological discussion of this research, see my author website www.Lynne-Haney.com.

2. Gerson and Damaske 2021.

3. For instance, some of these agencies required that my research undergo their own institutional reviews (in addition to NYU's) prior to working with me. And these reviews were not simply pro forma gestures—a few agencies actually concluded that their parents were too vulnerable, legally and otherwise, to be involved in research on support debt. For the full list of institutions and agencies I did work with and recruit through, see www.Lynne-Haney.com.

4. For more on this reform work see Haney and Mercier 2021 as well as www.Lynne-Haney.com.

Bibliography

Abramovitz, Mimi. 1988 [2017]. *Regulating the Lives of Women: Social Welfare Policy from Colonial Times to the Present*. Boston: South End Press.

Aharpour, Delara, Lindsay Ochoa, Jill Stein, and Marykate Zukierwicz. 2020. "State Strategies for Improving Child Support Outcomes from Incarcerated Parents." ASPE Research Brief. Washington, D.C.: Office of the Assistant Secretary for Planning and Evaluation, US Department of Health and Human Services.

Anderson, Elijah. 1978. *A Place on the Corner*. Chicago: University of Chicago Press.

Anderson, Helen. 2009. "Penalizing Poverty: Making Criminal Defendants Pay for the Court Appointed Counsel through Recoupment and Contribution." *University of Michigan Journal of Law Reform* 42(2): 323–80.

Apel, Robert. 2016. "The Effects of Jail and Prison Confinement on Cohabitation and Marriage." *Annals of the American Academy of Political and Social Science* 665: 103–26.

Arditti, Joyce. 2012. *Parental Incarceration and the Family*. New York: NYU Press.

———. 2018. "Parental Incarceration and Family Inequality in the U.S." In *Prison, Punishment, and the Family*, edited by Rachel Condry and Peter Scharff Smith. New York: Oxford University Press.

Arthur, Joey. 2018. "Do Parents Who Owe the Most Child Support Debt Have Reported Income?" Washington, D.C.: US Department of Health and Human

Services, Administration for Children and Families, Office of Child Support Enforcement. www.acf.hhs.gov/css/ocsedatablog/2018/07/do-parents-who-owe-the-most-child-support-debt-have-reported-income.

Austin, Bobby William. 1996. *Repairing the Breach: Key Ways to Support Family Life, Reclaim Our Streets, and Rebuild Civil Society in America's Communities.* New York: W.K. Kellogg Foundation.

Aviram, Hadar. 2015. *Cheap on Crime: Recession-Era Politics and the Transformation of American Punishment.* Berkeley: University of California Press.

Bach, Amy. 2009. *Ordinary Justice: How Americans Hold Court.* New York: Picador.

Bales, William, and Daniel Mears. 2008. "Inmate Social Ties and the Transition to Society: Does Visitation Reduce Recidivism?" *Crime and Delinquency* 3: 43–50.

Bartfeld, Jodi, and Daniel Meyer. 1999. "The Changing Role of Child Support among Never Married Mothers." Institute for Research on Poverty, Discussion Paper no. 1200-99. Madison: University of Wisconsin Institute for Research on Poverty. http://www.ssc.wisc.edu/irp.

Battle, Britanny. 2018. "Deservingness, Deadbeat Dads, and Responsible Fatherhood: Child Support Policy and Rhetorical Conceptualizations of Poverty, Welfare, and the Family." *Symbolic Interaction* 41(4): 443–64.

———. 2019. "They Look at You like You're Nothing": Stigma and Shame in the Child Support System." *Symbolic Interaction* 42(4): 640–68.

Beatty, Jack, Sheldon Danziger, Peter Edelman, Robert Rector, and Jason Turner. 1997. "Welfare: Where Do We Go from Here?" *Atlantic Unbound* 12(25) (March). www2.theAtlantic.com/unbound/forum/welfare/intro.htm.

Beckett, Katherine. 2018. "The Politics, Promise and Peril of Criminal Justice Reform in the Context of Mass Incarceration." *Annual Review of Criminology* 1: 235–59.

Beckett, Katherine, and Alexes Harris. 2011. "On Cash and Conviction." *Criminology and Public Policy* 10(3): 509–37.

Bennett, William. 2001. *The Broken Hearth: Reversing the Moral Collapse of the American Family.* New York: Random House.

Berg, Mark, and Beth Huebner. 2010. "Reentry and the Ties That Bind: An Examination of Social Ties, Employment, and Recidivism." *Justice Quarterly* 28: 382–410.

Berger, Lawrence, and Callie Langton. 2011. "Young Disadvantaged Men as Fathers." *Annals of the American Academy of Political and Social Science* 635(1): 56–75.

Bersani, Bianca, and Elaine Eggleston Doherty. 2018. "Desistance from Offending in the 20th Century." *Annual Review of Criminology* 1: 311–34.

Black, Timothy, and Sky Keyes. 2021. *It's a Setup: Fathering from the Social and Economic Margins.* New York: Oxford University Press.

Blank, Rebecca. 1997. "The 1996 Welfare Reform." *Journal of Economic Perspectives* 11(1): 169–77.

———. 1998. *It Takes a Nation: A New Agenda for Fighting Poverty*. Princeton: Princeton University Press.

Blankenhorn, David. 1995. *Fatherless America*. New York: Harper Perennial.

Braman, Donald. 2004. *Doing Time on the Outside: Incarceration and Family Life in Urban America*. Ann Arbor: University of Michigan Press.

Brayne, Sarah. 2014. "Surveillance and System Avoidance: Criminal Justice Contact and Institutional Attachment." *American Sociological Review* 79(3): 367–91.

Brito, Tonya. 2000. "The Welfarization of Family Law." *University of Kansas Law Review* 48: 229–63.

———. 2012. "Fathers behind Bars: Rethinking Child Support Policy toward Low Income Fathers and Their Families." *Journal of Gender, Race, and Justice* 15: 617–35.

———. 2013. "What We Talk about When We Talk about Matriarchy." *Michigan State Law Review*, 1263–89.

———. 2019. "The Child Support Debt Bubble." *UC Irvine Law Review* 9(4): 953–88.

———. 2020. "Producing Justice in Poor People's Courts: Four Models of State Legal Actors." *Lewis and Clark Law Review* 24: 145–89.

Bryner, Gary. 1998. *Politics and Public Morality: The Great American Welfare Reform Debate*. New York: W.W. Norton.

Burton, Linda, Dorian Burton, and Bobby Austin. 2016. "Repairing the Breach: A Focus on Families and Black Males." In *Boys and Men in African American Families*, edited by Linda Burton, Susan McHale, Jennifer Van Hook, Dorian Burton, and Valary King, 1–3. New York: Springer.

Cadigan, Michele, and Gabriela Kirk. 2020. "On Thin Ice: Bureaucratic Processes of Monetary Sanctions and Job Insecurity." *RSF: The Russell Sage Foundation Journal of the Social Sciences* 6(1): 113–31.

Camissa, Anne Marie. 1998. *From Rhetoric to Reform? Welfare Policy in American Politics*. Boulder: Westview Press.

Cammett, Ann. 2006. "Expanding Collateral Sanctions: The Hidden Costs of Aggressive Child Support Enforcement against Incarcerated Parents." *Georgetown Journal on Poverty Law and Policy* 13: 313–40.

———. 2011. "Deadbeats, Deadbrokes, and Prisoners." *Georgetown Journal on Poverty Law and Policy* 18(2): 127–68.

———. 2014. "Deadbeat Dads and Welfare Queens: How Metaphor Shapes Poverty Law." *Boston College Journal of Law and Social Justice* 34(2): 233–65.

Cancian, Maria. 2013. "Discouraging Disadvantaged Fatherhood." *Journal of Policy Analysis and Management* 32: 758–84.

———. 2017. "Should Incarcerated Fathers Owe Child Support? Evaluating a

Policy Option." Madison: University of Wisconsin Institute for Research on Poverty.

Cancian, Maria, Carolyn Heinrich, and Yiyoon Chung. 2009. *Does Debt Discourage Employment and Payment of Child Support? Evidence from a Natural Experiment*. Madison: University of Wisconsin Institute for Research on Poverty.

Cancian, Maria, and David Meyer. 2002. *W-2 Child Support Demonstration Evaluation Report on Nonexperimental Analyses*, vol. 2. Madison: University of Wisconsin Institute for Research on Poverty.

——. 2018. "Reforming Policy for Single-Parent Families to Reduce Child Poverty." *RSF: The Russell Sage Foundation Journal of the Social Sciences* 4: 91–112.

Cancian, Maria, Daniel Meyer, and Emma Casper. 2008. "Welfare and Child Support: Complements, not Substitutes." *Journal of Policy Analysis and Management* 27: 354–75.

Cancian, Maria, Daniel Meyer, and Eunhee Ha. 2011a. "Child Support: Responsible Fatherhood and the Quid Pro Quo." *Annals of the American Academy of Political and Social Science*, 635(1): 140–62.

——. 2011b. "The Regularity of Child Support and Its Contribution to the Regularity of Income." *Social Service Review* 85(3): 401–19.

Cancian, Maria, Daniel Meyer, and Jennifer Roff. 2007. *Testing New Ways to Increase the Economic Well-Being of Single-Parent Families: The Effects of Child Support Policies for Welfare Participants*. Madison: Institute for Research on Poverty.

Carlson, Marcia, Sara McLanahan, and Paula England. 2004. "Union Formation in Fragile Families." *Demography* 41: 237–61.

Carson, E. Ann. 2020. *Prisoners in 2019*. Washington, D.C.: US Department of Justice, Bureau of Justice Statistics.

Cassetty, Judith. 1978. *Child Support and Public Policy: Securing Support from Absent Fathers*. Lexington: Lexington Books.

——. 2002. "Child Support Disregard Policies and Program Outcomes: An Analysis of Microdata from the CPS." In *W-2 Child Support Demonstration Evaluation Report on Nonexperimental Analyses*, vol. 3: *Quantitative Nonexperimental Analyses*: *Background Reports* (chapter 2). Madison: University of Wisconsin Institute for Research on Poverty.

CDC (Centers for Disease Control). 2013. "Fathers' Involvement with Their Children: United States, 2006–2010." National Health Statistics, 20 December 2013. www.cdc.gov/nchs/data/nhsr/nhsr071.pdf.

CDCSS (California Department of Child Support Services). 2017. *The Use of Contempt across California Counties*. Sacramento: CDCSS.

——. 2018. *Comparative Data for Managing Program Performance, Federal Fiscal Year 2018*. Sacramento: CDCSS.

Center for Law and Social Policy. 2005. *Every Door Closed: Facts about Parents with Criminal Records*. Washington, D.C.: Community Legal Services.

Chambers, David. 1979. *Making Fathers Pay: The Enforcement of Child Support*. Chicago: University of Chicago Press.

Chettiar, Inimai, and Priya Raghaven, eds. 2019. *Ending Mass Incarceration: Ideas from Today's Leaders*. New York: Brennan Center for Justice, New York University.

Chondry, Rachel, and Peter Scharff Smith, eds. 2018. *Prison, Punishment, and the Family*. New York: Oxford University Press.

Clair, Matthew. 2020. *Privilege and Punishment: How Race and Class Matter in Criminal Court*. Princeton: Princeton University Press.

Clayton, Obie, Ronald Mincy, and David Blankenhorn. 2003. *Black Fathers in Contemporary American Society: Strengths, Weaknesses, and Strategies for Change*. New York: Russell Sage Foundation.

Clear, Todd. 2007. *Imprisoning Communities: How Mass Incarceration Makes Disadvantaged Communities Worse*. New York: Oxford University Press.

Collins, Patricia Hill. 1990. *Black Feminist Thought*. New York: Routledge.

Comfort, Megan. 2007. "Punishment beyond the Legal Offender." *Annual Review of Law and Social Science* 3: 271–96.

———. 2008. *Doing Time Together: Love and Family in the Shadow of the Prison*. Chicago: University of Chicago Press.

———. 2012. "It Was Basically College to Us: Poverty, Prison, and Emerging Adulthood." *Journal of Poverty* 16: 308–22.

———. 2016. "'A Twenty Hour-a-Day Job': The Impact of Frequent Low-Level Criminal Justice Involvement on Family Life." *Annals of the American Academy of Political and Social Science* 665: 63–79.

Comfort, Megan, Tasseli McKay, Justin Landwehr, Erin Kennedy, Christine Lindquist, and Anupa Bir. 2016. *Parenting and Partnership When Fathers Return from Prison: Findings from Qualitative Analysis*. Washington, D.C.: US Department of Health and Human Services, Office of the Assistant Secretary for Planning and Evaluation.

Cook, Karen S. 2001. "Trust in Society." In *Trust in Society*, vol. 2, edited by Karen S. Cook. New York: Russell Sage Foundation.

———. 2005. "Networks, Norms, and Trust: The Social Psychology of Social Capital." *Social Psychology Quarterly* 68: 4–14.

Cook, Karen S., Russell Hardin, and Margaret Levi. 2005. *Cooperation without Trust?* New York: Russell Sage Foundation.

Cook, Steven. 2015. *Child Support Enforcement Use of Contempt and Criminal Nonsupport Charges in Wisconsin. Report to the Wisconsin Department of Children and Families*. Madison: University of Wisconsin Institute for Research on Poverty.

Cook, Steven, and Jennifer L. Noyes. 2011. *The Use of Civil Contempt and*

Criminal Nonsupport as Child Support Enforcement Tools: A Report on Local Perspectives and the Availability of Data. Madison: University of Wisconsin Institute for Research on Poverty.

Corcoran, Mary, Sandra K. Danziger, Ariel Kalil, and Kristin S. Seefeldt. 2000. "How Welfare Reform Is Affecting Women's Work." *Annual Review of Sociology* 26: 241–69.

Cozzolino, Elizabeth. 2018. "Public Assistance, Relationship Context, and Jail for Child Support Debt." *Socius* 4(1): 1–25.

Curran, Laura, and Laura Abrams. 2000. "Making Men into Dads: Fatherhood, the State, and Welfare Reform." *Gender and Society* 14(5): 662–78.

Curtis, Anna. 2019. *Dangerous Masculinity: Fatherhood, Race, and Security inside America's Prisons.* New Brunswick: Rutgers University Press.

Dagan, David, and Steven M. Teles. 2014. "Locked In? Conservative Reform and the Future of Mass Incarceration." *Annals of the American Academy of Political and Social Science* 651(1): 266–76.

———. 2016. *Prison Break: Why Conservatives Turned Against Mass Incarceration.* Oxford: Oxford University Press.

deVuono-powell, Saneta, Chris Schweidler, Alicia Walters, and Azadeh Zohrabi. 2015. *Who Pays? The True Cost of Incarceration on Families.* Oakland: Ella Baker Center, Forward Together, Research Action Design.

Doar, Robert. 2017. "Empowering Child Support Enforcement to Reduce Poverty." Washington, D.C.: American Enterprise Institute.

Dunier, Mitchell. 1999. *Sidewalk.* New York: Farrar, Straus and Giroux.

Edin, Kathryn. 1995. "Single Mothers and Child Support: The Possibilities and Limits of Child Support Policy." *Children and Youth Services Review* 17(1–2): 203–30.

Edin, Kathryn, Paula England, and Kathryn Linnenberg. 2003. "Love and Distrust among Unmarried Parents." Paper presented at National Poverty Center conference on Marriage and Family Formation among Low-Income Couples. Washington, D.C., 4–5 September.

Edin, Kathryn, and Maria Kefalas. 2005. *Promises I Can Keep: Why Poor Mothers Put Motherhood before Marriage.* Berkeley: University of California Press.

Edin, Kathryn, and Timothy Nelson. 2013. *Doing the Best I Can: Fatherhood in the Inner City.* Berkeley: University of California Press.

Edin, Kathryn, Timothy Nelson, and Rechelle Paranal. 2004. "Fatherhood and Incarceration as Potential Turning Points in the Criminal Careers of Unskilled Men." In *Imprisoning America: The Social Effects of Mass Incarceration,* edited by Mary Patillo, David Weiman, and Bruce Western, 46–75. New York: Russell Sage.

Edin, Kathryn, and H. Luke Shaefer. 2015. *$2.00 a Day: Living on Almost Nothing in America.* New York: Houghton Mifflin Harcourt.

Ellwood, David. 1996. "Welfare Reform as I Knew It: When Bad Things Happen to Good Policies." *American Prospect* (May–June): 22–29. http://epn.org/prospect/26/26ellew.html.

Emory, Allison Dwyer, Lenna Nepomnyaschy, Maureen Waller, Daniel Miller, and Alexandra Haralampoudis. 2020. "Providing after Prison: Nonresident Fathers' Formal and Informal Contributions to Children." *RSF: The Russell Sage Foundation Journal of the Social Sciences.* 6: 84–112.

England, Paula, and Kathryn Edin. 2007. *Unmarried Couples with Children.* New York: Russell Sage Foundation, Project MUSE.

———. 2010. "Unmarried Couples with Children: Why Don't They Marry? How Can Policy-Makers Promote More Stable Relationships?" In *Families as They Really Are*, edited by Barbara Risman, 307–12. New York: W.W. Norton.

Enos, Sandra. 2001. *Mothering from the Inside: Parenting in a Women's Prison.* Albany: SUNY Press.

Estacion, Angela, and Andrew Cherlin. 2010. "Gender Distrust and Intimate Unions among Low-Income Hispanic and African-American Women." *Journal of Family Issues* 31(4): 475–98.

Faludi, Susan. 1999. *Stiffed: The Betrayal of American Men.* New York: William Morrow.

Fernandez-Kelly, Patricia. 2015. *The Hero's Fight.* Princeton: Princeton University Press.

Financial Justice Project. 2019. *The Payback Problem.* San Francisco: Department of Finance.

———. 2020. *Criminal Justice Administrative Fees: High Pain for People, Low Gain for Government.* San Francisco: Department of Finance.

Flavin, Jeanne. 2009. *Our Bodies, Our Crimes: The Policing of Women's Reproduction in America.* New York: NYU Press.

FOCSA (Florida Office of Child Support Administration). *Florida's Child Support Bench Handbook 2012.* Tallahassee: Florida Office of State Court Administrator.

———. 2017. *Review and Update of Florida's Child Support Guidelines.* Report Submitted to the Florida Legislature. Tallahassee: Department of Economics, Florida State University.

Fourcade, Marion, and Kieran Healy. 2007. "Moral Views of Market Society." *Annual Review of Sociology* 33: 285–311.

Fraser, Nancy. 2016. "Contradictions of Capital and Care." *New Left Review* 100: 99–117.

Fraser, Nancy, and Linda Gordon. 1994. "Dependency Demystified: Inscriptions of Power in a Keyword of the Welfare State." *Social Politics* 1: 4–31.

Freeman, Richard, and Jane Waldfogel. 2001. "Dunning Delinquent Dads: The Effects of Child Support Enforcement Policy on Child Support Receipt by Never Married Women." *Journal of Human Resources* 36(2): 207–25.

Furstenberg, Frank. 2001. "The Fading Dream: Prospects for Marriage in the

Inner City." In *Problem of the Century: Racial Stratification in the United States*, edited by Elijah Anderson and Douglas Massey, 224–46. New York: Russell Sage Foundation.

Galbi, Douglas. 2015. "Incarcerating Parents without the Benefit of Counsel." http://purplemotes.net/2011/03/22/persons-in-jail-for-child-support-debt.

Garfinkel, Irwin. 1992. *Assuring Child Support: An Extension of Social Security*. New York: Russell Sage Foundation.

Garfinkel, Irwin, Sarah McLanahan, and Phillip Robins, eds. 1994. *Child Support and Child Well-Being*. Washington, D.C.: Urban Institute.

Garfinkel, Irwin, Daniel Meyer, and Sara McLanahan. 2001. "A Brief History of Child Support Policies in the United States." In *Fathers under Fire: The Revolution of Child Support Enforcement*, edited by Irwin Garfinkel, Daniel Meyer, Sara McLanahan, and Judith Selzter, 14–27. New York: Russell Sage Foundation.

Garfinkel, Irwin, and Lenna Nepomnyaschy. 2010. "Assuring Child Support: A Re-assessment in Honor of Alfred Kahn." In *From Child Welfare to Child Well-Being*, edited by Sheila B. Kammerman, Shelley Phipps, and Asher Ben-Arieh, 231–53. New York: Springer.

Garland, David, ed. 2001. *Mass Imprisonment: Social Causes and Consequences*. London: Sage.

Geller, Amanda, Carey E. Cooper, Irwin Garfinkel, Ofira Schwartz-Soicher, and Ronald B. Mincy. 2012. "Beyond Absenteeism: Father Incarceration and Child Development." *Demography* 49: 49–76.

Geller, Amanda, Irwin Garfinkel, Carey E. Cooper, and Ronald B. Mincy. 2009. "Parental Incarceration and Child Wellbeing: Implications for Urban Families." *Social Science Quarterly* 90: 1186–1202.

Geller, Amanda, Irwin Garfinkel, and Bruce Western. 2011. "Paternal Incarceration and Support for Children." *Demography* 48: 25–47.

Geller, Amanda, Kate Jaeger, and Garrett Pace. 2016. "Surveys, Records, and the Study of Incarceration in Families." *Annals of the American Academy of Political and Social Science* 665: 22–43.

Georgia Department of Human Services. 2019. *Parental Accountability Court Program Fact Sheet*. Atlanta: Department of Human Services.

Gerson, Kathleen. 1994. *No Man's Land: Men's Changing Commitment to Work and Family*. New York: Basic Books.

Gerson, Kathleen, and Sarah Damaske. 2021. *The Science and Art of Interviewing*. New York: Oxford University Press.

Gilens, Martin. 1999. *Why Americans Hate Welfare: Race, Media, and the Politics of Antipoverty Policy*. Chicago: University of Chicago Press.

González, Killeen. 2011. "Anniversary of Bradley Amendment Continues Child Support Discussion." *Fugitive Nation*, 4 May. https://fugitivenation.wordpress

.com/2011/05/05/anniversary-of-bradley-amendment-continues-child-support-discussion.

Gordon, Linda. 1994. *Pitied but Not Entitled: Single Mothers and the History of Welfare*. Cambridge, MA: Harvard University Press.

———. 2001. "Who Deserves Help? Who Should Provide?" *Annals of the American Academy of Political and Social Science* 577: 12–25.

Gottschalk, Marie. 2006. *The Prison and the Gallows: The Politics of Mass Incarceration in the United States*. New York: Cambridge University Press.

———. 2016. *Caught: The Prison State and the Lockdown of American Politics*. Princeton: Princeton University Press.

Grall, Timothy. 2020. *Custodial Mothers and Fathers and Their Child Support: 2017. Current Population Reports*, 60–269. Washington, D.C.: US Department of Commerce, US Census Bureau.

Green, David. 2015. "U.S. Penal-Reform Catalysts, Drivers, and Prospects." *Punishment and Society* 17(3): 271–98.

Griswold, Esther. 2001. "Child Support in the Criminal Justice System." Working paper. Denver: Center for Policy Research.

Griswold, Esther, and Jessica Pearson. 2003. "Twelve Reasons for Collaboration between Departments of Correction and Child Support Enforcement Agencies." *Corrections Today* 65: 87–90.

———. 2005. "Turning Offenders into Responsible Parents and Child Support Payers." *Family Court Review* 43(3): 358–71.

Griswold, Esther, Jessica Pearson, and Lanae Davis. 2001. *Testing a Modification Process for Incarcerated Parents*. Denver: Center for Policy Research.

Griswold, Esther, Jessica Pearson, Nancy Thoennes, and Lanae Davis. 2004. *Fathers in the Criminal Justice System*. Denver: Center for Policy Research.

Gustafson, Karen. 2011. *Cheating Welfare: Public Assistance and the Criminalization of Poverty*. New York: NYU Press.

Ha, Yoonsook, Maria Cancian, Daniel R. Meyer, and Eunhee Han. 2008. *Factors Associated with Nonpayment of Child Support* [Report to Wisconsin Department of Workforce Development]. Madison: University of Wisconsin Institute for Research on Poverty.

Hagan, John, and Holly Foster. 2012. "Children of the American Prison Generation: Student and Spillover Effects of Incarcerating Mothers." *Law and Society Review* 46(1): 37–69.

Hager, Eli. 2015a. "Why Was Walter Scott Running?" *The Marshall Project*, 10 April. www.themarshallproject.org/2015/04/10/why-was-walter-scott-running.

———. 2015b. "For Men in Prison, Child Support Debt Becomes Crushing Debt." *The Marshall Project*. https://www.themarshallproject.org/2015/10/18/for-men-in-prison-child-support-becomes-a-crushing-debt.

———. 2016. "Child Support Relief Coming for Incarcerated Parents." *The Mar-*

shall Project. www.themarshallproject.org/2016/12/20/child-support-relief-coming-for-incarcerated-parents.

Haggerty, Kevin, and Richard Ericson. 2000. "The Surveillant Assemblage." *British Journal of Sociology* 51(4): 605–22.

Hahn, Heather, Kathryn Edin, and Lauren Abrahams. 2018. *Transforming Child Support into a Family-Building System*. Washington, D.C.: US Partnership on Mobility from Poverty.

Hahn, Heather, Daniel Kuehn, Hannah Hassani, and Kathryn Edin. 2019. *Relief from Government-Owed Child Support Debt and Its Effects on Parents and Children*. Washington, D.C.: Urban Institute.

Halushka, John. 2016. "Work Wisdom: Teaching Former Prisoners How to Negotiate Workplace Interactions and Perform a Rehabilitated Self." *Ethnography* 1: 72–91.

———. 2017. "Managing Rehabilitation: Negotiating Performance Accountability at the Frontlines of Reentry Service Provision." *Punishment and Society* 19(4): 482–502.

———. 2020. "The Runaround: Punishment, Welfare, and Poverty Survival after Prison." *Social Problems* 67(2): 233–50.

Handler, Joel, and Yeheskal Hasenfeld. 1997. *We the Poor People: Work, Poverty, and Welfare*. New Haven: Yale University Press.

Haney, Lynne. 1996. "Homeboys, Babies, Men in Suits: The State and the Reproduction of Male Dominance." *American Sociological Review* 61(5): 759–78.

———. 2008. *Offending Women: Power, Punishment, and the Regulation of Desire*. Berkeley: University of California Press.

———. 2013. "Motherhood as Punishment: The Case of Parenting in Prison." *Signs* 39(1): 105–30.

———. 2018. "Incarcerated Fatherhood: The Entanglements of Child Support Debt and Mass Imprisonment." *American Journal of Sociology* 124(1): 1–48.

Haney, Lynne, and Nathan Link. 2017. "Child Support Arrears and Incarceration: Understanding the Relationship." Proposal prepared for and submitted to the California Department of Child Support Services.

Haney, Lynne, and Miranda March. 2003. "Married Fathers and Caring Daddies: Welfare Reform and the Discursive Politics of Paternity." *Social Problems* 50(4): 461–81.

Haney, Lynne, and Marie Mercier. 2021. *Child Support and Reentry*. Washington, D.C.: Department of Justice and National Institute of Justice.

Hansen, Drew. 1999. "The American Invention of Child Support: Dependency and Punishment in Early American Child Support Law." *Yale Law Journal* 108(5–13): 1123–53.

Harding, David. 2010. *Living the Drama: Community, Conflict, and Culture among Inner-City Boys*. Chicago: University of Chicago Press.

Harding, David, Jeffrey Morenoff, Cheyney Dobson, Erin Lane, Kendra Opatovsky, Ed-Dee Williams, and Jessica Wyse. 2016. "Families, Prisoner Reentry, and Reintegration." In *Boys and Men in African American Families*, edited by Linda Burton, Susan McHale, Jennifer Van Hook, Dorian Burton, and Valary King, 105–60. New York: Springer.

Harding, David, Jessica Wyse, Cheyney Dobson, and Jeffrey Morenoff. 2014. "Making Ends Meet after Prison." *Journal of Policy Analysis and Management* 33: 440–70.

Harris, Alexis. 2016. *A Pound of Flesh: Monetary Sanctions as Punishment for the Poor*. New York: Russell Sage Foundation.

Harris, Alexis, Heather Evans, and Katherine Beckett. 2010. "Drawing Blood from Stones: Legal Debt and Social Inequality in the Contemporary United States." *American Journal of Sociology* 115(6): 1753–99.

Harris, Kathleen Mullen. 1997. *Teen Mothers and the Revolving Welfare Door*. Philadelphia: Temple University Press.

Hays, Sharon. 1996. *The Cultural Contradictions of Motherhood*. New Haven: Yale University Press.

———. 2004. *Flat Broke with Children: Women in the Age of Welfare Reform*. New York: Oxford University Press.

Healy, Kieran. 2006. *Last Best Gifts: Altruism and the Market for Human Blood and Organs*. Chicago: University of Chicago Press.

Heimer, Carol A. 2001. "Solving the Problem of Trust." In *Trust in Society*, edited by Karen Cook, 40–88. New York: Russell Sage Foundation.

Heinrich, Carolyn, Brett Burkhardt, and Hilary Shager. 2011. "Reducing Child Support Debt and Its Consequences: Can Forgiveness Benefit All?" *Journal of Policy Analysis and Management* 30: 729–74.

Henrichson, Christian, and Ruth Delaney. 2012. "The Price of Prison: What Incarceration Costs Taxpayers." *Federal Sentencing Reporter* 25(1): 68–80.

Hobson, Barbara, and David Morgan. 2002. "Introduction." In *Making Men into Fathers: Men, Masculinities, and the Social Politics of Fatherhood*, edited by Barbara Hobson. Cambridge, MA: Cambridge University Press.

Holzer, Harry. 2009. "The Labor Market and Young Black Men: Updating Moynihan's Perspective." *Annals of the American Academy of Political and Social Science* 621: 47–69.

hooks, bell. 2004. *The Will to Change: Men, Masculinity, and Love*. New York: Washington Square Press.

Huang, Chien-Chung, and Hillard Pouncy. 2005. "Why Doesn't She Have a Child Support Order? Personal Choice or Objective Constraint." *Family Relations* 54: 547–57.

Irwin, John. 1987. *The Felon*. Berkeley: University of California Press.

Johnson, Earl, Ann Levine, and Fred Doolittle. 1999. *Fathers' Fair Share: Helping Poor Men Manage Child Support and Fatherhood*. New York: Russell Sage.

Justice, Jan, 2007. *Modifying Child Support Orders of Incarcerated Parents to*

Prevent the Build-Up of Debt. Washington, D.C.: Center for Law and Social Policy.

Kantorowicz-Reznichenko, Elena. 2015. "Day Fines: Should the Rich Pay More?" *Review of Law and Economics* 11: 481–501.

Kaye, Kerwin. 2019. *Enforcing Freedom: Therapeutic Communities and the Intimacies of the State*. New York: Columbia University Press.

Kirk, David, and Sarah Wakefield. 2018. "Collateral Consequences of Punishment: A Critical Review and Path Forward." *American Review of Criminology* 1: 171–94.

Kiviat, Barbara. 2017. "The Art of Deciding with Data: Evidence from How Employers Translate Credit Reports into Hiring Decisions." *Socio-Economic Review* 17(2): 283–309.

Kohler-Hausman, Issa. 2018. *Misdemeanor Land: Criminal Courts and Social Control in the Age of Broken Windows*. Princeton: Princeton University Press.

Kotova, Anna. 2018. "Time, the Pains of Imprisonment, and 'Coping.'" In *Prisons, Punishment, and the Family: Towards a New Sociology of Punishment?* edited by Rachel Condry and Peter Scharff Smith, 244–57. New York: Oxford University Press.

Koven, Seth, and Sonya Michel, eds. 1993. *Mothers of a New World: Maternalist Politics and the Origins of Welfare States*. New York: Routledge.

Krause, Harry. 1989. "Child Support Reassessed: The Limits of Private Responsibility and the Public Interest." *University of Illinois Law Review* 2: 367–98.

Lara-Millan, Armando. 2014. "Public Emergency Room Overcrowding in the Era of Mass Imprisonment." *American Sociological Review* 79(5): 866–87.

Lara-Millan, Armando, and Nicole Gonzalez van Cleve. 2017. "Interorganizational Utility of Welfare Stigma in the Criminal Justice System." *Criminology* 55(1): 59–84.

LeBaron, Genevieve, and Adrienne Roberts. 2010. "Toward a Feminist Political Economy of Capitalism and Carcerality." *Signs* 36(1): 19–44.

Legler, Paul. 1996. "The Coming Revolution in Child Support Policy: Implications of the 1996 Welfare Act." *Family Law Quarterly* 30(3): 519–63.

Legler, Paul, and Vicki Turetsky. 2006. "More Child Support Dollars to Kids: Using New State Flexibility in Child Support Pass-Through and Distribution Rules to Benefit Government and Families." Washington, D.C.: Center for Law and Social Policy.

Levine, Judth. 2013. *Ain't No Trust: How Bosses, Boyfriends, and Bureaucrats Fail Low-Income Women and Why It Matters*. Berkeley: University of California Press.

Levingston, Kirsten, and Vicki Turetsky. 2007. "Debtor's Prison: Prisoners' Accumulation of Debt as a Barrier to Reentry." *Clearinghouse Review* 41(3–4): 186–97.

Lewis, Nicole, and Beatrix Lockwood. 2019. "The Hidden Costs of Incarceration."

The Marshall Project, December. www.themarshallproject.org/2019/12/17/the-hidden-cost-of-incarceration.

Liebow, Elliot. 1967. *Tally's Corner: A Study of Negro Streetcorner Men*. New York: Little, Brown.

Link, Nathan, and Caterina Roman. 2017. "Longitudinal Associations among Child Support Debt, Employment, and Recidivism after Prison." *Sociological Quarterly* 58: 140–60.

Lippold, Kye, Austin Nichols, and Elaine Sorenson. 2013. *Evaluation of the $150 Child Support Pass-Through and Disregard Policy in the District of Columbia*. Washington, D.C.: Urban Institute.

Liu, Lin, and Christy Visher. 2021. "Decomposition of the Role of Family in Reentry: Family Support, Tension, Gender, and Reentry Outcomes." *Crime and Delinquency* 67(6–7): 970–96.

MacKinnon, Catherine. 1989. *Toward a Feminist Theory of the State*. Cambridge, MA: Harvard University Press.

Maldonado, Solangel. 2006. "Deadbeat or Deadbroke: Redefining Child Support for Poor Fathers." *UC Davis Law Review* 39: 991–1023.

Marsiglio, William, and Kevin Roy. 2012. *Nurturing Dads: Fatherhood Initiatives beyond the Wallet*. New York: Russell Sage Foundation.

Martin, Courtney. 2019. "Child Support vs. Deadbeat States." *New York Times*, 10 September. https://www.nytimes.com/2019/09/10/opinion/child-support-states.html?referringSource=articleShare.

Martin, Karin. 2018. "Monetary Myopia: An Examination of Institutional Response to Revenue from Monetary Sanctions for Misdemeanors." *Criminal Justice Policy Review* 29(6–7): 630–62.

Martin, Karin, Sandra Smith, and Wendy Still. 2017. *Shackled to Debt: Criminal Justice Financial Obligations and the Barriers to Re-Entry They Create*. Washington, D.C.: US Department of Justice, National Institute of Justice.

Martin, Karin, Bryan Sykes, Sarah Shannon, Frank Edwards, and Alexes Harris. 2018. "Monetary Sanctions: Legal Financial Obligations in US Systems of Justice." *Annual Review of Criminology* 1(1): 471–95.

Martinson, Karin, and Demetra Nightingale. 2008. *Ten Key Findings from Responsible Fatherhood Initiatives*. Washington, D.C.: Urban Institute.

Maruna, Shadd. 2011. "Reentry as a Rite of Passage." *Punishment and Society* 13: 3–28.

May, Rebecca, and Marguerite Roulet. 2005. *A Look at Arrests of Low-Income Fathers for Child Support Nonpayment*. Madison: Center for Family Policy and Practice.

McIntosh, Mary. 1978. "The State and the Oppression of Women." In *Feminism and Materialism: Women and Modes of Production*, edited by Annette Kuhn and AnnMarie Wolpe, 254–89. London: Routledge and Keagan Paul.

McLaughlin, Michael, Carrie Pettus-Davis, Derek Brown, Christopher Weeh, and

Tanya Renn. 2016. *The Economic Burden of Incarceration in the US*. Tallahassee: Institute for Justice Research and Development. https://ijrd.csw.fsu.edu/publications/author/michael-mclaughlin.

McLean, Rachel, and Michael Thompson. 2007. *Repaying Debts*. Washington, D.C.: US Department of Justice, Bureau of Justice Assistance; and New York: Council of State Governments Justice Center.

McLeod, Branden, and Aaron Gottlieb. 2018. "Examining the Relationship between Incarceration and Child Support Arrears among Low Income Fathers." *Children and Youth Services Review* 94: 1–9.

Mead, Lawrence. 2011. *Expanding Work Programs for Poor Men*. New York: AEI Press.

Mellgren, Linda, Tasseli McKay, Justin Landwehr, Anupa Bir, Amy Helburn, Christine Lindquist, and Kate Krieger. 2017. *Earnings and Child Support Participation among Reentering Fathers*. Washington, D.C.: US Department of Health and Human Services.

Meyer, Daniel, Maria Cancian, and Melody Waring. 2020. "Use of Child Support Enforcement Actions and Their Relationship to Payments." *Children and Youth Services Review* 110: 1–11.

Meyer, Daniel R., Yoonsook Ha, and Mei-Chen Hu. 2008. "Do High Child Support Orders Discourage Child Support Payments?" *Social Service Review* 82(1): 93–118.

Meyer, Daniel R., and Emily Warren. 2011. *Child Support Orders and the Incarceration of Noncustodial Parents*. Madison: University of Wisconsin Institute for Research on Poverty and School of Social Work.

Miller, Daniel, and Ronald Mincy. 2012. "Falling Further Behind? Child Support Arrears and Fathers' Labor Force Participation." *Social Service Review* 86(4): 604–35.

Miller, Ruben. 2014. "Devolving the Carceral State: Race, Prisoner Reentry, and the Micro Politics of Urban Poverty Management." *Punishment and Society* 16(3): 305–35.

Mincy, Ronald, Monique Jethwani, and Serena Klempin. 2015. *Failing Our Fathers: Confronting the Crisis of Economically Vulnerable Nonresident Fathers*. New York: Oxford University Press.

Mincy, Ronald, and Elaine Sorensen. 1998. "Deadbeats and Turnips in Child Support Reform." *Journal of Policy Analysis and Management* 17(1): 44–51.

Mink, Gwendolyn. 1995. *The Wages of Motherhood*. Ithaca: Cornell University Press.

———. 1998. *Welfare's End*. Ithaca: Cornell University Press.

———. 1999. "Aren't Poor Single Mothers Women? Feminists, Welfare Reform, and Welfare Justice." In *Whose Welfare?* edited by Gwendolyn Mink, 171–88. Ithaca: Cornell University Press.

Minow, Martha. 2001. "How Should We Think about Child Support Obligations?" In *Fathers under Fire: The Revolution of Child Support Enforcement*, edited by Irwin Garfinkel, Daniel Meyer, Sara McLanahan, and Judith Selzter, 302–30. New York: Russell Sage Foundation.

Morenoff, Jeffrey, and David Harding. 2014. "Incarceration, Prisoner Reentry, and Communities." *Annual Review of Sociology* 40: 411–29.

Morris, Monique. 2018. *Pushout: The Criminalization of Black Girls in Schools*. New York: New Press.

Moynihan, Daniel Patrick. 1965. *The Negro Family: The Case for National Action*. Washington, D.C.: US Department of Labor.

Mpondo-Dika, Ekedi. 2021. "The Intimate Costs of Hardship: Support and Ambivalence among the Truly Disadvanatged." Talk at Department of Sociology, New York University, January.

Murphy, Jane. 2005. "Legal Images of Fatherhood: Welfare Reform, Child Support Enforcement, and Fatherless Children." *Notre Dame Law Review* 81(1): 325–86.

National Fatherhood Initiative. 2018. *Responsible Fatherhood Toolkit: Resources from the Field*. www.fatherhood.gov/toolkit/work/non-residential-fathers/partnerships.

National Research Council. Committee on Law and Justice. 2014. *The Growth of Incarceration in the United States: Exploring Causes and Consequences*, edited by Jeremy Travis, Bruce Western, and Steve Redburn. Washington, D.C.: National Academies Press.

NCSL (National Conference of State Legislatures). 2013. "Child Support Guideline Models by State." Washington, D.C. www.ncsl.org/research/human-services/guideline-models-by-state.aspx.

———. 2014. "License Restrictions for Failure to Pay Child Support." Washington, D.C.

———. 2017. "Behind Bars, Behind in Payments." *National Conference of State Legislatures Magazine*, June 2017. https://www.ncsl.org/bookstore/state-legislatures-magazine/parents-prison-child-support-debt.aspx.

———. 2019a. "Interest on Child Support Arrears." Washington, D.C. www.ncsl.org/research/human-services/interest-on-child-support-arrears.aspx.

———. 2019b. "Child Support and Incarceration." Washington, D.C. https://www.ncsl.org/research/human-services/child-support-and-incarceration.aspx.

———. 2020a. "License Restrictions for Failure to Pay Child Support." Washington, D.C. https://www.ncsl.org/research/human-services/license-restrictions-for-failure-to-pay-child-support.aspx.

———. 2020b. "Child Support Pass-Throughs and Disregard Policies for Public Assistance Recipients." Washington, D.C. https://www.ncsl.org/research/human-services/state-policy-pass-through-disregard-child-support.aspx#50-State%20Chart.

Nelson, Timothy. 2004. "Low Income Fathers." *Annual Review of Sociology* 30: 427–51.

Noyles, Jennifer, Maria Cancian, and Laura Cuesta. 2012. *Holding Child Support Orders of Incarcerated Payers in Abeyance: Final Evaluation Report*. Madison: University of Wisconsin Institute for Research on Poverty.

Noyles, Jennifer, Maria Cancian, Laura Cuesta, and Vanessa Rios Salas. 2017. *Holding Child Support Orders of Incarcerated Payers in Abeyance: Four Year Outcomes*. Madison: University of Wisconsin Institute for Research on Poverty.

Nurse, Anne. 2002. *Fatherhood Arrested: Parenting from within the Juvenile Justice System*. Nashville: Vanderbilt University Press.

NWLC (National Women's Law Center). 2002. *Dollars and Sense: Improving the Determination of Child Support Obligations for Low-Income Mothers, Fathers, and Children*. Washington, D.C.

NYCHRA (New York City Department of Human Resources). 2014. "Manage Your Child Support." http://www.nyc.gov/html/hra/downloads/pdf/services/child_support/manage_your_child_support.pdf.

———. 2021. "Programs to Assist Noncustodial Parents Avoid or Manage Child Support Debt." https://www1.nyc.gov/assets/hra/downloads/pdf/services/child_support/manage_your_child_support.pdf

NYC Independent Budget Office. 2015. "A Shift in Priorities and Caseload at the City's Office of Child Support Enforcement." https://ibo.nyc.ny.us/iboreports/2014childsupport.html.

O'Connor, Alice. 2001. *Poverty Knowledge: Social Science, Social Policy, and the Poor in 20th Century History*. Princeton: Princeton University Press.

OCSE (Office of Child Support Enforcement). *Annual Reports* (fiscal years 1994–2020). Washington, D.C.: Department of Health and Human Services, Administration of Children and Families.

———. 2004. *The Story Behind the Numbers: Who Owes Child Support Debt?* Washington, D.C.: Department of Health and Human Services, Administration of Children and Families.

———. 2006. *Incarceration Reentry and Child Support Issues: National and State Research Overview*. Washington, D.C.: Department of Health and Human Services, Administration of Children and Families.

———. 2007. *Working with Incarcerated and Released Parents. Lessons from OCSE Grants and State Programs*. Washington, D.C.: Department of Health and Human Services, Administration of Children and Families.

———. 2011. *State Child Support Agencies with Debt Compromise Policies*. Washington, D.C.: US Department of Health and Human Services, Administration of Children and Families.

———. 2012. *"Voluntary Unemployment," Imputed Income, and Modification Laws for Incarcerated Noncustodial Parents*. Washington, D.C.: US Depart-

ment of Health and Human Services. Administration of Children and Families.
———. 2014. "Major Change in Who Is Owed Child Support Arrears." *The Story behind the Numbers*. Child Support Fact Sheet #4. Washington, D.C.: Department of Health and Human Services, Administration of Children and Families.
———. 2017a. *Who Owes Child Support*? Washington, D.C.: Department of Health and Human Services, Administration of Children and Families, Office of Child Support Enforcement. https://www.acf.hhs.gov/css/ocsedatablog/2017/09/who-owes-the-child-support-debt.
———. 2017b. *Final Rule Resources Flexibility, Efficiency, and Modernization in Child Support Programs Final Rule*. https://www.acf.hhs.gov/css/resource/final-rule-resources.
———. 2017c. *Child Support Caseload Trends 1999–2016*. Washington, D.C.: Department of Health and Human Services, Administration of Children and Families. https://www.acf.hhs.gov/css/map/child-support-caseload-trend-reports.
———. 2018. *State Child Support Agencies with Debt Compromise Policies*. Washington, D.C.: US Department of Health and Human Services, Administration of Children and Families. https://www.acf.hhs.gov/css/state-child-support-agencies-with-debt-compromise-policies-map.
———. 2020. *Economic Impact Payments under the Coronavirus Aid, Relief, and Economic Security (CARES) Act*. https://www.acf.hhs.gov/css/resource/economic-impact-payments-under-the-coronavirus-aid-relief-and-economic-security-cares-act.
———. 2021. *Certified Child Support Arrears Show Sharp Decline*. Washington, D.C.: Department of Health and Human Services, Administration of Children and Families. https://www.acf.hhs.gov/css/ocsedatablog/2021/05/certified-child-support-arrears-shows-sharp-decline.
OIG (Office of Inspector General). 2000. *State Policies Used to Establish Child Support Orders for Low Income Non-Custodial Parents*. OEI-05-99-00391. Washington, D.C.: US Department of Health and Human Services.
———. 2007. *State Use of Debt Compromise to Reduce Child Support Arrearages*. Washington, D.C.: US Department of Health and Human Services.
Oldrup, Helene. 2018. "Falling Out of Time: The Challenge of Synchrony for Children of the Incarcerated." *Child and Society* 32(1): 27–37.
Orloff, Ann Shola. 1993. "Gender and the Social Rights of Citizenship: The Comparative Analysis of State Policies and Gender Relations." *American Sociological Review* 58(3): 303–28.
———. 1996. "Gender in the Welfare State." *Annual Review of Sociology* 22(1): 51–78.
———. 2006. "From Maternalism to 'Employment for All': State Policies to

Promote Women's Employment across the Affluent Democracies." In *The State after Statism: New State Activities in the Era of Globalization and Liberalization*, edited by Jonah D. Levy, 230–68. Cambridge, MA: Harvard University Press.

Orloff, Ann, and Renee Monson. 2002. "Citizens, Workers, or Fathers? Men in the History of US Social Policy." *Making Men into Fathers: Men, Masculinities, and the Social Politics of Fatherhood*, edited by Barbara Hobson. Cambridge, MA: Cambridge University Press.

Pager, Devah. 2003. "The Mark of a Criminal Record." *American Journal of Sociology* 108: 937–75.

———. 2007. *Marked: Race, Crime, and Finding Work in an Era of Mass Incarceration*. Chicago: University of Chicago Press.

Paperno, Barry. 2016. "How Delinquent Child Support Affects Credit Scores." *Creditcards.com*, 11 August. https://www.creditcards.com/credit-card-news/delinquent-child-support-credit-score.php.

Pate, David. 2016. "The Color of Debt: An Examination of Social Networks, Sanctions, and Child Support Enforcement Policy." *Race and Social Problems* 8: 116–35.

Patterson, Elizabeth. 2008a. "Civil Contempt and the Indigent Child Support Obligor: The Silent Return of Debtor's Prison." *Cornell Journal of Law and Public Policy* 18(1): 95–142.

———. 2008b. "Unintended Consequences: Why Congress Should Tread Lightly When Entering the Field of Family Law." *Georgia State University Law Review* 25: 397–434.

Pearson, Jessica. 2004. "Building Debt While Doing Time: Child Support and Incarceration." *Judges' Journal* 1(43): 5–12.

Pearson, Jessica, and Lanae Davis. 2002. *An Evaluation of Colorado Arrears Forgiveness Demonstration Project*. Denver: Center for Policy Research.

Pearson, Jessica, Nancy Thoennes, and Lanae Davis. 2003. *OCSE Responsible Fatherhood Programs*. Denver: Center for Policy Research and Policy Studies.

Pearson, Jessica, Nancy Thoennes, and Rasa Kaunelis. 2012. *Debt Compromise Programs: Program Design and Child Support Outcomes in Five Locations*. Denver: Center for Policy Research.

Perry, Leah. 2016. *The Cultural Politics of US Immigration: Gender, Race, and Media*. New York: NYU Press.

Pew Research Center. 2019. "8 Facts about American Dads." 12 June. https://www.pewresearch.org/fact-tank/2019/06/12/fathers-day-facts.

Phelps, Michelle. 2016. "Possibilities and Contestation in 21st Century Criminal Justice Downsizing." *Annual Review of Law and Social Science* 12: 153–70.

———. 2020. "Mass Probation from Micro to Macro: Tracing the Expansion and Consequences of Community Supervision." *Annual Review of Criminology* 3: 261–79.

Phelps, Michelle, and Devah Pager. 2016. "Inequality and Punishment: A Turning Point for Mass Incarceration?" *Annals of the American Academy of Political and Social Science* 663: 185–203.

Pirog, Maureen, and Kathleen Ziol-Guest. 2006. "Child Support Enforcement: Programs and Policies, Impacts and Questions." *Journal of Policy Analysis and Management* 25(4): 943–90.

Pleggenkuhle, David. 2018. "The Financial Cost of Criminal Conviction." *Criminal Justice and Behavior* 45: 121–45.

Poletta, Francesca, and Zaibu Tufail. 2014. "The Moral Obligations of Some Debts." *Sociological Forum* 29(1): 1–28.

———. 2016. "Helping without Caring: Role Definition and the Gender-Stratified Effects of Emotional Labor in Debt Settlement Firms." *Work and Occupations* 43(4): 401–33.

Putze, Dennis. 2017. "Who Owes the Child Support Debt?" Washington, D.C.: US Department of Health and Human Services, Administration for Children and Families, OCSE. https://www.acf.hhs.gov/css/ocsedatablog/2017/09/who-owes-the-child-support-debt.

Quadagno, Jill. 1994. *The Color of Welfare: How Racism Undermined the War on Poverty*. New York: Oxford University Press.

Randles, Jennifer. 2013. "Repackaging the 'Package Deal': Promoting Marriage for Low-Income Families by Targeting Paternal Identity and Reframing Marital Masculinity." *Gender and Society* 27(6): 864–88.

———. 2020. *Essential Dads: The Inequalities and Politics of Fathering*. Berkeley: University of California Press.

Reese, Ellen. 2005. *Backlash against Welfare Mothers: Past and Present*. Berkeley: University of California Press.

Rhodes, Lorna. 2004. *Total Confinement: Madness and Reason in the Maximum Security Prison*. Berkeley: University of California Press.

Rios, Victor. 2011. *Punished: Policing the Lives of Black and Latino Boys*. New York: NYU Press.

Roberts, Dorothy. 1993. "Racism and Patriarchy in the Meaning of Motherhood." *American University Journal of Gender and Law* 1(1): 1–38.

———. 1997. *Killing the Black Body: Race, Reproduction, and the Meaning of Liberty*. New York: Random House.

———. 2002. *Shattered Bonds: The Color of Child Welfare*. New York: Basic Books.

Roberts, Paula. 2000. "Child-Support Issues for Parents Who Receive Means-Tested Public Assistance." *Clearinghouse Review: Journal of Poverty Law and Policy* 34: 182–96.

Robles, Frances, and Shaila Dewan. 2015. "Skip Child Support. Go to Jail. Lose Job. Repeat." *New York Times*, 19 April. https://www.nytimes.com/2015/04/20/us/skip-child-support-go-to-jail-lose-job-repeat.html.

Roman, Caterina, and Nathan Link. 2015. "Child Support, Debt, and Prisoner Reentry: Examining the Influences of Prisoners' Legal and Financial Obligations on Reentry." Final report to the National Institute of Justice, Grant #2012-IJ-CX-0012, NCJ 248906.

———. 2017. "Community Reintegration among Prisoners with Child Support Obligations: An Examination of Debt, Needs, and Service Receipt." *Criminal Justice Policy Review*, 28(9): 896–917.

Rothman, Barbara Katz. 2005. *Weaving a Family: Untangling Race and Adoption*. Boston: Beacon Press.

Roy, Kevin. 2005. "Transitions on the Margins of Work and Family for Low-Income African American Fathers." *Journal of Family and Economic Issues* 26(1): 77–100.

———. 2006. "Father Stories: A Life Course Examination of Paternal Identity among Low-Income African American Men." *Journal of Family Issues* 27(1): 31–54.

Sabol, William, and Miranda Baumann. 2020. "Justice Reinvestment: Vision and Practice." *Annual Review of Criminology* 3: 317–39.

Sampson, Robert. 2011. "The Incarceration Ledger: Toward a New Era in Assessing Societal Consequences." *Criminology and Public Policy* 10: 819–28.

Schept, Judah. 2016. *Progressive Punishment: Job Loss, Jail Growth, and the Neoliberal Logic of Carceral Expansion*. New York: NYU Press.

Schlafly, Phyllis. 2006. "Repeal the Bradley Amendment." *Townhall.com*, 27 February. http://townhall.com/columnists/phyllisschlafly/2006/02/27/repeal_the_bradley_amendment.

———. 2009. "Family Court Injustices to Men." *World Net Daily*, 22 July. www.wnd.com/2009/07/104624.

Schnittker, Jason, and Andrea John. 2007. "Enduring Stigma: The Long-Term Effects of Incarceration on Health." *Journal of Health and Social Behavior*. 48(1): 115–30.

Schnittker, Jason, Michael Massoglia, and Christopher Uggen. 2011. "Incarceration and the Health of the African American Community." *Du Bois Review* 8(1): 133–41.

Schroeder, Daniel, and Nicholas Doughty. 2009. *Texas Non-Custodial Parent Choices: Program Impact Analysis*. Austin: University of Texas, Lyndon B. Johnson School of Public Affairs.

Schroeder, Daniel, and Amna Khan. 2011. *Non-Custodial Parents Choices: Establishment Pilot, Impact Report*. Austin: University of Texas, Lyndon B. Johnson School of Public Affairs. https://raymarshallcenter.org/files/2005/07/NCP_Choices_Estab_Sep2011final.pdf.

Smeeding, Timothy, Irwin Garfinkel, and Ronald Mincy. 2011. "Young Disadvantaged Men: Fathers, Families, Poverty, and Policy." *Annals of the American Academy of Political and Social Science* 635: 6–21.

Solinger, Rickie. 2005. *Pregnancy and Power*. New York: NYU Press.
Solinger, Rickie, Paula Johnson, Martha Raimon, Tina Reynolds, and Ruby Tapia. 2010. *Interrupted Life: Experiences of Incarcerated Women in the United States*. Berkeley: University of California Press.
Solomon-Fears, Carmen. 2016. *Child Support Enforcement: Program Basics* (CRS Report no. 7-5700). Washington, D.C.: Congressional Research Service.
Solomon-Fears, Carmen, Alison Smith, and Carla Berry. 2012. *Child Support Enforcement: Incarceration as the Last Resort Penalty for Nonpayment of Support* (CRS Report no. R42389). Washington, D.C.: Congressional Research Service.
Solow, Robert. 1998. *Work and Welfare*. Princeton: Princeton University Press.
Sorensen, Elaine. 1997. "A National Profile of Nonresident Fathers and Their Ability to Pay Child Support." *Journal of Marriage and the Family* 59(4): 785–97.
———. 2004. "Understanding How Child-Support Arrears Reached $18 Billion in California." *American Economic Review* 94(2): 312–16.
———. 2010. "Child Support Plays an Increasingly Important Role for Poor Custodial Families." Washington, D.C.: Urban Institue. https://www.urban.org/sites/default/files/publication/29421/412272-Child-Support-Plays-an-Increasingly-Important-Role-for-Poor-Custodial-Families.PDF.
———. 2019. "TANF Arrears Continue to Decline." Washington, D.C.: Office of Child Support Enforcement." https://www.acf.hhs.gov/css/ocsedatablog/2019/10/tanf-arrears-continue-to-decline.
Sorensen, Elaine, and Ariel Halpern. 1999. "Child Support Enforcement Is Working Better Than We Think." No. A-31 of *The New Federalism: Issues and Options for States* Series. Washington, D.C.: Urban Institute. http://www.newfederalism.urban.org/html/anf_31.html
Sorensen, Elaine, and Ariel Hill. 2004. "Single Mothers and Their Child Support Receipt: How Well Is Child Support Enforcement Doing?" *Journal of Human Resources* 39: 135–54.
Sorensen, Elaine, Heather Koball, Kate Pomper, and Chava Zibman. 2003. *Examining Child Support Arrears in California: The Collectability Study*. Sacramento: California Department of Child Support Services.
Sorensen, Elaine, Liliana Sousa, and Simone Schaner. 2007. *Assessing Child Support Arrears in Nine Large States and the Nation*. Washington, D.C.: Urban Institute. https://www.urban.org/research/publications/assessing-child-support-arrears-nine-large-states-and-nation/view/full_report.
Sorensen, Elaine, and Chava Zibman. 2001. "Getting to Know Poor Fathers Who Do Not Pay Child Support." *Social Service Review* 75(3): 420–34.
Soss, Joe, Richard Fording, and Sanford Schram. 2011. *Disciplining the Poor*. Chicago: University of Chicago Press.

Southern Center for Human Rights. 2013. "Criminalization of Poverty." *SHCR.org*.

Spencer-Suarez, Kimberly. 2021. "Reintegration in the Red: Navigating Child Support Arrears after Prison." PhD diss., Columbia University, School of Social Work.

Spjeldnes, Solveig, Hide Yamatani, and Maggie Davis. 2015. "Child Support Conviction and Recidivism: A Statistical Interaction Pattern by Race." *Journal of Evidence-Informed Social Work* 12: 628–36.

Stack, Carol. 1974. *All Our Kin: Strategies for Survival in a Black Community*. New York: Basic Books.

Stanlie, James. 1993. "Mothering: A Possible Black Feminist Link to Social Transformation." In *Theorizing Black Feminisms: The Visionary Pragmatism of Black Women*, edited by Stanlie James and Abena Busia, 44–54. London: Routledge.

Stuart, Forrest. 2016. *Down, Out, and under Arrest: Policing Everyday Life in Skid Row*. Chicago: University of Chicago Press.

Sum, Andrew, Ishwar Khatiwada, Joseph McLaughlin, and Sheila Palma. 2011. "No Country for Young Men: Deteriorating Labor Market Prospects for Low Skilled Men in the US." *Annals of the American Academy of Political and Social Science* 635: 24–55.

Sykes, Gresham. 2007. *The Society of Captives: A Study of a Maximum Security Prison*. Princeton: Princeton University Press.

Takayesu, Mark. 2011. *How Do Child Support Order Amounts Affect Payments and Compliance?* Orange County, CA: Department of Child Support Services, Research Unit.

Thoennes, Nancy. 2002. *Child Support Profile: Massachusetts Incarcerated and Paroled Parents*. Denver: Center for Policy Research.

Townsend, Nicholas. 2002. *Package Deal: Marriage, Work, and Fatherhood in Men's Lives*. Philadelphia: Temple University Press.

Travis, Jeremy. 2014. "Assessing the State of Mass Incarceration: Tipping Point or the New Normal?" *Criminology and Public Policy* 13(4): 567–77.

Turetsky, Vicki. 2007. "Staying in Jobs and Out of the Underground: Child Support Policies That Encourage Legitimate Work." Washington, D.C.: Center for Law and Social Policy.

———. 2008. *Voluntary Unemployment and Other Reentry Policies*. Washington, D.C.: Center for Law and Social Policy.

Turetsky, Vicki, and Maureen Waller. 2020. "Piling on Debt: The Intersections between Child Support Arrears and Legal Financial Obligations." *UCLA Criminal Justice Law Review* 4(1): 117–41.

Turner, Kimberley, and Maureen Waller. 2017. "Indebted Relationships: Child Support Arrears and Nonresident Fathers' Involvement with Children." *Journal of Marriage and Family* 79: 24–43.

Turney, Kristen. 2015. "Liminal Men: Incarceration and Relationship Dissolution." *Social Problems* 62: 499–528.
Turney, Kristin, Jason Schnittker, and Christopher Wildeman. 2012. "As Fathers and Felons: Explaining the Effects of Current and Recent Incarceration on Major Depression." *Journal of Health and Social Behavior* 53: 467–83.
US Department of Health and Human Services. OCSE. 2002. "Essentials for Attorneys in Child Support Enforcement." Washington, D.C.
———. 2018. "About the Office on Child Support Enforcement." Washington, D.C. https://www.acf.hhs.gov/css/about.
US House of Representatives. 1996. 104th Congress—*The Personal Responsibility and Work Opportunity Act of 1996: Hearing before the Committee on Commerce.* Congressional Publications. Washington, D.C.: US Government Printing Office.
Visher, Christy. 2013. "Incarcerated Fathers: Pathways from Prison to Home." *Criminal Justice Policy Review* 24: 1–18.
Visher, Christy, and Jeremy Travis. 2003. "Transitions from Prison to Community: Understanding Individual Pathways." *Annual Review of Sociology* 29: 89–113.
Visher, Christy, Jennifer Yahner, and Nancy La Vigne. 2010. *Life after Prison: Tracking the Experiences of Male Prisoners Returning to Chicago, Cleveland, and Houston.* Washington, D.C.: Urban Institute.
Vogel, Lisa Klein. 2020a. "Help Me Help You: Identifying and Addressing Barriers to Child Support Compliance. *Children and Youth Services Review* 110: 1–14.
———. 2020b. "Barriers to Meeting Formal Child Support Obligations: Noncustodial Father Perspectives." *Children and Youth Services Review* 110: 1–10.
Wacquant, Loic. 2002. "Scrutinizing the Street: Poverty, Morality, and the Pitfalls of Urban Ethnography." *American Journal of Sociology* 107(6): 1468–532.
Wakefield, Sara, Hedwig Lee, and Christopher Wildeman. 2016. "Tough on Crime, Tough on Families? Criminal Justice and Family Life in America." *Annals of the American Academy of Political and Social Science* 665: 8–21.
Wakefield, Sara, and Christopher Uggen. 2010. "Incarceration and Stratification." *Annual Review of Sociology* 36: 387–406.
Wakefield, Sara, and Christopher Wildeman. 2013. *Children of the Prison Boom: Mass Incarceration and the Future of American Inequality.* New York: Oxford University Press.
Weaver, Kent. 2000. *Ending Welfare as We Know It.* Washington, D.C.: Brookings Institution.
Weimer, Douglas Reid. 2000. "The Bradley Amendment: Prohibition against Retroactive Modification of Child Support Arrearages." *Congressional Research Service*, RS 20642.

Western, Bruce. 2006. *Punishment and Inequality in America*. New York: Russell Sage Foundation.
———. 2018. *Homeward: Life in the Year after Prison*. New York: Russell Sage Foundation.
Western, Bruce, Anthony Braga, Jaclyn Davis, and Catherine Sirois. 2015. "Stress and Hardship after Prison." *American Journal of Sociology* 120(5): 1512–47.
Western, Bruce, and Becky Petit. 2010. "Incarceration and Social Inequality." *Daedalus* 139: 8–19.
Western, Bruce, and Christopher Wildeman. 2009. "The Black Family and Mass Incarceration." *Annals of the American Academy of Political and Social Science* 621: 221–42.
Wheaton, Laura, and Victoria Russell. 2004. *Literature Review for: Benefits and Costs of Child Support Passthroughs and Disregard Policy*. Report prepared for the US Department of Health and Human Services. Washington, D.C.: Urban Institute.
Wherry, Frederick. 2012. *The Culture of Markets*. London: Cambridge University Press.
Wherry, Fredrick, Kristin Seefeldt, and Anthony Alvarez. 2019. *Credit Where It's Due: Rethinking Financial Citizenship*. New York: Russell Sage Foundation.
Wildeman, Christopher. 2009. "Parental Imprisonment, the Prison Boom, and the Concentration of Childhood Disadvantage." *Demography* 46: 265–80.
Wildeman, Chistopher, and Christopher Muller. 2012. "Mass Imprisonment and Inequality in Health and Family Life." *Annual Review of Law and Social Science* 8: 11–30.
Wimberly, C. 2000. "Deadbeat Dads, Welfare Moms, and Uncle Sam: How the Child Support Recovery Act Punishes Single-Mother Families." *Stanford Law Review* 53(3): 729–66.
Yee, Lucy. 1979. "What Really Happens in Child Support Cases: An Empirical Study of Establishment and Enforcement of Child Support Orders in the Denver District Court." *Denver Law Journal* 57: 21–68.
Young, Alfred. 2004. *The Minds of Marginalized Black Men: Making Sense of Mobility, Opportunity, and Future Life Chances*. Princeton: Princeton University Press.
———. 2011. "Comment: Reactions from the Perspective of Culture and Low-Income Fatherhood." *Annals of the American Academy of Political and Social Science* 635: 117–22.
———. 2016. "Safe Spaces for Vulnerability: New Perspectives on African Americans who Struggle to Be Good Fathers." In *Boys and Men in African American Families*, edited by Linda Burton, Susan McHale, Jennifer Van Hook, Dorian Burton, and Valary King, 173–83. New York: Springer.
Zatz, Noah. 2016. "A New Peonage? Pay, Work, or Go to Jail in Contemporary

Child Support Enforcement and Beyond." *Seattle University Law Review* 39: 3.
———. 2021. "Better Than Jail: Social Policy in the Shadow of Racialized Mass Incarceration." *Journal of Law and Political Economy* 1(2): 212–38.
Zatz, Noah, and Michael Stoll. 2020. "Working to Avoid Incarceration: Jail Threat and Labor Market Outcomes for Noncustodial Fathers Facing Child Support Enforcement." *RSF: The Russell Sage Foundation Journal of the Social Sciences* 6(1): 55–81.
Zelizer, Vivanna. 2005. *The Purchase of Intimacy*. Princeton: Princeton University Press.
———. 2010. *Economic Lives: How Culture Shapes the Economy*. Princeton: Princeton University Press.
———. 2012. "How I Became a Relational Economic Sociologist and What Does That Mean?" *Politics and Society* 40: 145–74.

Index

Figures are marked by page numbers in *italics* while tables are marked by **bold** page numbers.